THE SEEDS WE SOW

Kindness That Fed a Hungry World

THE SEEDS WE SOW

Kindness That Fed a Hungry World

GARY BEENE

SANTA FE

Sunstone books may be purchased for educational, business, or sales promotional use.
For information please write: Special Markets Department, Sunstone Press,
P.O. Box 2321, Santa Fe, New Mexico 87504-2321.

Book and Cover design ¤ Vicki Ahl
Body typeface ¤ California FB
Printed on acid free paper

Library of Congress Cataloging-in-Publication Data

Beene, Gary, 1951-
  The seeds we sow : kindness that fed a hungry world / by Gary Beene.
     p. cm.
Includes bibliographical references.
  ISBN 978-0-86534-788-5 (softcover : alk. paper)
1. Food supply--Social aspects. 2. Hunger--Prevention. 3. Agriculture--United States--History-
-20th century. 4. Humanitarianism. 5. Carver, George Washington, 1864?-1943. 6. Wallace,
Henry A. (Henry Agard), 1888-1965. 7. Borlaug, Norman E. (Norman Ernest), 1914-2009. I. Title.
  HD9000.5.B4135 2010
  363.8'5--dc22
                        2010048819

WWW.SUNSTONEPRESS.COM
SUNSTONE PRESS / POST OFFICE BOX 2321 / SANTA FE, NM 87504-2321 /USA
(505) 988-4418 / ORDERS ONLY (800) 243-5644 / FAX (505) 988-1025

To:

My brothers, Bill and David, who found kindness in this life;
and my daughter, Carissa, who was born with it.

CONTENTS

PREFACE__11
PROLOGUE__13

PART I
The Tilling__15

1 Bushwhacked__17
   George Washington Carver's kidnapping, rescue, and early childhood.
2 The Attractor__26
   The kindness influences in Carver's early life.
3 Jump Jim Crow__41
   Reconstruction, Black Codes, and Jim Crow.
4 The Pursuit__53
   Carver's early life educational quest.
5 The Butterfly's Egg__60
   Dr. Edward Lorenz and the "butterfly effect" research.
6 Metamorphosis__63
   Carver's benefactors, college education, and influence on Henry A. Wallace.
7 Where Buffalo Roamed__80
   Abuse of the soils, animals, and peoples of the Great Plains.

PART II
The Sowing__83

8 A Better Corn__85
   The hybridization of corn.
9 A Better Man__97
   The emergence of a unique American voice.
10 By Their Fruit__107
   Wallace as a young adult, Wallaces' Farmer, and HiBred Corn Company.

11 Little Norway's Little Cornhuskers__124
    The Borlaug family, farming in "Little Norway," and Norman Borlaug's
    early life.
12 Hard Knocks__134
    Politics of the Great Depression.
13 Odds and Ends__158
    Wallace is chosen the "New Deal" Secretary of Agriculture.
14 A Country Boy Goes To DC__166
    Wallace, as secretary of Agriculture, responds to the broken farm economy.
15 Where Grasses Grew__175
    The much abused Great Plains become the Dust Bowl.
16 A Farm Kid Goes To Town__189
    Borlaug leaves the farm and goes to the University of Minnesota.
17 Grit In The Teeth__203
    Wallace's war on the Dust Bowl.
18 Only Butterflies are Free__215
    The completion of Dr. Lorenz' work on chaos theory and the butterfly
    effect.
19 Storm Clouds__222
    Profits: The reason to fight.
20 The New Deal's Mystic__238
    Wallace becomes the New Deal's unofficial "spiritual leader-philosopher."

Part III
The Harvest__243

21 Destiny's Appointment__245
    Borlaug's Great Depression adventures that shaped a man who would feed
    the world.
22 Mr. Secretary__257
    The political metamorphosis of Secretary Wallace.
23 Enigmas of Opulence__269
    Henry Ford, Mohandas Gandhi, Eleanor Roosevelt—not as remembered.
24 Mr. Vice President__276
    Wallace becomes Vice President of the United States and tours Mexico.
25 The Farm Boy At DuPont__296
    Dr. Norman Borlaug's work at DuPont during World War II.
26 Benevolence__308
    Establishment of the Rockefeller Foundation.
27 Comestibles Por Mexico__310
    Vice President Wallace pitches an idea to feed Mexico—the Rockefeller
    Foundation establishes the Mexican Agricultural Project.

28 Winning The Peace__320
    Vice President Wallace's role during World War II.
29 A Moment of Grief__332
    Vice President Wallace learns of George Washington Carver's death.
30 M.A.P. To The Future__334
    "You can't build a peaceful world on empty stomachs and human misery."
31 Abundance__344
    "We began by observing that 'hope is always buried in tragedy'. Maybe strife in return arrives with success."
32 Always A Good Boy__355
    The Nobel Peace Prize.
33 The Evil Men Do__362
    Kindness and evil juxtaposed.
34 The Harvest__373
    "Norman Borlaug is the living embodiment of the human quest for a hunger free world."

Epilogue__377
From the chaos of kindness to warm and caring environments.
A Word Personal__381
Dr. Borlaug's passing on September 12, 2009.
Appendix__383
Perpetrators of twentieth century democides.

Notes__378
Acknowledgements__405

Preface

This work is an account of cross generational change embellished with fictionalized conversations among historical figures. With regard to genre, it is non-traditional in its use of history and biography as vehicles for examining kindness as an attitude toward the world.

All of the characters who are identified by two or more names are historical figures. A few characters identified by a single name are fictional, primarily because the main players in the historical events being described are not known. The book uses the lives of three great men, (George Carver, Henry Wallace, Norman Borlaug) and the research of another (Edward Lorenz) to tell the story of how kindness is passed and enhanced across generations by virtue of the "butterfly effect."

The "butterfly effect" maxim emerged from the title of a paper Dr. Lorenz presented at the American Association for the Advance of Science annual conference in 1972. He had originally submitted his paper to the conference program committee without a title. One of his friends on the committee was ribbing Dr. Lorenz when he added to the conference program booklet the facetious title "Predictability: Does the Flap of a Butterfly's Wings set off a Tornado in Texas?" In his opening remarks, Dr. Lorenz' response to the question posed by the title was, "If the flap of a butterfly's wing can be instrumental in generating a tornado, it can equally be instrumental in preventing a tornado." Whatever it is called, Dr. Lorenz' theory is at once both exquisitely simple and intricately complex. The implication is that given enough time every event, indeed every expression of energy everywhere, ripples through time and space to impact every subsequent event and expression of energy everywhere, forever—the "butterfly effect."

While this book offers considerable detail about the lives of these men, it is not a series of biographies. Rather, it is the story of the impact they had on each other, and all of humanity, as they pursued the hybridization of the plants that feed us and the hybridization of the way we interact with each other and the environment. Because George Washington Carver, Henry Agard Wallace, and Norman Ernest Borlaug lived, so do we. This book tells that story.

Prologue

At the Carver farm Mary Washington, with the enthusiastic and meticulous assistance of her "mistress" and friend, Susan Carver, had given birth to her second son. That evening they did not realize that baby George was not born a slave. In Jefferson City earlier in the day, Governor Thomas Fletcher had signed the Missouri Ordinance of Emancipation.

It was unseasonably warm on January 11, 1865 and folks in and about Diamond Grove, in the southwest corner of Missouri, were enjoying the day—enjoying it at least as much as the sad times of a broken nation would allow. The Civil War had by now claimed the lives of over 570 thousand people. The war had raged for years through Missouri and along the Mississippi River but had retreated toward the southeastern seaboard. Though it was in its waning days the battles of Fort Fisher, Hatcher's Run, Bentonville, and others were yet to be fought and another 50 thousand lives would be sacrificed to forsaken causes.

Some war refugees, white and black, from north and south, had decided to take up the federal government on the proposition codified in the Homestead Act that President Lincoln had signed into law in 1862. They were moving westward onto the Great Plains where native "old growth" perennial grasses had been living continuously and growing in sod several feet thick for untold thousands of years.

In 1865 this new wave of humans found herds of bison numbering in excess of 15 million animals. The bison continued their ancient yearly migrations across the plains eating the annual foliage produced by the grasses and fertilizing the next year's growth with 11 billion pounds of manure.

The human descendants of Europe and Africa also found "indigenous" peoples, descendants of Asia, whose cultures had evolved to synchronize with the seasons of the grasses and the migrations of the bison. These human cultures clashed violently around widely differing ideas and attitudes of how the lands bounty should be used—and no one yet understood that those ideas, attitudes, and clashes would change everything—forever.

PART I

The Tilling

1

Bushwhacked

George Washington Carver's kidnapping, rescue, and early childhood.

The tear streaked expression of anger and fear on Susan's face flickered in the light cast by the fire of the torched pig pen. She shrieked at Mary, "Throw me the baby!" A hooded man, with a handful of her wiry hair, yanked Mary into the buckboard. Her reason surrendered to the instincts of a mother. Every fiber of her being clung desperately to the ten day old infant, as she was thrown to her back on the bed of the wagon. Susan's screamed plea was of no avail—Mary did not toss the baby to her friend.

As the wagon wheeled wildly out of the farm yard the hooded man reached to grab the baby from his mother's arms. Without a sound, Mary bit deeply into the man's hand and clamped her jaw shut with no intention of letting go. Over the sound of the squeaking wheels the driver heard Seth's startled scream—then a sickening crunch, turn to a splash, as the butt of the bushwhacker's rifle liquefied the bones of Mary's eye orbit. Falling instantly into unconsciousness her teeth released their hold, and so too her arms relinquished their grasp. The baby George plopped violently to the floor boards of the wagon beside his mother's convulsing body.

Jim, the nominal leader of this band of ruffians, rode up quickly on his horse and angrily chastised Seth for likely killing the only profit they were going to make of this night's "work." Driving the team, Richard turned his attention from the horses for a moment to peruse the goings-on in the bed of the wagon. Already furious that Seth had shot the sow, as well as the black man who had opened the pig pen, Richard was made nauseous by the sound of the crushing blow and the squalling of the baby. Figuring that as long as the woman remained alive she would still produce some milk, Jim scornfully ordered Seth to shut the baby up by putting him on his mother's tit.

Meanwhile, on the driver's bench, Richard had returned most of his attention to guiding the team down the wagon path illuminated by the waxing quarter moon. 'Most of his attention'—but he was still seething with anger at Seth's bloodlust. Profit was made by kidnapping blacks near the state line and spiriting them as quickly as possible into Arkansas where there were still those willing to pay for slaves, albeit only a fraction of their prewar worth. The dead black man lying in the Carver's barnyard, the gravely injured wench, and an infant pickaninny in the wagon were worth nothing. They did not even get away with any fresh meat. For this band of Missouri bushwhackers, it had been a very poor night indeed.

As Jim spurred his horse up ahead of the wagon, Richard sat fuming holding the draft horse reins and refusing to look back at either Seth or their dying cargo. "And why the hell did you shoot that sow?" was all Richard could think to say.

"When that boy flung open the gate to let her free, I saw he had a gun so I figgered I'd just lay 'em both low."

Richard responded with barely controlled malice dripping from his voice, "You damned fool! Next time you pull a stunt like that, I'm gonna lay you low!"

Sulking, Seth dropped to his knees, grabbed the squalling baby and stuck him on Mary's breast.

¤ ¤ ¤

Contrary to popular history, the blood-letting of the Civil War did not begin on April 12, 1861, in Charleston, South Carolina. It began on November 21, 1855, along the border of Missouri and Kansas in what became known as "Bleeding Kansas," a term coined by Horace Greeley of the New York Tribune. Early nineteenth century Missouri had seen an influx of slave holding southerners who moved up the Mississippi and Missouri Rivers. Missouri had been admitted to the Union as a slave state under the auspices of the Missouri Compromise of 1821. A second wave of settlers, primarily of German and Irish descent, began arriving in large numbers soon after Missouri's statehood. Most did not share any great fervor for the institution of slavery. In 1854 the Kansas-Nebraska Act nullified the Missouri Compromise and stipulated the two states should decide on their own whether to be free or slave states. This resulted in the de facto start of the Civil War between pro-slavery residents, known as border ruffians or bushwhackers, and anti-slavery forces called jayhawkers. Ostensibly, the goal of their violence was to influence how Kansas would choose to enter the Union.

By the late 1850s the state of Missouri was itself almost equally divided among those who opposed and those who supported slavery. Thus, it quite literally waged a civil war upon itself. During the Civil War, Missouri did not secede from the Union but rather settled upon a policy of "armed neutrality." Of course, by virtue of the fact that the population was not really neutral and most certainly was armed, Missouri suffered over twelve hundred armed clashes, more than any other state either north or south of the Mason-Dixon line. Because the vigilante nature of both the bushwhackers and the jayhawkers put them outside the control of either the regular Union or Confederate armies, the Civil War in Missouri and Kansas devolved into horrific and bloody guerrilla warfare.

There can be little doubt that in modern psychological parlance, many of the individuals riding with the bushwhackers and jayhawkers would have been diagnosed with "Antisocial Personality Disorders" (sociopaths). The bushwhackers counted almost five hundred among their ranks, approximately thirty of whom murdered each other during and after the war. Subsequent to the war, at least thirty-five were known to pursue crime as their primary profession, including bank robbery, stagecoach and train hold-ups, murder, and prostitution. Most famous of this ilk were Jesse and Frank James along with Henry and Cole Younger.

Even during the Civil War the roving bands of marauders were less about the principles of their espoused pro- and anti-slavery positions and more about equal parts of profiteering and mayhem. These pirates on horseback proved to be ruthlessly proficient in both endeavors. Employing guerrilla warfare tactics, they primarily waged war against the civilian sympathizers of their enemy by raiding, killing, and burning property. The most notorious raid occurred August 21, 1863. William Quantrill led a band of about 450 raiders in an assault on Lawrence, Kansas, where they murdered 183 men and boys, some as young as ten years of age. They dragged the victims from their homes and forced the women and girls to watch the slaughter. After stealing all of the money and liquor that could be found, they torched most buildings of the town.

Variable penetrance is an observable, albeit subjective, aspect of sociopathic behavior. At one end of the spectrum one might find individuals who exhibit an almost orgasmic pleasure in blood-letting and at the other end zealots who can justify their violence as an acceptable means to a political end. Somewhere in the middle are those who murder and maim for profit. These narcissistic individuals often use raw and violent force to sate their greed and impose their will, while feeling little or no empathy for their victims. The entire gamut was likely represented among the various bands of bushwhackers that raided the farm of Moses and Susan Carver near Diamond Grove, Missouri. The last of three such "visits" occurred in January, 1865.

¤ ¤ ¤

The Carver's farm house was nestled in a little grove which hid it from the road even when the winter's ground had claimed the foliage. A house and a small cabin were situated on the south side of the complex that also hosted a rather large barn with an attached horse stable; four sizable pens for cattle, oxen and mules; six smaller pens for swine; and seven coops for fowl. Immediately to the west of the barnyard was an eleven acre oat-hay pasture with a horse exercise track grooved around the perimeter. (*Moses Carver dabbled with breeding and raising race horses throughout his life.*) Beyond that on about sixty acres of cultivated land lay the vestiges of last year's corn, wheat, and potato crops. No more than a hundred yards north of the house grew a dense wood of mixed deciduous hardwood trees.

Following the ugly events of the night, Moses Carver had slept fitfully for a couple of hours, distressed by recurring dreams of Mary walking into the kitchen holding the baby none the worse for wear. The dreams belied his fear of much worse. He crawled out of bed at dawn and went out to saddle a horse. As he mounted and headed up the path to the road, he saw John Bentley rounding the bend toward the house on his large dappled mare.

Moses dismounted and stood still, with sad, sad eyes cast in the direction of his approaching neighbor. John Bentley, often accompanied by two black men, had served as a scout for the Union army during the fighting in Missouri and Arkansas. In roughly equal parts due to the nature of guerrilla warfare and the nature of how they were deployed, the term "scout" was a euphemism for spy, assassin, or enforcer, depending upon the particular assignment. Scouts were generally rough characters and only nominally mustered into and out of the armed services. Alexander and Wesley had enlisted in the 1st Kansas Colored Infantry regiment and were both mustered in on May 1, 1863. They fought in the battles at Cabin Creek (July 1 – 2, 1863) and Honey Springs (July 17, 1863). However, these two young men were extraordinary marksmen, had skills with horses that exceeded most cavalry officers, and a certain turn of wit that uniquely qualified them for work as scouts. They were surreptitiously redeployed and mysteriously dropped from the muster roles of Company H. It is equally mysterious how they came to be in the company of one John Bentley. Regardless, theirs' was a relationship forged in battles fought across the Border States.

Moses Carver had wrapped Wesley's body in a blanket and had just been on his way to fetch John Bentley. He was somewhat mystified that John already knew of the preceding night's raid, but was discrete enough to squelch any curiosity about John's covert sources of information. Moses, voice choked by the lump in his throat, was unable to manage a verbal greeting for his neighbor. He pointed to where the wrapped body was laid out. John climbed down from his horse and for a fleeting second looked into the eyes of the older man. His face haloed in white hair and beard, Moses looked more weathered than usual. Overcome with emotion John quickly looked east toward the brightening horizon and said only, "Well."

Gathering enough composure to free his voice, Moses explained, "He'd just dropped by to check on Mary and see her new baby. Oh—John—I am so sorry. They shot him over by the pig pen. We knew it was bushwhackers when we heard the wagon and too many horses. I grabbed my gun and ran little Jim off to hide in the woods. Wes hollered that he'd turn out the stock. I looked up from behind the wood pile and saw him opening the pig pen about the time one of the bushwhackers came around the corner of the barn with a torch. He dropped it and laid aim on the run away sow. He fired on the pig then spun and saw Wes raising his gun and quicker than I can say it, Wes was on his back. He coughed a couple of times and then was gone. I shot once but I don't think I hit him. That son of Satan ran to the wagon and dragged Mary aboard by her hair. John—I'm just so damned sorry." The breaking day glistened off the tear soaked bags beneath Moses' eyes.

John Bentley, Wesley and Alexander had fought together since the battle at Pine Bluff and over the ensuing months had engaged the enemy, most often bushwhackers rather than regular units of the Confederate States military, in ways that can speciously be described as unconventional. In warfare of this type, the fighters were likely to engender a special enmity among foes. If the person was known, vengeance was often sought by the enemy on or off the battlefield, during or subsequent to the cessation of formal hostilities. This reality necessitated a circumspect existence, coupled with armed vigilance. For that reason, John had always insisted that both his compatriots carry a side arm when out and about. At that moment, his angst led him to consider the possibility that had Wes not been armed, he may not have been so brave—he may have run to hide in the woods with little Jim.

Only able to whisper and not able to think of anything else to say, Moses offered, "I've got some lumber over there. I'll help you make a box if you'd like and we can take him over to bury him at your place."

¤ ¤ ¤

As distraught as the two men were about the carnage wrought the night before, their grief did not compare to that of Moses' wife, Susan. Though attempting to attend to the daily routine, fearing the worst for her dearest friend and baby George, Susan was unable to maintain her composure and had crumpled to the floor sobbing. Moses and John found her thus when they entered the house after making the casket for Wesley.

Susan was a quiet woman. Although active in the affairs of the church, which her husband generally refused to attend, she was always more comfortable in her own home surrounded by those she considered family. The Carvers had no children of their own, but before the war they had raised three nephews and nieces whose parents' lives had come to untimely ends. They were Unionist who did not support slavery, yet quixotically had purchased Mary Washington in 1855. However, like her nieces and nephews, Susan considered Mary more family than servant and by all accounts loved her as a sister. One might conjecture that it was Susan's loneliness, after the youngest of her nieces had married and moved away, that motivated her husband to purchase the fourteen year old black girl.

Unable to cry anymore, Susan sat on the floor gulping air in spasms. Moses and John gathered her up and laid her upon the bed.

John Bentley knew how to acquire information from the most likely and many not-so-likely sources. As they loaded the casket onto the wagon to which they had harnessed the dappled mare he said, "I'll do what I can to find Mary and the babe."

"That would give my wife much comfort—I'll let her know when she wakes." And as John pulled himself up onto the driver's bench Moses added, "I'll make it worth your while."

"No need for you to come over for the burying. You stay here and tend to Mrs. Carver. I'll ask Alexander to bring the wagon back tomorrow." Turning slightly and pointing with his nose and a nod of his head toward the dead hog still laying in the barn yard, "You'd better cure that sow—best not waste the meat. Alexander can bring you some of his salt brine when he returns the wagon."

¤ ¤ ¤

The expressions of the men sitting around the fire attested to their different levels of disgust as they listened to Seth's grunts coming from the tent where the still unconscious black woman laid with her baby. Richard stood and walked over beside a large oak tree, leaned against it and wretched. Stepping out of the tent, Seth wiped the saliva from his grin with the back of his left hand and urged the others to jump in the tent for a quick "change of luck, before the wench was dead and good for nothing at all."

Out of the corner of his eye Jesse saw Richard raising his hand. He quickly looked over at the log where his friend had sat cleaning his gun and saw that the prized flintlock pistol, with the gold inlay grip, was not laying there. Too late he screamed, "DON'T RICHARD!"

Through the blue smoke of exploding black powder, the men at the campfire could almost make out the massive musket ball slamming into Seth's sternum and literally lifting him off his feet, throwing him backwards on top of the tent he had just exited. As shattered bits of bone flew through his heart, lungs, and aorta, his life ended within seconds of landing on his back. Without a flicker of remorse Richard walked over and grabbed Seth by the boots, "This pig ain't worth digging a hole for." He dragged Seth's body down the hill, leaving it unburied for the critters.

¤ ¤ ¤

Knowing that they could not sell an unconscious black woman and a sick baby, the bushwhackers had arranged a ransom with the Carvers, through the efforts of John Bentley. However, when John had learned the identities of bushwhackers, he told Moses that he would not be able to go himself. If the ruffians recognized him, they would kill him for sure. Obliquely he explained that it had something to do with espionage and the death of one of their band of brothers at the battle of New Madrid. In fact, John wondered aloud to Moses whether they had recognized Wesley, which may have been why he lay dead rather than kidnapped and sold down the

— 23 —

river. On reflection though, he decided that was not likely, given that Wes was just about as dark as the surrounding night. So, even this thought did not salve his sense of guilt about the loss of his friend.

Giving Moses the meeting time and a map to the appointed rendezvous near the Sugar Creek crossing just south of Pineville, John cautioned him to "ride a good horse, go armed and be careful."

¤ ¤ ¤

Jim and Jesse laid Mary and the baby in the back of the wagon, but she was dead within a mile and the baby's cough seemed to foretell that he would soon follow. They quickly dug and placed the woman in a shallow grave, put the baby in the flour sack that had served as Seth's hood on the night of the raid and wrapped that in a blanket. They unhitched and saddled the horse, planning to return for the wagon later. Jim carried the swaddled baby in his arms as he, Jesse, Richard, George and Ike rode horseback north from Sulphur Springs, Arkansas.

Moses had taken some of John's advice. He was armed and he was being careful, but he had not saddled his best horses. In fact, he later gave his best filly to John and Alexander who reportedly made considerable money racing her and her foals. Instead, Moses was riding an eight year old sorrel gelding and was leading a mare he had purchased in 1855. While not absolutely certain of her age he figured she was almost fourteen years old. Mary had been riding her since she had come to live at the Carver's farm. He had brought the mare saddled for Mary's return trip, which she would never make.

The first indication that he was approaching the rendezvous was the sound of the mill wheel. Though the use of hydro-electric power was still three generations hence, people had long since begun to use the force of gravity and falling water as a source of power. Thus, many large springs throughout the Ozarks were fitted with mill wheels for grinding flour and cornmeal in quantities that had fueled the earliest stages of the conversion of agriculture from a subsistence endeavor, to a commercial enterprise. Within a couple of minutes of hearing the sounds of the wheel, he arrived at the creek.

About 150 yards downstream of the mill pond was a clearing in the woods. Moses reined in the horses at the edge and sat silently listening. Hearing nothing he slowly dismounted, remaining vigilant with all of his senses. Within seconds of planting both feet, he heard and saw three men step out of the brush no more than twenty yards to his left. The flour sacks they wore on their heads shone a spooky iridescence in the pale bluish light of the moon, which also reflected off the barrels of two rifles and a pistol pointed at him. The man with the pistol walked over and gathered up the reins of both horses. A fourth man stepped out of the brush just a few feet from Moses and tossed a flour sack at him. Moses lunged forward to catch the sack and immediately dropped to one knee. Laying it carefully on the ground, he tore the bag open. In that instant Moses knew that Mary was gone, and they would never see her again. He pulled baby George from the sack, opened his knee length duster coat and his shirt and laid the sick, almost dead, baby against his warm skin. Closing his shirt and coat, he turned on a heel and without a word began the seven hour walk back to Diamond Grove.

The kidnappers had failed to deliver the ransomed woman. As Moses walked, he wondered at what sense of "honor" would lead men to rob and kill innocents, but not steal the $130 they knew he carried simply because they had been unable to hold up their end of the ransom agreement. His anguished curse roused baby George—but just barely.

Back at their farm, Susan and Moses Carver moved Mary's two boys, Jim and George, into the main house to live with them. Though interracial adoption was not legally recognized, out of love for the children and a sense of duty to Mary, they committed to raising those boys as they would their own. The boys would not truly remember their mother, but the Carvers taught them to love and respect her, knowing full well that even that would never make things right.

The rescue of George, and nursing him back from the edge of death, were the first of many great kindnesses that he attracted throughout his life—which he repaid by changing the world.

2

THE ATTRACTOR

The kindness influences in Carver's early life.

Even from infancy, George was a lightening rod through which giant bolts of kindness flowed. These acts of kindness were neither small nor insignificant. They were often giant acts of courage, sacrifice and long term commitment. Not only did Moses Carver undertake to find George and his mother, but he mounted a rescue effort that entailed no small degree of personal courage.

Miguel de Cervantes' novel, *Don Quixote de la Mancha* was first translated into English in 1620. Moses was a well read man, but it is not known whether he ever read the most famous Spanish novel. However like the novel's protagonist, Moses was long and lean with high cheekbones, deep-set eyes, collar length gray hair and a beard trimmed close to the jaw line but extending at least four inches below the chin. He always carried a long straight cane with no crook in the handle. Applying only a modicum of imagination allows the mind's eye to transfigure that cane into a lance. From there it is only a short leap of fancy to visualize Moses on horseback jousting with windmills. Perhaps many considered his Quixotic decision to parent two black children was just such an exercise.

The Carvers were considered "different" by their neighbors in the Diamond Grove area. Moses, in particular, was known as being more than a bit eccentric. Some of this was perhaps due to the fact that he was a good deal more literate than most of his contemporaries. Folks also looked askance, and murmured amongst themselves, at the fact that Moses would not attend the interdenominational Locust Grove Church, which was only a mile from his farm. Much to the neighbor's relief, however, he was an active

Free Mason, thereby dispelling any notion that perhaps he was atheist— thank God for that.

Though private people, the Carvers welcomed company, and Moses especially enjoyed the children often giving them treats from the garden or his bee hives. Given that both Jim and George maintained a warm and caring lifelong relationship with their step-father, it can be safely assumed that he likewise treated them with kindness and respect. Moses was an accomplished musician who frequently played the fiddle at neighborhood gatherings. He also demonstrated a remarkable affinity with animals. Visitors would often find him with a pet rooster perched upon his shoulder and witnessed squirrels eating directly from his hand.

Not only was George the beneficiary of the Carver's child-rearing kindness, he embraced these acts and reflected them. His childhood fascination was growing vegetables and flowers. One day when seeing George tending the flower bed beside the house, a neighbor stopped and asked George how she could get flowers to grow like Mrs. Carver's. George replied simply, "Why, just love them."

Over and over people referred to George as "special." This seemed to manifest in many ways. He was known as the "boy who could talk to flowers." His thirst for knowledge led him into the woods for hours at a time, wandering by himself gathering plants and stones and frogs and insects. His pockets were always full of something. He would hide his "treasures" in the house, until finally one day Susan insisted that he build a storage shed outside. After that she still had to be vigilant to ensure that George always emptied his pockets on the porch before entering the house.

¤ ¤ ¤

"And just where are you off to in such a hurry this morning?" Susan called to George's back as he ran out the back door without breakfast.

"I'm going to get my knife!" he hollered excitedly over his shoulder.

Shielding her eyes from the glare of the rising sun with her left hand and wiping her right on the apron tied at her waist, she looked after her adopted son as he receded toward the woods. Susan shook her head in utter puzzlement and turned back toward the kitchen. She was learning to accept being mystified by George's thoughts and antics and could only hope that his unusual ways would not cause him too much trouble in his life—she hoped, but was by no means optimistic, in that regard. Though he had been pestering her for several weeks about wanting a pocket knife, his departing comment served only to further bewilder this woman who loved and worried about him so.

With a sense of excitement and anticipation, George hurried to the log on the far side of the livestock watering pond at the farm's west end. To his great disappointment there was no pocket knife there. He looked around and uttered under his breath, "This is not right." Stretching his memory deep into his subconscious he tried to retrieve the details of his dream.

It was misty. There had been a log with a watermelon sitting on top. An old, very dark skinned black man with closely cropped hair and mustache sprinkled with gray sat on a stump beside the downed tree. He wore round wire frame glasses and a heavy white apron over his coat, shirt and tie. When I ask him where he got such a big watermelon in May, he just smiled and waved me over toward the log. As I approached the log, I saw the pool of standing water on the other side. I looked up at the stump where the old man was sitting, and it had moved. Now he was sitting on the same stump, but it was in the mist on the other side of the pond. I looked at the watermelon, and stuck right in the middle was a four inch double-blade pocket knife. When I reached for it, the melon seemed to just disappear. Then as I looked back at the old man, who was still sitting there grinning at me, he seemed to fade into the mist. Then slowly the whole dream was consumed by a thickening fog.

When George woke he was certain the log had to be the one by the stock pond, because that was the only place where he knew a downed tree lay beside a pool of water. When he arrived, however, he gradually became aware this was not the right place. Things were not correct. In the dream the stump where the old man sat was on the edge of a thicket across the pond. Here there was only pasture opposite the downed tree, and no stump at all.

George wandered north through the woods for at least half an hour trying to reconstruct every detail of his dream. Then suddenly, there it was. The downed tree with a knife stuck in a large knot rather than a watermelon. On the opposite side of the tree was a pool of rain water that had fallen two days before and collected in a small hollow. The storm that dropped the rain had been accompanied by a howling wind that had toppled the tree, roots and all. The knife was a double bladed Barlow with some rust at the hinges. It had been stuck in the knot on the tree long before the tree fell. While the tree stood, the knife was lodged well above George's head. He would never have noticed it, though his ramblings through these woods brought him by this area many times. The pool was but temporary standing rain water and would soon be absorbed into the earth and the air. As George grabbed the knife and pulled it, he had a deep sense of wonder, bordering on awe, at the messages hidden in dreams. In the back of his mind he could hear Ma Carver's frequent refrain, "The mysterious messages of the Creator can only be heard by those who will listen."

Upon returning to the farmhouse he only told the Carvers that he had found the knife in the woods. It was many years later that he recounted the story of his dream to several people, including Rackham Holt, who in George's final years began writing the first of many biographies detailing this most extraordinary life.

¤ ¤ ¤

It was only a couple of months after finding the knife that George spent the better part of a day scouring the woods for two identical sticks; strong but light weight with perfect U shaped forks. He quickly found the first one, but coming by the match required several more hours of search. He found a few possibilities and did a bit of carving, before deciding that they would not meet his need. By mid-afternoon he had wandered far afield and suddenly, there lay the twin stick he sought. A wide grin crossed his face as he trotted over to the stump that propped his prize. Grabbing it he thumped it hard against the ground to be sure there was no dry rot, and that it had the heft to support the weight of an eighty-five pound boy.

He struck it a few times with his knife to be sure the wood would take the shape he envisioned whittling, but not so soft it would scratch and dent too easily with the rough use that a nine year old boy's crutch was likely to endure. Richard had taken a bad fall while helping his father repair the loft in their barn and had broken his left femur. He was severely injured, and had bled so much internally for several days, the family feared the need to amputate in order to cauterize the bleeding vessels. Fortunately, it appeared that the damage was primarily to veins rather than arteries. The bruising slowly began to improve, thus obliging the decision to save rather than amputate the leg. When George had visited his friend, almost eight weeks after the injury, he witnessed the awkward ambulation of hopping on one leg, and feared that a loss of balance would aggravate the injury or result in another. The next day George set out on his quest for the wood to make crutches.

When Moses saw George walking toward the shed with the two branches tucked under his arm he queried, "And what's this all about?" George told of his plan to whittle crutches for his friend and explained how he had spent the day looking for two forked sticks with branches to serve as hand holds and U shaped rather than V shaped forks at the top notch. Moses took up one of the sticks and whistled softly while giving it a close inspection. "Okay, let's go put this in the vice and you can use a rasp to knock off all the bark. Then tomorrow you can whittle it to shape." Moses Carver was a man who believed that kindness was a choice, and he knew it to be a decision that had to be coupled with action in order to be meaningful and successful. The fabrication of the crutches for their young friend, Richard, became a team effort. After George finished shaping the crutches with his considerable sculpting skills, Moses used pumice stone to smooth the wood almost to a gloss. Then they added actual gloss with several applications of linseed oil. Sneaking some quilt batting from Ma Carver's sewing supplies, they lashed it firmly into the notches so as to limit armpit chaffing.

In the long days of summer, the church would often host social events and worship on Wednesday afternoons with people departing at sundown to enjoy their twilight journeys home. George was particularly fond of this time, always fascinated by the profusion of fireflies that would cordon the mile walk with thousands of random greenish flickers of light produced in their chemically excited abdomens. On this evening he felt particularly good, as all four of the family strolled north toward the farm. Usually Moses did not participate in these gatherings, but on this evening they had presented Richard with the crutches meticulously manufactured over the preceding week. At first somewhat embarrassed with the gift, Richard shyly took the crutches from George's hands. After a moment studying the hand-made devices, he reached over with his left arm and drew George into a tight embrace. George looked up at Moses with pride and noted that as Richard's father shook Moses hand, his eyes brimmed with tears that he was too manly to allow to drain down his cheeks.

In many respects Moses Carver's influence manifested in his young son. Like Moses, George also became one of the most literate people of the area and the era. He too became an accomplished musician. His affinity for and understanding of life, albeit plant rather than animal, marked the course of his own future in a way that would shake the foundations of many mistaken notions dating back into antiquity. Perhaps most important, though, was the similar attitude George developed toward children. Ultimately, his influence on one very special child may have been his greatest contribution to humanity.

¤ ¤ ¤

George never fully regained his health after his bout in infancy with whooping cough and he struggled life-long with flare-ups of respiratory illness. His brother, Jim, on the other hand was strong and agile. Their playmates were primarily the neighbor children and the Carvers' great nieces and nephews. Unable to join in the more rambunctious play of youth, George was considered rather shy around other children. However, he clearly formed lasting bonds of friendship with many playmates of his childhood. It is known that he continued written correspondence with many of them for years after he left Diamond Grove.

Due to his poor health, he was unable to do the heavier farm work that Moses and Jim would do, so Susan taught him household skills such as sewing, laundry and cooking, which would serve him well during later years as a way of earning money while pursuing his education. She also recognized that he was "special" and spent time reading with him and working on other academic pursuits. In his own words he later recalled, "I wanted to know the name of every stone and flower and insect and bird and beast. I wanted to know where it got its color, where it got its life—but there was no one to tell me. I don't know how I learned to read or write, but I did in some way, thanks to the Carvers."[1]

He also wanted to know about his roots and would pester Susan for details, though her responses were most often short, evasive, and immensely unsatisfying. When asked about Mary Washington, George's mother, Susan would usually well-up and turn away. From that, George could only surmise great love and even greater grief. To some extent, her emotionalism may also have reflected some measure of guilt. It was clear from many things Susan said that she believed the institution of slavery had been an abomination, yet they had purchased Mary. About the only information George could get out of Moses Carver was that he and his mother had been kidnapped and that John Bentley had helped get him back. George would often stand wistfully beside his mother's old spinning wheel and conjure up images of his heritage. That spinning wheel and his mother's 1855 bill of sale would become two of his most prized possessions in his old age.

His efforts to quench the thirst for knowledge were frequently thwarted, but it was through these frustrating experiences that he learned that his "specialness" had more to do with a remarkable intellect than the color of his skin. Ironically, in their reconstruction fervor, the framers of the Missouri Constitution of 1865 required the provision of free schooling for black children, but not so for white. Of course, as is so often the case, even with noble ideas the devil resides in the details. The fact is, the infrastructure for free public education did not exist in Missouri in the late 1860s. School facilities, qualified teachers, and instructional materials were all in short supply or literally non-existent.

Additionally, while the education of black children was stipulated, the new constitution did not compel the integration of schools, thereby creating one of the conundrums that plagued education all over the nation for the next hundred years—separate but equal school systems for white and black children. Though not legally required, integrated education was not yet prohibited in the early 1870s. Some communities, recognizing the impracticality of funding duel school systems, initially offered education in the same classrooms for both white and black children.

George and his older brother, Jim, were allowed to enroll in the school at the church in Diamond Grove. Within the first year, it was clear that little George was the star pupil. While this impressed his teacher, it distressed many parents. It was simply too great a challenge to the perceived natural order for a black orphan, being raised by two white immigrants, to be more intelligent and academically accomplished than American pure-blood white children.

The parents formed a school board, which of course did not include the parents of any black children. The Carvers did not serve on the board, perhaps because they were disinclined to do so, or perhaps because they were considered parents of black children, but most likely because George was the source of the parental consternation. Ostensibly, the purpose of the board was the governance of the school and the improvement of education. That said, their first action was to ban the enrollment of black children.

Likely because of the tenuous nature of their "adoption" of two black children, the Carvers were not willing to fight this decision. In fact, they never spoke of the decision outside of their home. They did, however, employ the services of one Steven Slane to privately tutor George for a while. It was clear, in short order, that George's own knowledge and academic potential outstripped Mr. Slane's ability to deliver challenging instruction. Even given this second educational frustration, George did not consider either his intellect nor his skin color a curse. Thus, from his point of view, there was no cause to surrender his quest for a formal education.

After much cajoling, at the age of eleven George coaxed the Carver's into allowing him to attend a school for black children eight miles away in the town of Neosho, Missouri. It was arranged that George would embark early enough on a Sunday afternoon to arrive before sundown at the house of some friends of the Carver's who lived in Neosho. Many people of the area were not entirely comfortable with the child rearing arrangements out at the Carver farm. Though this was rarely, if ever, articulated directly to the Carvers, both Jim and George sensed this reticence. Not wanting to confront these feelings directly, George managed to meander toward Neosho at such a slow pace as to arrive in town well after dark. Rather than disturb the appointed family at such a late hour, he went to the school to await the next day. That night he bedded down in a hay loft in the barn next to the school. The barn and house next door were owned by a black couple, Andrew and Mariah Watkins. Early the next morning Mariah saw George standing at the corner of the barn staring shyly at the one room school house. She asked what he was doing there and he responded, "Waiting for school to start."

She told him, "Well, I suppose you better wash up and come on inside for some breakfast—you ain't gonna learn much if your stomach is growling at ya."

When she asked his name he responded, "Carver's George."

"Why, aren't you the son of a woman named Mary Washington who is now long gone? If I recall correctly, you was kidnapped, but Mr. Carver brought you back and they raised you boys out there on their farm. Ain't that right?" When George responded that indeed her account was correct, she told him that she had known his mother well and said, "No sir, you are not to call yourself Carver's George. Your name is George Washington Carver."

George questioned, "And why do I need all three names?"

"Because it will remind you of who you are and three reasons to always be your best." Looking squarely into George's puzzled expression, Mariah explained, "First, you must be proud of yourself, so you do good for 'George.' Second, your mama was a fine woman and you should honor her. You do good for 'Washington.' And finally, the Mister and Missus have done right by you and your brother. You, and everything you do, should make the Carvers proud."

He was George Washington Carver for the remainder of his life.

Like the Carvers, the Watkins had no children of their own and, for all intents and purposes, they too took George into their family, but more as a kindly aunt and uncle rather than parents. In fact, George referred to Mrs. Watkins as Aunt Mariah. Like Moses Carver, she disdained wastefulness and continued reinforcing the lessons of thrift which Moses had instilled in young George. She also expanded George's eclectic spiritual exposure by introducing him to his first black congregation in the local African Methodist Episcopal Church.

No doubt he entered school on his first day with high hopes and butterflies in his stomach. This was his first experience interacting within an all-black community. On this first day George met his teacher, a young black man named Stephan Frost. A very nice man, certainly literate, but by no means prepared to teach someone with young George's aptitude. For the most part George's classmates were not literate and, therefore, the lesson plans consisted of learning the alphabet, rudimentary reading, and arithmetic. Mr. Frost could not be faulted for his lack of preparation as a teacher. The reality was that in most places teaching a slave to read had been illegal prior to the Emancipation Proclamation. In the case of Mr. Frost, someone had obviously decided to disregard the law. The mere fact that he knew how to read "qualified" him to be a teacher of black students, and therein lay the main dilemma regarding implementation of the Missouri Constitution's mandatory education requirements.

Though his educational experience at the school provided little, and left young George wanting, he had once again been extended the helping hand of kindness and was beginning to see this emerge as a major theme in his life. He was by no means cavalier in accepting or expecting these expressions and was always heartfelt in his efforts to respond in-kind.

Education in the post-Civil War Midwest was elusive, at best, for a young man of such considerable intellect. After staying with the Watkins in Neosho for almost two years, George struck out on an odyssey in search of knowledge which led him to Fort Scott, Olathe, Minneapolis, Highland, and Beeler, all in the state of Kansas.

¤ ¤ ¤

George was part of a migration of black people from all over the south into what was still known as "Free Kansas." The migration was fueled in part perhaps by this moniker, but also by the mythic tales of "heroics" by the famous abolitionist, John Brown. In 1856 Brown led parties of jayhawkers in combat against much larger forces of Missouri bushwhackers at Palmyra and Osawatomie. The way Brown and his troops accounted for themselves in these battles became legendary. Much more controversial, however, was his involvement in what became known as the Pottawamie Massacre. During the night of May 24, 1856 John Brown and some of his fellow zealots dragged five of their pro-slavery neighbors (James Doyle, William Doyle, Drury Doyle, Allen Wilkinson, and William Sherman) out of their cabins and hacked them to death.

A contemporary and friend of John Brown, Fredrick Douglas, was known as the "Sage of Anacostia" for the historic Washington, DC neighborhood where he resided. Douglas was the most famous and influential African-American abolitionist of the era. In 1859 Brown invited Douglas to participate in the ill-conceived raid upon the U.S. Army Arsenal at Harper's Ferry, Virginia. Fortunately for Douglas, he decided that discretion was the better part of valor and declined Brown's invitation. In the poorly executed assault, two of Brown's sons were fatally wounded on the evening of October 17, 1859. Brown himself was captured and tried. He was found guilty of murder and treason and hung from a gallows on December 2, 1859. Also captured, tried and executed for their parts in the ill-fated raid were John E. Cook, John Anthony Copeland, Edwin Coppac, Shields Green, Albert Hazlett, and Aaron D. Stevens. In reflecting upon his decision to not participate, Fredrick Douglass commented, "I could live for the slave, but he [John Brown] could die for him."

Three years and a month later, on January 1, 1863 "John Brown parties" were held all across the nation in celebration of President Lincoln's signing of the Emancipation Proclamation. On that day Major General Robert H. Milroy, commanding the Railroad Division of the Union Army, VIII Corps, Middle Department, read the signed proclamation to his troops. No doubt aware of the historical significance of their duty station at Harper's Ferry, the troops spontaneously broke into a popular verse sung to the tune of "The Battle Hymn of the Republic":

John Brown's body lies a-mouldering in the grave;
John Brown's body lies a-mouldering in the grave;
John Brown's body lies a-mouldering in the grave;
His soul's marching on!
> Glory, halle—hallelujah! Glory, halle—hallelujah!
Glory, halle—hallelujah! his soul's marching on!
> He's gone to be a soldier in the army of the Lord!
He's gone to be a soldier in the army of the Lord!
He's gone to be a soldier in the army of the Lord!
His soul's marching on!
> John Brown's knapsack is strapped upon his back!
John Brown's knapsack is strapped upon his back!
John Brown's knapsack is strapped upon his back!
His soul's marching on!
> His pet lambs will meet him on the way;
His pet lambs will meet him on the way;
His pet lambs will meet him on the way;
They go marching on!
> They will hang Jeff. Davis to a sour apple tree!
They will hang Jeff. Davis to a sour apple tree!
They will hang Jeff. Davis to a sour apple tree!
As they march along!
> Now, three rousing cheers for the Union;
Now, three rousing cheers for the Union;
Now, three rousing cheers for the Union;
As we are marching on![2]

After reading the Emancipation Proclamation and hearing the voices of his men on that day, General Milroy later recounted, "That hand-bill order gave freedom to the slaves through and around the region where old John Brown was hung. I felt then that I was on duty, in the most righteous cause that man ever drew sword in."[3]

One of the most enigmatic and controversial characters in American history, John Brown was, depending upon one's point of view or life circumstance, either a heroic symbol of sacrifice—one of God's warrior saints; or conversely a murderer, thief, and insane fanatic. Abraham Lincoln considered him a "misguided fanatic" while W.E.B. Du Bois in his 1909 biography referred to Brown as "the man who of all Americans has perhaps come nearest to touching the souls of black folk."[4]

When the thirteen year old George climbed on the wagon departing Neosho for the seventy-five mile ride north to Fort Scott, Kansas he carried with him one of the more aggrandizing versions of the John Brown story which his teacher Mr. Frost had given him. *Echoes of Harper's Ferry* was written by one of Brown's personal friends, James Redpath, and published in 1860 by Thayler and Eldridge Publishing Company of Boston. Also publishing abolitionist literature authored by Walt Whitman and William Douglas O'Connor, the political sentiments of Misters Thayler and Eldridge were quite clear.

George also carried a tattered and weather-worn copy of Ralph Waldo Emerson's "Boston Hymn." Always concerned that he remembered who he was, and from whence he came, Aunt Mariah had stuffed the famous work in his bag as she hugged him farewell. About the third time George pulled the poem out to reread it, one of his companions in the wagon asked, "What you got that you keep reading on there, boy?" With no more prodding than that, George commenced to give voice to the famous poet's words:

> The word of the Lord by night
> To the watching Pilgrims came,
> As they sat by the seaside,
> And filled their hearts with flame.
> God said, I am tired of kings,
> I suffer them no more;
> Up to my ear the morning brings
> The outrage of the poor.
> Think ye I made this ball
> A field of havoc and war,
> Where tyrants great and tyrants small
> Might harry the weak and poor?
> My angel,—his name is Freedom,—
> Choose him to be your king;
> He shall cut pathways east and west
> And fend you with his wing.
> Lo! I uncover the land
> Which I hid of old time in the West,

As the sculptor uncovers the statue
When he has wrought his best;
  I show Columbia, of the rocks
Which dip their foot in the seas
And soar to the air-borne flocks
Of clouds and the boreal fleece.
  I will divide my goods;
Call in the wretch and slave:
None shall rule but the humble.
And none but Toil shall have.
  I will have never a noble,
No lineage counted great;
Fishers and choppers and ploughmen
Shall constitute a state.
  Go, cut down trees in the forest
And trim the straightest boughs;
Cut down trees in the forest
And build me a wooden house.
  Call the people together,
The young men and the sires,
The digger in the harvest-field,
Hireling and him that hires;
  And here in a pine state-house
They shall choose men to rule
In every needful faculty,
In church and state and school.
  Lo, now! if these poor men
Can govern the land and sea
And make just laws below the sun,
As planets faithful be.
  And ye shall succor men;
'Tis nobleness to serve;
Help them who cannot help again:
Beware from right to swerve.
  I break your bonds and masterships,
And I unchain the slave:
Free be his heart and hand henceforth

As wind and wandering wave.
      I cause from every creature
His proper good to flow:
As much as he is and doeth,
So much he shall bestow.
      But, laying hands on another
To coin his labor and sweat,
He goes in pawn to his victim
For eternal years in debt.
      To-day unbind the captive,
So only are ye unbound;
Lift up a people from the dust,
Trump of their rescue, sound!
      Pay ransom to the owner
And fill the bag to the brim.
Who is the owner? The slave is owner,
And ever was. Pay him.
      O North! give him beauty for rags,
And honor, O South! for his shame;
Nevada! coin thy golden crags
With Freedom's image and name.
      Up! and the dusky race
That sat in darkness long,—
Be swift their feet as antelopes.
And as behemoth strong.
      Come, East and West and North,
By races, as snow-flakes,
And carry my purpose forth,
Which neither halts nor shakes.
      My will fulfilled shall be,
For, in daylight or in dark,
My thunderbolt has eyes to see
His way home to the mark.[5]

The family in the wagon was thrilled that George could read. While not literate themselves, in their minds there was no mistaking Emerson's message. When the reading was done, the wagon-bound audience sat in deafening silence for several moments, then suddenly, just as the front wheels bounced through a water cut rut in the road, they all started whooping shouting. Two of the teenage passengers leapt to the ground and danced laughing alongside the wagon for a quarter mile, celebrating the "angel of freedom" who was "cutting the pathway" toward their anticipated promised land.

3

Jump Jim Crow

Reconstruction, Black Codes, and Jim Crow.

Come, listen, all you gals and boys,
I'm just from Tuckyhoe;
I'm gwine to sing a little song,
My name's Jim Crow.
Wheel about, an' turn about, an' do jis so;
Eb'ry time I wheel about, I jump Jim Crow.[1]
—A song and dance from 1828 that was done in blackface by white comedian Thomas Dartmouth "Daddy" Rice

Abraham Lincoln flatly rejected the notion of post-war punishment of the south. He even rejected the idea that the southern states had to be readmitted to the Union. It had always been his contention that states could not constitutionally secede, and any effort to do so was therefore illegal. It was his position, as an attorney and the President, that since the southern states were not allowed to leave the union in the first place, there was no reason for readmission because they had never legally ceased to be member states of the Union.

The political parties of 1864 were as divided on this question as the nation. The chasm among the Democrats ran between those who supported the war effort, War Democrats, and those who opposed it, Peace Democrats. They nominated a War Democrat, General George C. McClellan for President, a Peace Democrat, former Congressman Thomas H. Seymour, for

Vice President, and had a party platform that leaned strongly toward the Peace Democrat point of view. Having a presidential candidate who did not support the party platform and therefore was not supported by the Vice Presidential nominee, was a formula for political impotence.

The Republicans were divided along the lines of moderates, who wanted to win the war and implement a rapid and harmonious reconciliation, against the Radical Republicans who also wanted to win the war and then extract a pound of flesh from the secessionist states. Some were even opposed to allowing the southern states to reenter the Union and take seats in the nation's Congress. The Republican convention of 1864 was a disaster. At its conclusion they had renominated President Lincoln who was a moderate and had nominated a War Democrat, Andrew Johnson, to run as the Vice President. Lincoln himself was pleased with the selection of Johnson, but in order to distance themselves from the Radical Republican element of that party, the two men chose to run on the National Unity ticket rather than as Republicans.

Reconstruction and reconciliation efforts had actually begun well before the end of the Civil War. As early as April 10, 1863 President Lincoln issued the Amnesty Proclamation that offered pardons to those who had not held a Confederate civil office, had not mistreated Union prisoners, and would sign an oath of allegiance to the United States of America. It also decreed that a state could be reintegrated into the Union when only ten percent of voters casting a ballot during the 1860 elections had taken the oath of allegiance and pledged to abide by the Emancipation Proclamation of January 1, 1863.

The Radical Republicans came out furiously against the Amnesty Proclamation with its ten percent clause. They pushed the Wade-Davis bill through Congress on July 2, 1864. The bill made re-admittance to the Union for former Confederate states contingent on a majority of white males in each Southern state signing the "Ironclad Oath." The oath required white males to swear that they had never voluntarily borne arms against the United States, had voluntarily given no aid, countenance, counsel or encouragement to persons in rebellion and had exercised or attempted to exercise the functions of no office under the Confederacy. Candidly, far less than fifty percent of the white males in the states of the south could honestly and in good conscience sign that oath. This would have required southerners to decide between perjuring themselves or accepting that their state could not be readmitted to the Union. President Lincoln vetoed the act, and the Radical Republicans developed an acute case of apoplexy.

Everything changed on Good Friday, April 14, 1865. The assassination of Abraham Lincoln was not merely the murder of the President. It was a poorly executed coup d'état.

Just as John Wilkes Booth was mortally wounding the President in Ford's Theatre, one of his co-conspirators, Lewis Powell, attacked Secretary of State William Seward who was convalescing in his home from a broken arm, broken jaw, and concussion suffered in a carriage accident a few days earlier. Powell forced entry to the Secretary's bedroom by bludgeoning the butler. He stabbed Seward numerous times with a Bowie knife and stabbed four other individuals, including both Seward's son and daughter, while making his escape from the house. Though seriously injured, Secretary Seward survived the attack, as did all of the other victims.

At the same hour, another of the conspirators, George Atzerodt, was deployed to kill Vice President Andrew Johnson at Kirkwood Hotel, in Washington. He lost his nerve and got drunk, or he got drunk and lost his nerve. Either way, the attack on the Vice President never occurred.

John Wilkes Booth never stood trial for Lincoln's assassination. Twelve days after the failed coup, he was killed by Union soldiers in an effort to capture him in a barn at the farm of Richard Garrett. In all, eight persons were tried by a military tribunal for their participation in the conspiracy to overthrow the United States Government. During the seven week trial, 366 witnesses were called to provide testimony. All eight of the accused were found guilty. George Atzerodt, David Herold, Lewis Powell, and Mary Surratt were all hanged in the Old Arsenal Penitentiary on July 7, 1865. Mary Surratt was the first woman the United States government put to death by hanging.

Samuel Mudd, Michael O'Laughlen and Samuel Arnold were all sentenced to life in prison. Edmund Spangler was sentenced to a six year term of imprisonment. In 1867, O'Laughlen died of yellow fever while in prison. President Andrew Johnson, whose would be assassin had been hanged, pardoned Mudd, Arnold, and Spangler in February 1869, just days before the end of his presidency.

John Wilkes Booth and his co-conspirators believed that an overthrow of the U.S. government would result in a negotiated peace with treaty terms more favorable for southern states than they would likely get from the

Lincoln administration. They were obviously so blinded by their zeal they were unable to count votes. The fact is that the Radical Peace Democrats, known as Copperheads, and the Republicans who supported a negotiated peace absent a clear Union victory, were a small minority in Congress, at the political party's national conventions, and among the voting public.

Andrew Johnson, as president, tried to continue Lincoln's policies geared toward reuniting the nation as quickly and painlessly as possible. However, Johnson lacked Lincoln's political power and panache. The Radical Republicans held that the states which seceded had technically forfeited their statehood rights, and after the war should be administered as territories under military occupation and rule. As president, Andrew Johnson proved inept in forwarding the kinder and gentler reconciliation envisioned by his predecessor.

So it was that just four months after George Washington Carver's birth, all hope of an amicable reconciliation among the warring states shared President Lincoln's death bed. The result of the failed coup was disastrous for the south, the nation, and the cause of civil rights. George Carver, everyone in his generation, and generations yet unborn would suffer the consequences of that fateful night. The results of the assassination were precisely the opposite of what the conspirators, who were Confederate sympathizers, had intended. This can only be considered one of the most tragic ironies of this nation's history.

¤ ¤ ¤

The issues of reuniting the divided nation were complex to be sure. Reconstruction efforts had to address how secessionists states would reestablish state governments and be reseated in Congress, the civil status of the former leaders of the Confederacy, and the constitutional and legal status of freedmen, particularly their civil rights and whether they would have the right to vote. All of these issues were controversial, especially so in the South.

The Reconstruction's legal framework is found in the thirteenth, fourteenth, and fifteenth Amendments to the United States Constitution:

AMENDMENT XIII

(Passed by Congress January 31, 1865. Ratified December 6, 1865.)

Section 1.

Neither slavery nor involuntary servitude, except as a punishment for crime whereof the party shall have been duly convicted, shall exist within the United States, or any place subject to their jurisdiction.

AMENDMENT XIV

(Passed by Congress June 13, 1866. Ratified July 9, 1868.)

Section 1.

All persons born or naturalized in the United States, and subject to the jurisdiction thereof, are citizens of the United States and of the State wherein they reside. No State shall make or enforce any law which shall abridge the privileges or immunities of citizens of the United States; nor shall any State deprive any person of life, liberty, or property, without due process of law; nor deny to any person within its jurisdiction the equal protection of the laws.

AMENDMENT XV

(Passed by Congress February 26, 1869. Ratified February 3, 1870.)

Section 1.

The right of citizens of the United States to vote shall not be denied or abridged by the United States or by any State on account of race, color, or previous condition of servitude.[2]

These Constitutional Amendments were augmented by the passage of the Civil Rights Act of 1866. The passage of this Act was primarily intended to nullify the "Black Codes," which most southern State Legislatures had passed almost immediately after the cessation of Civil War hostilities.

Historians typically point to the Black Codes, and the almost simultaneous emergence of the "Invisible Empire of the South," as an expression of southern racism. As the primary causal factor, racism has always been the easy culprit, but not necessarily historically very accurate. In point of fact, the causal factors likely had more to do with commerce, profits, and access to cheap labor, than with attitudes of racial superiority. To wit, the Mississippi Black Code required that "Negroes must make annual contracts for their labor in writing; if they should run away from their tasks, they forfeited their wages for the year. Whenever it was required of them they must present licenses (in a town from the mayor; elsewhere from a member of the board of police of the beat) citing their places of residence and authorizing them to work. Fugitives from labor were to be arrested and carried back to their employers. Five dollars a head and mileage would be allowed such Negro catchers. It was made a misdemeanor, punishable with fine or imprisonment, to persuade a freedman to leave his employer, or to feed the runaway. Minors were to be apprenticed, if males until they were twenty-one, if females until eighteen years of age. Such corporal punishment as a father would administer to a child might be inflicted upon apprentices by their masters. Vagrants were to be fined heavily, and if they could not pay the sum, they were to be hired out to service until the claim was satisfied. Negroes might not carry knives or firearms unless they were licensed to do so. It was an offense, to be punished by a fine of $50 and imprisonment for thirty days, to give or sell intoxicating liquors to a Negro. When Negroes could not pay the fines and costs after legal proceedings, they were to be hired at public outcry by the sheriff to the lowest bidder."[3]

Likewise, the South Carolina Black Code was primarily concerned with labor issues. "In South Carolina persons of color contracting for service were to be known as 'servants,' and those with whom they contracted, as 'masters.' On farms the hours of labor would be from sunrise to sunset daily, except on Sunday. The Negroes were to get out of bed at dawn. Time lost would be deducted from their wages, as would be the cost of food, nursing, etc., during absence from sickness. Absentees on Sunday must return to the plantation by sunset. House servants were to be at call at all hours of the day and night on all days of the week. They must be 'especially civil and polite to their masters, their masters' families and guests,' and they in return would receive 'gentle and kind treatment.' Corporal and other punishment was to be administered only upon order of the district judge or other civil magistrate. A vagrant law of some severity was enacted to keep the Negroes from roaming the roads and living the lives of beggars and thieves.[4]

Of course, it would be inaccurate to say that racism was not a factor in the reconstruction debate. It clearly was, but it was a national issue rather than isolated to the south. The poster below appeared during the 1866 Pennsylvania election campaign. It alleged that Freedman's Bureau money was being lavished on lazy freedmen at the expense of white workers. In the small text it states, "Negro Estimate of Freedom!... Whar is de use for me to work as long as dey make dese appropriations."[5] The racist tone of the text and artwork could not have been more clear.

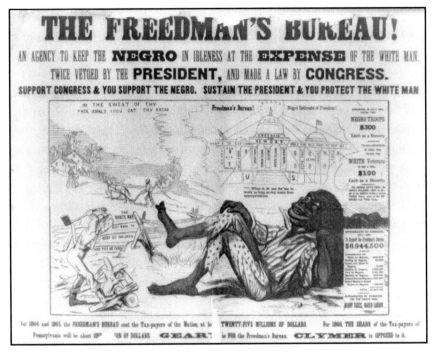

1866 Pennsylvania Campaign Poster. Library of Congress Rare Book and Special Collections Division Washington, DC

Pennsylvania sent over 360 thousand soldiers to fight for the Union, 33,183 of whom died in the war to end slavery, yet the state's politicos cynically used racism "to get out the vote." The poster appeared only a single year after General Lee surrendered to General Grant at Appomattox, with thousands of Pennsylvania troops bivouacked among the Army of the Potomac just a couple of miles away.

¤ ¤ ¤

Reconstruction would not have been easy under the best of circumstances. The Radical Republicans won control of both houses of Congress during the elections of 1866, and they made absolutely certain that the "best of circumstances" did not prevail. It is almost incomprehensible that 359,528 United States soldiers gave their lives during the Civil War to preserve the union. Yet soon after the war, the political leaders of the north could not have intentionally designed a plan more likely to tear the nation asunder had that been their stated intention.

With the Radical Republicans in control of Congress, they passed and overrode presidential vetoes four bills that came to be known as the Reconstruction Acts. The essential components of these laws included: creation of five military districts in the secessionist states, not including Tennessee; congressional approval of new state constitutions, which was required for the former Confederate states to rejoin the Union; voting rights to all males, regardless of race or former slave status; and, ratification of the fourteenth Amendment by all former Confederate States.

In and of themselves, these requirements do not seem too draconian. However, among the military camp-followers were all manner of con artists and flim-flam men, out to make a fortune off the government's reconstruction expenditures. They carried their clothing and personal items in the popular and stylish cloth luggage that resembled the brightly patterned carpets of the era. They became known as "carpetbaggers," and their exploitation and excesses gave the term a negative connotation that yet survives 140 years later.

Their most effective scam was perpetrated by increasing property taxes five to ten fold. The money was to be used to rebuild the infrastructure of the South—roads, bridges, and particularly railroads. Of course, taxes can only be paid when people have income and money. Subsequent to the war, the large land owners of the south had no currency recognized by the United States Government. During the war, each of the southern states had minted their own money, which after the collapse of the Confederacy was utterly worthless. So, in order to pay their taxes, estate holders were forced to sell large tracks of land at bargain-basement prices. In some cases, carpetbaggers managed to buy all of the arable land of former plantations for only a few cents per acre.

In many cases, these "sales" were enforced by the occupying military forces, and the sellers were given the option of selling their land in order to retain their homes, or be forcibly evicted by Union troops. As if to add insult, the military-controlled local governments entered into contracts with many carpetbagger owned construction companies using the money raised through the inflated property taxes and the sale of the foreclosed estates. It is estimated that over half the money spent on infrastructure during the "Reconstruction" era was pocketed by con-men who skipped town, leaving no new roads or bridges behind. They elevated the art of scamming the government and profiteering from war to a new level. To say that the military occupation rankled the former southern aristocracy, as well as the bankers, merchants, and even the poor folks of the "old south" would be an absurd understatement.

In this environment, armed resistance and insurrection found fertile soil from which sprung "The Invisible Empire of the South." The "Empire" was a loose affiliation of paramilitary organizations including the likes of the Ku Klux Klan, the White League, the Knights of the White Camellia, and the Red Shirts. Though it may have had its origins as far back as 1859 in an organization known as the Knights of the Golden Circle, which operated primarily in Texas and New Mexico, the most likely scenario is that these organizations sprung up rather spontaneously, and autonomously, in places all across the southern states. The best documented story of origin is the 1867 meeting in Memphis of former Confederate Generals George Gordon and Nathan Bedford Forrest with a group of like-minded ex-confederates. In short order, Nathan Forrest was named the first Grand Wizard of the Ku Klux Klan.

General Forrest soon realized that the Klan was not the Confederate army, and military discipline did not exist. By its nature, the organization attracted roughnecks from anti-black vigilante groups, disgruntled poor white farmers, wartime guerrilla fighters, displaced Democratic politicians, whiskey bootleggers, white workmen fearful of black competition, employers trying to enforce labor discipline, common thieves, sadists and rapists. The local groups, known as "klaverns," were so violent and uncontrollable that the chagrined "Grand Wizard," Nathan Forrest, officially disbanded the organization in 1868. Of course, the proclamation doing so was somewhat akin to closing the barn door after the horses have gotten out. Though its leader had disaffiliated himself with their activities, the Invisible Empire waged terrorist warfare for another decade.

¤ ¤ ¤

The Presidential election of 1876 pitted Rutherford B. Hayes, Republican from Ohio, against the New York Democrat, Samuel J. Tilden. With 47.9% of the popular vote, Hayes claimed 185 electoral votes, whereas, Tilden carried 51.5% of the popular vote but only 184 electoral votes. The vote counts in Florida, South Carolina, and Louisiana were disputed. The nation faced a constitutional crisis and teetered on the threshold of a second Civil War.

In a tacit acknowledgement of military defeat and the failure of the Reconstruction effort, the Radical Republicans agreed to the Compromise of 1877. In this unwritten deal, the White House was awarded to their candidate, Rutherford Hayes, with the understanding that he would immediately upon taking office order the withdrawal of all occupying federal troops in the southern states. Within months of their departure, a flurry of legislation codifying racial discrimination emanated from state houses all across the south. Once the "Jim Crow" tide was released, it did not stop at the Mason-Dixon line. Below are excerpts from various states' Jim Crow legislation.

Alabama: "All passenger stations in this state operated by any motor transportation company shall have separate waiting rooms or space and separate ticket windows for the white and colored races."

California: Voter rights [Constitution] "No native of China" would ever have the right to vote in the state of California.

Miscegenation [Statute] Made it illegal for white persons to marry a "Negro, mulatto, or Mongolian."

Colorado: Miscegenation [Statute] Marriage between Negroes and mulattoes, and white persons "absolutely void." Penalty: Fine between $50 and $500, or imprisonment between three months and two years, or both.

Georgia: "All persons licensed to conduct a restaurant, shall serve either white people exclusively or colored people exclusively and shall not sell to the two races within the same room or serve the two races anywhere under the same license."

"It shall be unlawful for any amateur white baseball team to play baseball on any vacant lot or baseball diamond within two blocks of a playground devoted to the Negro race, and it shall be unlawful for any amateur colored baseball team to play baseball in any vacant lot or baseball diamond within two blocks of any playground devoted to the white race."

Maryland: "All railroad companies and corporations, and all persons running or operating cars or coaches by steam on any railroad line or track in the State of Maryland, for the transportation of passengers, are hereby required to provide separate cars or coaches for the travel and transportation of the white and colored passengers."

Mississippi: "Any person…who shall be guilty of printing, publishing or circulating printed, typewritten or written matter urging or presenting for public acceptance or general information, arguments or suggestions in favor of social equality or of intermarriage between whites and Negroes, shall be guilty of a misdemeanor and subject to fine not exceeding $500 or imprisonment not exceeding six (6) months or both."

Missouri: "Separate free schools shall be established for the education of children of African descent; and it shall be unlawful for any colored child to attend any white school, or any white child to attend a colored school."

Ohio: Miscegenation [Statute] Unlawful for a person of "pure white blood, who intermarries, or has illicit carnal intercourse, with any Negro or person having a distinct and visible admixture of African blood." Penalty: Fined up to $100, or imprisoned up to three months, or both. Any person who knowingly officiates such a marriage charged with misdemeanor and fined up to $100 or imprisoned in three months, or both.

Oklahoma: Mining-bath facilities [Statute] "The baths and lockers for the Negroes shall be separate from the white race, but may be in the same building."

South Carolina: "It shall be unlawful for any parent, relative, or other white person in this State, having the control or custody of any white child, by right of guardianship, natural or acquired, or otherwise, to dispose of, give or surrender such white child permanently into the custody, control, maintenance, or support, of a negro."

Of course, the Jim Crow laws were from the 1800s; another era; a less enlightened time. Well, not exactly—codified racism held sway well into the twentieth century.

> **West Virginia:** "White and colored persons shall not be taught in the same school." This statement appeared in Article XII Section 8 of the state's constitution. Over the years, numerous attempts to remove this language from the constitution were defeated in the state legislature. It was finally repealed in November 1994.

> **Utah:** Miscegenation Marriage between "white and Negro, Malayan, mulatto, quadroon, or octoroon void." (State Code—1953)

> **Nevada:** Miscegenation—Gross misdemeanor for white to marry person of black, brown, or yellow race. (State Statute—1957)

> **Michigan:** Adoption required that race be used as a consideration in adoption petitions. (State Statute—1957)

> **Arizona:** Miscegenation Marriage of person of "Caucasian blood with Negro, Mongolian, Malay, or Hindu void." (State Statute—1956)[6]

> **United States:** In the Summer of 1948 President Harry S. Truman stated, "My forebears were Confederates. . . . But my very stomach turned over when I had learned that Negro soldiers, just back from overseas, were being dumped out of Army trucks in Mississippi and beaten."[7] The president ordered the end of racial segregation in the United States Military with Executive Order 9981 on July 26, 1948. It would be another six years before the last all black unit in the United States military was abolished.

It seems that for 120 years lawmakers were inordinately concerned with the racial overtones of integration, education, suffrage and sex. The legacy of the Radical Republican's failed version of Reconstruction was a travesty for the nation, for civil rights, and for George Washington Carver.

4

THE PURSUIT

Carver's early life educational quest.

Asserting historically inaccurate claims that Kansas was "the home of John Brown", who was actually born in Connecticut and raised in Ohio, soon after the Civil War enterprises owned by black individuals, such as the Edgefield Real Estate and Homestead Association, persuaded tens of thousands of disenfranchised black people to join in a large scale migration to the "Sunflower State." By 1879 the participants in this human torrent came to be known as "Exodusters." In 1861 there were but 625 free black persons living in Kansas. By 1870 their ranks had swollen to 17 thousand and to 43 thousand by 1880. Unfortunately, Kansas was not the lush prairie paradise many had envisioned. Winters of the late 1880s were some of the coldest ever recorded over the Midwestern heartland. In some places temperatures in January 1888 dipped to forty below zero. The Exodusters did not have much better luck with the agricultural economy. Corn prices in 1880 were pegged near 32^c a bushel. By the end of the decade, a Midwestern farmer was lucky to receive 19^c.

The influx of tens of thousands of black immigrants, a worsening economy, and extreme weather conditions had predictable effects upon the welcome mat put out by white Kansans. The black arrivals hopes of finding new lives, absent the malice of bigotry, did not pan out so well. Even had these conditions, which were beyond their control, been better the influx of so many poor people greatly exceeded the absorption capacity of local economies. Jobs were scarce, need was great, and Kansas was by no means an agricultural Eden. The Kansas Freedmen's Relief Association and Quaker relief organizations tried to meet the most dire needs of the new residents, but as is often the case competition for limited resources devolved into conflict drawn along the lines of race and culture. Through the efforts of people like Benjamin (Pap) Singleton, W.R. Hill and W.H. Smith, enclaves populated by the black immigrants sprung up and survived in places known as Nicodemus, Quindaro, Tennessee Town, Mud Town, Dunlop Colony, and the largest—Olathe.

At first George did not situate himself in one of these black communities. He stayed on in Fort Scott where he was taken in by the family of Felix Payne, the local blacksmith. He earned his room and board by cooking for the family. George put some money in his pockets by doing chores for Stadden Grocery and doing laundry for Wilder House Hotel patrons. Time and again throughout the odyssey of his life, he was taken into the homes of black and white families whom he had never met. His time with the Payne family was just another iteration of the "kindness attractor" theme that ran through his life.

He employed his cooking, laundry and sewing skills to earn money at each stop in this long and frustrating journey toward knowledge. In that quest, however, not all lessons were pleasant. As the influx of black Exodusters in Kansas grew, Fort Scott became a hotbed of racial tension. It was there, on March 26, 1879, that George was first exposed to vicious human cruelty. A black man accused of raping a white thirteen year old girl was dragged from the county jail by a group of about thirty hooded men. He was lynched from a lamp post and his corpse set ablaze over a fire of dry-goods boxes and coal oil. Over sixty years later George recalled, "As young as I was, the horror haunted me and does even now."[1]

Vomiting immediately was small relief as George battled nausea all the way back to the Payne home. There he found family members and guests vociferously arguing the virtue and vice of public lynching. Though in this house lynching proponents were outnumbered by those who considered it an act of evil depravity, George could not accept that anyone espousing Christianity could even condone the discussion. He stealthily retired to his room, where he packed his belongings and exited through the window— never looking back—never to return.

George walked through much of the night, cold and hungry. On this night he was not alone in the northerly exodus. Other blacks, individuals and families, moved furtively away from Fort Scott. There was little talking amongst the refugees, and George spoke not at all. But he kept his eyes open and his ears tuned. He did overhear some quiet conversations about where to go. Most seemed to concur that the safest place would be Olathe, being the largest black community in Kansas, as there was likely some strength in numbers. There also seemed to be some sense that they were safer in Kansas than in Missouri. This puzzled George as he had never seen the kind of atrocity they had witnessed a few hours earlier during his first thirteen years living in Missouri's southwest corner. Of course, he had no memory of his own mother's brutal slaying.

In the early morning hours of March 27th, there was word that violence had also flared in the community of Hammond. During the night a family had offered to carry George's two bags on their two wheel wagon. They carried too heavy a load to also offer him a ride. Regardless, he was glad to have his load lightened and walked ahead of the mule drawn cart much of the time.

In the grey light of early dawn George noticed legs and boots extending from the brush on the side of the road. He stepped off the path for closer inspection, thinking that perhaps the person needed assistance. For the second time in twelve hours the horror of what he found induced violent nausea. The body dumped in the brush had half his skull knocked away, and his brains lay hemorrhaged upon the ground. Dropping to his knees and vomiting violently, George passed out from the combination of emotional shock, lack of food, water, sheer exhaustion, or perhaps his mind just needed somewhere to hide for a while. A large man who, like George, had not spoken a word during the preceding night, picked George up and silently carried him on down the road.

Fearing that passing through the small town of Fulton might incite a similar incident, the parties of refugees decided to circumnavigate the community on an infrequently used by-pass path just to the east. When they arrived at Little Osage Creek at midday they made camp. George, revived with some food and water, awoke in time to hear the finalization of plans to travel only at night in hopes of avoiding confrontations on the way to Olathe. Only two of the individuals present had made this trek before, but they believed that night travel would be easy given the terrain. However, a journey in the dark is slower than in the light of sunshine—the remaining sixty-seven mile trek to Olathe would take most of five nights.

George was befriended by Richard, the gentle giant who had carried him for several hours. When they arrived in Olathe, Richard introduced

George to his sister and brother-in-law. Lucy and Ben Seymour had a laundry business and, thanks to Susan Carver, George had laundry and sewing skills. He moved in and helped with their business while attending the community school. Once again, he was far more advanced academically than his classmates.

Educational lesson plans are nothing if not a real-world demonstration of the statistical phenomenon known as "regression to the mean." By necessity the lion's share of the teacher's time and energy was focused on the development of the most basic literacy skills among her charges. Often George was asked to assist by tutoring a few students, which he very much enjoyed, but he knew that his own long-term educational goals would not be met in Olathe.

After a couple of years the Seymours moved some 180 miles west to the predominately white community of Minneapolis, Kansas, where Ben took up farming full time. George soon followed and upon arriving borrowed about $150 from a local bank to set up his own laundry business. Lucy worked as a nurse and over the next four years the three of them prospered in their business ventures. George was welcomed at the four room school in town where he was the only black student.

During the years in Minneapolis, George became close friends with a fellow student, Chester Rarig and his family. He was often invited to dine with the Rarigs after church on Sundays. So, in 1885 when Chester and George moved to Kansas City to work at Union Depot, it was only natural that they assumed they would continue to dine together when opportune. This assumption led to their exposure to an insidious, though less horrific form of racial prejudice than the experiences in Fort Scott several years prior. One morning the two of them entered a hotel restaurant for breakfast. Chester was told that he could be served but that his "friend" could not. They both left the restaurant, but George urged Chester to return seeming more embarrassed for his white friend than for himself.

Scenes similar to this played out time and again as a sub-text of George's life. It is ironic that in years to come he would receive honors and accolades, and be invited to speak in restaurants and assembly halls, where he would not be served on any other occasion, owing to his very dark skin. George would not live long enough to see the end of the Jim Crow era. White only restaurants, hotels, restrooms, train station waiting rooms, and "colored" drinking fountains were a form of discrimination that he would endure for the remainder of his life.

Jim Crow's protection against interracial cooties at the Streetcar terminal in Oklahoma City. Library of Congress Prints and Photographs Division Washington, DC

A more painful encounter with racial discrimination occurred when he was accepted to attend a Presbyterian College in Highland, Kansas. His application and letters of reference were all in order, his Christian faith was undeniable, and his admission test scores assured intellectual and academic potential to successfully matriculate. All of the paperwork and correspondence between George and the college had been handled by the United States Post Office. In 1885 the Postal Service employed thirty-four African American Postmasters, fifty-six African American Letter Carriers, and forty-two African-American Post Office Clerks. Upon his arrival at the college, the administration realized that George was African-American and denied him final admission.

Disappointed right up to the threshold of serious depression, George suspended his educational quest for several years. He did remain in Highland where he was befriended by, and worked for, the Beeler family. Again, being on the receiving end of institutionalized bigotry had not altered his willingness and ability to befriend white people. When one of the Beeler sons moved to Ness County in western Kansas to open a store, George soon followed.

In most ways George was a typical western Kansas settler. He obtained a 160 acre homestead relinquishment. He went to work for and lived with a man named George Steeley. He built a sod house on his homestead and moved into it on April 18, 1887 with a cook stove, bed, cupboard, two chairs, a table and his laundry equipment. George continued to rely on Steeley for farming implements and water, which had to be retrieved from a well three-fourths of a mile from his field. George cultivated twenty-seven acres for the planting of corn and vegetables.

Like most settlers, George found life on the plains tough, but the rigors of that life did create a communal spirit of cooperation among neighbors, which for the most part seemed to be color blind. Always willing to help and share his knowledge of how to coax crops from the land, George was viewed as being a most remarkable person, as well as the best educated in the area. He pursued his interests in art and literature through the Ness County Literary Society. The society frequently hosted music events, plays and debates. George was even elected assistant editor for the group. The following comments, which appeared in the Ness County News, leave little question that his color was still an issue, though it may have enhanced rather than diminished the recognition of "specialness" among his friends and neighbors. "When I was in the presence of that young man Carver, as a white man, of the supposed dominant race, I was humiliated by my own inadequate knowledge compared to his." . . . "He is a pleasant and intelligent man to talk with, and were it not for his dusky skin—no fault of his—he might occupy a different sphere to which his ability might otherwise entitle him."[2]

Perhaps these two observations captured a kind of inescapable truth—though George continued to try. The seemingly aimless relocations throughout his youth likely had more to do with his need for intellectual stimulation than lack of acceptance. That is not to say that there were not very intelligent people among the settlers of rural Kansas in the 1880s, rather it is simply a matter of arithmetic that the critical mass of erudite people necessary to form an intelligentsia, with whom George would find a cadre of peers, did not exist in communities of only a few hundred souls. So, once again after only two short years, he pulled up stakes and moved on in his restless quest to escape one of the most burdensome realities of his genius—loneliness.

The next stop in his fitful wanderings found him in Winterset, Iowa. However, this interlude would be different than all the preceding stops along the way. Though technically "freed" on the date of his birth, it was in Winterset that George Washington Carver would begin his voyage of emancipation.

Carver's genius stood in stark contrast with the popular image of the shiftless, uneducated negro lacking the intelligence necessary to vote. Library of Congress Rare Book and Special Collections Division Washington, DC

5

The Butterfly's Egg

Dr. Edward Lorenz and the "butterfly effect" research.

The three colleagues sat at a round table in a small conference room with a door directly to the hall and another that entered from the Department secretary's office. Overcast sunlight filtered through a small window. A small single bulb incandescent lamp adorned the table. Barry Saltzman had driven the two hours from Hartford to Cambridge to visit friends at his alma mater. He had been intending to do so for a few weeks, but the call earlier in the week from Edward Lorenz had created intrigue enough to instigate the visit. The third person in the room was a younger graduate student named Ellen Fetter. She had been assisting Dr. Lorenz with many numerical computations and graphical presentations of data.

It was late spring of 1962, at the Massachusetts Institute of Technology, Meteorology Department located in Building #24. For the purposes of testing various theoretical models, Dr. Lorenz had been one of the first among his colleagues to embrace the computer's potential to "quickly" run calculations. "So, tell me again exactly what we are looking for here." Dr. Saltzman inquired.

Leaning back in his chair Lorenz began, "We were using the computer to run a twelve variable non-linear model simulation of atmospheric weather conditions. I wanted to extend the forecast, so I ran a second simulation with the same parameters and conditions as the first model. I entered exactly the values for the variables that were on the printout from our previous run. Naturally, I expected the results to be exactly replicated over the first portion of the model, with the only difference being the extended time tacked onto the end of the original results. The machine is loud and prints about one page every two minutes. So, I figured I could escape the bedlam..."

"He really doesn't like noise, you know." interrupted Ms. Fetter with a slight smile and roll of her eyes.

"Well, yes, and given that we expected eight pages, I figured I had at least a quarter hour of clackity-clack that could be avoided by going to get a cup of coffee. I returned in about thirty minutes and the printer was still running. I was puzzled, so I started scanning the results. It was immediately obvious that the trajectories had shifted radically from our previous run."

The three colleagues were at a loss to understand the anomaly that now lay before them on the table in the form of computer printouts. For the next hour and a half they stared at, shuffled through, and puzzled over the stacks of papers with only an occasional word. A barely audible, "Oh my." from Ms. Fetter intruded upon the group's studious quietude.

Both Drs. Saltzman and Lorenz looked up and simultaneously, "Oh my, what?"

"Well, I'm not certain," replied Ms. Fetter hesitantly. "When I was preparing the initial computations, we had calculated out to six decimal places." Sliding the sheet in front of Dr. Lorenz and pointing at the number .506, "The printout from the results of our most recent run only shows three decimal places."

The three of them immediately retreated to the computer, which occupied an entire room down the hall. It was being used by a professor from the planetary sciences department, so they waited until the following morning to access the machine. They found that the numerical value for the variable stored in the computer's memory was .506127. The computer itself did not actually round to the nearest one thousandth. Rather, the printer could not accommodate the number of columns necessary to print all of the data, so it simply deleted the last three digits. For the second run of the model calculations, Dr. Lorenz had entered .506, which was the number exactly as shown on the printout.

Dr. Lorenz wondered aloud, "Could there be something wrong with the formulas that we entered for the calculations? Or perhaps the model itself requires further refinement. It just does not seem possible that one hundred twenty-seven millionths, could result in such an huge difference in the resulting weather forecast." With a touch of ironic mirth in his voice he added, "Well, when I was a kid my grandfather used to say anyone who tried to predict weather in New England was either a damned fool or a newcomer.

I was born in West Hartford forty-five years ago. I'm no newcomer, so maybe I'm a fool."

Chuckling, Dr. Saltzman urged, "Don't be too quick to despair your findings. I'd recommend that you take a careful look at the recent research on non-periodic solutions of convection equations. Then go back and play around with your computer some more, Ed, and run several models with very tiny changes in the initial variables. I've got a hunch about this." As it turned out, Dr. Saltzman's hunch was prescient.

¤ ¤ ¤

Like almost all veterans from the World Wars, Edward Lorenz brought home ghosts that from time to time haunted memories and dreams. Though a mathematician at the onset, Mr. Lorenz had served his country in the weather services of the Army Air Corp. As a soldier he had frequently been distressed by the lost lives and materiel on missions made futile, not by enemy fire, but by a failure to predict the weather with acceptable accuracy. Planes and ordinance ditched at sea because explosive thunderstorms that were too large to fly around or over seemed a terrible waste. He did not blame himself, nor did he suffer with survivor guilt, but he did resolve that it could be done better. This resolve led him to resume his studies at the Massachusetts Institute of Technology after the war, this time focusing on meteorology rather than mathematics.

In the March 1963 edition of the Journal of Atmospheric Sciences, Dr. Edward Lorenz published an article titled "Deterministic Nonperiodic Flow" and acknowledged his two colleagues, Dr. Barry Saltzman and Miss Ellen Fetter for their assistance with this research project. He determined, in part, that "Nonperiodic solutions are ordinarily unstable with respect to small modifications, so that slightly differing initial states can evolve into considerably differing states." He further concluded, "When our results concerning the instability of nonperiodic flow are applied to the atmosphere, which is ostensibly nonperiodic, they indicate that prediction of the sufficiently distant future is impossible by any method, unless the present conditions are known exactly. In view of the inevitable inaccuracy and incompleteness of weather observations, precise very-long-range forecasting would seem to be non-existent."[1]

These findings were the opening salvo in a career that changed our understanding of meteorology, physics, and indeed every expression of energy; everywhere, forever.

6

METAMORPHOSIS

Carver's benefactors, college education, and influence on Henry A. Wallace.

As was his custom, one of the first things George did upon arriving in Winterset was attend a local church service. Though members of the congregation may have looked at him inquisitively, it would have been unacceptable in most Methodist congregations to invite a fellow to leave a service of worship. This was particularly so for a young man whose eyes shone with a disarming intellect, and whose expressions exuded an affability for all to see. His faith led him to church, but on this day his poor health betrayed his normally unobtrusive presence. The painful cough that racked his body finally drove him from the sanctuary. He slowly walked to a bench that sat under a large mulberry tree with shiny leaves gracing the front lawn of the church. Within moments of taking a seat, his sad and troubled ruminations about his health and situation were interrupted by a rather deep and kindly voice. "You are not well, young man."

"No sir, I am told I had whooping cough as an infant, and I have endured frequent respiratory distress in all the years since."

Dr. Milholland raised an eyebrow at this young black man, obviously wondering at the articulate response. "Well, I am the town's doc and as soon as Mrs. Milholland comes out of the church we will walk over to the house and see if we can round-up some food and medicine that may help that cough of yours."

"Pleased to meet you Doctor. I appreciate your kindness and would be much obliged for the help." Accustomed to thanking people for their kindness, one can now only wonder if he sensed that this meeting was unprecedented in his life. Dr. and Mrs. Milholland would open doors for George through which whole swarms of butterflies would pass for generations yet unborn.

First, they nursed him back to health, then they helped him secure employment at the St. Nichols Hotel. They also helped him once again open a laundry service. Over the course of the next several weeks, the Milhollands invited George to dine with them and others in the congregation after Sunday services. As usual, George enchanted the other guests with his unassuming but utterly infectious personality and intellect.

One Sunday as the congregation was leaving church, Mrs. Milholland pulled George aside and informed him that their normal Sunday dining plans had changed somewhat. Henry and Nancy Wallace were in town for the weekend, and they along with several others from the Presbyterian Church had been invited for fellowship and dinner at the Milholland home. Though they had yet to meet, George knew that Henry Wallace was the controversial owner of the *Winterset Chronicle*, and now lived in Des Moines where he was also the editor and part owner of the state's largest newspaper, the *Iowa Homestead*. Unable to afford his own subscription, George was nevertheless an avid reader of the periodical. Week old copies were often given to him by patrons of his laundry business. Not only did it provide insightful political editorials, the paper often included articles about agricultural issues which George found particularly interesting.

Being sensitive to the racial implications of attending when other less familiar dining guests were invited, he excused himself to Mrs. Milholland with a fabricated story about needing to spend the afternoon cooking up a batch of soap for the laundry. Dr. Milholland walked up just as George was telling this "white lie" and recognized it as such. He chuckled and took George by the elbow as if to guide him in the direction of their house. As George began to voice his protest, Dr. Milholland replied, "No, I really insist that you be our guest just as last week and the week before that." With a somewhat sly grin he added, "This will give Henry Sr. a chance to demonstrate the broad-minded egalitarianism he preaches on the editorial page." He winked at his wife, who was looking askance at her husband's expression of mirth.

Having served as a chaplain in the Union Army during the final throes of the Civil War, Henry Wallace had seen the best and worst of humanity. He had long ago decided to conduct the affairs of his life without a hint of hypocrisy. He truly believed the prophesy inscribed in Luke 3. 5-6:

Every valley shall be filled,
and every mountain and hill shall be brought low,
and the crooked shall be made straight,
and the rough ways shall be made smooth;
and all flesh shall see the salvation of God.[1]

If the Wallaces were taken aback by the inclusion of a dark skinned person among the Milholland's guests, they never missed a stride. Quite to the contrary, Mr. Wallace engaged George in conversation and when he learned of the laundry business he asked about the cleaning of ink stained aprons from the print shop. George shared his idea of cooking up a special soap blend that might be used to wash the aprons in colder water. Often garments were boiled as part of the laundering process which seemed to set rather than remove ink stains. George not only impressed Mr. Wallace with erudite conversation on various topics, he also made a sale. Once a week for the next year the printer at the *Winterset Chronicle* delivered a set of aprons to George's laundry for cleaning.

There were actually three generations of Wallace's at the Milholland's table this Sunday afternoon. Henry and Nancy's son, Harry, their spunky daughter-in-law, May, and their one year old grandson, Henry Agard had come over from the family farm near Orient, Iowa. The farm lay on wide open, treeless prairie land some seventeen miles southwest of Winterset.

As an unsolicited demonstration of George's affinity with children, the youngest of the Wallace clan spontaneously climbed up on his lap. With his knee serving as a saddle and his fingers the reins, George gave baby Henry a good rough ride on a make-believe pony. The boy just grinned broadly but never laughed. His mother, May, came over and sat in the chair next to George and enjoyed an animated conversation throughout dinner. The relationship George struck that afternoon with the Wallace family would lay dormant for the next three years, but it would become an important friendship for all of them in the years ahead.

The Milhollands never failed to treat George as a man—with respect. As an expression of his gratitude, he gifted some pieces of his art work to Mrs. Milholland. She immediately noted an extraordinary, albeit uncultivated, talent. Recognizing a rare depth of intellect, talent and spirit, the Milhollands took it upon themselves to persuade George to apply for admission to Simpson College in nearby Indianola, Iowa. Simpson College, a Methodist institution of higher education, had a history of multi-ethnic matriculation. (*One black and three Asian students had preceded George in educational pursuits at Simpson*). Even so, Dr. Milholland, being a respected bellwether of the community and church, quietly advocated a positive reception by the college admissions committee. The Milholland's and George Washington Carver became lifelong friends, corresponding frequently and visiting when opportune over the next fifity plus years.

Arguably Dr. Milholland's intersession was not actually necessary once George cast the magic of his personality upon the committee membership. "Why do I want to attend college? Why do I want to study? The way I see it is that education opens our minds to possibilities. It allows us to conceive of things that would be impossible for the human intellect to grasp without the rigors of formal training. We have heard that knowledge is power, which may well be true, but it is also the precursor of opportunity and freedom. It allows us to perceive ideas that would otherwise be unfathomable. In a very real sense education is my emancipator, and ultimately it will be so for my people, who will only escape the bondage of second class citizenship through the pursuit and application of knowledge." With these words to the Simpson College admissions committee, George Washington Carver finally won acceptance to an institution of higher education, where on September 9, 1890 he was enrolled as a "select preparatory student." This designation indicated that he did not have a high school diploma. (*In 2009 there were at least eight schools in the United States named "George Washington Carver High School." Though in his life he would be awarded a Bachelor's degree, a Master's degree, and two Doctorate degrees, George Washington Carver was never to receive a high school diploma.*)

¤ ¤ ¤

George had become a deeply religious man. He had read the bible from the first verse of Genesis to the last verse of Revelations and had recited many of verse to memory. Having attended many different denominations of Christian churches in every community of his wandering young life, and through the pursuit of "scientific" research, he had developed an eclectic and unorthodox interpretation of the meaning of many scriptures. Throughout this life, many considered him more a mystic than a traditional Christian Protestant. He had come to believe that he was endowed with certain God-given gifts, which the Lord intended for him to use to facilitate the elevation of "his people." He had also come to realize that the most important manifestation of these "God-given gifts" was not his intellect, but rather his ability to relate to people in a manner that almost always paved the way to a truly unique kind of acceptance. He recognized that his very survival was a gift born of courageous kindnesses, and that this was perhaps the most important theme of his twenty-five year young life. Once again at Simpson College he found an extraordinary acceptance. Years later he recalled, "They made me believe I was a real human being."[2]

As usual, George used his laundry skills to earn money. When students would bring their dirty laundry, he would always invite them to have a seat for a few minutes of conversation. One of his fellows remembered, "He had no furniture so we sat on boxes the merchants in town had permitted him to take. I saw the old battered and broken cook stove which he had retrieved from the dump, and the boiler and wash tubs which he had secured on credit."[3] Clearly, other students also noted the circumstances of George's life. They took up a collection with which they procured a table, chairs and a bed that they placed in his shack one evening when he was not at home. George also recalled from time to time concert tickets and money were slipped under his door, though no one ever took credit for any of these acts, they were not random to be sure.

One of his classmates wrote, "[I]n young Carver, as we came to know him, we saw so much beyond the color that we soon ceased to sense it at all."[4] That was the measure of the man. Simply put, there was so much depth beyond his color that in an era when racism was codified in statutes, one of his attributes was the ability to quickly make friends of colleagues and have those friends soon cease to be aware of his skin. Because of his willingness and ability to share these gifts, the total number of recipients defies calculation.

The fact that George made creation of warm and caring environments a conscious choice seems to have had a profound impact on the kinds of people who were attracted to him, and the environmental choices those people tended to make. In retrospect it is impossible to know which came first in most of his relationships. Was he first the recipient or the purveyor of great kindnesses? Though the question this many years later can only be rhetorical, the answer probably is some of both.

Regardless of the answer, the question certainly seems applicable to the relationship that grew between George and Mr. and Mrs. W. A. Liston, who owned and operated the Indianola book store. George would visit, read and converse with the Listons frequently at their store. Soon he was being invited up to the house, where he recalled enjoying many hours sitting in the warm bay window studying. Mrs. Liston, who shared George's passion for art, "adopted" him as an unofficial member of the family. The two of them maintained a stream of correspondence for the remainder of Mrs. Liston's life. In closing her letters to George she always signed "Your Mother."

At Simpson College George studied grammar, arithmetic, essay writing, etymology, and he indulged his passion for the arts with courses in voice, piano, and painting. His art instructor was herself a recent college graduate, a young woman by the name of Etta Mae Budd. She harbored doubts about George's participation in her program, as it turns out not because of his race but rather his gender. All of the students in the Art Department at the college were female. Yet, as was usually the case, George quickly won over the lot.

Though George demonstrated that he was a natural artist with brush and palate, as well as needlework, what impressed Ms. Budd most were the plants that he brought to her, which he had cross-bred or grafted. She had grown up in a home with a unique appreciation for botany. Her father was the professor of horticulture at Iowa State. Though she admired George's natural artistic abilities, she became convinced that plants and soils, rather than brushes and needles, should busy his hands and his mind in the years ahead.

One day when he had brought some of his potted plants by for her to see, she finally worked up the courage to broach the subject, "George, you are a fine painter, but I have this sense that your future and your career lies more in the direction of botany than art. Have you ever considered studying agriculture?" In response George related the story of his acceptance and then rejection by the Presbyterian college in Highland, Kansas, "You see Ms. Budd, I have sought education wherever I've lived," chuckling somewhat to himself, "and I've lived in probably too many places, but never mind that—because of the color God saw fit to put on my skin, this is the first place that I have ever been allowed to actually attend college." Realizing that participation in her art program at Simpson College was not truly his choice, but rather his consolation, Etta Mae Budd wrote to her father in Ames and told him of a remarkable young man who should be enrolled at Iowa State. Yet again in George's life, the wheels of motion were spun by a benefactor with nothing to gain but the satisfaction of helping another human. Once again, the person helping George in his adventure could have no way of knowing the impact that this simple kindness would have on multitudes of people around the world.

¤ ¤ ¤

For every "daddy's girl" there is also a "girl's daddy." Though somewhat dubious, like many such fathers who love their daughters beyond all reason, Professor J.L. Budd would have agreed to almost any request from Etta Mae. When Etta Mae and George made the fifty-one mile journey from Indianola to Ames, they sat down to talk with Professor Budd. Any doubts the professor may have harbored were soon put to rest, and likely his notions of racial relations were severely challenged.

Professor Budd intervened on George's behalf at Iowa State, in much the same way as Dr. Milholland had at Simpson College a year earlier. In this case, however, it can safely be assumed that his intervention was likely necessary, for this college had neither history of, nor inclination to, establish a multi-racial admissions policy. The strength of his character and the power of George's gifts were not to be denied. In September 1891, George Washington Carver was to begin matriculating at Iowa State College of Agriculture and Mechanical Arts.

He packed to leave the supportive embrace of Simpson College with considerable trepidation, for good reason as it turns out. Early one September morning he boarded the train with his meager belongings in Indianola. He had a ticket that his friends at Simpson College had pitched in to buy for him. Later that day he disembarked in Ames to an environment on campus that ranged from being mildly scornful to outright hostility.

His first day on campus a group of students chanted "Nigger" at the sight of George making his way to class. By the end of the day he was tattered emotionally and physically. Though not initially welcomed by fellow students, Professor Budd and Professor James (Tama Jim) Wilson made up a room for George in an office space on campus. Years later George recalled Professor Wilson and his helping hand in this way, "The name of Hon. James Wilson is sacred to me. He was one of the finest teachers that it has ever been my privilege to listen to. . . . Being a colored boy, and the crowded condition of the school, made it rather embarrassing for some, and it made the questions of a room rather puzzling. Prof. Wilson said, as soon as he heard it, 'Send him to me, I have a room,' and he gave me his office and was very happy in doing so."[5]

When George's friends from fifty miles to the south heard of his troubles, they were not of a mind to allow the disdain of his reception at Iowa State to stand. Upon receipt of this news, Mrs. Liston took action. In her own words, "I immediately put on my best dress and hat and took the train for Ames. I then walked out all over campus with Carver and stayed with him all evening."[6] Years later George recalled, "The next day everything was different, the ice was broken, and from that moment on, things went very much easier."[7]

As different as the situation may have been, Etta Mae Budd was not satisfied with the degree of change she found when she went up to Ames to visit her family a few weeks later. She went down to the dining hall and did not find George there. Upon inquiring of the dining hall manager as to George's whereabouts, she learned that he was required to take his meals in the basement with the hired help. Indignantly, she fetched George from the basement, with his dishes containing his half eaten meal in hand; she plopped him down at a table in the dining hall and proceeded to sit with him, where she herself returned to take meals with her friend and former student for the next several days. Knowing that Etta Mae was faculty at a nearby college, and that her father was the "big cheese" in the horticulture department at Iowa State, the dining hall manager did nothing but sputter and spew that his instructions regarding George's dining accommodations had been vetoed thusly. Within days George found himself sharing tables with his fellow students. Once again, as his classmates came to know him, they found so much beyond the color that they "soon ceased to sense it at all."

¤ ¤ ¤

Academically George did not disappoint his many faculty benefactors during the course of his undergraduate studies at Iowa State. Indeed, he maintained correspondence with his supporters in both Winterset and at Simpson College. They had been instrumental in facilitating his educational aspirations, and he never forgot their support. It would be safe to say that he "made them proud" with his performance.

Though not liking mathematics and history, George managed to earn Bs in those courses. Interestingly, given the direction his career would take after leaving Iowa State for the Tuskegee Institute in Alabama, he only managed a B+ average in the Chemistry and Practical Agriculture courses.

In Botany and Horticulture, which were his favorite subjects, he never earned less than an A. Professor Wilson, the director of the Iowa State Agricultural Experiment Station wrote, "In cross-fertilization...and the propagation of plants, Carver is by all means the ablest student we have here. Except for the respect I owe the professors, I would say he is fully abreast of them and exceeds in special lines in which he has a taste."[8] When Professor Wilson wrote these comments, he had no earthly idea that he was watching the genesis of a new era in cross-fertilization and propagation of plants that would roil agriculture and human history in a few short decades. One can now only wonder what accomplishments Carver may have realized, had he maintained his focus on Botany and Horticulture.

In addition to his regular academic pursuits, George published three papers detailing the findings of his own original research: 'Grafting the Cacti', in Transactions Iowa Horticulture Society; 'Best Bulbs for the Amateur', in Transactions Iowa Horticulture Society; and, 'Plants Modified by Man', Senior Thesis Iowa State College of Agriculture.

As well as he did with his studies at Iowa State, perhaps his most remarkable accomplishments occurred outside the classroom. Being the only black student on the campus, indeed perhaps the only black person with whom most of the students had ever interacted as an "equal," he managed to not only earn acceptance, but he also became recognized as a leader among the student body. George and Professor Wilson established a weekly prayer group which evolved into the Young Men's Christian Association (YMCA). George was elected to serve as "missionary chairman" for two years. He was also selected to represent the college as a delegate to the National Students' Summer School at Lake Geneva, Wisconsin in 1893 and 1894. He participated in numerous other campus activities and organizations, including the Agricultural Society, the Welsh Eclectic Society, the debate club, the German Club, and the Art Club. Though not athletic himself, he supported the Iowa State football team by becoming their first trainer and masseur, which in the 1890s was known as a "rubber." He served as captain and quartermaster of Iowa States' Military Division and, as such, was selected to serve as a member of the state military escort for the Iowa Governor's visit to the Chicago World's Fair.

The environment on campus became, to a large extent, insulated from the effects of overt racism. However, when participating in the many different intercollegiate and other off-campus activities, George and his classmates were exposed to the bigotries of the "real world." This was by no means new to George, but for many of his classmates this was likely the first time they actually felt the barbs of hatred. Initially his classmates were reluctant to intervene, likely because of embarrassment, but this changed over time, and they made special efforts to include George in their activities and to defend his participation when challenged by others. His classmates were enraged when George was refused service at the Highland Park Methodist Episcopal eating house. Likewise, his fellow students voiced outrage when he was called "nigger" while serving as a member of the Governor's military escort. Perhaps they had forgotten that the same epithet had been used to "welcome" George to campus a scant two years earlier. An institutional culture evolved such that support of their black classmate became the expected norm at Iowa State. One student recalled how it was that this expectation was crafted and reinforced among the student body:

> After Carver became a teacher at Ames, he frequently took his meals with the students rather than with the faculty. He was a great favorite with the students. One day he brought his tray to a table where a student recently come from the South was eating. This student did not relish the idea of eating with a Negro, so he expressed his dissatisfaction by rattling his cutlery, scraping his chair etc. and finally gathered up his tray with his provisions and went to an adjoining table. The students at that table had been watching. So when the Southerner came to their table, they rattled their cutlery, scraped their chairs and gathered their trays and went to the table where Carver was sitting.[9]

Though not always so dramatic, George frequently encountered passive-aggressive expressions of racism. One such incident occurred when he was serving as a delegate at the National Students' Summer School conference. Willis Duke Weatherford later recalled the incident with these words, "Those of us from the South thought it a little queer that there should be a Negro delegate present."[10] Even with that recollection, Mr. Weatherford would have to admit that he too became caught up in the weaving of George's tapestry of kindness. Years later, Dr. Weatherford collaborated with Dr. Carver on projects to improve race relations in the South using the Young Men's Christian Association (YMCA) as the vehicle.

Though fully embracing Etta Mae Budd's admonition to pursue

agriculture rather than art, George did not forsake his love for artistic expression. In fact, he frequently presented his paintings as gifts to favored students and faculty. In 1892 Cedar Rapids hosted an exhibition of Iowan artists. George declined the exhortations of his classmates to enter some of his works in the exhibit. When they learned that his reticence was due to his wardrobe and the related expenses, he was spirited off campus by a group of his fellows who bought him a suit of clothes, a train ticket, and packed him aboard with a few of his best paintings. Their efforts resulted in George's painting "Yucca and Cactus" being among the collection selected for the Iowa display at the Columbian Exposition at the World's Fair in Chicago.

¤ ¤ ¤

"Carver, you must have a secret admirer—a big bouquet of flowers just arrived for you on The Dinky. They are awaiting your pick up over at the Hub. Why, you'll have enough lapel flowers to last a month," teased mathematics professor Maria Roberts.

"Do say, I better run over there and see who has fallen in love with me this time," responded George. He was in a particularly good mood on September 28, 1884, as he would finally be awarded his Bachelor's degree the following day, but this was only a partial reason for his sense of elation. Earlier in the day, Professor Pammel had informed him that Professor Wallace and President Beardshear had approved his appointment to the college faculty as an assistant in the Botany Department. He would begin at the start of the next semester and would be placed in charge of the college greenhouse. On this day, George was decidedly walking on air. "The Dinky" was the name given to the narrow gage train that ran from downtown Ames to the Hub on the Iowa State campus. It delivered mail, supplies and served as a commuter service for folks going to and fro. When George arrived and read the card that was attached to the large bouquet, tears welled in his eyes. The note read:

Knowing your love of flowers, we could think of no better way to congratulate you on the noteworthy accomplishment of your impending graduation. More importantly, we all wish you to know that we are so proud to have been part of your educational journey.—Your Simpson College friends.

¤ ¤ ¤

The pace of George's strides matched the briskness of the Saturday morning air. With his ever-present oval tin specimen can hanging across his shoulder by the well worn leather strap, he approached the group of students standing by the wagon. There was a detectable bit more excitement about this week's botany expedition than most previous trips, because today they were going far enough afield as to require a wagon ride. As instructed, they had also packed picnic lunches.

While Edward Sherman was busy hitching a two mule team to the buckboard wagon, George explained that they would be traveling about two miles north to the woods along Squaw Creek, where they would be gathering samples of tree bark. He gave instructions regarding how to note the type of tree, size, health, location and distance from surface water for each sample collected. They were also to collect and include in their notations any insects found on or under the sample of bark. While there was a certain lighthearted camaraderie among the six students present, they attended carefully to their professor's instructions, for they knew that these samples would be the crux of their studies in his classes for the next week or so.

George also welcomed his friend and colleague, Professor Louis Pammel, who was head of the Botany Department at the college. Later that year George and Professor Pammel would co-author an article for the Iowa Academy of Sciences conference titled "Fungus Diseases of Plants at Ames Iowa."[11] No doubt the samples of bark collected on this day would contribute to their knowledge of the fungi indigenous to the area.

"What about me?" questioned a precocious six year old Henry Wallace, the same Henry Wallace whom George had bounced on his knee one Sunday afternoon at the Milholland's house in Winterset, when he was but a year old toddler. Of course, Henry had no recollection of this encounter and only had vague memories of the farm in Orient. He and his parents had left the farm in 1892 in order for his father to further his formal education at Iowa State. 1895 found Professor Henry C. (Harry) Wallace head of the Dairy Sciences Department at the college. His son, the youngest Henry, was a serious though affable little boy, who wandered the campus and befriended many of his father's students and colleagues. He was, however, most taken by this black man with the high pitched voice. Henry was frequently seen around campus trotting along beside George, holding onto one hand and questioning his mentor about one thing and then another. George seemed ever-patient with his little protégé.

"And what about you?" George teased as he grabbed little Henry under the armpits and swung him into the back of the wagon. Henry grinned as he made a beeline to his favorite spot in the right front corner of the wagon box.

George was never particularly fond of driving a mule team. He climbed into the wagon and took his "designated" seat in the middle front with his back against the driver's bench. With little Henry on his left, Professor Pammel on his right, five students sprawled about the rest of the available wagon space, the picnic basket secured under the driver's seat and Edward at the reins, they lit out for Squaw Creek.

George did not talk much, but he greatly enjoyed listening to the excited chatter and laughter of the students. Though he was their professor, the "expert," he did not much care for lectures. He believed that people learn primarily from observation and patience—a lot of patience, because in observing the natural world sometimes change takes a long, long time. Though he considered it a necessary evil related to his chosen profession, he used lectures rarely. When he spoke, especially on these botany field trips, it was usually a story.

He told of times when he and his brother Jim would doodle fish with their bare hands out of the stream near the farm at Diamond Grove. This was only possible during a dry spell, when the water was very low and the fish had to rise to the surface to gulp air. He thought about that behavior for a long time and finally figured out why fish surfaced for air when the stream was so low.

George told of how he and Ma Carver would gather the tree bark every spring from the wood pile where Moses had split the winter's wood. They would pound it into small chips and course mulch and spread it over the beds where squash, black eyed peas, radish, beans and collard greens were planted. George had raked the mulch off of some of the beds to observe how it affected growth of the plants.

He told of the time that a late spring snow froze almost all of the peach blossoms, but the peaches that survived were huge. The next spring he decided to prune about half the green peaches on one tree when they were about the size of a knuckle. Papa Moses was not amused, but later they observed that tree produced much bigger and better peaches. Not only that, the total pounds of produce from that tree was approximately the same as the trees not earlier "abused" by the young Carver's thinning procedure. He remembered being surprised when the same technique did not seem to have any effect when applied to melon vines. He found no significant difference with size and quality of melons between the thinned and un-thinned vines.

Listening from the driver's seat, Edward questioned the reason for that.

George explained that he had come to believe that trees and perennial plants store energy for use by foliage, flowers, and fruit over extended periods of time. On the other hand, annuals take their energy directly from the soil, sun, and water, and then return the energy back to the soil at the end of each season in the form of decaying organic matter. Therefore, the melon vines will produce melons of a size and quality that directly corresponds with the soil, sun, and water conditions available each year.

Over the course of his long career, George came to see botany, indeed all of life, as an enormous interconnected system of energy exchange. His research related to this theory would revolutionize agriculture through the application of crop rotation and fertilization technologies.

¤ ¤ ¤

Frequently, George would go out on his botany expeditions in the early mornings or late afternoons. Quite often he would only be accompanied by his pint sized companion, Henry Wallace. One afternoon Henry and George came upon a decomposing tree in the woods, which was almost totally covered with mushrooms. George told how a root fungus had blocked the tree's uptake of energy from the soil and water. The tree was too heavy for the weakened roots and a wind uprooted the giant and toppled it to the ground. But even with its roots torn free of the earth, the tree had stored enough energy to pop buds and small leaves the following spring. Then with insufficient energy to sustain life, the tree died. He explained to Henry that death was not an instant in time, but rather a process that stretched over several years, and that the cycles of life and death were like "interwoven fingers of two hands folded in prayer. Now the tree gives the energy of its decomposing wood to the mushrooms, so that they may grow big and delicious."

Little Henry looked at the tree for a few moments and announced, "I don't like mushrooms."

George chuckled and replied, "I don't much care for them myself, but don't you tell your mama I said so."

"Why not, Dr. Carver?" Copying most of the students on campus, the six year old Henry called George 'Doctor Carver.' The students had taken to calling him in this way as a somewhat facetious indication of their genuine and profound respect. In reality, George was not to earn his master's degree until 1896 and the first of two doctorates in 1928.

"Well, every now and again she sends me over a pot of cream and mushroom soup." replied George.

"So, what do you do with that soup?" questioned Henry.

"Why, I eat it all up, of course."

"But how come you eat mushrooms you don't even like?"

"Well," George asked, "do you think your Mama loves you?"

"Yes she sure does!"

Now chuckling, "And does she 'sure' love your daddy?"

"Yes sir."

"I suppose she also 'sure' loves your sister, Annabelle and baby John?"

"My mama loves everybody." replied Henry somewhat impatiently.

"And so she cooks that soup with love you see, and soup spiced with love is delicious—in spite of the mushrooms."

Henry paused, studying the tree then looked up at George and said, "So you get the energy from the tree too."

George cast a surprised askance at the six year old and said, "**Yes sir, indeed I do.**"

A proud grin flashed across Henry's face as he turned to trot home. It always made him feel so good when George called him "sir." Many years later, the Secretary of the U.S. Department of Agriculture would often say "yes sir" or "yes ma'am" to subordinates at the department, who were frequently several years his junior. He may never have known how that made his colleagues feel, but there can be no doubt that he clearly remembered how those two little words of respect made that little boy in Ames, Iowa feel. Some fifty years later, Vice President Henry A. Wallace remembered his friend and mentor with these words:

> Because of his friendship with my father and perhaps his interest in children George Carver often took me with him on botany expeditions and it was he who first introduced me to the mysteries of plant fertilization. He seemed to have a great sympathy with me.
> . . . Later on I was to have an intimate acquaintance with plants myself, because I spent a good many years breeding corn. Perhaps

that was partly because this scientist, who belonged to another race, had deepened my appreciation of plants in a way I could never forget. Certainly because of his faith I became interested in things that today give me a distinct pleasure. I feel I must pay him this debt of gratitude.[12]

¤ ¤ ¤

By the time George obtained his Master of Agriculture Degree from Iowa State College in 1896, he had already accepted a position as Director of Agriculture at the Tuskegee Normal and Industrial Institute in Alabama. Dr. Booker T. Washington was Principal of the Institute and was adamant that the new department should be headed by a black man. Dr. Washington's position regarding the employment of black faculty dovetailed with George's own belief that the Lord had assigned him a special charge to use his life and gifts to help "his people." However, unbeknownst to George at the time, he was in many ways jumping out of the pot and into the fire of race relations.

George had been raised, befriended, and mentored by white benefactors time and again throughout his life. He had also witnessed and been the subject of racial bigotry, but in Ames he had created for himself a safe haven. At the Iowa State campus in particular, he thrived on an island virtually free of most forms of discrimination. He was moving to the deep south where overt racism was the norm, even codified in the laws of Jim Crow. Not only that, he arrived on the campus of a "Negro" institution, staffed exclusively by individuals of the "colored race," which in fact had a deeply ingrained pecking order predicated upon skin color, naturally favoring the lighter tones. George was very, very dark.

Over the next fifty-five years at the Tuskegee Institute, George Washington Carver, worked on plant hybridization, grafting, crop rotation, building and maintaining fertility in soils, and he went on to create 325 products from peanuts, more than a hundred products from sweet potatoes and hundreds more from a dozen other plants native to the South. Yet it is arguable that even acknowledging all of these professional achievements, the impact he had on the young Henry Wallace was perhaps the most influential accomplishment of his life. With kindness and respect he wove a tapestry in which he shrouded himself and almost all of those with whom he came in contact. Throughout his life, the environments he created influenced the remarkable lives of many of his protégés. As this story turns to the life of

Henry A. Wallace, it is important to note that though Dr. Carver is best remembered as the "peanut man," his life was most influential because he was a "gentle man."

7

Where Buffalo Roamed

Abuse of the soils, animals, and peoples of the Great Plains.

In 1874, Secretary of the Interior Delano testified before Congress, "The buffalo are disappearing rapidly, but not faster than I desire. I regard the destruction of such game as Indians subsist upon as facilitating the policy of the Government, of destroying their hunting habits, coercing them on reservations, and compelling them to begin to adopt the habits of civilization."[1] By the time George Carver arrived in Ames, Iowa, Secretary Delano's assignment with destiny was a fait accompli. In 1873 over 750 thousand hides were shipped on the Atchison, Topeka and Santa Fe Railroad. The indigenous peoples of the plains, whose lives and cultures had been so integrally linked to the bison, were not defeated in warfare by the military forces of the United States government. Instead, they were starved into internment on "reservations" by the commercial slaughter of at least 20 million American Buffalo during a fifteen year period ending in 1884—when there were virtually no animals of the species left to kill anywhere on the Great Plains.

By the time Henry A. Wallace graduated from Iowa State University in 1910, there were only about 1200 bison living on a ranch in South Dakota owned by James (Scotty) Phillips. Mr. Phillips almost single handedly saved the species from extinction.

Barbed wire had been introduced to the Great Plains in 1873, and by 1910 almost one half million square miles of plains had been sectioned and fenced into family farms and ranches. Crisscrossed by roads and rails, and soon joined by tractors capable of pulling moldboard plows, disc harrows, grain drills, binders, and thrashing machines, the Great Plains saw agriculture poised on the threshold of massive "single crop" factory farming.

In 1909 the United States Bureau of Soils published Bulletin 55. In this Bulletin, Professor Milton Whitney, Chief of the Bureau of Soils, proclaimed, "The soil is the one indestructible, immutable asset that the Nation possesses. It is the one resource that cannot be exhausted; that cannot be used up."[2]

Five years later in an article titled "Being Kind to the Soil" George Washington Carver espoused an opposing point of view. "Unkindness to anything means an injustice to that thing. If I am unkind to you I do you an injustice, or wrong you in some way. On the other hand, if I try to assist you in every way that I can to make a better citizen and in every way to do my very best for you, I am kind to you. The above principles apply with equal force to the soil. The farmer, whose soil produces less every year, is unkind to it in some way; that is, he is not doing by it what he should; he is robbing it of some substance it must have, and he becomes, therefore, a soil robber rather than a progressive farmer."[3]

Over the ensuing thirty years, human tilling of the ancient sod and replacing perennial old growth with annual crops and grasses on a massive scale, coupled with normal meteorological cycles, would put to the test which of these points of view held sway.

PART II

THE SOWING

8

A BETTER CORN

The hybridization of corn.

For three generations the eldest son of the Wallace family had been named Henry. Born in 1836, the patriarch Henry was of the first generation of Wallaces born in America. His life's journey took him from Pennsylvania, to Illinois, to Kentucky back to Illinois, and finally to Iowa. All his life he preached four gospels: 1) a liberal and tolerant form of Presbyterianism; 2) good farming; 3) clear thinking; 4) right living. He shared this from the pulpit and from behind the editor's desk of the *Winterset Chronicle*, in which he had purchased a fifty percent interest in 1878; the *Iowa Homestead*, where he was a thwarted editor and an unhappy thirty percent partner; and finally *Wallaces' Farmer*, which he founded in partnership with his sons. It was his work on the latter of these periodicals where he would become successful and much loved by farmers and their families. He became known affectionately as "Uncle Henry."

His son, Henry Cantwell Wallace, was born in 1866. Like his father, he grew to be a highly respected man of considerable honor and character. Most commonly called Harry, during the course of his life he served as editor of the family owned agricultural journal, professor at Iowa State, and Secretary of Agricultural under Presidents Harding and Coolidge.

With a few notable exceptions, the Harding and Coolidge administrations were populated by scoundrels and scalawags. Not unlike the biblical moneychangers in the temple, these were men deployed by the "big business" establishment to use their presidential appointments to maximize every conceivable profit during this time of almost manic industrial prosperity. "Good Farming, Clear Thinking, Right Living"[1] was printed on the masthead of every issue of *Wallaces' Farmer*. Being the son of a minister, an Iowan farmer, and an agricultural journalist who lived by this credo, Harry Wallace found little comfort among this ilk. Harry died in 1924, while serving as Secretary of Agriculture. It is a safe assumption that his final four years were probably the only truly unhappy times of his life.

It is important to note that in a much happier time, this was the same Professor Harry Wallace who took the young George Washington Carver under wing and made sure he had a job at Iowa State while Carver pursued his Master's Degree—the same Harry Wallace whose son would tag along with Carver on his botany expeditions, and whose wife would have Carver over for dinner and occasionally send him home with mushroom soup.

¤ ¤ ¤

In 1865 Gregor Mendel presented "Experiments on Plant Hybridization" at two meetings of the Natural History Society of Brünn in Moravia. His paper was published in 1866 in Proceedings of the Natural History Society of Brünn. It had little impact and was cited only three times over the next thirty-five years. Mendel's research had not been well understood by his contemporaries, and almost no one at that time seemed to understand the implications of his hybrid peas. As a result, his research papers were virtually lost for an entire generation. After being appointed abbot of the Augustinian Abbey of St. Thomas in Brno in 1868 his administrative duties superseded curiosity, and he was no longer able to press his scientific research.

While some of Mendel's results have since been disputed, the rediscovery of his work in the 1890s by the likes of Hugo Marie de Vries, a Dutch botanist, and Carl Correns, a German botanist, set the stage for the agricultural discoveries of the early twentieth century. At the turn of the century various pseudo-sciences were much enamored with the mythology of genetic superiority predicated upon an organism's appearance—cosmetics and aesthetics. This idea not only manifest in relations between races of humans, but also in the way humans practiced agriculture.

Dating back to the first corn producers, the indigenes of Meso-America, farmers would set aside the kernels from the ears of corn that looked best as the seed stock for the following year. So certain were farmers that this was the optimum method for seed selection, the whole process was elevated to a competitive art form by the time of the 1893 World's Fair in Chicago. Over the ensuing few years the "ideal" ear of corn was codified in standards governing competitions. Much ado was made of these "beauty contests" at state fairs all over the country, with the prescribed ideal ear of corn being 10.5 inches long, 7.5 inches in diameter, with twenty to twenty-two straight rows of perfectly symmetrical keystone shaped kernels. Furthermore, it was a "known fact" that these prize winning ears would produce more, higher quality corn when used for seed stock than their less fortunate, ugly cousins. These "Corn Shows" awarded prize money for the winning ears, and their kernels sold at premium prices to seed the next year's crop.

¤ ¤ ¤

By the early 1900s, *Wallaces' Farmer* had begun to prosper in earnest. Their circulation grew from twenty-thousand to almost forty-thousand subscribers. They had revenue enough to purchase a four story building in Des Moines to house their burgeoning publishing company. Whether or not they were true believers in the "Corn Shows," the newspaper was heavily invested in promoting them. It was good business, after all. People were interested in the outcomes: the shows appealed to the friendly competitive nature of farmers; they paid prize money, which is always newsworthy; people would buy copies of the paper to keep track of the contests.

In the spirit of promotion, the elder Henry Wallace was able to secure the services of Perry G. Holden. The flamboyant and erudite little man traveled the Midwest, Iowa in particular, promoting corn shows in general and the ideal ear of corn in particular. He became known as the "Corn Professor." The honorary title was not altogether unjustified, as he was quite remarkable in his ability to bring education to the masses of farmers in the corn belt. For almost eight years the "Corn Train," which was sponsored by *Wallaces' Farmer*, made whistle stop tours across the American heartland. In towns large and small Perry G. Holden promoted Reid Yellow Dent as the nation's best corn variety.

His educational efforts with the Midwestern farmer began in January 1903, with a short course offered in very rural Hull, Iowa. This offering is historically credited as the watershed event leading to the development of agricultural extension services, which evolved into a national system under the auspices of the Smith-Lever Act of 1914. Perhaps more than anything else, the Corn Professor can be credited with promoting a more scientific form of agriculture, which ultimately would expose the fallacies underpinning his much touted corn shows.

From the age of ten the third Henry, Henry Agard Wallace, had been a gardener. On a plot of ground behind the Wallace home on the west side of Des Moines he raised tomatoes, cabbage, celery, and strawberries—most especially strawberries. The young Henry Wallace loved strawberries. By the time he was fourteen though, he had become fascinated with corn and it had come to dominate the space allocated for different vegetables in his garden.

Though the corn shows would last another twenty years, January 1904, was the beginning of the end—and that from a most unlikely source. That month found the Corn Professor offering a short course for farmers at Iowa State. At fifteen years of age, Henry was able to persuade his parents to allow him to travel the twenty-seven miles north to Ames for the two week course. Young Henry and Perry Holden shared a mutual fondness, and Henry was actually a guest at the Professor's home that January. Nevertheless, young Henry was among a small minority of corn show skeptics. For two weeks Professor Holden happily evangelized the ancient corn grower's gospel:

pretty, symmetrical ears of corn = good
ugly, snaggletooth ears of corn = bad

That being the case, the best possible corn were ears of perfectly shaped Reid Yellow Dent. Young Henry Wallace was not persuaded. Toward the end of the course, the quiet, serious young man raised his hand.

"Yes, Mr. Wallace, you have a question." Professor Holden.

"Professor, what's looks to a hog?" questioned the fifteen year old Henry Agard Wallace. And for the next hour, in front of a packed auditorium, they argued amicably, for they genuinely did like each other, that the farmer's goal should be yield tonnage rather than corn ear aesthetics. The Corn Professor contended that aesthetics and yield were essentially one and the same. He held forth the most lovely ear of corn contained the kernels with the most vitality, and would produce both the highest quality and largest yield when used to seed the next year's crop. The Professor challenged Henry to test the theory. Without a moment's hesitation the challenge was accepted. Confident that the best looking ears would produce the best crop and the worst-looking ears the poorest crop, Perry Holden sowed the seeds of his own demise when he gave Henry the thirty-three ears of corn, which had been used as visual aids during the lecture.

The youngest Henry disembarked from the train (The Dinky) in Des Moines carrying a bag full of Reid Yellow Dent. When asked by his father what the extra cargo was all about, the youngest merely stated that he would need to use the five acres of land that laid fallow behind their house. He planted the seed from each ear in two rows and carefully recorded the source ear for each pair of rows. Much of the summer of 1905 Henry spent tending the sixty-six rows of corn being fastidiously careful to weed, thin, and water each row exactly the same. He also controlled for self-pollination by eliminating the plant's male sex organs. By hand he detasseled the entire five acres every single day. Henry literally committed many hundreds of hours work to his crop. Of course, in 1904 the experimental plot of corn did not have to compete with video-games and surfing the internet for the young man's attention.

The fall harvest was piled in thirty-three carefully marked and numbered squares drawn on the floor of the garage. Henry spent many more hours in that garage weighing, recording and calculating per acre yields for the progeny of each of the ears of corn. His methodology was impeccable; the calculations checked, double checked, and checked again were accurate; the numbers did not lie. The yields ranged from thirty-three to seventy-nine bushels per acre. Some of the "poorest" looking ears produced the highest yields, and the ear adjudicated the most beautiful of the bunch, settled in at twenty-fourth place in production per acre.

In terms of agricultural economics, tonnage matters and pretty doesn't. The corn beauty pageants were a fraud. "What's looks to a hog?"

At the turn of the twentieth century no one could have imagined that the skepticism of the fifteen year old Henry Wallace in Des Moines, Iowa would change the practice of agriculture, land use, food production, and food distribution almost everywhere on the planet. The findings of young Henry's study finally appeared on the pages of *Wallaces' Farmer* in 1907, three years after the results were in. The article titled "Productiveness vs. Prettiness in Corn"[2] was not the least bit self-effacing or apologetic about the publication's continued sponsorship of the Corn Professor and his Corn Shows.

¤ ¤ ¤

Now, the notorious inaccuracy of eye witness accounts proves hindsight is anything but 20x20. However, contemplating the ripple effect of Henry's study and its publication can only be appreciated from a retrospective perch many decades subsequent to the event. Therefore, it is likely that Professor George Harrison Shull, of the Carnegie Institute, did not even fully appreciate the importance of the study as he pursued his own work on "Hybrid Vigor" in 1908.

Professor Shull began with crossing various strains of corn, but it was more than just that. By continuing the cross breeding process for generations, he produced pure strains, which when mated resulted in almost explosive yield increases. This was, in the truest sense of the term, "pure science," because the resulting seeds were of no commercial value. Henry A. Wallace arrived at the same conclusion from his continued experimentation with cross breeding corn in his behind-the-house garden. The results of both Shull's and Wallace's experiments demonstrated that the spectacular production enjoyed by crossing two varieties in the first year, resulted in dismal production from the cross-bred seeds planted the second year. The scientific understanding of genetics in that era led Henry to an erroneous conclusion regarding why that was happening. Regardless of the cause, the yield data was undeniable. The production of a hybrid corn required detasseling which Henry knew was an extremely labor intensive activity. If the resulting seeds would only produce good yields for a single year, the cost of producing the seeds would be exorbitant, and simply too expensive to lure purchase by early twentieth century farmers.

At about the same time, 1200 miles due east of where young Henry Wallace had challenged the consensus mythology of corn culture, other scientists were raising red flags regarding food value of certain isolated seed proteins. Two chemists, Thomas B. Osborne at Yale University and Lafayette Mendel (no known relation to Gregor) at the Connecticut Agricultural Experiment Station in New Haven, Connecticut were experimenting with the nutritive value of seed proteins. They found that rats fed a mixture of pure protein, salt, starch and lard would not survive. They added lactose, gliadin from wheat, and zein from corn. These diets could not support the health of the animals. They realized that the diets must provide certain amino acids, which the rat's bodies could not synthesize. For example, they learned that without the protein lysine in the diet the rat's growth was stunted. When lysine was added to the diet, the normal growth rate resumed. They also realized that certain amino acids are necessary to maintain health, just as others are required for growth. These essential proteins must be present in the food that is consumed. Unhealthy rats recovered when they added butter to the diet, "as if a substance exerting a marked influence upon growth were present in butter."[3] Their work indicated that a nutrient of some sort was present in fats, without which the animals did not thrive and were susceptible to eye diseases.

In remarkably similar work at the University of Wisconsin Department of Agriculture, Elmer Verner McCollum and Marguerite Davis learned that rats would sicken and die when the butter in the diet was replaced by lard, olive oil, or bleached cottonseed oil. These findings became the scientific underpinnings of modern concepts of nutrition and "vitamin theory." By 1913, they had isolated "factor A" which later became known as vitamin A.

An interesting sidebar related to this study is the fact that Dr. McCollum was aware of, and in some respects replicating, the work of Doctors Osborne and Mendel. After obtaining his doctorate degree in biochemistry from Yale, McCollum had stayed at the University for an additional year to continue working with Osborne, Mendel, and their rats.

In his first research assignment at the University of Wisconsin, McCollum had been charged with determining why corn-fed cows were healthier than those fed only wheat or oats. Like his colleagues in Connecticut, he had decided to use rats as the experimental mammals because of their rapid reproduction and short lifespan, as well as the expedience of needing very little space and not much money for feed. When he informed the Dean of Agriculture, Dr. Harry Russell, that they would be experimenting with rats rather than cows, the dean was mortified and is reported to have said in essence that if the alumni heard the Ag school was studying (and feeding!) vermin, they'd have his head. Lacking formal approval, Dr. McCollum and Ms. Davis captured wild rats in the campus horse barn. Of course, wild rats bite! They proved to be far too vicious to safely handle in a laboratory setting. However, this miscalculation did buy them enough time to convince Dean Russell of the research benefits of using rats rather than cows, which resulted in a quick trip to a Chicago pet store to purchase domestic albino rats.

In her recollections years later, Ernestine Becker McCollum, Dr. McCollum's wife, said of that era, "The idea of food having anything to do with pathological conditions was incredible—If you had enough to eat, you were well-fed."[4] There can be no question that as a result of their collective research, these four individuals were among the first to produce the idea that some diseases are caused not by germs, but rather by a deficiency in certain essential nutrients called "vitamins."

While Doctors Osborne and Mendel were alternately starving and fattening rats through diet manipulation, two geneticists, Edward M. East and his student, Donald F. Jones, arrived at the Connecticut Agricultural Experiment Station and continued Professor Shull's earlier work on corn hybridization. Corn provides an ideal subject for study in this area because, being open-pollinated, each kernel may be fertilized with pollen from a different plant. Therefore, each kernel in a single ear of corn may be the product of an entirely unique gene pool. This variability provides the researcher with easily measured characteristics including those of most commercial interest such as number, size, color and shape of the kernels. Driven by those commercial interests, the focus of their research was to develop a vigorous, high-yield hybrid. Donald Jones is credited with moving the normal single-cross breeding method to the next level by breeding two hybrid corn lines. This process became known as "double-cross."

Now, all of this was happening long before the microchip and the World Wide Web allowed double click access to almost any research being done almost anywhere in the world. So, whether these individuals were aware of the details of their simultaneous efforts, separated by half the continent, is questionable. Whether aware or not, their collective energies were swirling forward toward a nexus that would return to and land squarely in the lap of Henry A. Wallace.

¤ ¤ ¤

Perhaps more than anything else, World War I was the spasmodic last gasp of an old world order dominated by despotic monarchs. Beginning violently with the French Revolution and continuing for a century, monarchs all around the world were being replaced by revolutions and constitutions. One could argue that the actual beginning of the end can be traced all the way back to 1215. In that year the Archbishop of Canterbury, Stephen Langton, forced the hand of King John of England, who reluctantly signed the Magna Carta. The document codified the first significant restraints imposed upon a monarchy as well as stipulating certain civil rights for commoners. Whatever the causes, the execution of World War I followed historical patterns—rich men profited and poor men were cannon fodder. Also like most preceding wars, civilians were almost as likely to die as soldiers, most to disease and starvation.

When the German Imperial Army invaded Belgium during the late summer of 1914, they immediately seized, and appropriated for their own use, all livestock and food crops. This was not an enormous cache for the Germans, since Belgium imported almost eighty percent of what they ate. In response, Britain felt compelled to blockade Belgian harbors in order to keep additional rations out of the hands of the opposing military. Belgians began starving by late Autumn of 1914, and a long winter lay in store.

The first camera to take full frame 24 x 36 mm negatives was introduced in the United States in 1914 under the brand name Simplex. The following year Levy-Roth of Berlin introduced the Minigraph—just in time for journalists to start recording the gruesome details of war in a new, more compelling format. A picture is indeed worth a thousand words, and photos splashed across the pages of newspapers graphically changed war correspondency. Viewing the photographs of shredded soldiers was bad enough, but the American public had no stomach for starvation's images of hollow-eyed children with distended bellies. Action was demanded—enter from stage right, Herbert Hoover.

Hoover was born in Iowa on August 10, 1874. From an early age, he was a when-in-doubt-do-something, go-getter kind of a man. A mining engineer by training, in 1897 he took a job with a London firm, Bewick, Moreing & Co. In that capacity, he moved to Australia and oversaw the operations of half a dozen gold mines. Within four years he was made a partner. In 1905 he figured out how to apply the "froth flotation" process to extract zinc from mine tailings. This process alone made millions.

Hoover also is credited with recruiting Italian immigrants to work the underground mines of Australia. He fostered an atmosphere of not-so-friendly competition and described the immigrant workers as "fully twenty per cent superior" to Australian miners. Determined to cut costs by crippling the Australian Labor movement, Hoover stated, "the ensuing rivalry between the Italians and the other men was of no small benefit."[5] This statement captured an attitude about the laboring classes that would be thematic throughout the course of his long career. By 1909, when Hoover returned stateside, he was already a multi-millionaire.

Recognizing his "kick-ass and take-names" approach was likely the only way to save the Belgian people, the Chairman of the Committee for Relief of Belgium, Emile Francqui, turned to Hoover to lead the effort. And lead he did! On day one of his new job he ordered 10 million bushels of wheat at the Chicago Commodity Exchange. For the next three years this pacifist from a family of Quakers finagled, cajoled, and bullied almost every power broker on all sides of the European conflict. It was a sight to see. The press and their readers loved the story.

With a goal of providing 1800 calories daily for every adult and more for children, 2.5 million free meals were provided in Belgium each day. Hoover, like the other 130 thousand workers, was a volunteer and accepted no pay for his efforts. In the end, they administered over $200 million in donations and delivered over 2.5 million tons of food. They saved a people. They saved a nation.

In the midst of all of this, something quite catastrophic happened back on the farms of the Midwest. In the summer of 1916, millions of acres of wheat from Manitoba to Missouri just up and died. Heretofore, the Marquis strain of wheat had been resistant to wheat rust. But beginning a couple of years earlier the dreaded black stem rust had begun a natural microbial mutation. In 1916 it succeeded in penetrating the stems of North America's wheat. The rust went viral. The result was a virtual one hundred percent North American wheat crop failure in 1916.

Outside of the states south of the Mason-Dixon line, few people were accustomed to eating cornbread. In Belgium it was a rare person who had ever even tasted the stuff. Of course, the same can be said for the much maligned, but altogether delicious, bowl of grits. By 1917 hunger pangs induced the massive consumption of this "livestock feed" by millions of people in Europe and North America. Out of this devastating necessity, a new market for corn was born. Corn prices soared.

Upon his triumphant return from Europe in 1917, the Republican Herbert Hoover was appointed Director of the Office of Food Administration by the Democrat President, Woodrow Wilson.

¤ ¤ ¤

When the eldest Henry Wallace (Uncle Henry) died suddenly in church at the age of seventy-nine, *Wallaces' Farmer* did not die with him. It was still on the ascending cusp of both circulation and prosperity. However, the situation down on the farm was not looking so good. Though farmers were clearly profiting from prices inflated by World War I, the Wallaces saw the handwriting on the wall and predicted very difficult economic times ahead for the American farmer.

These predictions were not predicated upon their moral queasiness about profiting from the slaughter on the European continent. (*World War I's total casualties, both military and civilian, numbered about 37 million: 16 million deaths and 21 million wounded, many as a result of the first wartime deployment of poisonous gases. The number of deaths included 9.7 million military personnel and 6.8 million civilians. The Entente Powers (Allies) lost 5.7 million soldiers and the Central Powers lost about 4 million.*) Rather, Henry A. Wallace, always enamored with statistics, used data to show the economic debacle that was in store for farmers. The wheat crop failure pushed corn prices to $2.10 per bushel. At that price, Henry calculated that farmers would lose $5.70 per hundred pounds on hogs which were selling at $17.45 per hundredweight on the Chicago market.

Both surviving Henry Wallaces, in their own ways, pled the farmer's case to the newly appointed director of the Office of Food Administration. With data Henry A. demonstrated that given the average production cost of hogs, the price of 14.3 bushels of corn would equal 100 pounds of hog on the hoof. They advocated that a supply and demand market simply would not serve the farmer, and that for the sake of the nation there had to be some system of agricultural price fixing. In late 1917 Herbert Hoover took a timid step in that direction with the issuance of a proclamation:

> We will try to stabilize the price so that the farmer can count on getting for each 100 pound of hog ready for market, thirteen times the average cost of corn fed into the hogs. Let there be no misunderstanding of this statement. It is not a guarantee backed by money. It is a statement of intention and policy of the Food Administration which means to do justice to the farmer.[6]

The only part of this statement that Herbert Hoover intended to stand behind was the third sentence. In September 1918 the Food Administration established hog prices at a flat $17.50 per hundredweight. Farmers were losing almost 6ᶜ on every pound of pork they produced. Both Henrys felt bamboozled and feuded openly with Mr. Hoover. The conflict would never be resolved. Indeed, it would be greatly exacerbated by the economic turmoil that engulfed the globe over the next two decades.

The Wallace's tiff with Mr. Hoover did not ingratiate them with most of the American public, including many farmers. Not without good reason, Hebert Hoover was somewhat idolized by most Americans, who had for two years read almost daily newspaper accounts of the Herculean efforts of this most unlikely "war hero" who fed the Belgian people.

Meanwhile, the Wallace's reasoning for predicting an economic crisis on the farm, based on statistical machinations, was just too esoteric for most people to grasp. Misreading Mr. Hoover's intent, farmers farrowed record numbers of hogs in 1918. As he had plainly said, the "guarantee was not backed by money" and within a year the hog market collapsed. Thousands of pig farmers went broke in a matter of months. The agricultural community, at least, returned to the Wallace's side of the brouhaha.

¤ ¤ ¤

All the while, Henry A. Wallace remained committed to, and obsessed with, the idea of producing a better corn. As fate would have it, one day in 1919 Dr. Edward East walked into his office unannounced. He had just departed the Connecticut Experimental Station for a position at Harvard University. Before taking up permanent residence at Cambridge, East had undertaken a journey to Des Moines for the sole purpose of meeting with the editor of Wallaces' Farmer. He proposed formation of a partnership to market hybrid corn seed. Perhaps distracted by the on-going battle with Herbert Hoover, or perhaps because of his own doubts about the economic feasibility of producing and marketing hybrid seed, Henry was not yet ready to entertain the idea of a seed company partnership. Dr. East did, however, leave Henry with a copy of a report prepared by his colleague and former student, Donald Jones.

The twenty-five year old geneticist, Jones, had taken the hybridization process to the next level. Like his predecessors, Henry Wallace and George Shull, Jones had produced various hybrid lines of corn through crossbreeding. When he then crossbred two of the hybrids, the offspring demonstrated the much sought after "hybrid vigor." The "double-cross" hybrid corn did not have a yield collapse in the second generation.

When Wallace made time to read the report, he immediately understood why the "double-cross" method worked, and beat himself up a bit for not having seen the solution sooner. It was so simple, after all. He also realized the commercial implications. It would now be economically feasible to produce hybridized seed for a better corn.

9

A BETTER MAN

The emergence of a unique American voice.

Equaling, or perhaps exceeding, the energy invested in making a better corn was Henry Wallace's commitment to making himself a better man. He included all aspects of his life in this quest—physical, intellectual, spiritual. With that said, however, he was a complicated man. The various aspects of his life were intertwined in a manner that makes easy description using the compartmentalization imposed by the lexicon exceedingly difficult.

For example, starting in adolescence and for the remainder of his life, Henry experimented with various diets. No one really knew whether these experiments were born of intellectual, physical, or spiritual motivations; or whether Henry even considered them in those terms at all. What is known is that the diets became an expression of eccentricity. Some of them were downright strange. With one experiment he tried to determine the most economical diet possible using the minimum amount of soil necessary to grow food enough for one person. He ate only corn, soy beans, cottonseed meal, linseed meal, and rutabagas. A few years later, when he read the nutrition and vitamin theory studies of Osborne, Mendel, McCollum and Davis, he would understand why this diet did not work out so well.

This was not the only time that his lack of understanding of essential vitamins and minerals resulted in a diet leading to malnutrition. One regimen consisted of only strawberries and cornmeal. Henry's mother intervened to terminate this draconian menu. Once, while a student at Iowa State, he read of fasting and decided to give it a try. He quit eating altogether. He would drink water, walk two or three miles each day, attend classes, and study. He commented, "It is amazing how much time you can pick up if you don't eat."[1]

After about six days of fasting he was out on a walk in the nearby woods. He happened on a downed tree that was almost totally decayed. Then he noticed a black man sitting at what was once the root end of the tree. The bespectacled man was very dark and lean, with a touch of gray appearing in his mustache and along his temples. Drawing closer he recognized his old friend. "Dr. Carver—but how?" The old man responded only with a grin. A vague awareness of his surroundings had been growing in Henry then suddenly, "This is the tree—this is the mushroom tree!" The old man threw back his head and chuckled silently as he faded into the ethers. Henry promptly returned to the campus dining hall and sat down to a meal, saying only that his fasting had resulted the development of "rather an abnormal state of mind."[2] Dr. Carver remained much on his mind for the next several weeks.

¤ ¤ ¤

Henry was always a walker. At six years of age he had walked and trotted many miles with George Washington Carver on their botany expeditions around the periphery of the Iowa State campus. Years later while attending college, rather than use the train on some weekends, he would walk the twenty-seven miles from the campus in Ames to his parent's home in Des Moines.

In 1910, his first summer after graduating from the university, the young Henry's shoe soles logged hundreds of miles on a walking tour of Iowa. He would stride along the back roads until he saw a farmer in a field or in a barnyard. Quiet, even reserved, but never really shy, Henry would just walk up, introduce himself and start up a conversation. Sometimes they talked about the weather, or the draft horse, or perhaps the family's diet. Often they talked about corn. Always they talked about farming. As soon as he had enough material written for his guest column, he would mail the article detailing his journey's observations to his father for publication in *Wallaces' Farmer*.

One such stop happened on a long lonely stretch of road about halfway between Lawler and Cresco, some two hundred miles northeast of Des Moines. About a mile north of Saude, a small village populated by Norwegian farmers, Henry happened on a man a couple of decades his senior, and just about the prettiest little three year old girl he had ever laid eyes on. Thomas was at the corner mail box gathering the post. They exchanged greetings and, making small talk, Henry asked if he had any exciting mail today.

"Nope, it looks like about the same old thing, but I see we got the *Wallaces' Farmer*. I'll just read it tonight and take it on up to Nels' house in the morning."

"No kidding, may I take a look?" Henry requested. Without hesitation Thomas handed the paper to Henry who quickly thumbed through each page.

"You read mighty fast."

Henry chuckled, "Well, not that fast, I was just looking to see if they had included my most recent article." Thumping the paper with the back of his right hand, "Yep, there it is—page five."

"Your article? Let me see that." Thomas narrowed his eyes and looked a Henry with a squint canted slightly to the left. Introductions were made and Thomas was astounded that one of **the** Henry Wallaces of Iowa was standing right in front of him. Thomas had been reading *Wallaces' Farmer* for years and was absolutely delighted to meet "Uncle Henry's" grandson.

Henry's grandfather had been ordained as a Presbyterian minister in 1863. He had something of a checkered history with the Presbyterian Church orthodoxy. After a dozen years in the pulpit his health was failing badly. His doctor, also a close friend, finally counseled, "It's either out of the pulpit or into the bone yard!"[3] So it was, at forty years of age, Henry Wallace left the ministry, but he did not leave his faith nor his need to proselytize a bit. Toward that end, beginning in 1898, he laid claim to page 2 of the family owned *Wallaces' Farmer*. There readers found "Uncle Henry's Sabbath School Lessons,"[4] which was by far the most popular feature in the paper. His weekly contribution to the spiritual well-being of the readers probably sold more subscriptions than anything else printed therein.

Ironically, he likely found a more receptive audience among the comparatively liberal Lutherans of Norway, than the brimstone breathing congregations he had served as a minister. His theology of kindness, expressed by material and spiritual generosity, was enthusiastically embraced by *Wallaces'* readers. They came to feel that they knew "Uncle Henry" as a personal friend and mentor.

For this and other reasons, *Wallaces' Farmer* was a fixture among the Borlaug families. A single edition was passed around from house to house to save on the cost of multiple subscriptions, which was $1.00 per year. Lucky was the Borlaug who went to the mail box on the day it arrived. He would enjoy crisp newsprint, and each successive reader would make do with a more tattered read.

Thomas looked up the road and saw his nephew Henry coming with six empty milk cans rattling around in the back of the buggy. "Yonder comes my brother Nels' son. Normally I'd hide the paper from him, so I could enjoy the first read at my leisure. If he sees it he will be wanting to take it on up to his house. But given the circumstances I am going to have to show it to him today."

Thomas had a circumspect grin on his face as his nephew pulled up the horse drawn buggy. "Henry, let me introduce you to another Henry." Nodding his head in Wallace's direction, "This here is Henry Wallace."

Henry Borlaug replied with casual politeness, "It's a pleasure to meet you."

Thomas handed Henry his mail with *Wallaces' Farmer* laid on top. He said with a hint of hero worship in his tone, "You'll find an article this gentleman wrote on page five."

Now it was Henry Borlaug's turn to frown and squint at the young Mr. Wallace, as he opened the paper to the stated page. "So, you are Henry Wallace?!"

"Well, I am not the Henry Wallace. I'm just the third Henry Wallace."

"Uncle Henry is your dad?"

"My granddad."

"Well, I'll be." replied Henry Borlaug as he looked down at the bottle of milk and block of cheese Wallace had just purchased at the Creamery in Saude.

It was already late in the day and thirteen miles to the nearest town, Cresco. Henry had resigned to sleeping under the stars somewhere up the road. Cheese and milk would be dinner. "I saw you buying your provisions at the Creamery a while ago. I figure you haven't got a place to stay tonight." Borlaug observed.

"No, but I'm fine—I'm walking around the whole state of Iowa this summer, so I've planned to spend a good many nights out."

Borlaug explained, "Now I have to say that if I tell Dad I met Uncle Henry's grandson and did not bring him by for a visit, he may want to tan my hide. Besides, we have room to put you up for the night."

The little girl had a precocious air, and thus far had listened silently to the adult's conversation, "You can sleep in Oscar bed. He not home," she added with a matter-of-fact, wide-eyed expression.

"Is that right?" Henry questioned teasingly, "And what is your name?"

"I am name Sina Bolaug."

"Well, Sina Borlaug, I might just take you up on that kind offer."

"You can sleep in a bed," she added again, just in case he had missed that point the first time.

The three men laughed, as Thomas swung his daughter into the buggy. He and Wallace clambered aboard as well. "We can stop by my house to grab the fishing poles and walk up Little Turkey Creek to Nels' house," Thomas suggested, as he looked toward the afternoon's descending sun, "We should get there about the time the fish start biting."

"I don't know much about fishing, but I can try." Wallace replied as he made a mental note of Thomas Borlaug's mail box route number. With his next article submission, he would include a dollar and ask his father to have another subscription sent to the Borlaug family.

They decided to forgo fishing, realizing other members of the Borlaug clan would want to spend the evening visiting with their special guest. Visitors were rare enough in the far northwest corner of Iowa, particularly one as special as the revered Uncle Henry's grandson.

That evening quite a crowd gathered at Nels' and Emma's house. In addition to Henry, Clara, and Ned, they were joined by Nels' brother Thomas, his wife Johanna, their oldest son Carl and their two youngest daughters, Hanna and Sina. Thomas and his family lived about a mile away. Their other four children, Semon, Ollis, Thomas, and Annie, had stayed behind to feed the livestock and milk the cows.

Emma Borlaug was the statuesque matriarch of the Borlaug clan. As a Scandinavian farm wife she was not at all prone to sentimentality. Nevertheless, she made much ado of the young Henry Wallace's visit. So much so, that Nels teased her just enough to cause a blush to cross her striking face. Over a dinner of homemade bread, beans and salt pork, carrots and cabbage, and a delicious raspberry pie, the Borlaugs pried everything possible out of their "urbane" guest. It is interesting that many of his Iowa State classmates considered Henry something of a bumpkin, but these farm folk saw him as sophisticated and worldly. After several attempts, Henry managed to turn the subject back to the Borlaug family, their farming, and their lives. He was a roving correspondent for Wallaces' Farmer after all, and it was his job to get a story and write it. Toward that end, Nels and Thomas

Borlaug acquiesced and told of the Borlaug family and how they came to be Iowans.

Their parents had spent six weeks crossing the Atlantic on a sail ship. They did not have the money to afford passage on a steamer, which would have only required two weeks to make the crossing. They were chased away from Norway's Sogn Fjord region by hunger born of the late-blight potato famine that swept through Ireland in 1845, the Scottish Highlands in 1846, and then Scandinavia after jumping the English Channel in 1847. In reality times had been tough even before the potato famine for the Borlaug family. They were scratching subsistence out of less than five rocky acres, and the fish they could catch in the Fjord.

Upon arriving in North America, they continued their journey up the St. Lawrence River and disembarked at Green Bay, Wisconsin. They broke ground on a small farm at Norway Grove, Wisconsin for a few years. Thomas and Nels were brought screaming into this world at that little farm. The family then pulled up stakes and migrated over seven hundred miles west in Conestoga wagons, across the states of Illinois and Iowa. They settled on the banks of the Missouri River where it exited the Dakota Territory, about forty miles northwest of Sioux City.

From time to time during the course of the telling, Nels would interrupt Thomas or vice versa. They would lapse into Norwegian to remind each other of some detail or to correct the other's recollection on some point. Then, both nodding their heads vigorously, one or the other would return to telling the story in accented English.

The farming had been good on the banks of the Missouri River, but being pacifists of Scandinavian descent, they disdained warring with the indigenous peoples of the northern plains. Sadly, if they planned to continue living there, choosing peace was not an option. The Sioux already considered the Europeans invaders. As the United States policy of waging war by slaughtering the buffalo became more effective, the indigenes became more hostile and raided farms for food and scalps.

The Borlaugs, along with twenty-two other Norwegian families, loaded their wagons and retreated to Iowa. They sunk roots in the northeast corner of the state and named their settlement "New Oregon."

Wallace chuckled, "New Oregon, huh? I take it there was a bit of tongue in cheek irony in that choice of name."

"Yes, I suppose there was," responded Nels with a wry grin.

"Seriously, why did your family choose to back track against the trend of migration toward Oregon and California?" questioned Wallace.

Nels sat quietly for a moment with a distant look in his eyes, "I remember them talking about it. I was quite young at the time. All the families got together and discussed plans on several occasions. There was consensus among the community about the need to move. They were not willing to live in fear and did not want to engage in on-going war. Where to go was not so easy. In the end, they opted to farm rather than pan gold, cut timber, or mine coal. I also think that in the minds of some, they hoped for a return visit to Norway at some time later in life. A move further west seemed to foreclose that option permanently. Of course, none of us have ever made that trip. Now, in looking back after all these years, I think by eighteen sixty-five they were just plain tired of chasing the sun for food."

Wallace took his pencil and notepad out of his pocket and quickly scribbled the title of his next article—"Chasing the Sun for Food."

In the summer of 1910, young Henry Wallace would have scores of conversations with Iowan farmers and their families. He would be invited to share meals dozens of times and often offered the spare bed or the hay loft as a place to bunk for the night. Over the next thirty-six years, as editor of *Wallaces' Farmer*, Secretary of both the Agriculture and Commerce Departments, and as Vice President of the United States, he would literally have tens of thousands such conversations. In early September 1946 Henry Wallace would meet a young agronomist from Iowa at the International Maize and Wheat Improvement Center in Champingo, Mexico. It is little wonder that Mr. Wallace did not make the connection that on one warm evening, three dozen years prior, he had shared dinner and conversation with Dr. Norman Borlaug's parents and grandparents. That evening had been exactly three years and nine months before Norman's arrival in this world.

¤ ¤ ¤

I addition to walking Wallace also took up the sports of tennis and volleyball. While not a graceful player, he became rather good at both. He was not overly aggressive or competitive, but when he played, he played to win. Toward that end, he knew that the final score was all that mattered. While he may not have been pretty to watch, he took solace in the fact that just like the "corn shows," pretty did not count when the points were tallied. If given the choice to win ugly or look good losing, he chose ugly every time.

¤ ¤ ¤

George Washington Carver had spent much of his first three decades in an often frustrating but ultimately successful educational quest. The consensus view of the era held that a black person would likely not benefit by an education, that being the case, she/he had no need for an education, and therefore, any education for black children, even if dramatically inferior, would more than suffice.

The impact of implementing these notions in George's early life was that for him every single educationally appropriate and intellectually stimulating placement was integrated, with him being the sole student of his race. Because education for black children was either absent or woefully inadequate and permission to access education in an integrated setting was often forbidden, his educational pursuit was a long and hard fought ordeal.

In contrast, educational opportunity was a virtual birthright for the third Henry Wallace. Access to the best education available was guaranteed and success was expected almost from the time he took his first toddling steps on the family farm in Adair County. The home was full of books, both parents were college educated, and from the age of four he virtually grew up wandering the campus of Iowa State College of Agricultural and Mechanic Arts. Education was ubiquitous in his life. So much so, that it could be easily taken for granted. Of his tenure at West High School in Des Moines, Henry commented later in his life, "Probably no one got more out of a school and gave less to it than I did from September of 1902 until June of 1906."[5]

Though Henry graduated with a Bachelor's Degree near the top of his Iowa State class in 1910, he continued to demonstrate some disdain for the formal education that had been George Carver's obsessive aspiration. He never seriously contemplated attending graduate school. To his father he explained that this decision was rooted in his belief that graduate school would only slow down the pace of his learning and corn breeding experiments.

Henry's father and grandfather supported this decision, because they had come to recognize that like his childhood mentor, Henry was "different"—different in a way that ultimately validated his reasoning for not pursuing graduate studies at a university. In point of fact, that effort likely would have slowed rather than enhanced his unique learning process.

In his first year out of school, Henry came to realize that no one really had any idea what factors affected the prices for agricultural products or why those prices fluctuated dramatically over time. He purchased *Economic Cycles: Their Laws and Cause*, a book by Professor Henry Moore of Columbia University. He did not understand it. He went to Drake University in Des Moines for help. He went to the Des Moines Public Library for help. Finally, he found a calculus text book, wrote on the inside cover "what one fool can do, another can,"[6] which became his lifelong motto, and set about the task of teaching himself the intricacies of correlation coefficients, regression lines, dependent and independent variables, and even the concept of initial conditions.

He performed statistical analyses of almost everything he could think of, and his articles in *Wallaces' Farmer* soon reflected his newly acquired expertise. So much so, that even without a graduate degree, Henry was invited to become a part-time professor at his alma mater, where on Saturdays he taught post-graduate statistics classes. In 1923 he co-authored a reference book entitled *Correlation and Machine Calculation*, which was issued by Iowa State University Press in 1925 and again in 1931.

With the support of his family, Henry's education also included a concerted effort to understand the world and its many cultures. Though he checked-out and read a stack of books from the public library each week, they reasoned that some knowledge had to be experienced firsthand. Fortunately, by the time he was a young man, his family had the means to support Henry's continuing education and cultural enlightenment. In 1909, the twenty-one year-old Henry was sent alone on a three month tour of the American west. Encouraged by his father and grandfather, the trip was paid for by *Wallaces' Farmer*. He traveled by almost every mode of transportation available—bicycle, automobile, train, horseback, mule drawn wagon, and foot. At each stop he submitted straight forward, plainly written reports for publication, detailing the discoveries of his journey. Most of the reports were agricultural in nature, but some ventured into his observations of the social and cultural differences he noted in the various locales. Most important in this regard were his observations of how irrigation imposed a "culture of cooperation" among western farmers. This exposure had a profound impact upon his thinking about people, cultures, and agriculture—when imposed by necessity, people could and would choose to get along.

By 1912, whether or not they were becoming worried that young Henry's brain was becoming too much like the pushbutton mechanical calculator that sat on his desk, it was certain that there was need to move him out of the self-imposed cloister that had become his office at *Wallaces' Farmer*. The two older Henrys insisted that he take a hiatus from his office full of statistical machinations. They packed him off to France, Holland, Belgium, Germany and finally Ireland. In Dublin he connected with his roots and met his grandfather's old friend, George Russel. An agrarian mystic, Mr. Russel found a kindred spirit in the young Wallace. They struck up a friendship that was to last twenty-five years and continue to influence Henry's thinking for the remainder of his life.

As a result of these travels, it can be said that Henry had a greatly expanded world view. He returned home no longer just a smart farm kid from Iowa. His provincial blinders removed, his understanding of George Carver's lessons about the connectedness of all things took on a global aspect.

Years later, at the behest of a President, Henry's journey though life would include many trips around the globe. These travels were greatly enhanced by his fascination with, and study of, languages. Inspired by a high school German teacher, he developed a life-long love of languages. He came to believe that language was not just a means of expressing ideas but was, in and of itself, an expression of a people's culture. Consistent with his normal modus operandi, he eschewed the classroom in his pursuit of this fascination. Regardless of exactly how he studied, during the course of his life he managed to become conversant in German, Portuguese, Italian, and Spanish. It was his command of the latter that is of most importance to this story. In fact, Henry Wallace's mastery of plant hybridization and the Spanish language was the vehicle that carried George Washington Carver's load of butterflies into the next generation.

10

By Their Fruit

Wallace as a young adult, Wallaces' Farmer, and HiBred Corn Company.

While on his decades-long pursuit of enlightenment, Henry's family also grew and changed. He married a beautiful woman, Ilo Browne, in 1914 and they had a loving, though not overtly demonstrative relationship. Their family included three children: Henry Browne Wallace, born on September 18, 1915; Robert Browne Wallace, born on July 13, 1918; and, Jean Browne Wallace born on June 20, 1920. As his career grew from editor of *Wallaces' Farmer*, to Secretary of Agriculture, to Vice President of the United States, and Secretary of Commerce, the demands on his time would absent him from his family for extended periods. Regardless, they loved each other and in the end, he had done well by his family and they by him.

In the years before television became the dominant force in American family life, people were pretty much left to their own devices with regard to evening entertainment and stimulation. Henry took on the role of intellectual mentor. He invented games that he played with the children. He read with them and tutored his oldest son in Latin. He encouraged intelligent and stimulating dinner conversation.

Henry also modeled the idea that people should and could communicate, and even disagree, with civility. He helped organize the "Pow-Wow Club" in Des Moines. Perhaps best likened to today's Toastmasters Club. The membership of twenty to thirty people met once each month to listen to one members presentation and then engage in discussion. Controversial topics and presentations were the expected norm.

Henry was egalitarian in his approach to friendships. Though reserved to the point of being considered shy, he was the center, perhaps in an odd way the alpha-male, of a circle of friends that included the proverbial butcher, baker, and candlestick maker—with a few farmers and lawyers thrown in. The group would often get together on Sunday afternoons for friendly games of tennis, volleyball, or just long hikes. From this, his children took the notion that people, regardless of station, are worthy, that friends of various backgrounds bring into play a diversity that is both stimulating and valuable.

Though quite different in temperaments, Henry Agard Wallace and his father Henry Cantwell (Harry) Wallace genuinely liked each other. They found little to argue about, because their shared values led to very similar positions on most matters of philosophy, politics and business. In 1921 the younger Henry assumed the role as chief editor of *Wallaces' Farmer* when his father, with much reticence, accepted President Harding's appointment as Secretary of Agriculture.

Henry C. Wallace evidenced his mixed feelings about entering the political realm, on the editorial page of *Wallaces' Farmer*, under the heading "A Word Personal":

> I am about to leave the surrounding in which I have spent twenty-six happy years and move into a strange place and an unfamiliar atmosphere. That is to say I have accepted the invitation of President Harding to become Secretary of Agriculture.
>
> It has long been a tradition of our family to not seek political office. Not that we consider the seeking or holding of public office as discreditable or unpraiseworthy; quite the contrary. But in our case the opportunity for service seemed larger outside than in it. In becoming the head of the United States Department of Agriculture I do not feel that I am breaking this tradition. I did not seek the office directly or indirectly, as a large number of my friends who have wanted to help me to it will testify. . . .
>
> I go to Washington with less reluctance because from the beginning President Harding has taken an advanced stand for a sound national policy as it relates to agriculture, and I am sure he will do everything the Chief Executive can do to promote that end. Therefore he has a right to the help of everyone of us as we can help best.

As to *Wallaces' Farmer*, this will make no difference in the paper. My absence will impose an additional burden and real sacrifice upon my brother, John P. Wallace, to give the business of the paper more confining attention for a while at least. But it is a burden he is fully capable of bearing and a sacrifice he makes willingly.

So far as the editorial conduct of the paper is concerned, the responsibility will rest upon my son, Henry A. Wallace. He has been in the editorial work for ten years, and has been doing more of it than is generally realized. That he is fully equal to this larger responsibility our readers will discover for themselves.

I wish it were possible for me to acknowledge personally the many expressions of confidence and good will that have come to me from all parts of the country. As for my work in the Department that must speak for itself. I will do the best I know. If I fall short of what is fair to expect of me, the failure must be charged not to lack of an earnest desire, but to my own personal limitations.[1]

Though reticent, Harry had some reason for his guarded optimism. During the presidential campaign, he had been asked to draft most of candidate Harding's speeches regarding agriculture. Being allowed to author the public pronouncements of the future President implies a considerable amount of sway and influence.

He also had some reason to believe that the Congress was willing to act on behalf of the agricultural community. In 1920 U.S. markets were being flooded by inferior quality peanuts from China. The United Peanut Association of America was invited to plead their case with Congress. On January 21, 1921, exactly six weeks before Harding's inauguration, George Washington Carver addressed the House Ways and Means Committee. His selection to represent mostly white peanut growers was a strategic stroke of genius. His appearance before the committee initially bewildered the Congressmen, who had never before hosted a black witness. Watching him arrange the many visual props he had brought on the table before him, the Committee Chairman curtly announced that Carver would have ten minutes for his presentation. The Chairman then cracked wise, "If you have anything to drink, don't put it under the table." To which Dr. Carver quickly responded, "Drinks will come later if my ten minutes are extended." The room erupted in laughter which won his first ten minute extension.

At one point, while Carver was explaining how a combination of peanuts and sweet potatoes offered a perfectly balanced diet, Congressman Tilson of Connecticut asked, "Do you want a watermelon to go with that?" Ignoring the racial barb the witness responded, "Watermelon would make a good dessert, but you know we can get along pretty well without dessert." This response drew a mixed reaction—laughter from some, but one can only imagine the thoughts that went through the heads of others present at this demonstration of a black man's nimbleness of wit. The word "uppity" comes to mind.

Congressman John Garner of Texas cautioned the committee and the audience, "Let us have order. This man knows a great deal about this business." Supportive throughout the testimony, Garner time and again moved for an extension of time allotted for Dr. Carver's presentation.

The Committee became increasingly captivated as Carver went on and on demonstrating previously unheard of uses for the peanut. Reflecting his life-long spirituality, as well as his approach to science, he concluded his remarks, "If you go to the first chapter of Genesis, we can interpret very clearly, I think, what God intended when he said 'Behold, I have given you every herb that bears seed. To you it shall be meat.' This is what He means about it. It shall be meat. There is everything there to strengthen and nourish and keep the body alive and healthy."

At this point the Chairman, perhaps still incredulous that a black man had just spent two hours sharing his knowledge with the august body, asked, "Dr. Carver, how did you learn all of these things?"

Carver answered: "From an old book"

"What book?" asked the Chairman.

Carver replied, "The Bible."

The Chairman inquired, "Does the Bible tell about peanuts?"

"No, Sir" Dr. Carver replied, "It tells about the God who made the peanut. I asked Him to show me what to do with the peanut and He did."

With this the members of the committee and the audience stood slowly at first, one here and one there, and then all—all clapping—a remarkable show of appreciation and respect. Afterward Congressman John Garner commented in a newspaper interview, "This was one of the most interesting talks I have ever heard before the committee and one of the most effective."[2]

There were likely white men who could have given an equally

informative presentation, but the press loved the subtext of this story. A black professor from Tuskegee Institute was the spokesman for the United Peanut Association of America. The story was carried in papers all across the country. The association's gambit paid off, the Fordney-McCumber Tariff bill passed out of the House Ways and Means Committee including a four cent per pound tariff on imported peanuts. The peanut industry had found a most unlikely patron and George Washington Carver became the "peanut man."

¤ ¤ ¤

So it was that Harry Wallace had grounds for reasonable optimism for the agriculture agenda. But being a man of clear moral values and high ethical standards, he was not a great fit in either the Harding or Coolidge administrations. He was almost alone among the Cabinet and presidential advisers in his calls for fairness and equity. His colleagues on the cabinet were, for the most part, "owned" by big business. Increasing their own wealth and that of the richest benefactors of the industrial revolution was, with few exceptions, the intent of public policies issued by these administrations.

This inclination was evidenced by the activities of the "Ohio Gang"(Warren G. Harding, Albert B. Fall, Harry M. Daughtery, Charles Forbes, Edwin C. Denby, Thomas W. Miller, and Jess Smith).

It was Albert Fall who was most involved in what became known as the "Teapot Dome Scandal." This was not the first nor the last "pay to play" scheme hatched by the unscrupulous among America's political folk, but it was a doozy. A geological formation about fifty-five miles north of Casper, Wyoming looks just like a teapot dome. Under this cap rock lay an enormous oil reserve on public lands.

President Taft, who had served as Secretary of War before ascending to the presidency, had set aside the oil at Teapot Dome and Elk Hills California as reserves for the Navy in 1913. This decision had been bitterly contested by Senator Fall of New Mexico.

Upon achieving statehood, New Mexico sent two Republicans, Thomas Catron and Albert Fall, to the United States Senate. After moving to New Mexico in 1866 and taking the Bar Exam in 1867, Thomas Catron, through a whole variety of chicanery, obtained "clear" title to thirty-four Spanish and Mexican land grants totaling almost 3 million acres.

Albert Fall, arrived in New Mexico in 1889. Soon thereafter, Fall met Catron, who almost immediately became his benefactor. Fall was admitted to the New Mexico Bar in 1891 and, leveraging Mr. Catron's influence, was appointed judge in the third judicial district two years later. During his five years of "service" on the bench, Albert Fall became one of the wealthiest land owners in the New Mexico Territory.

While in the Senate, Fall found company of like minds among the Ohio Gang. In 1921, the newly elected President Harding appointed Senator Fall the Secretary of Interior. The President also appointed another one of the "gang," Edwin C. Denby, Secretary of the Navy, though Denby had only achieved the rank of Major in the U.S. Marine Corps.

Later that same year, by executive order, President Harding transferred control of the Naval oil reserves at Teapot Dome and Elk Hills from the Navy Department to the Department of the Interior. In 1922, Secretary Fall leased, without competitive bids, the Teapot Dome fields to Harry F. Sinclair and the field at Elk Hills, California, to Edward L. Doheny. In 1921, Doheny had "lent" Fall $100 thousand, interest-free, and upon Fall's retirement as Secretary of the Interior, in March 1923, Sinclair also "loaned" him another $100 thousand.

These transactions became the subject of a Senate investigation. The investigation led to a series of civil suits and criminal charges related to the scandal. In 1927 the Supreme Court ruled that the oil leases had been corruptly obtained and invalidated the Elk Hills lease in February of that year and the Teapot Dome lease in October. The Navy regained control of the Teapot Dome and Elk Hills reserves as a result of the Court's decision. Another significant outcome of this entire brouhaha was the Supreme Court decision in the McGrain v. Daugherty case, which for the first time, explicitly established Congress' right to compel testimony.

Albert Fall was found guilty of bribery in 1929, fined $100 thousand and sentenced to one year in prison, giving him the inauspicious distinction of being the first Presidential cabinet member ever sentenced to prison for his actions in office. Harry Sinclair, who refused to cooperate with the government investigators, was charged with contempt, fined $100 thousand, and received a short sentence for jury tampering. Edward Doheny was acquitted in 1930 of attempting to bribe Fall. In fact, Mr. Doheny was not only acquitted on the charge of bribery, but Doheny's corporation foreclosed on Fall's home in Tularosa Basin, New Mexico, for failure to repay the $100 thousand interest-free loan made nine years prior, way back in 1921.

Secretary of the Navy Denby was never indicted on any criminal charges, but on March 10, 1924 he was forced to resign as a result of the scandal.

The Teapot Dome shenanigans were not all President Harding's Cabinet members were up to in the early 1920s.

The President had appointed his old Ohio Gang crony, Harry M. Daugherty, as the fifty-first United States Attorney General. During his three years in this post, Daugherty's name was connected with veterans bureau irregularities, alien property conspiracies, as well as his role in the pardoning of Eugene V. Debs for his conviction of violating the Espionage Act of 1917. However, it was the Senate investigation of his knowledge of a kickback scam involving bootleggers that led to his resignation on March 28, 1924, just two weeks after Secretary Denby's resignation. Like Denby, Daugherty was never found guilty of criminal wrong-doing. His aide and fellow member of the Ohio Gang, Jess Smith, committed suicide at the height of the investigation in 1923.

Meanwhile, Charles R. Forbes had been appointed the first director of the Veteran's Bureau by President Harding in 1921. Forbes' résumé indicates that he achieved the rank of Colonel in the US Army. Other records seem to show that he deserted from the Army in 1912, but later showed up in the Marine Corps where he served during World War I. While serving as Director of the Veteran's Bureau, he was accused of selling supplies from veterans' hospitals for a fraction of their worth. In the three years Forbes held this position, it was estimated that he embezzled close to $250 million, mainly in connection with the building of veterans' hospitals. He sold supplies intended for the Bureau and pocketed kickbacks from contractors. The total Veteran's Bureau budget for those three years was $1.3 billion, of which Forbes siphoned off fully nineteen percent for personal gain. He was indicted, prosecuted, and convicted of conspiracy to defraud the government. The chief witness for the Government, Elias H. Mortimer, also intimated that Mr. Forbes had incurred his enmity by seducing his wife. Forbes served a two year sentence in a federal penitentiary.

The President also appointed another "gang" member, Thomas W. Miller, the Alien Property Custodian. In this capacity he was responsible for receiving, holding, administering, and accounting for all money and property in the United States due to or belonging to an enemy, or ally of an enemy. Mr. Miller was convicted of accepting bribes and served an eighteen month prison sentence.

Having neither the intellectual capacity, political power, nor strength of character to deal with these scandals, all President Harding was able to do was ruminate and eat, and eat, and eat. He put on about forty pounds and ballooned to over two hundred and fifty pounds. This was well before medical sciences had embraced the concept of 'morbid' obesity, but in the President's case his weight gain was indeed morbid—physically and emotionally.

Even as all of these scandals swirled around him, the ever-ethical Secretary Wallace plugged away at his vision of a fair and prosperous rural America. As it turns out Harry Wallace was a rather natural politician, and over a period of time had gained the ear and the confidence of the President. The agricultural community began to share a guarded optimism that there may be a light at the end of the tunnel of the Post-World War I economic woes "down on the farm." Whether or not their optimism was warranted by the facts, the light in the tunnel was abruptly snuffed out by President Harding's death of heart failure in San Francisco on August 2, 1923. Vice President Coolidge was sworn in as the nation's thirtieth President later that day by his father, who was Justice of the Peace in Plymouth Notch, Vermont.

A reformer, but by no means a radical, Secretary Wallace had been working tirelessly on a farm plan that would have aligned agricultural product prices with that of other commodities. In large measure this would have been brought about by the creation of a government export corporation to manage the international sale of domestic agricultural products. The bill to accomplish this was introduced in November 1923 by Senator Charles McNary of Oregon and Congressman Gilbert Haugen of Iowa in the House of Representatives. The moneychangers from Wall Street to Washington came out furiously against the bill. It carried a strong scent of mercantilism. Secretary Wallace offered crystal clear prophesy of the economic carnage that lay ahead for agriculture and the nation, absent passage of the farm bill. (*Between 1920 and 1932 one in four farms in the United States was lost in foreclosure.*) With no support from the White House, Wallace fought on alone amongst his Cabinet colleagues for the next eleven months—and then he just up and died.

For his son back in Iowa, the personal loss and grief were profound. Politically it was a watershed event in the younger Henry's life. Watching closely his father's discomfort and angst with Washingtonian and Wall Street avarice, had catalyzed his already changing attitudes. On the pages of *Wallaces' Farmer* Henry eulogized his father and vowed to continue the struggle.

The fight for agricultural equality will go on; so will the battle for a stable price level, for controlled production, for better rural schools and churches, for larger income and higher standards of living of the working farmers, for the checking of speculation in farm lands, for the thousand and one things that are needed to make the sort of rural civilization he labored for and hoped to see. He died with his armor on in the fight for the cause which he loved.[3]

With these words, three generations of Republican support by the Wallace family came to an end.

Though there was no support of any consequence in the Coolidge Administration for the McNary-Haugen farm bill, had President Harding still held the seat of power, there may have been some small hope for success. By November President Coolidge disabused the nation's farmers of any notion that his administration would support the measure, or that he would sign it into law should it ever reach his desk, "No complicated scheme of relief, no plan for government fixing of prices, no resort to the public treasury will be of any permanent value in establishing agriculture."

In 1927, when the bill finally did pass through both houses and reach the President's desk, Coolidge promptly vetoed the measure and issued a message chastising its supporters for trying to benefit "at the expense of other farmers and of the community at large."[4] Given the administration's support of tariffs protecting almost every kind of industrial product, the hypocrisy of the message was palpable.

Seeing Herbert Hoover's fingerprints all over the veto message expunged Henry A. Wallace's earlier disillusionment and replaced it with outright anger. From the pages of *Wallaces' Farmer* he railed against the Administration's hypocrisy and shortsightedness. It seems however that the Republican party did not need or care about the support of the most widely read agricultural periodical in the country. In 1924 President Coolidge had been easily reelected, and in 1928 the Republican Party overwhelmingly nominated the Wallace family's old nemesis, Herbert Hoover. He won by a landslide, carrying forty of forty-eight states. Much to Henry Wallace's chagrin, Iowa was among the states that lined up in Hoover's column.

¤ ¤ ¤

For Henry Wallace, the "Roaring '20s" were not only about outrage with the political high jinks of Washington. His fascination with corn continued unabated. In 1919 when Dr. Edward East had visited and proposed forming a partnership to develop and sell hybrid seed, Henry was not yet ready. But by May 1926 the science had changed and so had Henry's mind. He and his Uncle, Jim Wallace, invited some friends and colleagues to a meeting at the offices of *Wallaces' Farmer*. In addition to the two Wallaces there were three farmers, a lawyer, and a seed salesman in attendance. They likely did not realize that at this meeting they were, literally and figuratively, sowing the seeds of great wealth for themselves and their heirs.

They formed a corporation—Hi-Bred Corn Company. They agreed to sell themselves seventy shares of stock at $100 per share. By purchasing fifty shares himself, Henry was the majority stock holder. The other men purchased the remaining twenty shares. By the end of the first year the company had sold 650 bushels of hybrid seed corn, for a net profit of about $30. The partners were delighted. Uncle Jim teased, "We were in business—the largest hybrid seed corn company in the world!" It was the only hybrid seed company in the world.

By the time of the stock market crash in October 1929, *Wallaces' Farmer* had been a profitable family concern for almost three decades. In some quarters it was even factiously referred to as "Wallace's Gold Mine." That moniker was more hyperbole than reality. It had been profitable and three generations of Wallaces had managed a comfortable living from its proceeds, but by no stretch of the imagination were they wealthy people. When the markets crashed, banks failed, and the world sank into depression; *Wallaces' Farmer* did not come through unscathed.

After the election of Herbert Hoover in 1928 a malaise settled over the Wallaces. In late summer of 1929 Henry was invited to present papers at the First International Conference of Agricultural Economists in Great Britain. His participation and travel expenses were paid by a wealthy Englishman by the name of Leonard K. Elmhirst. Believing that a road trip would do him good, Henry accepted the invitation and decided to tack on some additional visits in eastern Europe. His sister Mary was married to the Swiss ambassador to Czechoslovakia and he stayed with them in Prague for several days.

While in Prague, Henry received a telegram from his Uncle John that *Wallaces' Farmer* had consummated a deal to purchase their primary competitor, the *Iowa Homestead*. Now, this was only a matter of weeks before the house of cards, upon which the worldwide banking systems had been built, would collapse. There could not have been a more inauspicious time to acquire a two million dollar debt. Nevertheless, there was nothing for Henry to do except try to make the best of it. Though Henry was the chief editor, *Wallaces' Farmer* was wholly owned by his Uncle John and his late father's estate.

The first edition of the new publication, *Wallaces' Farmer and Iowa Homestead*, rolled off the presses on Saturday, October 26, 1929. On the following Monday and Tuesday almost 26 million shares were traded and the Dow lost over 24.5% of its value. Thirty billion dollars of wealth just evaporated. The "Roaring '20s" were over. President Hoover responded to the crisis by supporting the Mexican Repatriation Act, which essentially forced the migration of nearly half a million Mexicans and U.S. citizens of Mexican American decent southward across the border.

When banks failed they quite literally over-night locked their doors, shuttered the windows and hung a "closed" sign outside. People could not withdraw the money they had deposited in the bank. In some cases the public was so naive as to believe their money actually still existed and was locked in the vaults of banks. Of course, banks had been loaning $30 or more for every $1.00 on deposit. Much of that money had been borrowed for speculative investments in the stock market, so there was no real property securing the loans. When the stock market crashed, well . . .

In some rural communities depositors broke the locks off the bank doors and stormed inside. One can easily imagine that in their desperation they had convinced themselves that surely their money was still there— perhaps in neat stacks of cash on a table in the vault, or locked inside safety deposit boxes by mistake. Maybe it had just been misplaced in a file drawer or under a desk. Of course, there was no money. No money to pay the bills; no money to buy shoes for the kids; no money to purchase food; no money to pay for the subscription to *Wallaces' Farmer and Iowa Homestead.*

Circulation fell like a weather vane blown off the roof of an Iowa barn. The paper allowed their sales staff to accept chickens as payment in lieu of the $1.00 per year subscription fee. Chickens don't pay the bills, so the paper retreated from weekly to biweekly publications. That decision had the ripple effect of substantially cutting advertising revenue. In turn, some staff were laid off and all new job applicants were turned away.

Within a couple of years, John Wallace realized the mistake of purchasing the *Iowa Homestead*. Though he had not bothered to consult Henry about this decision before closing the deal, he now turned to his nephew to enlist support in approaching Bernard Baruch about a financial lifeline. Mr. Baruch was a wealthy member of the New York Stock Exchange. Three of his most famous quotes are:

"I made my money by selling too soon."

"I never lost money by turning a profit."

"The main purpose of the stock market is to make fools of as many men as possible."[5]

These statements articulate why Mr. Baruch did not lose his fortune in October 1929. He got out "too soon."

Mr. Baruch agreed to meet with Henry on March 23, 1932 in New York City. In the Baruch offices Henry explained the situation in Iowa. They discussed *Wallaces' Farmer*, agriculture, financial matters, and politics. Henry returned to Des Moines to tell his Uncle John, "Baruch said what a shame it is to see young fellows ruined, but he is not interested in owning a share of our paper."[6]

So, in 1932 a three-generation epoch ended. The Wallaces lost their paper. It returned to Dante Pierce, who was the son of the founder of the *Iowa Homestead* and the principal holder of the debt incurred by the Wallaces to purchase the *Homestead*. He asked Henry to continue as the paper's editor. Interestingly, Pierce also changed the paper's name back to the original *Wallaces' Farmer*, though the Wallace family no longer owned any share of the publication. An offer to retain Uncle John Wallace as the business manager was not forthcoming.

¤ ¤ ¤

When, and by whom, the term was coined is not known, but the "Great Depression" was just that—a depression. By virtually every measure economic activity was depressed from its rambunctious highs of the 1920s. Thirteen million people became unemployed. Industrial production fell by forty-five percent. Home building dropped by eighty percent. Eleven thousand of the twenty-five thousand banks in the United States failed. The stock market lost almost ninety percent of its value. The gross domestic product dropped by about fifty percent.

Many people, just like the economy, became clinically depressed. In an individual the sadness of depression is characterized by a greater intensity, duration, and more severe symptoms and functional disabilities than is normal. One sociological symptom was the dramatic increase in suicide. Twenty-three thousand Americans took their own lives between November 1, 1929 and October 30, 1930, the highest number in a twelve month period on record. During the 1930s the suicide rate climbed to seventeen per 100 thousand in the general population. By way of comparison, in 2005 the rate was eleven per 100 thousand in the United States.

While many people sank into the paralysis of economic and emotional depression, Henry Wallace responded with what can best be described as a manic level of activity. He was making speeches at farm conferences; meeting with organizations representing agricultural interests; writing books and articles for *Wallaces' Farmer* as well as other journals; actively pursuing his spiritual quest; studying meteorology; developing a breed of chicken that would be more prolific egg producers; and, as always, trying to grow a better corn.

There is no question that the Great Depression financially pummeled *Wallaces' Farmer* as a business and Henry Wallace personally. Both were sliding into the pit of insolvency. Even as this was happening, like a north bound sail ship banking off a northwest wind, his instincts keeled toward kindness. As if to foreshadow the trauma that lay in store for the Midwest, Arkansas was stricken by a crop destroying drought in 1931. Corn was worth almost nothing anyway, so Henry organized a relief effort among Iowan farmers. They collected three railroad cars of oats and corn to send across Missouri to hungry Arkansans. After the cars were loaded, a Rock Island Line official informed Henry that the Red Cross did not have the funds necessary to pay the bill of laden. Elsewhere across the heartland huge stores of wheat and corn lay rotting and were being eaten by mice and rats, while people in cities all over America were going hungry. These events reinforced Henry's growing conviction that a nation which permitted starvation in the midst of plenty was seriously broken. Though he and his family could ill afford the expense, he paid the $420 to ship the food to Arkansas out of his own pocket.

¤ ¤ ¤

The Hi-Bred Corn Company had dawdled along for a few years, with none of the partners focusing too much attention and energy on its growth.

Oddly, the crash of the markets in 1929 served as the impetus that would bring a combination of talent and moxie to the company, which would result in its explosive growth even in the throes of the bitter economy.

Perhaps because they were unemployed and did not have anything else to do, perhaps because of their faith in Henry Wallace, or perhaps with motives more complex, a group of men slowly clustered around Hi-Bred Corn Company like a covey of quail huddled in a pile of brush for shared warmth on a cold November morning. People, like quail, need some warmth too, and in those times folks were often reduced to taking what little comfort they could find. These men felt blessed rather than resigned to their company with Henry and each other.

First came J.J. Newlin, a good ol' farm-boy through and through. He managed the farm.

Next was Nelson Urban, a college kid. He had recently graduated from Antioch College over in Yellow Springs, Ohio. Urban took to heart the admonition of Antioch's first president, Horace Mann, "Be ashamed to die until you have won some victory for humanity." With this attitude he was a natural fit in any company headed by Henry Wallace. He was the bookkeeper and head of company sales.

Then there was Raymond Baker who "hired on" while still a student at Iowa State. Like Henry, his most enduring fascination was, quite simply, corn. When asked to consider work at the company Baker told Henry, "I love corn breeding so much, I'd pay for the opportunity to do it."

"Well," replied Henry straight-faced, "that **might** not be necessary— we'll have to wait and see."

Baker went on to be recognized as an unparalleled innovator in the field of hybridization. In addition to corn, he also dabbled with watermelons and chickens. With chickens, Baker and Henry Wallace's sons would enjoy remarkable success in the decades ahead. They doubled, then tripled average egg yields. They formed Hy-Line Chickens, a subsidiary of the Hy-Bred Corn Company and at one point their company produced approximately seventy-five percent of all the egg-laying chickens sold commercially. By 1990, the progeny of their experimental chickens were laying almost half of all the eggs eaten worldwide.

Finally came the character Roswell "Bob" Garst and his life-long friend, Charley Rippey. It was late July in 1930 and the coming drought was not yet underway across the heartland. As if to belie the impending dust bowl, a strong summer thunderstorm was building just west of Rippey's farm near Des Moines. The smell of rain and ozone wafted on the winds of the squall line. Charley, Bob, and Henry Wallace were inspecting the corn that had been planted the previous Spring. Henry had given Bob Garst some of his hybrid corn seed, which he and Charley Rippey had planted in rows of two, interspersed with two rows of regular open pollinated corn.

Charley raised his voice to be heard over the occasional rumbles of thunder and the background noise of the wind swirling past their ears, "There does appear to be a bit more corn on the hybrids, but the proof is in the bushel basket—we'll see."

Just then a ferocious blast of cool wind ripped Bob's hat from his head and Henry gave chase, finally stomping a foot on the brim at least a hundred yards down the road. He turned to see the blank expressions on the faces of his friends, both mouths dropped open in the perfect ovals of awe. Quickly surveying the scene, they all realized that the proof was not only in the bushel basket. Before them they beheld a field with two rows of corn broken and laying on the ground, two rows standing, two rows down, two rows standing and so on across the whole crop. The stalks of the hybrid corn had flexed with the wind while the other stalks, being more brittle, had simply snapped.

For a moment nothing was said. A gust of breath passed through Bob's pursed lips, not strong enough to whistle, but ever so clear as an expression of amazement. In turn each man looked the other in the eyes, then back at the field of corn; fifty percent disseminated by the powerful down blast. Mother Nature's cough was the source of Bob's epiphany. "We need to talk, Henry." And thus began an historic and most remarkable marketing arrangement— an arrangement that would give voice to the gospel of hybridization.

Garst and Hi-Bred Corn Company entered into a franchise arrangement. Garst and Rippey grew seed corn. Garst would then sell the corn using the Hi-Bred Corn label and pay the company a royalty on each bushel sold. The fee was on a sliding scale decreasing in price up to 50 thousand bushels sold. When the deal was struck Wallace told Garst, "Bob, I just love you. You are such an optimist. There won't be 50,000 bushels of hybrid corn sold in our lifetimes."[8]

"Nah, Henry, you're wrong there. I'll hit fifty thousand bushels in five years."[9]

Henry replied, "There is a depression on man. What are you thinking?"

"Hide and watch." was all Bob said grinning as he turned to exit Henry's office.

Whether Roswell "Bob" Garst had already settled on his marketing scheme that day when he shook Henry's hand and walked out of the office, a Hi-Bred Corn Company franchisee, we cannot know. What we do know is that the idea was a stroke of inspiration at a time when farmers did not have even two coins in their pockets to jingle with nervous fingers.

In the early spring of 1931, while snow squalls still raked the Iowa farmlands, Bob Garst loaded bushel baskets of the hybrid corn that had survived that blast of wind months earlier in the back of a beat up old pickup truck and lit out across northern Iowa. He gave it all away! With any farmer willing, Garst would give them enough corn seed to plant half their crop. Alongside the farmer would plant the remaining half of their acreage with whatever variety they had already planned to use, most often Reid Yellow Dent. Then, come late summer, the farmer would give Garst one half of the increased yield produced by the hybrid seed. It worked like this:

The Johnson brothers regular corn produced twenty-three bushels an acre and the hybrid seed produced forty-one bushels. Garst was entitled to nine bushels per acre of the hybrid corn harvested. The Johnsons had planted the equivalent of thirty-six acres with hybrid corn, so Garst collected a total of 324 bushels.

41 (bushel yield from hybrid seed) − 23 (bushel yield from Johnson's seed stock) = 18 (bushels)

18 (bushels) X 36 (acres) = 648 (bushels)

648 (bushels) X .5 (Garth's share) = 324 (bushels)

The Johnson brothers were delighted with this arrangement. They harvested 648 more bushels than they would have produced with their regular corn. They had no additional outlay of cash up-front, which they did not have anyway. Their cash savings had all been deposited in the local bank. The bank had failed and closed its doors for good on the Wednesday before Thanksgiving of 1930.

At 81ᶜ per bushel of corn in 1929, farmers were maybe coming out a few pennies above break-even. By 1931 a bushel was being sold for less than 50ᶜ. Prices eventually sank to a low of just over 10ᶜ per bushel. It was cheaper to burn corn than wood or coal, and thus the first use of corn as a substitute for fossil fuel came in the stoves of farmer's homes during the depths of the Great Depression. Obviously, at those prices, Garst's marketing strategy could not pay Hi-Bred Corn Company's bills. What it did, however, was convince farmers that hybridization was a remarkable technology. As soon as they once again had money to spend, farmers were willing to pay the astounding price of over $6.00 per bushel for hybrid corn seed.

¤ ¤ ¤

Though Henry continued to serve as editor of the beloved *Wallaces' Farmer*, in his heart it had slipped away. On the other hand, Hi-Bred Corn Company was his. It had been his vision and now, with the right cadre to staff the various functions, it once again captured his imagination. Even given all he knew about corn and the science of hybridization, Henry Wallace and the original partners were an odd combination of ignorant and naive about the business. In 1926 the original owners had purchased $100 shares in the company, with no idea how to market seed.

When the Athenians approached Socrates with the message that the Oracle at Delphi had observed that he was the wisest man in Athens, the story goes that Socrates responded, "If I am the wisest man, it is because I know that I know nothing." It seems that in many respects Henry Wallace shared Socrates' brand of wisdom.

At the first Hi-Bred Corn Company staff meeting, Henry outlined some basic principles for the business. "First we must be totally honest with our customers. We will tell our customers everything we understand about a particular seed stock, its strengths as well as it flaws. In short order farmers will see that ethic in our company and will repay our honesty with loyalty." All present shook their heads with understanding. "Next, we must charge outrageously high prices for our seed." To a man, the listeners eyes popped open wide. Perhaps Henry had misspoke, or maybe they had just misunderstood. Henry went on, "Through high prices farmers will come to understand they are buying something special. Also only through high prices will we be able to sustain a robust research effort. Sales are important, but ultimately our company's vigor will hinge on research." With that said, henceforth Henry assumed a rather laissez-faire approach to the company, leaving the management of the business and its details to the experts.

And so it was that the "Green Revolution" had begun, yet no one in that room could yet fathom what that phrase would come to mean.

—— 123 ——

11

Little Norway's Little Cornhuskers

The Borlaug family, farming in "Little Norway,"
and Norman Borlaug's early life.

On August 14, 1935, when President Roosevelt signed the Social Security Act, over half of America's senior citizens were living in poverty. Though the original act included provisions for survivors and persons with acquired disabilities, its primary purpose was to obviate poverty among the elderly. A little understood fact is that poverty among old folks was at least as much due to the industrial revolution as the economic woes of the Great Depression.

Subsistence farmers had a form of social security which extended far back into antiquity. Their social security system was called "children." Farming before mechanization was done by beasts, brains, and brawn. To raise a bushel of corn without a tractor required approximately sixty-five hours of labor. An adult farm worker could produce about thirty-two bushels of corn per year. That corn could feed three people when augmented by a vegetable garden, some hunting and gathering, as well as judicious food production and menu planning. After fifty years of farming (120 thousand total hours of labor), most elderly person's backs and arms and legs could not maintain the rigorous pace necessary to produce thirty-two bushels of corn. As they had been before the age of twelve, most farmers somewhere in their mid-sixties became dependents once again. Of course, elderly people still worked as much as possible, but for most the fruit of their labors were not enough to feed themselves, let alone two additional people. To a large extent, the food set before them on the family table was produced by the labor of their children and grandchildren.

That is how social security worked in an agrarian society, but with the industrial revolution people were drawn from the farms to labor in urban factories and at the bottom of mine shafts. Within a single generation, city dwellers had surrendered the idea of gardening to raise even a modicum of the food they would consume. In the latter half of the nineteenth century corporations motivated by profit, rather than quality of life, had laborers from age seven to seventy working sixty plus hours per week in factories and mines for subsistence wages. Seldom was there any discretionary income for savings. Wages might support one worker and one dependent. Given this choice, young children were forced to work rather than attend elementary school. Given this choice, babies were supported and elderly parents and grandparents were left to fend for themselves. After a lifetime of wear and tear on the body, most sixty-somethings no longer had the strength or stamina to swing a pick ax or a sledge hammer all day. No work meant no money. After a lifetime of profit-producing labor for the corporate lords of capitalism, the "retired" elderly were consigned to a few years of abject poverty and hunger, and then they died—often without the resources necessary for a "proper burial."

Before 1900 most laborers did not live to see sixty years of age. The dilemma of poverty among the elderly was not so bad when people died young, but as life expectancy began to increase during the twentieth century the weight of starving old people became too heavy a burden for the collective conscience. Even with ardent opposition from the political right to much of Roosevelt's "socialistic" agenda, the Social Security Act enjoyed considerable support across the political spectrum. A 1934 Gallup Poll showed that seventy-three percent of workers approved the idea of a wage tax for the purpose of social security. After much wrangling and negotiating of fine points, the Social Security Act was supported in the House of Representatives with 372 yeas to 33 nays. On the Senate side, 77 voted for the bill with only 6 voting in opposition.

¤ ¤ ¤

One of the "fine points" of the bill's negotiation had been the exclusion of farm workers. So, just as it had been on March 15, 1914, the day of Norman Ernest Borlaug's birth, children continued to be a farm family's only viable social security plan. Norm's parents, Clara and Henry, and grandparents, Emma and Nels, shared the house where he was born. He was their first child and grandchild. They all loved him from the moment of his birth. But there can be little doubt that recessed somewhere in the back of their minds was an unspoken awareness that this baby represented some modicum of "security" for their old age.

In Norm's home and in the community of Little Norway, kindness was the norm. It was expected every bit as much as work and a willingness to support parents and grandparents in their old age. The culture of the Borlaug family was calm and gentle. As an adult Norm recalled this aspect of his family thus:

> The environment in our home was excellent. Everyone was kind, quiet and considerate. There never was any quarreling. My mother was a small woman. She was very shy. She was a good mother, an excellent cook, and a wonderful seamstress. Palma and Charlotte always looked nice in dresses home-sewn by Mother. Mother loved to bake bread, cakes, and pies; they were delicious. My sisters and I would go back in the woods on our farm and gather wild blackberries, raspberries and cherries for her. In the fall, she would preserve food for the winter by canning it in glass jars: corn, beets, peas, carrots, black currents, gooseberries, rhubarb, and even chicken.
>
> My father was a tall man—about six feet one inch. He worked incredibly long hours in the field—from sun-up to sun-down—during the spring, summer and fall. But he also loved to read—the daily newspapers, journals, and magazines, especially Wallaces' Farmer and National Geographic, all delivered by Rural Free Delivery to mail boxes a half mile from the farm. During a winter evening, Dad would often read a chapter of a book to us children.
>
> All the Borlaugs—uncles, aunts and cousins—would get together one Sunday each month for dinner, and also on the main holidays. Granddad played the accordion and violin, and the whole family would join in and sing. On Christmas, Thanksgiving and the 4th of July, Granddad Nels always gave each of us twelve grandchildren a silver dollar—he didn't like paper money.
>
> Mostly, we enjoyed life. We sang both English and Norwegian songs that we learned from our parents and grandparents. Dad and I even sang while we hand-milked our fifteen cows.[1]

On the Borlaug farms some fourteen miles south of the town of Cresco, Iowa a warm and caring environment prevailed. Warmed by wood stoves and a kindness of spirit, life for Norm's family as well as that of his aunts, uncles, and cousins was, none the less, Spartan. They raised in their fields or gathered from the woods almost everything they consumed. They bartered for items needed that they could not produce themselves. Norm's mom would trade eggs at the general store in Saude, a mile and a half from the farm, for sugar, salt, coffee, thread, yarn, needles, and cloth. Her cousin Greg Vaala ran the store.

The Blacksmith was next to the store and just to the south was the Creamery and Feed Mill. These too were staffed by Norm's aunts, uncles and cousins. The family produced a little cash by hauling six milk cans of cream to the Creamery every couple of days. The frequency of the "milk run" was necessitated by the lack of refrigeration. If held any longer at the farm, the cream was prone to spoil before being churned into butter. Any butter that was not needed locally was loaded on the train and sold in Chicago.

The Borlaugs also managed to sell a dozen hogs and half a dozen head of cattle to the stockyards in Chicago each year. The cattle were walked the ten miles to the train depot in Lawler during the summer. The hogs were loaded on a large sled drawn by two horses and delivered to the railroad car soon after snow and ice covered the road to Lawler.

From all these sources, the infant Norm's parents and grandparents secured enough food to eat, enough supplies to operate the family and the farm, and almost $680 cash in 1914. But survival was not just a matter for the nuclear family. Little Norway, like agrarian communities almost anywhere in the world, enjoyed a level of consanguinity unimaginable, and genetically improbable, in more urban cultures. In order to survive, communal cooperation and joint labor was absolutely necessary.

A trip into Cresco, for example, required harnessing the draft horse and hitching the wagon (1 hour); driving the wagon the fourteen miles into town (3 hours); unhitching the wagon, feeding and watering the horse (½ hour); conducting necessary business in town (2 ½ hours); rehitching the horse to the wagon (½ hour); driving the wagon fourteen miles back home (3 hours); unhitch the wagon, feed, water and groom the horse (1 hour). A trip to town was an eleven to twelve hour ordeal. If Nels Borlaug needed a bottle of vegetable tannin for tanning leather, he could ill afford an entire day from the farm to make that one purchase. So, folks in the community let it be known when they planned a trip into town. Knowing that his cousin Thomas was going into town next Tuesday, Nels would take a silver dollar over to Thomas' house and ask that he bring back the necessary chemicals.

Electric company executives scoffed at the idea of extending the power grid into rural America. Houses were too far apart, too many miles of wire would be required, and farmers did not have enough cash to be reliable customers anyway. "Why, our stockholders would never stand for it!" was a most common refrain. There was no electricity anywhere within shouting distance of Saude, Iowa. Like trips into town, the lack of electric power also fostered a commitment to communal action, particularly come harvest.

Winter wheat is planted in the autumn, sprouts roots in the winter, pops out of the ground in the spring and is ready to harvest from late July until early September. It must be harvested as soon as the heads of wheat mature, and it must be done quickly. Summer storms can lay waste an entire crop by stripping the valuable grain seeds and strewing them upon the ground.

In order to expedite the harvest, a small army of farmers was required to gather in the sheaves. First, the farmer and his horse would draw a binder through the field, which would cut and tie the wheat stalks in bundles. The picturesque bundles would be wind-rowed for a few days to dry. Eight to twelve bundles would then be stacked in piles called "shucks." At that point the neighbors would converge, en masse, on the designated farm. A huge threshing machine would be set up in the barn yard. There being no electricity, the machine was driven by a steam engine. The machine operator would arrive before breakfast to fire up the engine, so that there would be enough steam to run when the threshing began. He would eat breakfast with the host family while they awaited a head of steam and the assemblage of the harvest troops.

Soon after sunrise they would begin. About eight men would haul the wheat bundles by horse drawn wagons from the field to the thresher. There a crew of older boys would throw the bundles into the machine's mouth. With paddles the machine would beat the wheat kernels from the stalks. The stalks and kernels would fall onto a series of slotted conveyor belts which would sift the wheat from the chaff. Another man operated the grain elevator, which conveyed the kernels up to the grain bin. Several boys would be busied raking and piling the straw for livestock feed and bedding.

The women of Little Norway traveled from farm to farm with their husbands. They would spend the entire morning preparing large meals of fried chicken or pork chops, vegetables, homemade bread, cakes and pies. The afternoon would be used for cleaning up and preparing for the next day.

The younger children were deployed delivering snacks and jugs of water to the men and boys working the machine and the fields all day long.

This routine went on day after day for most of six weeks.

Thunderstorms, with strong winds and frequently laden with hail, are not uncommon across northern Iowa in late summer. Sometimes a farmer's entire wheat crop could be smashed in a few minutes of meteorological fury. When this occurred each farmer in the "thrashing circle" (fifteen to thirty neighboring farms) would donate their "fair share" to the family whose crop was lost. You did not sit by and watch your neighbor—your family—go hungry. As an adult Norman Borlaug recalled the Little Norway society into which he was born.

> Our village was named for a town in Norway's Telemark province from which most of our ancestors hailed. Saude was a family friendly place of shared lives, shared heritage and shared counties: Chickasaw and Howard. There, we felt an almost tribal sense of belonging: loyalties were local; decisions were collective; and ideals were shared. Individualism was suppressed, but we felt a sort of glory in being part of a whole that was larger than ourselves.[2]

Henry A. Wallace's grandfather, Uncle Henry, had welcomed him to full-time employment at Wallaces' Farmer in the summer of 1910 with a gift for his office, a *Webster's Unabridged Dictionary*. Henry may have read the definition of 'socialism' found on page 1722;

> sō'cial·ism, n. 1. the theory or system of ownership and operation of the means of production and distribution by society or the community rather than by private individuals, with all members of society or the community sharing in the work and the products.[3]

In 1914, Norman Borlaug was born into a community of agrarian socialists. To say the least, it was an austere life, but it was a life that, for

Norm, produced enough fond memories to fill the granaries of every Borlaug barn in Little Norway.

¤ ¤ ¤

As farming was a communal effort, so too was education in the American hinterlands of 1919. At the age of five, Norm began school at the one room New Oregon Rural District School #8. There were no school buses and even if they had been available, roads were often mud bogs, especially during the spring snow melt, so much so that they could not be traversed even by a horse drawn carriage. A bus? Nope, kids walked to school. Hence, the state of Iowa made an earnest attempt to situate schools in places where no student would have to walk more than two miles.

Two miles is a considerable walk for the pint size legs of most five year olds in good weather. Often the weather in northern Iowa is not all that good, particularly during the winter. It can be cold, snowy, windy, and miserable. For safety sake, parents insisted that the young folk walk in packs. During severe weather they would walk in single file with the oldest boy leading the way and the oldest girl walking the sweep position. He would scuff his feet along in order to make the foot path through the snow; She would sweep up any laggards.

On one occasion an arctic clipper roared out of Canada, through the Dakotas and plowed into Iowa during the middle of the day. That day the temperature dropped precipitously and the snow howled vertically. Even an adult, with at least some fat on the body, would have been cold—very cold, but a five year old boy, skinny as a rail, was dangerously so.

That afternoon's walk home made quite an impression on the young Norman Borlaug. Years later he described the scene.

> I was miserable. Icy drafts slipped through my clothes and sliced the skin like a scalpel. It was hard to get a breath. Snow clung to my face, mittens, jacket. The melt inside my boots numbed my feet. I began stumbling. Soon it became too much to bear. Weariness pervaded every sense, including common sense. There was just one thing to do: lay down to cry myself to sleep snuggled in the soft white shroud nature had so conveniently provided.
>
> Then a hand yanked my scarf away, grabbed my hair, and jerked my head up. Above me was a face tight-lipped with anger

and fright. It was my cousin Sina. "Get up!" she screamed. "Get Up!" She began slapping me over the ears, "Get up! Get up!" The other children were clustered around. There was fear in their voices. Some of the young ones were crying. Finally, Herbert Lee hoisted me onto my tired little legs. Sina took my hand and got me walking again. She was twelve, sweet-tempered, and filled with self-assured authority. I was in tears when we entered the warm kitchen. I knew I'd let everyone down. But Grandmother Emma was as calm and goodhearted as ever. She'd just emptied her big wood-fired oven and the house smelled of yeast and hot bread. I've never forgotten that comforting fragrance. No food was ever so sweet as those loaves Grandmother baked the day when I was five and nearly died.[4]

This was not the only time that his cousin, Sina, would have a profound impact upon Norm's life. But it is certain, at twelve years of age, she could not have imagined that the butterflies she freed by her actions on that painfully cold day would survive to change the history of the world. No one had yet even heard of the "butterfly effect," but perhaps at some level Sina Borlaug sensed that everything we do matters—forever.

¤ ¤ ¤

The state's commitment to minimize these kinds of dangers was manifest by the prolific number of schools that dotted the landscape. Thus, the one-room school house, with a single teacher providing instruction to students ranging from grades one through eight, was the rural norm. During any given semester the New Oregon Rural District School #8 would have about a dozen students enrolled. Sometimes a few more, sometimes a few less, depending upon the time of year and the number of tasks requiring attention at the family farms. Fortunately for Norm, his parents and grandparents prioritized school. This was particularly true of Granddad Nels, who was self-educated and, like George Washington Carver, saw in education the prospect of emancipation; the prospect of a better future.

In that little classroom their teacher provided opportunity, format and inspiration, but learning was the responsibility of the student. Much incidental learning occurred in the close quarters as students would overhear the instruction provided to other students as well as the oral reports being given to their teacher, Miss Lena Halvorson. Older students would help Miss

Halvorson by tutoring the younger ones and, of course, by doing so they learned the subject matter better for themselves.

In 1920 over 100 thousand of these one-room schools were strewn all across America. Paved roads, the baby boom, and administrative considerations folded this form of instruction into the pages of history. Interestingly, the idea that older students can be called upon to tutor and mentor younger students has, like a Phoenix, risen from the ashes of this old and lost pedagogy. Younger children have always learned from older children. In the last decade of the twentieth century, schools once again realized that they have a remarkable opportunity to leverage this natural inclination among the young and manage the educational message.

The responsibility to learn was taken seriously by Norm and his classmates because it was considered a civic duty, which reflected upon the family and the community. In Norm's case the family connection became even more compelling when at the end of his sixth grade year Miss Halvorson took another teaching job. She had been a good teacher for the kids in the Saude neighborhood, but at thirty years of age she was lured away by the bright lights of Nashau on the other side of the county. Gosh, almost a thousand people lived over there in 1925. While he absolutely adored Miss Halvorson's replacement, Norm knew he had to mind his p's and q's. His prodigious nineteen year old cousin, Sina, became the new teacher.

Sina had become a stunning beauty, with an extraordinary smile and a command presence. After only two years of teaching Norm, she decided that his next step was high school. Most farm boys returned to work the fields after the eighth grade. Cousin Sina convinced Norm's parents and grandparents that his place was in the classroom, rather than on the farm, for the next few years at least.

By way of congratulating Norm on completion of his primary education, and to encourage him with his next educational endeavor, Sina presented him with a plaque that was at once both inspirational and prescient. It read:

> Advance in learning as you advance in life.
> Good instruction is better than riches.
> Kindness is the noblest weapon to conquer with.[5]

The most compelling barrier for the Borlaugs regarding Norm's continued schooling was not commitment to education, but rather geography. The high school for New Oregon Rural School District was in Cresco, which in 1928 was still fourteen miles of unpaved road away from the Borlaug farm. Though some of the noisy contraptions had arrived in the area, Norm's family had not yet purchased one of Henry Ford's Model T's. A daily eleven hour round trip by horse and buggy was out of the question. The high school may as well have been a hundred miles away.

Sina's doggedness would not be denied, however. A combination of solutions was arranged. One of the neighbor families owned a car. Six students from the area shared a ride when weather and road conditions permitted, which they often did not. When the weather precluded commuting, the young folks boarded with different families in Cresco.

In addition to the commute, high school also absented Norm's labor from the farm for much of the year. In early 1929, before they bought one of his automobiles, Norm's dad and Uncle Oscar bought a steel wheel, kerosene driven Fordson Tractor. The hours of labor necessary to produce a bushel of wheat and corn was halved.

The next year Norman brought home a bunch of powdered nitrogen, phosphorus, and potassium that had been introduced to him by the new Voc-Ag class teacher, Harry Shroder. Mr. Shroder had just graduated from Iowa State, the alma mater of George Washington Carver, Harry Wallace, and his son, Henry A. Wallace. Norm coaxed his family into mixing a few pounds of this powdered stuff called "fertilizer" into the hundreds of tons of soil they were cultivating. Corn production jumped from around twenty-five bushels to almost fifty bushels per acre. The labor necessary to produce a bushel of corn was halved once again. By the end of 1930, the Borlaugs were beginning to think sending Norm off to school was just about the best thing they ever did. Within four decades hundreds of millions of starving people all over the world would second that notion.

12

Hard Knocks

Politics of the Great Depression.

In 1928 the Dow Jones Industrial Index average closing was 245.6 points, which was sixty-eight points (thirty-eight percent) higher than any preceding year in the history of the Index. As a result of a decade long increase in food grain production, stores were full to overflowing all across the nation. During the first eight years of the decade, average "real income" had risen in the United States by twenty-eight percent and wholesale prices had gone down by seven percent. In accepting the Republican Party's nomination for President, Mr. Hoover set the tone for his campaign and administration by predicting, "We in America today are nearer to the final triumph over poverty than ever before in the history of this land. . . . We shall soon with the help of God be in sight of the day when poverty will be banished from this land."[1] On November 6, 1928 Herbert Hoover was elected by a landslide, winning 58.2% of the popular vote and 444 electoral votes, over his Democrat opponent, Alfred Smith.

For a decade *Wallaces' Farmer*, observing changes in the agriculture industry, had been sounding alarms about the inherent dangers of excess. Those alarms were drowned out almost everywhere east of the Mississippi by the brassy jazz and swing bands of the "Roaring Twenties." Even without buffalo manure fertilizing the prairie, the soil continued to produce prodigious crops of corn and grains. Of course, the surpluses battered the prices and though the production per acre was, historically speaking, quite high, the farmer's net profit per acre was in free fall. In order to maintain their incomes, farmers defaulted to the intuitive wisdom, which was to increase production. In order to do that, almost one million additional acres of perennial native grasses were turned under the plow each year—but the rains continued to come, and the annual crops of grain grasses continued to yield; holding the soil in place, albeit not as firmly as in the preceding 30 thousand years. With all that said, the winds of change were getting ready for a big blow.

In 1929 the markets crashed. Within three years the United States stock markets lost approximately eighty-seven percent of their value. Billions of dollars of wealth just disappeared, banks closed and in 1933 one thousand homes were lost to foreclosure each day. By the end of that year, unemployment was running at about twenty-five percent nationwide. Cities across the nation were witnessing food riots, as the soup lines grew too long and hungry people were being turned away. Just three years earlier, immense stores of surplus corn and grain had been allowed to rot and be eaten by mice, rats and rabbits, rather than preserved and stored for people food. Pragmatic statesmanship was on a leave of absence.

¤ ¤ ¤

By the time of the 1929 crash, farmers had been going broke, more or less, for the better part of a decade. The cause was, purely and simply, the increase of food production made possible by the post-World War I mechanization of all sorts of farm jobs. Jobs that had for hundreds of years been done by mules and men were now being done by tractors, swathers, and combines. The resulting abundance of food on the market was good for most consumers, to the extent that these commodities were plentiful and cheap. Corn prices fell from $1.38 per bushel in 1919, to 67^c in 1920, and 42^c in 1921. When hogs sold at 17.5^c per pound, farmers were losing over a nickel per pound, which was a total loss of over $12 per hog sold. It was likewise with wheat. During the course of the decade, prices fell from over $2.25 per bushel to about 40^c per bushel.

By the 1920s, America's industrial revolution was well into its fourth generation. Most urban dwelling industrial workers no longer had any living ancestors with roots in, or personal memories of, life on the farm. These urban dwellers saw no downside to cheap food prices. However, over the course of the next few years the downside would become more evident and profound than anyone buying the cheap food could have ever imagined. Farm income plunged from $16.9 billion in 1919 to just over $13 billion in 1920, and then on down to $8.9 billion in 1921. The surpluses were also, in part, fueled by the loss of export markets. During that same period, America's agricultural export income fell from $4.1 billion to $1.8 billion.

Agricultural production of food and fiber is the bedrock industry of every economic system as a culture moves beyond the hunter-gatherer stage of development. When societies fail to support their farmers, those societies soon fail. Everywhere, people simply did not grasp the shift that was occurring on farms during the twentieth century's third decade. This lack of understanding led to a worldwide failure to develop a sustainable response to the agricultural crisis. This, in turn, contributed to the catastrophic collapse of 1929, which was so quick and so dramatic, virtually every industrial economy on the planet cascaded into ruin.

¤ ¤ ¤

Believing that additional degrees would only bestow meaningless prefixes and suffixes to his name, Henry Wallace opted out of the halls of formal education. With this decision, however, he by no means eschewed learning. He actively pursued his own education in the areas of calculus, statistics, genetics, agricultural economics, journalism, Spanish, Portuguese, history, and just about every other subject that bumped up against his streak of curiosity. In retrospect, one might consider these fields of study his vocational education. If that was so, then his Master's degree would be earned at the College of Hard Knocks between 1928 and 1932. To carry the analogy further, if his journalistic observation and reporting were his coursework, then his activism must surely have been his practicum. Like almost everyone pursuing a Master's degree, he could not have envisioned where his course of study would ultimately lead. He could not have foreseen or even imagined what these years of "education" were preparing him to do in the years ahead.

Wallace's initial foray into politics ended with a combination of frustration and humiliation. Having parted ways with the Republican party after his father's death, he actively campaigned for the Democrat's presidential nominee, Alfred Smith, during the 1928 campaign. Wallace's efforts were utterly futile as his long-time adversary, Herbert Hoover, was elected president, carrying every state except six in the deep south. While Henry may have viewed this outcome as bad for agriculture and the nation, it certainly left him with no lack of material to write about. The economic depression that had begun in rural America in 1920, went viral during the first year of the Hoover administration. Every sector of the economy, everywhere in the nation became infected, and the illness was debilitating.

Henry reported on the Hoover administration's anemic response to the financial meltdown. The Harding and Coolidge administrations had either lacked the intellect, or were simply too calloused, to act when farm folk cried for help. In Herbert Hoover's case, his intelligence was unquestionable. In fact, he was undeniably a brilliant man, who had proven an effective humanitarian during Holland's World War I food crisis. However, his dogma stood in the path of effective action during the early years of the Great Depression. Hoover genuinely believed that every man would get what he should get out of life. As farmers were going broke and losing their families' farms and homes all across rural America, Hoover declared, "If a man has not made a million dollars by the time he is forty, he is not worth much."

It is impossible to overstate the effect of presidential statements such as: "Americans are nearer the final triumph over poverty than ever before in the history of the land."—"No one has yet starved."—"Men are selling apples on street corners because it is easier and more profitable than holding down a regular job!"[2] The chill of these pronouncements froze in place those public servants working in the legislative and executive branches of government who had the imagination to envision possible effective actions. From the top there was no impetus for, nor even the acknowledgement that, governmental action was necessary. The possibility that government could be part of the solution, rather than the problem, was incomprehensible to the era's barons of business. On the pages of *Wallaces' Farmer* and several other publications, Henry reported on this failure of will, foresight, and leadership. The news was for the most part, well, bad.

Even before the stock market crash of 1929, banks and thrift institutions had been failing at a rate that should have sounded alarms that something was seriously amiss. (In 1926 the 956 banks that failed represented 3.4% of all banks in the nation.) However, in the prevailing anti-regulation atmosphere, a certain "survival of the fittest" Darwinian attitude existed. If people lost all of their money because they opened accounts in poor performing banks, well, some animals get eaten in the jungle. Never mind the fact that if a person in Carson City was going to use a bank, the only choice was the local bank. When the bottom fell out, bank failures soared (i.e. 1345 in 1930, 2298 in 1931, and 1456 in 1932).

As public confidence spiraled downward, panics occurred in state after state. There were "runs on banks" in which depositors lined up to withdraw the full value of their accounts. When the withdrawal demands exceeded the cash available, bankers simply locked their doors, hung out a CLOSED sign, pulled down the window blinds, and went home to worry through many sleepless nights.

These panics prompted state governments to declare "bank holidays" with mandatory bank closures for limited periods of time. There were no ATMs. There was no on-line banking. People did not have access to their accounts or their cash. States believed the bank holidays would temporarily relieve pressure on the banks and give people time to cool off, thereby averting runs on the banks. Ironically, the "holidays" had exactly the opposite effect. When people in Sioux Falls, South Dakota learned that the banks in Sioux City, Iowa had just closed, they made a mad dash to their local bank to withdraw their deposits. This effect rippled like some kind of plague back and forth across the nation. By March 1933 over half the states in the nation had declared bank holidays.

Down in Tuskegee, Dr. George Washington Carver had deposits of $2,344.29 and $31,290.51 frozen when the local banks closed. To liquidate their obligation to Dr. Carver, the Macon County Bank deeded over to him 120 acres of farm land that was being sharecropped. Probably never wild about being a landlord under these circumstances, Dr. Carver sold the land to the sharecropper five years later.

As if fate saved one last insult for the administration's bungling incompetence, on Herbert Hoover's last day in office the unimaginable happened—the nation's entire banking system completely collapsed.

Even though farmers had not been generating profitable crops for almost a decade, they were considered employed. So, the frightening unemployment statistics reported did not generally include farmers who were still living, and in some cases starving, on their farms.

> 1929: 1,550,000 unemployed
> 1930: 4,340,000 unemployed
> 1931: 8,020,000 unemployed
> 1932: 12,060,000 unemployed
> 1933: 12,830,000 unemployed

Even given all of the evidence to the contrary, in March 1930, President Hoover declared, "all the evidences indicate that the worst effects of the crash on unemployment will have passed during the next sixty days."[3] By November 1930 nearly six thousand unemployed individuals were selling apples for a nickel apiece on street corners in New York City. In February 1931 several hundred men and women smashed the windows of a grocery market in Minneapolis in order to snatch fruit, canned goods, bacon, and ham. The store's owner, stupidly, pulled a gun on hungry people trying to grab food for themselves and their children. He was bludgeoned and ended the day with a compound fracture of his arm. A hundred policemen were called out to quell the riot. Only seven people were arrested. By April 1932, over 750 thousand New Yorkers were dependent upon city relief. Because average expenditures for a person on relief ran about $8.20 per month, the city did not have adequate funds to feed the hungry. 160 thousand hungry New Yorkers were placed on waiting lists.

In turn, hunger led to serious labor unrest. In February 1931, unemployment in Los Angeles drove desperate people to abandon their senses—6,024 U.S. citizens of Mexican American decent were accused of stealing jobs from "real" Americans and deported to Mexico. A month later, three thousand unemployed workers marched on the Ford Motor Company plant in River Rouge, Michigan. Police and company guards attacked, killing four marchers and wounding many more.

Anxious to improve income, farmers decided that the only way to combat falling farm prices was by withholding produce. On May 3, 1932, a convention of three thousand farmers in Council Bluffs, Iowa, which was led by Milo Reno, voted to support a July 4th strike. The author of the Farmer's holiday theme song is not known, but the message was crystal clear.

> Let's call a Farmers' Holiday
> A Holiday let's hold
> We'll eat our wheat and ham and eggs
> And let them eat their gold.[4]

Farmer's holiday supporters built road blocks on routes leading to the agricultural markets. They dumped milk on the ground and turned back cattle trucks. The blockades did not prevent enough food from reaching urban markets to have any substantive impact on prices. In many places police were called out to remove the road blocks—and brawl with the "striking" farmers.

Even though farmers lost money most years during the 1920's on every bushel of corn and every hog sold, banks were more than happy to loan them money secured by their land and their houses. Most years, the farmers made enough to pay the interest, so the loans were extended. That changed with the onset of the Great Depression. Farm loan foreclosures skyrocketed to well over 100 thousand per year.

In 1931 about 150 people showed up for the Von Bonn farm foreclosure auction in Madison County, Nebraska. Almost all of these people were friends and neighbors—a few carried weapons. When the auctioneer opened bidding on an item one hand would go up and offer a ridiculously low amount. When another bid was offered, a burly fellow carrying a club approached the bidder and "reminded" him that he was not holding enough cash to cover the bid. The second bids were always withdrawn. By the end of the day, the bankers had collected a whopping $5.35 for the farm and all personal effects auctioned. The following day, all "purchased" items were gifted back to the Von Bonn family. It was such a success that the "penny auction" movement gathered steam and was repeated at farms all across the upper Midwest.

Up to 30 thousand people actively participated in this form of protest. Were they violating the law? Absolutely, in some cases perhaps even feloniously. Did the perpetrators feel justified? No doubt. They did not feel they had lost the fruits of their life's work. They felt their acquisitions had been stolen by greedy bankers. Did they go too far? In some cases. Even today human bone fragments may still lay at the bottom of deep rock quarries, that decades ago filled with dozens of feet of spring water.

Henry Wallace had plenty of news to fill the pages of *Wallaces' Farmer* during these sad and tumultuous years.

¤ ¤ ¤

In the congressional elections of November 1930, Republicans took a beating, but still retained slim majorities in both houses of Congress (six seats in the House of Representative and one in the Senate). By mid-December, the public was clamoring for more government action. In a most classic example of governmental disconnect with the people's reality, Congress passed a bill allocating a paltry $116 million for public works and $45 million for drought relief. While Hoover spoke of the public works project as a "new experiment in our economic life" and an "advance in economic thought and a service to our people," his government's number one concern continued to be a balanced budget.

The president, and the ideologues who surrounded him, clung to their belief in a form of laissez-faire capitalism that was epitomized by greed and excess. What the nation's leaders could not acknowledge, people who could not feed their children already knew—free market capitalism, in it purist form, had failed. Published in 1931, New Russia's Primer described in euphemistic and simple language the planned order of communism, which it portrayed as much preferable to the chaos of capitalism. New York Times correspondent, Walter Duranty, aggrandized the "grass is greener on the other side" perception of Russia's communism. Mr. Duranty was even awarded the 'Excellence in Journalism' Pulitzer Prize for his reports on the Soviet Union and its "successful development." In reality, Bolshevism under Stalin was already a horrifically brutal failure, and it was going to become much, much worse before the monster's death.

Hungry people are not terribly interested in ethical journalism. Desperate Americans flirted tempestuously with New Russia's Primer and Mr. Duranty's fallacious assessments. The book became a bestseller and Book-of-the-Month Club selection. Authored by Mikhail Ilin, it was translated from Russian into English by self-proclaimed socialists Nucia P. Lodge and George S. Counts. Revenue from sales made them both modestly successful capitalists. Among its hundreds of thousands of readers was one Henry A. Wallace in Des Moines, Iowa.

Hunger inclined many Americans to consider change, perhaps even radical change, a necessity. While many who stalked the halls of power in Washington, DC wanted to minimize the economic crisis ("Good times are just around the corner."—"No one has yet starved."), among themselves they discussed and feared the fact that historically, grinding poverty provides fertile soil for crops of revolt. They eyed the sales of New Russia's Primer with deep suspicion and more than a modicum of fear. It was their belief that the farmer's holiday, penny sales, and labor unrest were the ideas of and fomented by communists. Only fifteen years after the startlingly fast overthrow of Russia's Czar by unarmed and unruly mobs, a similar looking force descended upon Washington, DC.

¤ ¤ ¤

In 1914 the United States fielded a military force of only about 100 thousand men. With U.S. involvement in World War I looming, on May 18, 1917 Congress passed the Selective Service Act. By 1918 the total number of volunteers and conscripts who served in the armed forces numbered about 4 million, over half of whom were committed to the western front in France. About 13 thousand troops were deployed to northern Russia, where they fought Bolsheviks at Arkhangelsk Oblanst, Siberia and the Pacific sea port of Vladivostok.

The Central Powers began falling like dominoes in late September 1918. The Germans were the last to sign the armistice at 11:00am on November 11th. Two million dough boys boarded ships bound for America and were home in a matter of weeks. The soldiers deployed to fight communist in Russia were not so lucky. They finally departed on April Fool's Day, 1920, after it became clear that the Red Army of the Bolshevik revolution would prevail. During World War I, United States Forces suffered 264 thousand casualties (many as a result of inhaling poisonous gas) and 112,432 deaths (over 60 thousand died of disease).

For the majority of returning veterans the jobs they had held before the war did not await them upon their return. For many veterans the job prospects were bleak; for veterans with disabilities even worse. They had been paid, on average, about $1 per day for their active duty, a $60 discharge bonus, and a transportation allowance intended to help them return home.

Veterans' advocates claimed that they deserved a cash award to balance out the difference between their military pay and the wages enjoyed by civilian war workers. As legislators viewed the plight of unemployed and unemployable veterans, action was taken to alleviate the situation. In 1918, Congress passed P.L.65-178, the Vocational Rehabilitation Act, to provide for the retraining and job placement of disabled persons who had served in the U.S. armed forces. In 1922 Congress passed the Adjusted Service Compensation Act, which would have provided additional back pay to veterans of $1.25 per day for overseas service and $1.00 per day for domestic service. The measure was vetoed by President Harding, which was consistent with his administration's philosophy to avoid all "unnecessary" government spending, unless of course, a high ranking government official, or one of their millionaire friends, stood to gain an enormous fortune. Congress sustained the presidential veto.

To be sure, this was quite a setback, but efforts on behalf of World War I veterans were not dead. In the spring of 1924 Congress passed the

Soldiers' Bonus Act. The following provisions applied to veterans who had held the rank of captain or below:

- ¤ They would be paid $1.25 for each day of foreign service, up to $500 maximum, and $1.00 for each day served in the States, up to $625 maximum.
- ¤ These sums were not to be paid immediately. Rather, the funds would be used to create a twenty-year endowment at four percent interest, with an additional twenty-five percent added to the total due upon payment.
- ¤ In the short term, participants were entitled to borrow up to 22.5 percent of the value of the fund.
- ¤ Veterans owed $50 or less were paid immediately.
- ¤ Some 3,662,374 military service certificates were to be issued, with a face value of $3.638 billion.
- ¤ Congress would appropriate twenty annual installments of $112 million, which was to be put in a trust fund. These sums, with interest, would finance the $3.638 billion dollars needed for pay-out to veterans in 1945.

Like his predecessor, President Coolidge vetoed the bill, but this time the veterans had the congressional votes necessary to override the veto. While no immediate cash was forthcoming, in 1924 the economy was roaring, at least for urban dwellers, and most veterans were relatively well situated.

That changed dramatically with the onset of the Great Depression. By 1932 hundreds of thousands of World War I veterans and their families were absolutely destitute. The veterans reasoned that when their country had called, they had stepped forward to meet the need, so the reverse should also be true. Now they were in need and wished for the country to make good on the Soldiers' Bonus Act promissory notes, albeit thirteen years early.

A movement of activist veterans began clamoring for immediate cash redemption of the Adjusted Service Certificates. These certificates could be found in old shoe boxes in the attic, safety deposit boxes in now defunct banks, and tattered manila envelopes in the bottom of sock drawers. Led by a former army sergeant, Walter W. Waters, and encouraged by retired U.S.M.C. Maj. Gen. Smedley Butler, the veterans group came to be known as the "Bonus Army." The movement began in mid-May of 1932, when Waters and three hundred out-of-work veterans in Oregon jumped on trains headed for Washington, DC. With their certificates in hand, their goal was the passage of the Patman Bonus Bill, which would have fast forwarded the bonus pay-outs to World War I veterans.

The original three hundred were astounded by the exponential growth in their numbers, as they made their railroad trek across the northern tier. Looking back after all these years, their surprise is actually surprising. After all, like themselves veterans all across America were unemployed, underfed, and unable to care for their families. They did not really have anything better to do, so why not take a road trip to Washington? By mid-June almost 22 thousand Bonus Marchers had amassed in the nation's capitol. They occupied parks and a row of condemned buildings along Pennsylvania Avenue, between the White House and the Capitol. When new arrivals overflowed those sites, they put up a makeshift camp with scraps of lumber, canvas, and tin on the muddy Anacostia Flats, just a few blocks downhill from the historic home of the Civil War era's most famous abolitionist, Fredrick Douglas. They named their camp Hooverville.

Cheers roared from Hooverville on the afternoon of June 15th, when they received news that the House of Representatives had passed the Patman Bill by a vote of 209 to 176. The populism evidenced in the House was not found in the Senate two days later. The bill went down to overwhelming defeat with sixty-two nay votes and only eighteen Senators in support. The camp gave way to a kind of seething malaise. The Bonus Army leadership had 'deputized' their own three hundred man police force. They had required campers to provide proof of honorable discharge from the military, as a way to keep communist agitators out. Nevertheless, the mood was ugly on the night of June 17th.

It was in that volatile atmosphere that retired Major General Butler took the stage. He had always been an extremely popular leader among the rank and file, but never more so than on this night when he spoke of hope and persistence. He was not willing to give up on the fight to help the struggling War Veterans in Hooverville and across the nation. He stated flatly, "Nor should you surrender in the face of the Senate vote. We came home from France victorious, we came to our nation's capital for justice, we have come so far."

Butler, unlike many of his top brass military colleagues, had come to be far more concerned about possible fascist overthrow of the government than communist insurrection. In 1934, Butler alleged that a group of wealthy, pro-fascist industrialists were plotting a military led coup d'état against the government of President Franklin D. Roosevelt. In Congress the McCormack-Dickstein Committee (predecessor of the House Un-American Activities Committee) investigated Butler's allegations and corroborated most of the specifics of his testimony. Fortunately for the nation, apparently the mere reporting of the plan was enough; no one was ever indicted, no action was ever taken, no coup occurred, and Franklin Roosevelt went on to be elected to three more terms as President.

A veteran of seven overseas military campaigns, including World War I, the Major General was twice awarded the Medal of Honor. He was a true American hero. That being the case, there was little anyone could or would do about his post-military retirement gig. He became a pacifist lecturer and author. His book, *War is a Racket*, was published in 1935. His most famous quote:

> I spent 33 years and four months in active military service and during that period I spent most of my time as a high class muscle man for Big Business, for Wall Street and the bankers. In short, I was a racketeer, a gangster for capitalism. I helped make Mexico and especially Tampico safe for American oil interests in 1914. I helped make Haiti and Cuba a decent place for the National City Bank boys to collect revenues in. I helped in the raping of half a dozen Central American Republics for the benefit of Wall Street. I helped purify Nicaragua for the International Banking House of Brown Brothers in 1902 – 1912. I brought light to the Dominican Republic for the American sugar interests in 1916. I helped make Honduras right for the American fruit companies in 1903. In China in 1927 I helped see to it that Standard Oil went on its way unmolested. Looking back on it, I might have given Al Capone a few hints. The best he could do was to operate his racket in three districts. I operated on three continents.[5]

Expressing these thoughts and attitudes in lectures all over the nation, it is little wonder that Major General Butler's support of the Bonus Army so rankled the military and business leadership of the day. It is also little wonder that Army Chief of Staff, Major General Douglas MacArthur, decided to play the "commie" card when he reported that the Bonus Army had been taken over by "communists and pacifists." Communists were bad enough. But pacifists, well, they were totally anathema to General MacArthur and his boss, the Secretary of War, Patrick Hurley.

As the Veteran's occupation of the vacant Treasury buildings and Anacostia swamp drug on into late July, the historical comparisons to the spontaneous 1917 revolt in St. Petersburg, Russia were inevitable. A palpable sense of fear began to emanate from the west wing of the White House. The Bolsheviks, after all, were only minor actors with a cameo appearance in St. Petersburg that cold February of 1917. It was by sheer ruthless determination, and strategically applied violence that they seized all real power from the Provisional Government of Russia by the end of October.

With this recent history as the contextual background, a secret Army intelligence report was issued on July 5, 1932 by Conrad H. Lanza, Assistant Chief of Staff, to the Intelligence Officer of the Second Corps Area. Though there was never any evidence submitted to corroborate the report, it warned:

> Word has been passed around in Syracuse (New York) that the first bloodshed by the Bonus Army at Washington, is to be a signal for a communist uprising in all large cities thus initiating a revolution. The entire movement is stated to be under communist control, with branches being rapidly developed in commercial centers.[6]

Not wanting to miss the opportunity to exploit the situation and the paranoia, the Communist Party of the United States dispatched one John Pace. He organized and led a small group of veterans with communist leanings from Detroit to Washington, DC. He applied for a permit to hold a meeting in the ball park adjoining the big Anacostia camp. The District of Columbia Superintendent of Police, Pelham Glassford, was himself a veteran and had been sympathetic toward the beleaguered campers at Hooverville. He had even arranged private donations of medical supplies, clothing, and food. He also approved the permit application received from John Pace.

In reality, the majority of veterans camped on the Capitol's doorstep were staunchly anti-communist. Motivated by that sentiment, coupled with his fear that a communist rally would be used as pretext to forcefully expel the Bonus Army, Walter Waters requested a meeting with Police Superintendent Glassford and John Pace. Waters strongly protested the issuance of a permit to the communist contingent led by Pace.

"If they are allowed to speak, my men will tear him and his boys from limb to limb!" exclaimed Waters. With that, the gauntlet was thrown and a fist fight broke out. Superintendent Glassford waded into the middle and broke up the altercation. Glassford squared on Waters and told him face to face, "We're all veterans together, and I did not want to see any veterans fighting veterans." Continuing to stare at Walters, he pointed an index finger, crooked with age and abuse, at Pace and continued, "That man has a right to speak and express his views. Any one of you who doesn't want to listen to him had better go back to camp and play baseball."[7]

With those words, the Superintendent of Police for the District of Columbia demonstrated that he understood what veterans had fought and died for. He understood the First Amendment to the United States Constitution: "Congress shall make no law respecting an establishment of religion, or prohibiting the free exercise thereof; or abridging the freedom of speech, or of the press; or the right of the people peaceably to assemble, and to petition the Government for a redress of grievances."[8] In the days ahead, not all the powerful men in Washington would demonstrate a similar understanding of the Constitution they had sworn to uphold.

The buildings occupied by the Bonus Army were condemned federal office buildings. A firm date had not been set, but they were scheduled for demolition. With Congress in recess, and the communist scare at full tilt, the Hoover administration began casting about for a reason to dislodge the entrenched veterans. Proceeding post-haste with the building demolition was the strategy upon which they settled. On July 26, 1932 the Assistant Secretary of the Treasury, Ferry K. Heath, sent the following letter to the Commissioners of the District of Columbia:

> Under the date of July 23, 1932 this department served notice to W.W. Waters and Camp Commanders of the various areas to vacate on or before midnight of Monday, July 25, 1932, all land and premises belonging to the United States and under the jurisdiction and control of the U.S. Treasury Department.
>
> On Monday, July 25, 1932, counsel for the Bonus Expeditionary Force (B.E.F.) besought a 24 hour stay of the above order of vacation, in order to afford the B.E.F. an opportunity to offer a definite proposal for the vacation of the buildings occupied

by the veterans. This department has granted this stay, and nothing developed at the conference which warranted the order of vacation, and the contractors are under orders to proceed with the work.

It is planned to begin work on this area at 7:30am sharp, Wednesday, July 27, 1932, and it is requested that a sufficient detail of police be on hand to prevent any interference with the contractor or his workmen.[9]

When Superintendent Glassford and his police officers arrived at mid-morning on Thursday, July 28th with written orders to vacate the premises, they became the target of bricks and stones. One officer suffered a serious head injury when a brick crashed into his skull. As the melee got out of hand, an angry veteran, apparently feeling that Glassford had betrayed his fellow veterans, tore off the chief's gold police badge. Fearing for their safety, some police officers opened fire, killing one veteran immediately and mortally wounding another. The officers retreated, and Superintendent Glassford immediately sought the advice of his Board of Commissioners.

At the meeting he told the Commissioners what had transpired:

> I was about twenty yards away from the building when I heard a commotion. I went to the second floor. One officer had started up the steps, and near the rear I heard someone say, 'Let's get him.' The officer had attempted to stop a commotion between two veterans. As he started up the steps bricks started falling on him, and as I leaned over the railing above I saw him fall and draw his gun, firing two shots. Two other policemen rushed up with their guns in hand. I leaned over and shouted, 'Stop that shooting.' When I did that one of my men who apparently was dazed by the bricks thought I was a veteran about to throw at him. He turned his revolver straight at me. I ducked behind a pillar, for fear he might shoot before he realized who it was.[10]

The District of Columbia Commissioners were eager to rid themselves of this no-win situation, and the morning's events provided just such an opportunity. Early that same afternoon they hastily fired off a letter to President Hoover, effectively washing their hands of the entire mess.

Mr. President:

The Commissioners of the District of Columbia regret to inform you that during the past few hours, circumstances of a serious character have-arisen in the District of Columbia which have been the cause of unlawful acts of large numbers of so-called "bonus marchers" who have been in Washington for some time past.

This morning, officials of the Treasury Department, seeking to clear certain areas within the Government triangle in which there were numbers of these bonus marchers, met with resistance. They called upon the Metropolitan Police Force for assistance and a serious riot occurred. Several members of the Metropolitan Police were injured, one reported seriously. The total number of bonus marchers greatly outnumbered the police; the situation is made more difficult by the fact that this area contains thousands of brickbats and these were used by the rioters in their attack upon the police.

In view of the above, it is the opinion of the Major and Superintendent of Police, in which the Commissioners concur, that it will be impossible for the Police Department to maintain law and order except by the free use of firearms which will make the situation a dangerous one; it is believed, however, that the presence of Federal troops in some number will obviate the seriousness of the situation and result in far less violence and bloodshed.

The Commissioners of the District of Columbia, therefore, request that they be given the assistance of Federal troops, in maintaining law and order in the District of Columbia.
Very sincerely yours,
L. H. Reichelderfet
President, Board of Commissioners of the District of
Columbia"

The building demolition strategy was working perfectly. The Commissioner's letter made clear that some amount of "violence and bloodshed" was expected. President Hoover now had the cover he needed to unshackle the Secretary of War, who at 3:00pm on July 28, 1932 sent the following memorandum to General MacArthur:

To: General Douglas MacArthur

Chief of Staff, U.S., Army

The President has just now informed me that the civil government of the District of Columbia has reported to him that it is unable to maintain law and order in the District.

You will have United States troops proceed immediately to the scene of the disorder. Cooperate fully with the District of Columbia police force which is now in charge. Surround the affected area and clear it without delay.

Turn over all prisoners to the civil authorities.

In your orders insist that any women or children who may be in the affected area be accorded every consideration and kindness. Use all humanity consistent with the due execution of the order.

Patrick J. Hurley,

Secretary of War[12]

General MacArthur received these orders with glee and, as was typical throughout his career, he would not be denied this opportunity to grab the gaze of an adoring media. At 3:05pm he stepped out of his office and addressed his aids, Major Dwight D. Eisenhower and Major George S. Patton, "We got word to move 'em out. Call the stables and have them bring my horse up."

Major Eisenhower questioned, "Sir?"

"I said, have them bring my horse up. I am going to oversee the operation personally."

Knowing full well that a General's direct involvement in a domestic affair would be a serious breach of military tradition, Major Eisenhower counseled, "Sir, this standoff could easily devolve into a riot. It would be highly inappropriate for the Chief of Staff of the Army to be involved in anything like a local or street-corner embroilment."

"You are wrong about that Major. This is no street-corner affair. This is a matter of federal authority over the District of Columbia. Pacifism and its bedfellow communism are all around us, and they have laid siege to the nation's capitol."

Major Eisenhower persisted, "Sir, military protocol calls for the commanding officer to remain in headquarters. Besides, this could turn ugly and those men are honorably discharged vets who served with us in France."

"Dammit Ike, I'll bet not one man in ten out there are vets. They are a bunch of communist traitors. Incipient revolution is in the air and it is going to end today, and I will be at the front of our troops."

Realizing that the last words of the preceding statement spoke volumes about his commanding officer's character, Major Eisenhower acquiesced and requested his orders.

Eisenhower's fellow officer did not share this initial reticence about the operation. Concurring with General MacArthur's opinion that the Bonus Marchers were "a bunch of red agitators," Major Patton briefed his command before the operation. "If you must fire do a good job. A few casualties become martyrs, a large number an object lesson. When a mob starts to move keep it on the run. Use a bayonet to encourage its retreat. If they are running, a few good wounds in the buttocks will encourage them. If they resist, they must be killed."[13]

By 4:45pm four troops of cavalry, four companies of infantry, a mounted machine gun squadron, and six whippet tanks lined up on Pennsylvania Avenue near 12th Street. Thousands of Civil Service employees spilled out of their offices and lined the streets to watch. At first, and perhaps naively, the veterans assumed the military display was in their honor. They cheered! Suddenly the troopers turned and charged. In the lead rode General Douglas MacArthur, his medals shining on his immaculate uniform, his boots gleaming, his horse perfectly groomed. The bedraggled veterans being herded ahead of the onslaught viewed his magnificence with disdain. The flash bulbs of the press corps exploded in orgasmic frenzy—neither the General nor his mount flinched.

Once the civil servant spectators realized what was happening, they took up the chant, "Shame! Shame! Shame!"[14] Next followed soldiers with gas masks and fixed bayonets, hurling tear gas into the crowd. Bonus Marchers and spectators alike scattered in panicked confusion. As the scent of tear gas wafted across the rose garden, reporters at the White House were being told that the Secret Service had learned that those resisting eviction were "entirely of the Communist element."

At about 6:30pm General George Van Horn Moseley, Deputy Chief of Staff of the Army, received a call from Secretary of War Hurley. The Secretary was totally surprised, and mildly irritated, that General MacArthur was at the scene leading the troops. "George, get down there and make damned sure he understands that the President does not want the troops crossing the bridge. I want you to deliver that message personally—do you understand?" The Secretary knew that General MacArthur would have to meet with the Assistant Chief of Staff if he showed up on the scene, and doubted that he would be willing to meet with any lower ranking official.

General Moseley proceeded with haste to the scene. He found General MacArthur dismounted, standing with hands on his hips, chest thrown out, and an excited gleam in his eyes. Moseley pulled MacArthur aside and they walked back up the street for a private word. "General, I have received orders from the President, through the Secretary's office, that they do not want you to pursue the Bonus Marchers across the river."

"Goddammit George, they are a bunch of commies. We may never have the chance to clear the rabble out of town if we don't do it now!"

Looking his commanding officer square in the eye, General Moseley responded, "Douglas, I am delivering a message from the civilian command. I am only the messenger. Do you understand?"

"Yes." General MacArthur turned on a heel and strode back to where his horse was being held by a Private First Class, a young black man. Many of the stable hands were "Colored" soldiers and this private, having brought the General's horse up to Pennsylvania Avenue, stayed with several other horse handlers to tend the cavalry mounts.

Whether or not General Moseley agreed with the orders cannot now be known, but it is almost certain that he had doubts that MacArthur would comply, as did apparently the Secretary of War. Having delivered the message, Moseley returned to his office where almost immediately he received a call from a Presidential aide at the White House.

General Moseley, "Yes, I delivered the message personally."

White House aide, "Have the troops stopped shy of the bridge?"

General Moseley, "I am not certain that has happened."

The phone was hung up at the White House without another word.

Within ten minutes, General Moseley received another call from Secretary Hurley. He assured Hurley that the message had been delivered and that General MacArthur indicated he understood the orders. Secretary Hurley instructed, "This is not good." After a brief pause he continued, "I want the message sent again to assure that General MacArthur has received it before they cross the Anacostia Bridge."

This time General Moseley sent Colonel Clement Wright, Secretary to the General Staff. As Colonel Wright drew near he saw someone waving a white shirt as a flag of truce approaching General MacArthur and Majors Eisenhower and Patton. All three were standing on the bridge. Upon his arrival Col. Wright recognized the man holding the shirt. It was the Bonus Army's de facto leader, Walter Waters. Waters asked General MacArthur if the Hooverville campers would be "given an hour to form in columns, salvage their belongings, and retreat in an orderly fashion."[15]

MacArthur replied, "Yes, my friend, of course."[16]

For many of the Bonus Army and their families, all of their worldly possessions were stored haphazardly in the shanty town they had constructed on Anacostia Flats. They did not have cedar chests full of warm winter cloths stored in some little house with a white picket fence in Iowa. They did not have a bank account with funds to buy shoes for their children. They did not have a root cellar with stores of food for the coming winter. They were broke—flat broke.

The sun was setting as Mr. Waters turned and walked away toward Hooverville. Colonel Wright delivered the message, this time in the presence of two additional officers, Major Eisenhower and Major Patton. When he attempted to make it perfectly clear that these orders had come directly from the White House, General MacArthur cut him off, "Colonel, get out of my way, I am too busy and do not want my staff bothered by people coming down here and pretending to deliver orders."[17]

Stunned, Colonel Wright looked at the Majors, first one then the other. They both refused to make eye contact. He drew to attention and saluted. When no acknowledging salute was forthcoming from General MacArthur, Wright turned and walked back to his office.

Some of the Veteran's children had gathered a few hundred yards downstream and were skipping stones on the water. On the bridge, General MacArthur strode back and forth flipping a riding crop against his neatly pressed breeches. Barely fifteen minutes after promising Waters that the Hooverville campers would be given an hour to salvage belongings and clear out, MacArthur turned to his aides and said, "By damned, they are continuing to riot. I just saw some of them throwing rocks across the river." With that, the troops were ordered to lay down a volley of tear gas. They donned their masks and moved across the bridge.

A woman hiding in a nearby house with her family recalled, "One of the soldiers threw a bomb. We all began to cry. We got wet towels and put them over the faces of the children. About half an hour later my baby began to vomit. I took her outside in the air and she vomited again. Next day she began to turn black and blue and we took her to the hospital."[18]

As the troops marched through Hooverville the camp was torched. By daybreak, Anacostia flats was nothing but smoldering debris. The Bonus Marchers and their families had just melted away into the nearby neighborhoods and woods. No one knows for sure where most spent the night. In late July it is certain they were not cold, but equally certain many went hungry that night and for months to come.

From the scene on the bridge when MacArthur refused to receive orders from Col. Wright until daybreak the next morning, events seemed to catalyze a diminution of Major Patton's earlier enthusiasm and bravado. When it was over he described the action, "Sure there were some Bolsheviks in the mix. But for the most part they were poor, ignorant men, without hope, and without really evil intent. All in all, it was a most distasteful form of service." More than anything else, Patton seemed relieved that his troops had resisted the urge to discharge weapons, and the Bonus Army had chosen retreat rather than standing in for a brick throwing melee. It had been ugly, Patton understood that it could have been much, much worse.

¤ ¤ ¤

As witnessed by his instructions to troops at the onset, Patton's career was speckled by his emotional volatility. Even so, he was a man who absolutely revered military duty. No man has ever worn the uniform who took his oath more seriously.

> I, [George C. Patton], having been appointed a Major in the U.S. Army under the conditions indicated in this document, do accept such appointment and do solemnly swear that I will support and defend the Constitution of the United States against all enemies, foreign and domestic, that I will bear true faith and allegiance to the same; that I take this obligation freely, without any mental reservation or purpose of evasion; and that I will well and faithfully discharge the duties of the office on which I am about to enter, so help me God.[19]

Coupling the oath, with Article 2, Section 2, Clause 1 of the United States Constitution, which states in part, "The President shall be Commander in Chief of the Army and Navy of the United States, and of the Militia of the several States, when called into the actual Service of the United States;"[20] Patton knew full well that General MacArthur had willfully violated his military oath and the Constitution of the United States by refusing the orders of the President. This dereliction left a horrible taste in Patton's mouth. Within months he openly criticized the Army's tactics, stating "they violated every precept of how to handle civil unrest."[21]

Major Eisenhower had never shared any enthusiasm for the assignment, but unlike Patton, his colleague and friend, Eisenhower was always more politic and circumspect. He was never as direct in his criticism of MacArthur or the breakdown in command protocol. In retrospect, Eisenhower merely stated, "the whole scene was pitiful. The veterans were ragged, ill-fed, and felt themselves badly abused. To suddenly see the whole encampment going up in flames just added to the pity."[22]

¤ ¤ ¤

Still doing the peacock strut back at Anacostia, as dawn broke MacArthur began to realize that his megalomanic betrayal bordered on armed insurrection. The fact that a United States military force had disregarded direct orders of the President in the Nation's capitol, literally in the shadow of the White House, made matters worse. MacArthur took immediate steps to head off possible charges of treason. At about 6:30am, before anyone else in the administration had a chance to comment, MacArthur released the following statement to the press:

> It is my opinion that had the President not acted today, had he permitted this thing to go on for twenty-four hours more, we would have been faced with a grave situation which would have caused a real battle. Had he let it go on another week I believe that the institutions of our Government would have been very severely threatened. I think it can be safely said that he had not only reached the end of an extraordinary patience but that he had gone to the very limit of his desire to avoid friction and trouble before he used force. Had he not used it all that time, I believe he would have been very derelict indeed in the judgment in which he was handling the safety of the country. This was the focus of the world today; and had he not acted with the force and vigor that he

did, it would have been a very sad day for the country tomorrow.

I have been in many riots but I think this is the first riot I ever was in or ever saw in which there was no real bloodshed. So far as I know there is no man on either side who has been seriously injured.[23]

MacArthur's masterfully worded statement made it seem that the decision to "go all the way" had been solely the President's call—and a wise decision at that. Though that was an absolute lie by the Army Chief of Staff, the statement credited the President with extraordinary patience and judgment in his steadfast protection of the government and its institutions. The press, sharing the anti-communist paranoia of the era, ate it up. The President's hands were tied—he could hardly admit that he had opposed an action and had lost control of the military; an action that had "saved the union from communist insurrection."

General MacArthur's facts about bloodshed turned out to be another lie, and soon the press began to question the veracity of his statement. In reality nearby hospitals were overwhelmed. There were casualties.

¤ ¤ ¤

In Iowa, a young state champion wrestler named Norman Borlaug had obtained a copy of the Friday, July 31st Des Moines Register. He wanted to read the accounts of the previous day's opening ceremonies of the 1932 Summer Olympics in Los Angeles, California. He was sidetracked by the Associate Press article about the "Bonus Army Riot" in Washington, DC. The article reported the following statistics.

> Killed: 3
> Injured: 55 (5 seriously)
> Tear gas victims: 20
> Arrests: 135
> Still being held the next day: 55 (36 for immigration authorities, 10 for technical investigation, 9 for disorderly conduct and 1 for inciting a riot.)[24]

Folding the paper and setting it down on the kitchen table, young Borlaug said to himself as much as to his mother, "I suspect that whole bloody affair had more to do with hunger than politics."

¤ ¤ ¤

Because the Bonus Marchers' 1st Amendment rights, freedom of speech and assembly, had been trampled, a flurry of comments were released from the White House and Attorney General William Mitchell's office. They were trying to cast a net of damage control over the events of the evening of July 28th and early morning hours of July 29th. In New York Governor Roosevelt, sitting in his wheelchair, knew the damage had already been done.

In a letter to the *Washington Daily News* a disgusted reader expressed the sentiments of many. "I voted for Herbert Hoover in 1928. God forgive me and keep me alive at least till the polls open next November!"[25]

Already confident of success, Roosevelt now felt certain of victory in his 1932 campaign for President. He said to one of his aides as they ate breakfast in the Governor's mansion, "He should have invited a delegation into the White House for coffee and sandwiches."[26]

By his refusal to obey orders, General Douglas McArthur contributed, perhaps more than any other single person, to the election of Franklin Roosevelt. As if the economy was not bad news enough for Hoover, in the wake of the Bonus Army debacle, the presidential election was a fait accompli.

Roosevelt, realizing there was little need to mount an aggressive campaign against Hoover, pulled many of his aides off the campaign trail. He dispatched them to begin discussions regarding the filling of cabinet posts. Within days Professor M.L. Wilson, from Montana State Agriculture College, arranged a meeting between Henry Wallace and Rexford Guy Tugwell, one of Roosevelt's most trusted advisors. The handsome and erudite Tugwell was a professor of economics at Columbia University. His father had been a prosperous fruit farmer and canner. In his chest still beat the heart of a farmer.

Tugwell cottoned to Wallace from the get-go and just like the election, Wallace's position within the Roosevelt administration was already a done deal, though he was not yet aware of this fact. A few days after the meeting, Mary Huss, the administrative assistant at *Wallaces' Farmer*, walked into Henry's office with a broad smile on her face. In her hand she carried a personal invitation. Henry was going to have lunch with the Democratic nominee for president. They would be dining at Roosevelt's Hyde Park estate.

13

Odds And Ends

Wallace is chosen the "New Deal" Secretary of Agriculture.

Beginning as early as 1919, Henry Wallace had used statistical analyses to demonstrate that unmanaged free markets, by their very nature, would treat the farmer unfairly. He predicted that without control mechanisms this inherent unfairness would lead to a general collapse of the food and fiber production and distribution systems. As he watched urbanites go hungry in 1932, while massive surpluses of food rotted and was being eaten by vermin, his much maligned prognostications were sadly vindicated. Henry took no consolation in that fact, and one cannot find in the historical record a single "I told you so" in anything he authored during those years.

During the boom years of the Roaring '20s, Americans and their leaders worshiped at the altar of unfettered profits, which spawned a kind of avarice that Henry found abhorrent. It is natural, even after all these years, that one might blur the lines between the greed of the capitalists and the efficacy of capitalism. After all, by allowing agriculture to fail and farmers to go broke, while urban America frolicked in a decade of self-indulgent wealth, capitalists had ultimately betrayed capitalism. Rich men could not then and cannot now eat dollar bills, or clothe their families with buffalo nickels.

> The world is too much with us; late and soon,
> Getting and spending, we lay waste our powers;
> Little we see in Nature that is ours;
> We have given our hearts away, a sordid boon!
> This Sea that bares her bosom to the moon,
> The winds that will be howling at all hours,

And are up-gathered now like sleeping flowers,
For this, for everything, we are out of tune;
It moves us not.--Great God! I'd rather be
A Pagan suckled in a creed outworn;
So might I, standing on this pleasant lea
Have glimpses that would make me less forlorn;
Have sight of Proteus rising from the sea;
Or hear old Triton blow his wreathed horn.

—William Wordsworth (1807)[1]

Though in years hence, Henry would often share lunch with his personal friends, George William Russell and Robert Frost, he tended to view poetry with what might best be described as mild disdain. Regardless of that attitude, in the early 1930s he read Wordsworth's "The World Is Too Much with Us" over and over, as if to capture an articulation of his philosophical response to the Great Depression and its causes. More and more, his writing and his activism gave a prose voice to Wordsworth's poetic message. More and more, he was becoming an advocate of dramatic, perhaps even radical economic change. Though they had yet to meet, a Governor back in New York was keeping an eye on this Iowan. He was watching the gestation of a "New Dealer."

While Henry was delighted with the invitation to go to New York, he was a bit strapped for cash. He contacted friends at Cornell University and arranged a day of guest lectures. The University, having extended earlier invitations, was only too glad to host the renowned agriculturalist and author. They picked up the tab for his travel expenses.

As almost a cliché example of his eccentricity, Henry also took advantage of the trip to New York to visit with Iroquois shaman. He spent a day with them exploring his growing belief that he had lived a prior life among the Onondaga tribe of the Iroquois Confederation. Reportedly the shaman confirmed that indeed this was the case.

When Henry arrived at Hyde Park, he was not certain what to expect. He thought it likely that he would be introduced to Governor Roosevelt and would have the opportunity to share four or five minutes of pleasantries. To his surprise, he was scheduled for a full thirty minute sit down lunch with Governor Roosevelt and Henry Morgenthau, a trusted Roosevelt advisor, chairman of the New York State Agricultural Advisory Commission, and publisher of *The American Agriculturalist*. They dove right into the nation's agriculture problems. Henry learned that Roosevelt, a man born to wealth and refined culture, actually had a genuine interest in agriculture. In fact, he owned a farm in the red clay hills of west Georgia, just outside of Warm Springs.

Though it was to become much, much worse before the drought was over, gargantuan dust storms were already brewing in the Midwest. As if demonstrating his knack for prescience, Roosevelt foresaw the Dust Bowl and proposed the idea for planting "shelter belts" of trees all the way across the great plains to serve as wind breaks. They discussed the sharecropper tenancy problems and how that had been addressed in England and Ireland. Wallace recounted his impressions in the September 3, 1932 edition of *Wallaces' Farmer*.

> Roosevelt does not have the extreme pride of personal opinion that has characterized some of our more bull-headed presidents. He knows that he doesn't know it all and tries to find out all he can from people who are supposed to be authorities. He is such a likable humorous man that he is better fitted than most to draw the right kind of men to him.[2]

During their meeting Roosevelt's legendary people skills were in top form, and his empathic antennae were fully extended. The "half-hour" lunch had been underway for a full hour when Roosevelt suddenly remembered a vitally important task that required Morgenthau's immediate attention. Roosevelt had a knack for dismissing people in a way that made them feel good about it. Now in their privacy, Roosevelt and Wallace did not discuss agriculture, or politics, or cabinet appointments. The next president wanted to talk about mysticism with this spiritually eclectic visitor from Iowa. That afternoon they cast a spell on each other that would endure for their lifetimes.

When Henry boarded the train early that evening, no promises had been made—cabinet positions had not even been discussed. At this point, that was of no import to Henry. He was going home to do everything he could to get the New York Governor elected president. Consistent with his nature, he threw himself at this task with manic energy.

In 1928, Henry had not campaigned so much for Alfred E. Smith, as against Herbert Hoover. Not only had Hoover proven unsympathetic to the farmer's cause, Henry had not forgotten his father's bitter feud with the former Secretary of Commerce. Years later, he related his emotions during that campaign, "Do you know, I hope I never again feel as intensely antagonistic toward anyone as I did then. I felt, for a while there, I felt, almost, as if Hoover had killed my father." Such intense negativity were no doubt foreign and uncomfortable emotions for Henry Wallace.

This time, though the adversary was the same, Henry found himself campaigning whole-heartedly **for** Mr. Roosevelt rather than **against** Mr. Hoover. It was much easier to get out of bed in the morning and hit the campaign trail in 1932, than it had been four years earlier. Though the nation's farms were a tragic mess, Henry was a happier man asking those farmers to support the democratic presidential nominee. Receiving almost 23 million votes, Roosevelt won the November 8th election by a landslide. The democratic ticket carried forty-two states, including every state where Henry Wallace campaigned.

Not even a blip on the screen, General MacArthur's nightmare and nemesis, the much maligned Communist Party, garnered a paltry 103,307 votes (.3% of the total). So much for the ground swell of communist insurrection feared by the vanquishers of the Bonus Army, just four months earlier.

¤ ¤ ¤

Henry was excited when he awoke on the morning of November 9, 1932. Though thrilled with the election outcome, he obviously still chaffed at the heartbreaking loss of his family's newspaper earlier in the year. That morning he went downtown to his office and dictated a letter to Bernard Baruch.

> Dear Mr. Baruch,
>
> I am writing to you today to carry out a promise which I made to you as I was leaving your office on Wednesday, March 23. At that time, you will remember that you made the statement that Iowa would never go Democratic, that the prejudice of the middlewestern farmer was so deep that nothing could ever be done to shake it.
>
> I don't think you realized last spring and I doubt that you

realize now how mightily our people in this section of the country are being shaken.[3]

Just eight months prior Henry had gone to New York to solicit Mr. Baruch's financial support for *Wallaces' Farmer*. The capital needed for the Wallace family to retain ownership of the paper was not forthcoming. While in New York, the two men also discussed politics. As Henry was leaving the office Baruch suggested that they revisit their respective positions the day after the election. The letter, and its tone, was quite atypical of Henry Wallace. Mr. Baruch's refusal of financial support and the loss of the business, that had been a family fixture for three generations, rankled still.

More in keeping with his true personality, Henry also dictated a letter to the President-elect. Even though he knew his name was on the short-list for Secretary of Agriculture, his letter recommended George Peek for that position. During World War I, Peek had actually worked for Bernard Baruch at the War Industries Board. In subsequent years, he partnered with John N. Willys and General Hugh Johnson to marry the Moline Plow Company with Universal Tractor, a subsidiary of Willys-Overland Automobile Company. Peek dove into the political arena by drafting much of the McNary-Haugen Farm Relief Bill. For a decade he stalked the corridors of Congress as the most vociferous lobbyist for agricultural reform. Having made many political connections, and widely recognized as an expert in agricultural economics, he became one of the original members of Roosevelt's famous "Brain Trust." To Henry's way of thinking, Peek was a logical choice for the job.

When Henry received letters from people supporting his appointment as Secretary of Agriculture, his typical responses were coy, "If the job were offered to me, I suppose I would take it although it would be with considerable misgivings." To another advocate he responded, "I know from my father's experience just what this job means in times like the present." At one point he even went so far as to say, "I sincerely trust that fate will not carry me into that hell down at Washington."[4]

One might speculate that Henry's protestations were as disingenuous as Brer Rabbit. ("That's all right, Brer Fox. It'll hurt something awful, but go ahead and skin me. Scratch out my eyeballs! Tear out my ears by the roots! Cut off my legs! Do what'nsoever you want to do with me, Brer Fox, but please, please, please! Don't throw me in that briar patch!"[5]) There is also good reason to believe that Henry had genuine misgivings about diving into the political abyss that was Washington. In retrospect, even in his own mind, his emotions and motives were probably mixed. Either way, fate, in the personage of Raymond Moley, called on the telephone in late November. Henry Wallace quickly packed his doubts and his clothes and jumped on a train for a sixty-eight hour ride down to Roosevelt's farm just west of Warm Springs, Georgia. Sixty-eight hours is a long time to ruminate about the smörgåsbord of possibilities that seemed to lay ahead.

He arrived early and had breakfast with the "vacationing" president-elect. This time the meeting was very brief. Henry spent the remainder of the day in discussions with New York agriculturist, Henry Morgenthau, and Raymond Moley, yet another of the Ph.D.s on the original "Brain Trust." That evening Wallace saw, perhaps for the first time in his life, a true professional politician "work the room" for a couple of hours over cocktails, which were illegal by the way. (*Almost exactly one year later, on December 5, 1933, prohibition of alcoholic beverages would be repealed by the ratification of the 21st Amendment to the United States Constitution.*)

"Awed" is the only word that comes close to describing Henry's impression of what he had seen in the future president's style and panache. Henry described his experience at Warm Springs as, "A complete break with all that I had been and all that I had known, and a new outlook on life."[6] Still when he boarded the train the next morning no seat at the Cabinet table had been offered.

He went home to Des Moines to relax some with the family he had neglected somewhat during the campaign, and to catch up with a backlog of work at *Wallaces' Farmer*. On February 6, 1933 fate came knocking again, this time via U.S. Post.

> My dear Friend,
>
> Before I leave on a ten days' fishing trip I am going to ask you to assume a task which is one of the utmost importance to the whole Country. I want to have the privilege of having you as a member of my official family in the post of Secretary of Agriculture.[7]
>
> Please let me know of your decision by radio to the yacht Nourmahal. The Navy Department's communication office will be ready to patch your call through at your earliest convenience.
>
> With my warmest regards,
> Faithfully yours,
> Franklin D. Roosevelt

Henry agonized as he read the letter, and then he read it again, over and over for six days. On February 12th, President Lincoln's birthday, Raymond Moley called, "Henry, I know this is a difficult time and a difficult decision, but we must have your reply."

In recollecting the phone conversation years later Moley stated, "There was a long pause, which I vividly remember to this day. Finally, after a verbal prod from me, I got a hesitating and rather tremulous acceptance."[8]

The decision had been made and conveyed to the president-elect by Moley. All that was left for Henry was to pen a formal and typically succinct reply.

> Dear Mr. President,
>   Your invitation can have but one reply. I appreciate the honor and accept the responsibility. So far as it is in me I will carry my part of the 'family' burdens.
>   Sincerely,
>   Henry Agard Wallace[9]

To say the least, the agriculture community was thrilled. For Henry, however, packing up and moving to the nation's capitol was a sombrous affair, made worse by the fact that he could not access any cash, due to bank closures throughout Iowa. He made all necessary arrangements to leave the fledgling Pioneer Hi-Bred Seed company in the control of his partner and friend, Fred Lehmann. Like his grandfather and father before him, his next column bid the *Wallaces' Farmer* readers adieu. He did break with tradition by using a tagline other than the somewhat odd "A Word Personal," which both his father and grandfather had used for their farewells.

Odds and Ends

This is the last time, for a while at least, that I shall be writing this column. I am going to Washington, March 4, to serve as the Secretary of Agriculture in the Cabinet of President Roosevelt.

I remember how my father left home 12 years ago to take a similar position under President Harding. He accepted a cabinet place because he felt keenly the need of trying to restore the agricultural values smashed in the decline of 1920 – 21 and because he feared there would be a much more serious smash later on unless both the government and the city people of the United States became aware of their debt and duty to the farmer. In this cause he gave his life. . . .

While the situation of the world and of agriculture is far more desperate today than it was then, I have an advantage he did not have—a chief who is definitely progressive, entirely sympathetic toward agriculture, and completely determined to use every means at his command to restore farm buying power. . . .

Of course, every sensible man must realize that the new administration will labor under a terrific handicap. It is fairly easy to put out a fire before it gets much of a start. To put it out after the wind and time and neglect have fanned it into a flaming rage is a task of great difficulty. The new administration must make up for twelve years of lost time. . . .

Fortunately for the nation, President Roosevelt has exactly the right kind of temperament for this kind of situation. He rises to emergencies fearlessly and optimistically. And so, I will be working under a courageous man with a kindly heart. . . .

I will try to do my part in Washington. No doubt I shall make many mistakes, but I hope it can always be said that I have done the best I knew.[10]

And so it was with those words, Henry Wallace's life in Iowa was over. He would return to visit often, and made one of his most famous speeches at the Des Moines Coliseum, but he would never again reside in his home-state. He would never return to work for *Wallaces' Farmer*, though his name would remain on the masthead of the paper as "editor on leave" for the next thirteen years.

14

A Country Boy Goes To DC

Wallace, as Secretary of Agriculture, responds to the broken farm economy.

By inauguration day, March 4, 1933, it could be said that Henry Agard Wallace had received his Master's degree from the college of Hard Knocks. Still nothing in his training had prepared him to be Secretary of Agriculture during the Great Depression—not his Bachelor's degree from Iowa State, not his back yard experiments with Professor Perry Holden's Reid Yellow Dent corn, not his study of calculus and statistics, not his travels throughout the Western United States and Europe, not his job as Chief Editor of *Wallaces' Farmer*—nothing in this life, nor even some previous life among the Iroquois people, made him ready for what he was to encounter in Washington, DC.

Henry was a country boy. At that fateful inauguration in 1933, more people would crowd around the steps of the Capitol and out beyond 1st St. NE, than all the people living in Des Moines and Ames, Iowa combined. The day's activities started at 10:15 with a prayer service at St. John's Episcopal Church attended by the next President, Vice President, Cabinet designees and their families. After the service the attendees poured out onto the sidewalk directly across H Street from Lafayette Park. Never all that comfortable with crowds and small talk, the Wallaces milled around, introduced themselves to some of the other nominees for cabinet posts and their families, and wondered what to do next. Being an avid hiker, Henry had assumed the walk up to the Capitol, being slightly less than two miles, would be a pleasant stroll. He had no idea what it would be like trying to fight through a crowd of well over 100 thousand people. Others present were jumping in cars and zooming off at break neck speed. At last, only Henry, his wife Ilo, Francis Perkins and her daughter Susanna remained. Ms. Perkins, as Labor Secretary, was the first woman ever appointed to a Cabinet post in the United States. The political novices introduced themselves and decided to share a cab.

By now it was after 11:00 am. The U.S. Constitution stipulates that the swearing-in occurs at 12:00 noon. The cab was able to push through the throng of people only slightly faster than they could have walked. The driver dropped them off at the only place he could, the corner of Constitution and Louisiana, which was still more than a quarter of mile from their designated seating on the East Portico of the Capitol Building—a quarter mile filled with a sea of humanity. When Perkins and Wallace did finally succeed in pushing their way through to the stage, they found their "assigned" seats had been commandeered by people who had understood the necessity of early arrival. The two neophytes found a place to stand uncomfortably on the left side of the stage. From that vantage point, they were unable to see the swearing-in ceremony and could only catch bits and pieces of Roosevelt's famous speech.

> I am certain that my fellow Americans expect that on my induction into the Presidency I will address them with a candor and a decision which the present situation of our Nation impels. This is preeminently the time to speak the truth, the whole truth, frankly and boldly. Nor need we shrink from honestly facing conditions in our country today. This great Nation will endure as it has endured, will revive and will prosper. So, first of all, let me assert my firm belief that the only thing we have to fear is fear itself—nameless, unreasoning, unjustified terror which paralyzes needed efforts to convert retreat into advance. In every dark hour of our national life a leadership of frankness and vigor has met with that understanding and support of the people themselves which is essential to victory. I am convinced that you will again give that support to leadership in these critical days. . . .[1]

Many who had traveled to Washington to observe the inauguration had found notices in their hotel rooms the prior evening stating that checks drawn on out-of-town banks would not be honored. State after state had declared "bank holidays" following panicked withdrawal demands over the previous four days. Demands that could not be met. What most of the audience did not know was that President-elect Roosevelt had received word, just minutes before being sworn in, that every state in the union had declared a bank holiday earlier in the day. Into the black hole of a collapsed banking system the new president spoke these words during his inaugural address:

> The money changers have fled from their high seats in the temple of our civilization. We may now restore that temple to the ancient truths. The measure of that restoration lies in the extent to which we apply social values more noble than mere monetary profit.[1]

From the stage-left wings, Henry's contemplations reflected the day's cold, damp skies. As he craned his neck to watch the proceedings he noted "a feeling of imminent, dire crisis." He wondered whether the team assembled that day, on that stage "could find the technical means to get out of the crisis in a hurry . . . because people were so desperate."[2] Interestingly, over seventy-five years later, though we survived as a nation, radio and television pundits continue to debate that question. We wonder still.

Almost missing his president's inauguration was not Henry's only stumble during this first year in Washington. But the Secretary of Agriculture job was not a sprint. It was a long distance race, and in distance running a stumble at the start does not make or break the runner. Indeed, what was amazing is how fast the country boy from Iowa found his stride. Not just that, but he was able to set a torrid pace unmatched by Department of Agriculture staff or any of the other Cabinet secretaries for that matter.

The depression of agricultural economics was, by 1933, a full twelve years old. During all of those years Henry had come to understand that there were but few mechanisms available to prop up fair prices for the commodities farmers brought to market.

First was to control prices by executive fiat. After the 1919 debacle of setting hog prices at a level almost 6¢ per pound below production costs by the federal Office of Food Administration, Henry did not trust that price fixing by the executive branch would always be reasonable.

Second was to establish mechanisms of market management. In large measure the McNary-Haugen Farm Relief bill would have endeavored to manage markets through the application of tariffs and other means. Though it came close a number of times, the bill never had the necessary political support to pass both houses of congress and be signed into law by the president. At the time, Henry had supported the measure as the best alternative available, but he never viewed it as a panacea for agriculture.

Next was to create new markets for agricultural products. George Washington Carver spent most of his career working in his laboratory at Tuskegee Institute in the effort to produce new products that would have value in the market place. Though he would obtain patents on 325 products made from peanuts, more than a hundred from sweet potatoes, and dozens more from other plants, his efforts had very little impact on commodity market prices. Looking back one almost has to wonder if his career, in fact, took a turn onto a dead end street in that Tuskegee chemistry lab. Perhaps he should have stuck with horticulture, his first love—he could "talk to flowers," after all. Meanwhile in Washington, Henry came to believe the only way to significantly impact the creation of new markets was through the export of agriculture products to foreign countries. He recognized that this methodology had some **serious** downsides. It would likely exacerbate tariff driven international trade wars.

Finally, control of production was viewed as the most likely way to support fair farm commodity prices. A man whose passion was creating a better corn—a corn with greater per acre yield, enigmatically settled on the belief that production limits had to be imposed in order for farmers to receive fair prices in the open market place. The Hoover Administration's core agricultural program had been a $500 million revolving fund administered by a nonpartisan Farm Board. The fund was used to stabilize commodity prices primarily through cooperative marketing. The board would establish government corporations that would buy and hold farm commodities. Theoretically, this mechanism would be used to sustain farm prices a bit above international levels. Henry concluded, that without a mechanism to restrict production, this plan would fail. It did. In order to stabilize farm prices long-term, there had to be a way to restrict production. The question was, how?

¤ ¤ ¤

Rex Tugwell had arranged Henry's first meeting with Roosevelt. Through years of support, and effective campaign efforts, there is no doubt that Mr. Tugwell had earned a spot in the new administration. To everyone's complete surprise, he asked "to go over to agriculture and work for that chap Wallace." Very different men of temperament and style, Wallace and

Tugwell fit like a picture in a frame. They made a great team, and their first job was to find some way to stabilize farm commodity prices at the highest sustainable level.

No one loves a crisis. Yet historically, if coupled with the right leadership, crises have offered opportunities to revisit the paradigms that govern societies. Farms had been in trouble since 1920; in crisis since 1929; and, along with the banking system, had essentially collapsed in March 1933. The "right leadership" had converged at the Department of Agriculture, and bold action was absolutely necessary.

Rex Tugwell advised that protracted congressional wrangling could be avoided by an omnibus emergency bill authorizing the proposals being pushed by competing lobbyists. On March 8, 1933 they made an appointment to visit with Roosevelt. They asked the President to consider expanding the scope of his congressional proposals, to include the agricultural crisis in addition to the financial services industry legislation. Tugwell counseled the president, "Decisions could thus be deferred and perhaps altogether removed from legislative bickering. Successful action, we believe, might smother arguments; and, best of all, we might actually be able to get to work!"[3]

The President loved the idea, particularly the flexibility it offered in terms of tailoring responses to meet different regional needs, as those needs changed with the changing winds of the times. He also liked the political advantage of moving farm legislation first stating, "It will give Congress something to do while we prepare bills on other fronts."[4]

Henry agreed to set up an "emergency conference" of farm leaders within two days, noting that immediate action was essential, "cotton is sprouting on expanded acreage, winter wheat is ripening, spring wheat is being planted, and hog and cattle numbers are nearing record levels—we must act now."[5]

With a wry grin the President commented, "Well, I hope some of your farm boys are old-fashioned enough to keep some cash buried in a tin can. Otherwise, with all the banks closed, they won't be able to buy a train ticket to come to your meeting."

Two days later, on Friday, March 10, 1933 the heads of the American Farm Bureau, the National Grange, the Secretary and Assistant-Secretary of Agriculture, and about fifty farm leaders from across the country met in a cramped conference room at the Department of Agriculture building. Three hours into the meeting Henry was summoned to give a live radio interview. In part he stated, "Today, in this country, men are fighting to save their homes. That is not just a figure of speech. That is a brutal fact, a bitter commentary on agriculture's twelve years' struggle. What do we propose to do about it? . . . Emergency action is imperative."[6]

The meeting continued for several more hours and at the close of the day a consensus statement was issued, "The farm leaders were unanimous in their opinion that the agricultural emergency calls for prompt and drastic action. . . . The farm groups agree that farm production must be adjusted to consumption and favor the principles of the so-called domestic allotment plan as a means of reducing production and restoring buying power. . . . "[7]

Unbeknownst to the farm leaders group, their choice of words, "prompt and drastic action," was a precise harbinger of the following sequence of events that would unfold over the next few weeks:

On March 16th the Agricultural Emergency Act to Increase Farm Purchasing Power (H.R.3835) was introduced by Congressman Marvin Jones of Texas. Representative Jones chaired the House Agricultural Committee.

On March 22nd the house approved the bill by a vote of 315 to 98 without amendments and sent it on to the Senate.

Farmers' Union president John Simpson provided testimony in the Senate opposing the bill. He stated that farmers would be better served by what was known as the "cost of production" plan. The Senate embraced this idea in large part because it was easy to understand. If average farm cost for producing a bushel of corn went up 17ᶜ, so would the amount paid for the corn.

Secretary Wallace and Assistant Secretary Tugwell lobbied against this amendment with the obvious question, "What incentive would the agriculture industry have to control production costs?" They were convinced that whether or not that issue could be managed, the automatic "cost of production" price adjustment method was certain to create an inflationary spiral that would last ad infinitum or until rescinded. The Senate turned a deaf ear and on April 13th the Senate voted forty-seven to forty-one to amend H.R.3835 to include the "cost of production" idea into the bill. What seemed like a sure legislative victory three weeks earlier was slipping away, but "drastic" actions brewed and boiled over back in the heartland.

In Le Mars, Iowa on April 27th radicalism erupted into violence. A mob of militant farmers had successfully thwarted a foreclosure with their "penny sale" strategy. Buoyed by their success they crowded into Judge Charles C. Bradley's courtroom, where he was hearing a case testing the constitutionality of Iowa's foreclosure moratorium. When the judge ordered the men to remove hats and stop smoking, several hotheads charged the bench, overpowered the bailiff, and dragged the judge from the courtroom. At that point, a mob mentality took over. They tied Judge Bradley in the bed of a pickup and took him to an intersection where a large tree stood just outside of town. He was humiliated by being undressed and threatened with genital mutilation. The mob expected the Judge to capitulate to their demand to cease foreclosures. He responded with as much courage and dignity as a naked man in front of a mob can muster, "I will do the fair thing to all men to the best of my knowledge." Hearing that, a couple of men put a noose around his neck. At that point a local newspaper man stopped reporting and started making news. His appeal dampened down the homicidal inclinations of the mob. They did however, fill a hubcap with grease, put it on Bradley's head, and dumped the sixty year old judge in the bar-ditch beside the road.

On April 28th Iowa Governor Clyde Herring declared martial law and dispatched troops to Le Mars. Military authorities arrested eighty-six men.

On April 29th the story of the Iowa "cowardice and rebellion" was denounced on the front page of the New York Times.

On May 1st Iowa militia raided the Communist Party headquarters in Sioux City and made several arrests. No charges were ever filed, and all those arrested were released within twenty-four hours.

Though officials were unable to find a link with the Communist Party, the Farmer's Holiday movement had crossed the line, and Farmer's Union President John Simpson's sway with Congress plummeted.

Henry Wallace again appealed for prompt action defending H.R.3835 as "a course of action between the status quo and radicalism."

On May 10th the Senate passed the measure with the "cost of production" amendment intact by a vote of 48 to 33.

Secretary Wallace was not happy with the amendment. The House of Representatives was not happy with the amendment. The House refused to accede to the Senate version of the bill.

By May 11th everyone knew time was running out. The Senate blinked and gave final approval to the measure, as it had been originally introduced in the House.

On May 12, 1933 President Roosevelt signed the 'Agricultural Emergency Act to Increase Farm Purchasing Power' into law.

Secretary Henry Wallace reported that "the twelve-year effort by farmers to build a modern vessel with which to reach the new world has finally succeeded. The craft was launched on May 12, 1933, and immediately set on a course toward social justice."[8] By any reckoning, the law gave the Secretary of Agriculture the most sweeping powers ever allowed an appointed public official in United States history. Secretary Wallace had the de facto authority to levy taxes, regulate production by prescription, and order the destruction of crops as well as the slaughter of livestock in excess of production ceilings.

People did not like the idea of killing piglets and plowing up cotton sprouts. To those who vociferously made their concerns known, Secretary Wallace responded, "The plowing under of 10 million acres of cotton in August 1933 and the slaughter of 6 million little pigs in September, 1933 were not acts of idealism in any sane society. They were emergency acts made necessary by the almost insane lack of world statesmanship during the period from 1920 to 1932."[9]

The little pigs were not wasted. The recently established Federal Surplus Relief Corporation distributed one hundred million pounds of pork and pork by-products, such as soap and lard, to the needy, and in 1933 there were a lot of "needy."

Under the auspices of the Agriculture Emergency Act, Henry Wallace and Rex Tugwell put in place and oversaw a system to regulate agricultural production, thereby employing the principles of supply and demand to enhance the possibility of profitable farming. In the throes of the Great Depression that likelihood still seemed a long way off, but through the efforts of the Agricultural Adjustment Administration (AAA) at least the door was cracked open. Actual cash income for farmers rose by thirty percent during that first year. Clearly Wallace, Tugwell, and the Department of Agriculture "New Dealers" were making progress with job #1—managing production in order to stabilize farm prices.

The over-supply of farm commodities reaching the market was a problem that had been building for twelve years. Secretary Wallace's Job #2 was much sneakier, and its solutions much more vexing. Human impact on the environment had been building for generations. The winds of change were swirling in the jet stream far overhead and setting up for a big blow that would last most of a decade.

15

WHERE GRASSES GREW

The much abused Great Plains become the Dust Bowl.

The "dry spell" that began in 1931 had grown into a full-fledged drought by 1934. On the High Plains it was far too dry to grow wheat and corn and, with no native grasses left, the soil simply could not hold its own against the onslaught of the spring winds. Like some medieval plague, starvation had migrated out from the cities and now even farmers could not find food enough to fill their bellies.

If one were to ask almost anybody who grew up on a farm in the western half of North America, during the latter half of the twentieth century, for an opinion about Salsola Kali the response would likely be nothing much more than a blank stare. If the question were posed substituting Russian Thistle for Salsola Kali, quite a few of us "farm kids" would at least know what was being asked. But if one asked for an opinion of the Tumbleweed, the almost unanimous response would be, "It's a pain in the ass!"

The Russian Thistle (tumbleweed) is actually a misnomer. Its scientific classification is:

Kingdom: Plantea
Division: Magnoliphyta
Class: Magnoliopsida
Order: Caryophyllales
Family: Chenopoliacae
Subfamily: Salsoloideae
Genus: Salsola[1]

Thistles are of the Order Asterales, rather than Caryophyllales. For example, the Milk Thistle is classified:

Kingdom: Plantae
Division: Magnoliophyta
Class: Magnoliopsida
Order: Asterales
Family: Asteraceae
Subfamily: Carduoideae
Tribe: Cynareae
Genus: Silybum[2]

In point of fact, the tumbleweed is more closely related to spinach than to thistle. Milk Thistle is a much touted folk medicine prescribed to treat, and believed to cure, all manner of pathology related to jaundice, colitis, pleurisy, the spleen, liver, bile ducts, and gall bladder. Whereas, spinach is primarily known for giving Popeye the strength to beat-up Bluto and get out of all kinds of tight spots.

How Russian Thistle arrived in North America from the steppes of Russia is not known precisely, but the best conjecture is that the weed stowed away with flax seeds imported from Russia by South Dakota Mennonites around 1877. In Bon Homme County, South Dakota, the Mennonites who had recently arrived from Russia themselves, readily recognized the noxious plant when it first sprouted in and amongst the sown flax. Unfortunately, the flax did not adapt well to the dry environment and efforts to cultivate it as a cash crop were abandoned within a few years. However, with each mature plant scattering up to 200 thousand seeds, the Russian Thistle rolled across the prairie much as Genghis Khan's armies had rolled across the Russian steppes 650 years earlier. Like the conquering Mongol empire, the Russian Thistle left devastation in its wake. By 1891 farmers abandoned the eastern half of South Dakota, surrendering the land to the onslaught of the rolling tumbleweeds. By 1895 it had rolled as far south as New Mexico and as far west as the Pacific coast of California. Today it is found in forty-eight states, sparing only Florida and Alaska.

Regardless of the fact that Salsola Kali is not actually thistle, and whether or not it is now considered a "pain in the ass," it was about the only thing that could grow reliably across the rainless and wind bludgeoned

Midwestern prairies of the 1930s. Therefore, consuming the much maligned tumbleweed became life's ultimate option. In 1932 farmers had started grinding it, adding salt and feeding it to the livestock. By 1933 people were reduced to pulling the plants while still green and canning the "thistles" in brine. Like its cousin spinach, tumbleweeds are high in iron and chlorophyll. It may not have made people as strong as Popeye, but it kept them alive.

Hunger is not just a sensation of emptiness in the stomach. It is painful. In the extreme, it will double over even the toughest person with excruciating gut pain. Tumbleweed may have kept folks alive, but it did not fill the empty. While the eyes may indeed be windows to the soul, there can be little doubt that the hollow eyes seen in the photos of dust bowlers were windows to the emptiness of their bellies—an emptiness that cried out for meat. People would never pass up a fresh piece of road kill, but more dependable than finding the occasional carcass in the "bar ditch" were the rabbit drives.

In addition to worship, Sundays were "Rabbit Drive" days, unless of course dust storms precluded either prayer or slaughter. On a good Sunday afternoon a thousand people could drive mostly black tailed jackrabbits (another misnomer for the Lepus californicus melanotis is actually a hare) from a square mile of land into a fenced enclosure and club several thousand to death. The jackrabbits, also sardonically called "Hoover Hogs," had become so populous that they decimated any crops that the wind had not totally dehydrated. In the minds of the Dust Bowl farmers, the slaughter was justified as the only means of population control.

The largest recorded "rabbit" drive was near Dighton, Kansas. It enlisted the participation of ten thousand drivers. Encircling an eight square mile area, the drivers herded the animals into the netted enclosure, and there they clubbed an estimated thirty-five thousand rabbits to death. Five or six rabbits and canned tumbleweed did not truly satiate the hunger of a family, but for one more week it would stay starvation's execution.

¤ ¤ ¤

April 14, 1935, "Black Sunday," awoke crystal clear all across the nation's heartland. The *Boise City News* declared it a "grand and glorious" day for a rabbit drive. The national weather bureau had recorded forty-nine dust storms over the preceding three months, but this day at least seemed to be a blessed respite. Now this was long before satellite imagery had showed us how the generally west to east flow of high altitude wind, the jet-stream, is frequently interrupted by enormous north-south detours sometimes extending two thousand miles before resuming the eastward course. Occasionally, these winds will even turn back on themselves, angling to the west, and spinning off gargantuan eddies in the atmosphere. For the most part, all of this happens several thousand feet above our heads. But on some days the uplift of rapidly warming surface temperatures climbs into those currents aloft and sometimes, if the rising air is unseasonably warm and the air overhead is unseasonably cold, the clashing air masses engage violently, sucking the jet stream off of its sky perch and slamming it into the ground—never more furiously than on this Palm Sunday, 1935.

A not altogether unusual arctic air mass caught a quick ride on a powerful southern express of winds aloft and streamed across Saskatchewan Province on April 13th. By most accounts, it violently ran into the warm air mass somewhere over North Dakota in the pre-dawn hours of April 14th. The cold air crashed into the earth with such force as to create the metaphorical equivalent of a horizontal tornado, stretching almost 190 miles west to east, and rolling south at a rate of over sixty miles per hour. Further south the brilliant sunshine heated the dry air to near 90° Fahrenheit. The resulting lift in the atmosphere carried more dirt skyward and intensified the violence of the clashing air masses.

Eye witnesses standing at ground level, in general, offer notoriously poor subjective estimates of the altitude of any object suspended aloft. Various eyewitness reports offer estimates of the height of the dust cloud bank ranging from 200 to 8000 feet. However, a far more objective report came from Laura Ingalls, who was flying one of the fastest and most powerful airplanes of the era built by Lockheed. Crossing the Texas Panhandle she sighted the dusty onslaught. She endeavored to jump the storm and reported an altimeter reading of 23 thousand feet before deciding that she could not safely fly over the top. In addition to sucking dangerous amounts of harmful dust into the engine, these storms produced so much static electricity that they frequently shorted out the ignition systems of 1930s vintage internal combustion engines. That, of course, was dangerous enough for the automobiles caught below with all four tires on the ground, but for a plane at 23 thousand feet—well. Actually Miss Ingalls' reported depth of the storm provides a rational explanation for the thousands of reports of blackness at midday darker than the darkest night.

Black Sunday arrives at Spearman Texas. Courtesy of Amarillo Public Library

"On April 14, 1935, around four or five in the evening, a bad dust storm approached the area. . . . Dave was on his way home from the neighbors. It became pitch black, so dark you couldn't see your hand in front of your eyes. Dave had to crawl home a half mile in the bar ditch . . . and got dust pneumonia afterwards."

—Barbara A. Unruh, Perryton, Texas[3]

Ms. Ingalls was able to fly fast enough to put sufficient distance between the plane and the cusp of the storm and luckily found a safe place to land. Later she commented, "It was the most appalling thing I ever saw in all my years of flying."[4] Like many other eyewitness accounts, she also reported seeing thousands of birds winging southward before the storm. Unlike the earth-bound witnesses though, her airplane mimicked the birds in their panicked retreat.

"[We] were driving home . . . on this beautiful Sunday afternoon. [We] were caught out in the approaching storm. There were thousands of frightened birds flying, rabbits running, and tumbleweeds blowing ahead of the dirt cloud."

—Kathleen (Allen) Lewis, Perryton, Texas[5]

Black Sunday dust storm rolls across Texas panhandle. Courtesy of Amarillo Public Library

In fact, in the storm's wake cattle, wildlife, and bird carcasses were strewn across the landscape. Other accounts of the storm appeared in various news reports over the next several days. They provide a fascinating array of information, misinformation, and some outright "spin."

> LIBERAL, Kans., April 14 (AP)—The worst dust storm in history brought premature and complete darkness to this city in midafternoon today. The weather was delightful thirty minutes previous.
>
> Swirling in suddenly from the Southwest, the storm struck during a funeral at a local church, putting the crowd into a panic. Three people fainted as the dust swept inside the church.
>
> Long distance telephone wires are reported out of order and the weather turned colder tonight with the storm still raging.[6]

This account contained both information and misinformation. The precipitous arrival of the storm was consistently reported all along its length, but obviously the north to south trajectory of the maelstrom precluded an arrival in Liberal, Kansas from the Southwest.

Ochiltree County Herald, Perryton, Texas, April 18, 1935
BLACK BLIZZARD BREAKS ALL RECORDS
Visibility Goes to Zero; Many Are Caught On Highways and on Picnic Parties
Was Worst in History
Worst Duster in History Followed Ideal Spring Day; Hit Here About Five o'clock

The worst dust storm in the memory of the oldest inhabitants of this section of the country hit Perryton at five o'clock Sunday afternoon, catching hundreds of people away from their homes, at the theatre, on the highways, or on picnic parties. The storm came up suddenly, following a perfect spring day.

In just a few minutes after the first bank appeared in the north, the fury of the black blizzard was upon us, turning the bright sunshine of a perfect day into the murky inkiness of the blackest night. Many hurried to storm cellars, remembering the cyclone of July, two years ago, which followed a similar duster.

Without question, this storm put the finishing touch of destruction to what faint hopes this area had for a wheat crop. Business houses and homes were literally filled with the fine dirt and silt driven in by this fifty mile an hour gale.

The storm started in the Dakotas and carried through with diminishing fury into Old Mexico. Borger reported the storm struck there at 6:15 p.m.; Amarillo at 7:20 p.m.; Boise City, Oklahoma, at 5:35 p.m.; and Dalhart at 5:15 p.m.[7]

WHEAT & DUST
Monday, Apr. 22, 1935

A farmer isn't happy unless he has sand in his beard. Last week farmers in ten Midwestern States had sand in their beards, in their hair, in their ears, in their eyes, in their mouths, in their pockets, in their pants, in their boots, in their milk, coffee, soup and stew. Dust poured through the cracks in farmhouse walls, under the doors, down the chimneys. In northwest Oklahoma a hundred families fled their homes. Every school in Baca County, Colo, was closed. In Texas the windswept hayfields were alive with blinded sparrows. Methodist congregations in Guymon, Okla. met three times a day to pray for rain. Originally confined to a 200-mile strip between Canada and Mexico, last week's dust storm suddenly swirled eastward over Missouri, Iowa and Arkansas, crossed the Mississippi to unload on Illinois, Indiana, Kentucky, Tennessee and Louisiana.[8]

By chance, on the morning of April 14th, an Associated Press reporter and a staff photographer had departed from Denver headed southeast across the plains of Colorado toward the Oklahoma panhandle.

WRITER CAUGHT IN DUST
by Robert Geiger
(EDITOR'S NOTE: Of all types of soil blowing, the black duster provides the most awe-inspiring manifestation of the power of the prairie wind. It moves with express train speed and blots out the sun so darkness prevails at midday. Such a storm was that which swept over part of Southwest Sunday. An Associated Press correspondent caught in the cloud tells of the experience.)
BOISE CITY, Okla., April 14 (AP) – Old timers say it's the worst storm to hit this part of the country, dust ridden though they've been in recent weeks. The cloud caught us, Staff Photographer Harry Eisenhand and I, on the highway about six miles north of town.
"What a swell picture," Harry said. We stopped at a knoll, took several pictures, then turned the car around for flight.
The great cloud of dust rose a thousand feet into the air, blue gray. In front of it were six or seven whirling columns of dust, drifting up like cigar smoke.
We went down the road about 60 miles an hour to keep ahead of it. We had seen an old couple at a dilapidated farm house, and stopped there to warn them, but they had already gone.
Speeding on, the car was suddenly engulfed by a flank movement of the cloud. Momentarily the road glimmered ahead like a ribbon of light in a tunnel, then the dust closed it. It became absolutely black as night. We slammed on the brakes and turned on the car lights. Exploring by touch, we found the car in a dust drift.
Backing out and keeping a door open to watch the edge of the highway, we took two hours to move the remaining six miles

into Boise City. En route we picked up Jack Atkins of Hunter, Colo., his wife and three children from their stalled car. "Without doubt," said Atkins, "this is the worst blow that ever hit this section."

Undoubtedly hundreds of cars were stalled throughout the area by the dust, seemingly semi-solid in the darkness.

Lights can barely be seen across the street. It took the storm just one hour 45 minutes to travel the 105 miles airline from Boise City to Amarillo, Texas.

The funeral procession of Mrs. Loumiza Lucas, enroute from Boise City to Texhoma, Okla., was caught eight miles out and forced to turn back. Mrs. Lucas was the mother of Fred Lucas, well known Texhoma rancher, and E.W. Lucas of Boise City.

Half a dozen small boys and girls sought by police as missing were found to have been lost on the way from their home – they started when skies were clear – to a drug store.[9]

In another news article the following day, Roger Geiger is credited with coining the term "dust bowl." He reported, "Three little words, achingly familiar on a Western farmer's tongue, rule life in the dust bowl of the continent – if it rains."[10] Though despised by most "dust bowlers," the phrase caught on and stuck. It is still the most common term used to describe the area and the era.

From the *Amarillo Daily News*, April 15, 1935
WORST DUSTER WHIPS ACROSS PANHANDLE
FARMERS PRAY FOR RAIN BUT WIND ANSWERS
NORTHER STRIKES SUNDAY TO BLOT OUT SUN, TURN DAY INTO NIGHT
SETS RECORD PACE
KANSAS GOVERNOR SAYS SOIL UNDAMAGED
STORM HITS SOUTH TEXAS
(Associated Press)

North winds whipped dust of the drought area to a new fury Sunday and old timers said the storm was the worst they'd seen. Farmers prayed through dust filmed lips for rain. A black duster—sun blotting cloud banks—raced over Southwest Kansas, the Texas and Oklahoma Panhandles, and foggy haze spread about other parts of the southwest. Easter services at Lindsborg, Kansas, opening with a chorus singing "The Messiah" were carried on in dust-laden air.

MAKES RECORD TRIP

The black duster made the 105 miles from Boise City, Okla., to Amarillo, Texas, in 1 hour 45 minutes. Hundreds of Sunday motorists lured to the highways by 90 degrees temperatures and crystal clear skies were caught by the storm. Farmers and agricultural officials of the dust area, Southwest Kansas, Southeast Colorado, Northeastern New Mexico and the Texas and Oklahoma Panhandles, reported the soil was not damaged and that crops could still be made this season if it would rain. Governor Alf M. Landon of Kansas pointed out top soil ranges from 10 to 30 feet deep at many points in the area.

STORM TURNS CITY INTO TOTAL DARKNESS

Blotting out every speck of light, the worst dust storm in the history of the Panhandle covered the entire region early last night. The billowing black cloud struck Amarillo at 7:20 o'clock and visibility was zero for 12 minutes.

Gradually it cleared and Weatherman H. T. Collman said the storm would be over by morning. The black, ominous cloud rolled over the Panhandle from the north, an awe-inspiring spectacle.

INTO CENTRAL TEXAS

The storm continued southward and had moved into Wichita Falls by 9:45 o'clock, the Associated Press reported. A large area west and southwest of Temple was reported feeling effects of the duster, which moved onward into South Texas.

Warning of the terrible storm reached Amarillo about 45 minutes before it struck. It came from a woman in Stinnett. The woman called Sheriff Bill Adams. He did not learn her name. "I feel that you people of Amarillo should know of the terrible dust storm which has struck here and probably will hit Amarillo," the woman said, "I am sitting in my room and I cannot see the telephone."

8000 FEET HIGH

A gentle, north breeze preceded 8,000-feet-high clouds

of dust. As the midnight fog arrived, the streets were practically deserted. However, hundreds of people stood before their homes to watch the magnificent sight.

Darkness settled swiftly after the city had been enveloped in the stinking, stinging dust, carried by a 50-mile-an-hour wind. Despite closed windows and doors, the silt crept into buildings to deposit a dingy, gray film. Within two hours the dust was a quarter of an inch in thickness in homes and stores.

Reports from the north at 10:30 o'clock last night by the Santa Fe dispatcher said that the moon could be seen at Woodward, Okla., showing that the storm was clearing rapidly.[11]

This article provides a level of detail that other reports missed. In addition to the times of arrival and departure of the storm, the article actually reports a twelve minute period of zero visibility. Most interesting, however, is the blatant "spin" of the facts related to soil and crop damage. Ever mindful of property values, and aware that this Associated Press article would be picked up by newspapers all over the country, officials reported that soil was not damaged and crops could still be raised. Governor Alf M. Landon of Kansas went so far as to say that "top soil" in the area ranges from ten to thirty feet deep. In reality, the storm carried twice as much dirt as was dug across the Isthmus of Panama to excavate the famous canal. The canal took seven years to dig; the storm required about seven days to roar from Saskatchewan south to New Mexico then east to Washington, DC. More than 300 thousand tons (600 million pounds) of Great Plains topsoil was cast into the air on April 14th. Five million acres of the fledgling grain and corn crops of 1935 were laid waste.

The following December, at a meeting in Pueblo, Colorado, experts estimate that 850 million tons of topsoil had blown off the Southern Plains during the course of the year, and that if the drought continued, the total area affected would increase from 4,350,000 acres to 5,350,000 acres in the spring of 1936. C.H. Wilson, of the Resettlement Administration, proposed buying up 2,250,000 acres and retiring it from cultivation.

Some of the spin on events of that day was not quite so mercenary and bears witness to the strength of people and humor in the throes of unimaginable adversity.

Examples of tall tales that were told:

> "Kansas farmers had to pay taxes in Texas because that's where their farms had blown."
> "Farmers would have to wait until spring to plow when the south winds would blow their farms back to them."
> "A salesman saw a prairie dog twenty feet above ground digging frantically downward trying to get back to earth."
> "Prairie dogs thought they had been buried. So, they dug UP through the dust to get out. Later, the dust storm settled, and for three hours it rained prairie dogs."[12]

The almost apocalyptic nature of the events during the last week of 1935's Lenten season provides a backdrop for hearkening back to the observations of the deeply religious George Washington Carver. During his whole life he "preached" by example that through kindness humans have the power to affect, change, and create environments. He described his understanding and attitude with these words.

> "Unkindness to anything means an injustice to that thing. If I am unkind to you I do you an injustice, or wrong you in some way. On the other hand, if I try to assist you in every way that I can to make a better citizen and in every way to do my very best for you, I am kind to you. The above principles apply with equal force to the soil. The farmer, whose soil produces less every year, is unkind to it in some way; that is, he is not doing by it what he should; he is robbing it of some substance it must have, and he becomes, therefore, a soil robber rather than a progressive farmer."[13]

The idea that kindness applied to everything, including the soil, was simply too foreign for most people of the era to embrace. Even more so was the idea that humans actually have the power to dramatically impact environments, especially on a scale as unfathomable as the dust bowl. That lack of understanding, coupled with the political skepticism of the massive government intervention proposed by the Roosevelt Administration's "New Deal," led one Congressman to question, "If God can't make it rain in Kansas, how can the New Deal hope to succeed?"[14]

There were, however, some people in the Department of Agriculture who understood Dr. Carver's admonitions. Dr. Hugh Bennett, the head of the Soil Erosion Service, used the events of Black Sunday as a clarion call for action as he lobbied Congress in support of Public Law 74-46. He agreed that President Roosevelt was not God and could not make it rain in Kansas, but he added, "One man cannot stop the soil from blowing, but one man can start it!"[15] He was invited to present the case in support of an orchestrated national soil conservation policy in testimony to the Senate Public Lands Committee. The date was April 19, 1935. In his biography of Hugh Hammond Bennett, Wellington Brink described the almost legendary events of what transpired that morning in Room 333 of the Senate Office Building.

The witness was not cheerful, but he was persistent, informed, and courageous. He told a grim story. He had been telling it all morning. Chapter by chapter, he annotated each dismal page with facts and figures from a reconnaissance he had just completed. . . . The witness did not hurry. He did not want to hurry. That extra ace he needed was not yet at hand. Well he realized that the hearing was beginning to drag. Out of one corner of his eye, he noted the polite stifling of a yawn, but Hugh Bennett continued deliberatively. . . . Bennett knew that a dust storm was on its way. He had newspaper items and weather reports to support this knowledge. But it seemed mighty slow arriving. If his delaying tactics were successful, the presence of the swirling dust—material evidence of what he was talking about—ought to serve as a clincher for his argument. Presently one of the senators remarked—off the record—"It is getting dark. Perhaps a rainstorm is brewing." Another ventured, "Maybe its dust.'"

"I think you are correct," Bennett agreed. "Senator, it *does* look like dust." The group gathered at a window. The dust storm for which Hugh Bennett had been waiting rolled in like a vast steel-town pall, thick and repulsive. The skies took on a copper color. The sun went into hiding. The air became heavy with grit. Government's most spectacular showman had laid the stage well. All day, step by step, he had built his drama, paced it slowly, risked possible failure with his interminable reports, while he prayed for Nature to hurry up a proper denouement. For once, Nature cooperated generously.[16]

Dr. Bennett later recalled, "When it arrived, while the hearing was still on, we took a little time off the record, moved from the great mahogany table to the windows of the Senate Office Building for a look."[17] Standing at the window with the Senators staring at nature's wrath he concluded his remarks for the day, "This, gentlemen, is what I'm talking about. There goes Oklahoma."[18]

The Seventy-fourth Congress passed PL74-46 without a single dissenting vote. The new law declared that soil erosion was a menace to the national welfare and authorized broad powers to the Soil Conservation Service (SCS), which was the predecessor of the Natural Resources Conservation Service (NRCS). The bill was signed into law by President Roosevelt on April 27, 1935.

Even though Black Sunday, and the events of that week, provided for a Congressional epiphany on Good Friday of 1935, there remained a profound lack of understanding about the etiology of the troubles across the heartland. People simply could not grasp that the dust bowl was not about the absence of rain. It was about four generations of treating the indigenous peoples, the buffalo, the soils, and the grasses of the high plains unkindly.

16

A Farm Kid Goes To Town

Borlaug leaves the farm and goes to the University of Minnesota.

During his high school years, the political and economic landscape outside the safe confines of his home and school were utterly bewildering to Norman Borlaug. His Uncle Oscar, being something of a self-educated agricultural economist, had predicted the Great Depression after reading an economics text from Cornell University. He urged his father and brothers to take their cash out of the bank and invest in building their much needed new barn, purchasing a tractor, and making other improvements needed at the house and farm. They finished building the barn in late August 1929. The stock market crashed just two months later. Soon thereafter, two of the three banks in Northeastern Iowa failed. All of their depositors lost every dime they had placed in those institutions for "safe keeping."

Some farmers had decided not to tap their cash reserves and instead had borrowed money to buy a couple of Fords. What happened next just did not make sense to Norm. Within a year those farmers who had borrowed money for a Fordson tractor and a Model A truck were no longer able to make payments, because there was no viable cash market for their produce. Due to bank closures their deposits were lost, yet creditors were still trying to get their money out of the equipment loans. The old saw, "You can't squeeze water from a rock," was the way locals articulated their befuddlement.

Regardless of how it seemed, the law was on the side of the creditors. The problem was that no one had enough money to pay top dollar for the tractor or truck at auction, so repossessing the equipment could not generate enough cash to retire the debt. Hence courts would order foreclosure on the entire farm and the local sheriffs were responsible for arranging "sheriff sales." Farmers were evicted from property and homes that had been in their family for generations, and still the revenue produced from the auction of the house, barn, land, equipment and livestock was not enough to settle the debt on a single truck or tractor that had been purchased before 1929. It was local a sham. It was a national shame.

Though protected from this economic calamity by his Uncle Oscar's foresight and providence, as well as his family's hard work and thrift, Norm was both troubled and curious about what was happening on neighboring farms. One day, he and a couple of his high school buddies decided to drive the twenty miles east to Saratoga to see one of the sheriff sale auctions for themselves. What they witnessed was at once inspiring and distressing.

The word had gotten out—the "penny sale" was on. Most neighborhood farmers and many of their wives were there. When an item was on the block, there was only one bid—a penny, perhaps a nickel. The entire auction raised less than five dollars.

It is important to understand that sheriffs had no choice but to implement the orders of the court, as they were sworn to do. That does not mean they had to like it. Often these foreclosures, and the accompanying evictions, were extremely distasteful duties for a sheriff and his deputies. One deputy commented, "I feel just like my wife's cat—I have to lick my butt to get the taste out of my mouth!" The farmers standing around shared a laugh and an understanding of the sentiment. On this day, the Sheriff was clearly an accomplice in a form of disdain for the court's orders, which any judge would likely view as malfeasance by Howard County's highest ranking law enforcement officer.

Norm had been raised to believe that it is one's civic duty to support and obey the law. The ambiguity of holding these core values and yet admiring the kind-hearted motives behind the unanimous complicity of violating the law was deeply troubling. This was Norm's first, but by no means his last, encounter with the equivoque that laws serve and protect societies, but sometimes their implementation does not engender justice.

The day after the sale, all of the bidders "gave" the purchased property back to the foreclosed family.

¤ ¤ ¤

High School years flew by for Norm. He was a good student. He was a good athlete. He had fun. But for the class of 1932 the normal dignitaries who frequent graduation events were hard pressed to deliver optimistic and inspirational commencement addresses. In 1932, these young people graduated into the very center of a national malaise. Eleanor Roosevelt had given voice to the national fear that this was likely to be a "Lost Generation," and that everything possible needed to be done to save them. Almost seven decades later, Tom Brokaw would rightly call them the "Greatest Generation," and no small amount of credit is due Mrs. Roosevelt for making it so.

With no money and no prospects, Norm went home to the farm after graduation. He wanted to go to college. His family supported the idea, particularly Grandfather Nels, "When you're young you'd better study to put information in your brain that you will use later in life to improve not only your well-being but that of your neighbors and friends."[1]

The Borlaug family was clearly given to prescience. The plaque Norm's cousin Sina had given him upon completion of grammar school was inscribed with these words, "Advance in learning as you advance in life. Good instruction is better than riches. Kindness is the noblest weapon to conquer with." Tucked inside Grandfather Nels' and cousin Sina's admonitions lay the motto for the Rockefeller Foundation, "To promote the well-being and to advance the civilization of the peoples of the United States and foreign lands in acquisition and dissemination of knowledge, in the prevention and relief of human suffering, and the promotion of any and all elements of human progress."[2] Whether or not Nels and Sina even knew about the Rockefeller Foundation cannot now be known. Regardless, it seems they had some sense of Norm's future.

Norm, however, did not have a sense of his future. He knew what he wanted to do, he just did not see any way to make that happen. If high school had seemed an impossible dream four years prior, college now seemed even more remote.

During the summer the Bonus Army was camped in the parks of the nation's capitol, two million of their fellow citizens had become nomads in search of their next meal. Knowing that a quarter of a million of those wanderers were his age or younger, Norm understood that he "had it good" living on the farm. This knowledge though did little to quench his own cravings. He wanted to continue his education and he did everything he could to make that happen. He worked on the farm, worked for the neighbors, and set traps along the creek for furs He even caught a mink. That pelt brought a whopping $10. That winter he cut trees and sold fence posts and firewood. By the summer of 1933, he had managed to save a veritable fortune—$60.

As a former state high school wrestling champ, the Midwestern Amateur Athletic Association extended the courtesy of inviting Norm to wrestle in the University Wrestling Tournament as an athlete "Unattached to Any Institution." This opportunity was, in large part, offered to stir local interest in the tournament, as it was being hosted at Norm's former high school in Cresco. Regardless of the reason, this was a huge honor and an extremely rare opportunity. It was the first time an individual not affiliated with a university was allowed to compete in a sporting event sponsored by the Association. Norm was ecstatic, too much so—he failed to sleep well for days in advance of the tournament. Fortunately, his hard labor had kept him fine tuned physically, so he did not have to sweat off pounds to make the 135 weight class. He knew, however, that even though physically fit, his mental readiness and technique had suffered during the nine months since his graduation from High School. He also knew that college coaches would be everywhere in his old high school gymnasium. He made up for the loss of honed skills during his hiatus with a preponderance of desire.

Norm won match after match in the single elimination tournament. Though he did not have a team cheering him on, his family and friends were going wild in the bleachers. He made it to the final bout where he was matched against the regional champion, a senior at Iowa Teachers College. At the end of the three regulation rounds the match was tied. In overtime his opponent scored one point on an escape. Was Norm disappointed? Sure, but also proud of his performance, given that he had not practiced a single day since the end of his senior year season.

As he left the gym, his opponent's coach approached Norm, "If you'll come to Teachers College next year, I'll see about getting you situated with a job." Athletic scholarships were unimaginable—a job, often working for a college alumnus, was as good as gold. He started making plans immediately to move sixty-five miles south to Cedar Falls. It was the most exciting summer of his young life.

¤ ¤ ¤

When Norm stepped outside early on Saturday, September 2, 1933, he was immediately aware that a cool front had passed through sometime during the night hours. It was by no means cold, but the air held the crispness that every year foretells autumn's approach. The almost full moon was setting just as the dawn broke. It was a beautiful morning, made even more so by virtue of the fact the Norm's crystal ball was perfectly clear. He knew exactly where he was going, what he was going to do, and what he was to become.

In a couple of weeks his family would proudly pack him off to Teachers College. He was going to be a high school science teacher and athletic coach. Probably after about a decade of doing that, he would become a school principal, maybe even a superintendent of an Iowa school district. His future was certain and it was bright. But even at this early hour a butterfly was flapping its wings up in Cresco.

An All-America running back for the University of Minnesota Golden Gophers football team was gathering the tools to change the oil in his pride and joy, a Model A Roadster. After that, he would gas up and drive south on ten miles of gravel road to County Line Road. There he'd turn right and drive another three and a half miles over to Henry and Clara Borlaug's farm. They did not have a telephone, so his visit would come unannounced.

The wheat harvest had been completed a week earlier. That morning Norm had just mucked out the cattle pens and replaced the old bedding with fresh straw. He was tidying up the pile of chaff as George Champlin rounded the turn into the driveway and pulled up by the house. Norm recognized the car as belonging to Cresco's hometown hero and was perplexed by the unexpected visit.

"Hello George."

"Hi Norm, how you doing?" In small communities folks know each other. Folks know each other's folks; parents, grandparents, and siblings. But George Champlin and Norm were not contemporaries, there being four years difference in age. Norm had seen Chaplin play football when he was a high school star at Cresco, but that was a year before Norm enrolled at Cresco High. Likewise, Chaplin had watched Norm wrestle a couple of times when home from the University of Minnesota for Christmas break. Their total number of prior conversations could be counted on one hand. This visit was quite a surprise.

George Champlin was extremely confident and carried it quietly in his posture, stride, and manner. However, he was a young man of his era and had little facility, or even inclination, for small talk. He dove right in, "Norm, I'm headed back to Minneapolis tomorrow and I want you to come try out for the football team."

If a bolt of lightning had pierced the clear blue sky and struck him square on the head, Norm could not have been more thunderstruck. He did not even know what to say. He was a wrestler. He was a baseball player. Football?

The conversation was probably much like watching Henry Wallace play tennis. It was not pretty, but ultimately effective. Norm would serve up an objection, Champlin would deftly put the ball back in Norm's court. He could get Norm into school—he could get Norm some work—he already had an apartment near campus with two double beds. It was a little pricey, but with four guys sharing costs, rent would be a manageable $5 per month each.

Champlin could tell he was softening Norm up a bit, and with the timing of an elite athlete, he figured it was time to put an end to the waffling. The coup de grace—Norm's best friend and fellow state high school wrestling champion, Erv Upton, had already agreed to go! With that Norm's instinctive conservatism, along with the last vestiges of his resistance, dissolved.

As destiny's messenger drove out the driveway, Norm went in the house to announce the change of plans. His family was simultaneously dumbstruck and excited.

The next morning George Champlin returned soon after breakfast to pick up Norm for the 160 mile journey to the Twin Cities. No one present was more excited than Grandfather Nels. After giving Norm a farewell bear-hug, Nels reached in his pocket and pulled out his coin purse. With an index finger he hooked Norm's pants pocket and dumped in eleven silver dollars. Seeing his first grandson, the first Borlaug, off to a university was, for Grandfather Nels, a dream come true. Within eighteen months Nels would succumb to stomach cancer, but his life-long influence on Norm's tenacity and educational appetite would have a profound impact upon generations yet unborn.

¤ ¤ ¤

Things did not proceed quite as smoothly in Minnesota as the young men had hoped. Erv and Norm were both missing two prerequisite courses, one math and one science. They had taken the courses, and done very well in both, during their ninth grade year. The problem lay in the fact that in Iowa, ninth grade courses were not included on high school transcripts. No amount of explanation seemed to satisfy the University's admissions office. In lieu of documentation of successful completion of the required courses, Norm and his buddy, had to take a placement exam. Erv easily managed to ace the exams—not so for Norm. It had been well over a year since he had graduated from high school. Being out of practice with test taking, as well as the doubts he harbored about choosing the University of Minnesota over Iowa Teachers College, combined to serve up a heaping plate full of test anxiety.

Norman Borlaug failed to qualify to matriculate at the U of M. He was clearly not university material. Perhaps he could still pack his bags and hitch-hike down to Cedar Falls, Iowa. With their lower entrance requirements, surely the offer to attend Iowa Teachers College and wrestle for the Panthers was still a viable option.

George Champlin would have none of it. He marched Norm into Assistant Dean Frederick Hovde's office and forcefully, albeit rather disparagingly, advocated his fellow Iowan's case. "Something's wrong with the way you Minnesotans test. This guy's not as dumb as you think."

For a moment the office seemed as frigid as a January snow storm. Norm wanted nothing so much as to slink out the door and just keep walking south. Perhaps a loaf of his grandmother's homemade bread would salve his battered spirit, the way it had warmed his near frozen body the day Sina dragged him home through the blizzard, all those years ago. Not so fast, Norm—just like Sina's rescue, Champlin's brazen resolve carried the day. Hovde agreed to admit Norm to the newly established "General College" at the University of Minnesota. (*Minnesota's "General College" was the first tentative step to serve "different though not inferior" students, and over the next several decades this effort evolved into the national Junior College system.*)

At once, Norm was greatly relieved <u>and</u> somewhat humiliated. He felt certain he had what it took to pursue a bachelor's degree, and by God, he was going to prove it. Which is exactly what he did. After the first semester his performance and grades were outstanding, and Dean Hovde was easily able to approve the transfer into a course of study that would lead to a bachelor's degree. However, the Professor was not much enamored of Norm's choice of majors—forestry. Not so much because he did not respect the profession, but rather the students who populated that department might best described as the University's radical fringe. Hovde cautioned Norm that most of them sported beards, wore plaid flannel shirts, and joined the Society of American Foresters. Radicals indeed! (*The Society's founder, Gifford Pinchot, was the first director of the U.S. Forest Service, and in 1933 was Governor of Pennsylvania. He was likely button-busting proud of his Minnesota protégées activist reputation.*)

In December 1933, once again Norm was absolutely certain of his future. Four months earlier he was going to be a high school teacher and coach. Now there was no doubt, he was going to become a forester. In retrospect, it is amusingly clear that Norm had not inherited the Borlaug sense of the future.

¤ ¤ ¤

In addition to pursuing a bachelor's degree in his chosen major, matriculation within the regular University system would bestow another perquisite that was of great importance to the young Borlaug. He would now be allowed to wrestle for the Golden Gophers. His former high school principal and wrestling coach, David Bartelma, would soon move to the Twin Cities to pursue his doctorate in psychology. He would also take over the coaching duties for the almost defunct University of Minnesota wrestling team.

Within three years, he and the core of young men on that first team would develop the University of Minnesota program into a national powerhouse. They would host and defeat the national champion University of Iowa team in January 1937. Norm would win his bout in that tournament. Two of the Golden Gopher wrestlers went on to win Big Ten Conference and AAU championships. Norm himself made it to the semifinal bout of the Big Ten tournament in 1937. Fifty-five years later Dr. Norman Borlaug would be inducted as an "Outstanding American" into the National Wrestling Hall of Fame.

¤ ¤ ¤

Those wrestling laurels were yet years in the future. During that fall semester of 1933, the specter of hunger was always just one meal away. As difficult as that reality was physically, for Norm the intellectual and emotional impact was even greater. The source of his angst could be found in equal parts his own hunger pangs and the hunger of the citizenry, whom Norm saw laying in parks and on sidewalks. They had nothing to do, nowhere to go, and no energy to do anything anyway, which is the nature of depression. Almost all depressed people know they need to exercise to break the cycle of darkness, but they frequently lack the energy to make themselves do so. The nation's economy in 1934 was like that. People knew they needed to work, earn, and spend to roll the economy toward recovery, but the economy itself was just too depressed to offer up the opportunities.

Norm found the whole scenario so surrealistic as to be utterly unfathomable. He observed how hunger became the source of fear and desperation. One day, while walking a few blocks off campus, Norm saw grown men strewn all over Gateway Park, idle men, saying little and doing nothing. He approached one wearing a white shirt, black pants, hair closely cropped and a three day growth on his face. The man sat with his arms wrapped around his knees and a vacant stare in possession of his face. Norm had only recently arrived in the cities. He had seen poverty, but rural poverty did not look, or feel, or smell like this.

Dropping to both knees a few feet away, he just had to know, "Excuse me sir, I was wondering, what are all these men doing here?"

"Waiting."

"Waiting for what?"

The man pointed with his nose and a nod of his head toward the garbage cans barely visible around the corner, "In a while when the markets get ready to close there will be some scraps and rotted fruit thrown away." (*In 1933 diarrhea was the tenth leading cause of death in the United States.*)

"Do you ever get a real meal?" Norm asked.

"Son, it has been so long since I've sat down to a dinner that I wouldn't recognize the taste of home cooked food."

The man had sold wire until about 1930—baling wire, barbed wire, and even a little electric wire, to farmers and merchants across Minnesota and the Dakotas. Starting in about 1929 folks quit buying wire. All of his cash had been invested in his inventory, which he carried around in the back of a large truck. He could not eat wire. The bank took his truck. He was just waiting.

¤ ¤ ¤

Living in the city, Norm observed and spoke with many destitute urban dwellers. Seeing their plight, and hearing their stories, brought about a gradual enlightenment about the nature of economy. He knew that the farms of Little Norway were not worth as much money since the crash of the stock markets and the collapse of the banking system. However, they were no less valuable. This dichotomy began to make sense to Norm with the growing awareness that the poor people of Minneapolis and St. Paul had more cash than his family had ever had as he was growing up. The farm's value was not measured in cash, but rather in terms of whether it could provide the means of food, shelter, and clothing for its occupants. The land could produce food, the raw materials for housing, and the materials for clothing.

On the other hand, the city dwellers were able to provide for themselves these bare necessities only by selling their time, skills, and strength for money. All of their food, shelter, and clothing had to be purchased with cash. Prior to 1929, Americans had enjoyed spending and investing billions of dollars of cash that did not really exist. People had borrowed money to buy homes at values above the intrinsic value of the property. Banks had loaned money, often to the bank officials themselves, to purchase stocks at share prices far above the company's profitability potential or real property value. People borrowed money to buy cars and conveniences that heretofore had not existed. The banks handed out loan checks for almost any desired purchase. Borrowers did not really understand that checks were not cash. Since sellers and other banks accepted the checks as if they were real money, borrowers simply did not bother to worry about it.

It seemed to Norm that, in essence, banks were printing money. When the stock market crashed, sellers of goods and services started demanding "real money"—cash. Prior to the stock market crash, that would not have been a major problem, as the banker could simply sell some of the stock he had purchased with money borrowed from the bank to raise the cash. But when the stock values did not even approximate the face value of outstanding loans, bankers had to scramble to raise capital. When depositors heard rumors of their local banker casting about for money, they became nervous and went to the bank to withdraw the cash they had put in bank accounts. Banks offered to print more money, but by now no one was very interested in checks drawn on the bank or other types of bank notes—they wanted currency printed by the federal government. Banks did not have the cash to honor their depositors requests for withdrawal. They were also unable to recover their "money" by foreclosure, because people did not have enough cash to pay even half the outstanding debt on the house, or car, or farm being auctioned.

Article 1. Section 8. of the United States Constitution states that "The Congress shall have power . . . To coin money, regulate the value thereof." Article 1. Section 10. states "No State shall . . . coin Money; emit Bills of Credit; make any Thing but gold and silver Coin as Tender in Payment of Debts . . ."[3]

Norm came to suspect that banks had, in essence, usurped the federal government's constitutional authority to print money, by loaning "money" that did not exist. The farm boy wondered how it was that banks had been allowed to "coin money" and loan it based on an appraised property value that had nothing to do with production of food, shelter, or clothing. He also wondered why the federal government did not just print a bunch of money and put it in circulation, since the nation had for a long time been living on and spending money that did not really exist anyway. As long as people agreed to accept the U.S. dollar as the medium of exchange, he could see no harm in printing enough dollars to let people withdraw the amounts of money they had deposited in their local banks for "safe keeping." Since farms could produce enough food and fiber for the nation, it seemed to him that all these desperately poor city folks needed was enough cash to buy the essentials. He did not think it would be a government give-away, since it really was "money" people had earned and saved prior to depositing it, naively perhaps, in the banks.

Norm realized that there just had to be a flaw in his logic. Surely, it could not be that simple, otherwise President Hoover's advisors would not be so idle, while so many people were in such desperate straits. How he wished he could talk with his Uncle Oscar, whom the young Norm believed understood economics better than almost anybody.

¤ ¤ ¤

While those who sat waiting in Minneapolis' Gateway Park would have thrilled at the opportunity to work, many laborers in the Twin Cities felt the economy's chicanery in a different sort of way. The truck drivers, who daily delivered milk, produce, and commodities to mills and markets, had seen their pay cut steadily during the Great Depression's early years. It was common for them to begin work by 5:00am and work until 6:00pm, six days per week. In 1933 they were being paid $12 per week for sixty plus hours of work. They endeavored to organize and strike for better wages and work conditions. But with the enormous contingent of men willing to work for food, it was easy enough for company bosses to fire anyone who even used the word "union" in a sentence and replace him with any one of a dozen men desperately hungry enough to willingly venture across a picket line. It was a formula for violence.

The equation was fairly simple: men + hunger + a sense of being diddled + a willingness to exploit the situation for profit = desperation, anger, and bloodshed.

—— 199 ——

One afternoon soon after his conversation in the park with the wire salesman, young Borlaug witnessed the equation's real-life application. Like their country cousins who had staged "farmers holidays" in 1932 by dumping good milk on the side of the road, the milk truck drivers on this Autumn day in 1933, were refusing to deliver the perishable dairy products absent adequate pay. As Norm meandered around the city's Warehouse District, he rounded a corner on an ugly standoff. On one side were drivers who were blocking the gate through which the milk trucks exited for their assigned rounds. They were squared off against police, company security guards, and men desperate enough to drive the trucks through the picket line for the food their bellies craved. Quite by accident a photographer fell through the rag-top roof of a convertible automobile, upon which his camera tripod was perched. The photographer's commotion was like a match struck to explosively dry tinder.

In the ensuing baton swinging melee, Norm was washed away by the retreating wave of desperate humanity. He ducked into a doorway alcove and observed the milk trucks seize the opportunity hysteria presented. They lurched through the gate toward their appointed routes. People lay on the ground, heads cracked open and bleeding. Others screamed to vent the frustrations born of rage and fear. Ambulances arrived as Norm ran from the scene, profoundly distressed by what he had witnessed. He had been raised in a home and community that valued kindness and cooperation above all else. Farmers gave a share of their crops to a neighbor who had lost his to weather's wrath—they did not allow folks to go hungry. Norm had rarely been witness to uncontrolled anger and never seen violence on a massive scale. The experience had a profound impact upon his world view, as witnessed by these recollections years after the events of that fateful afternoon:

> I ran back toward campus, trembling, frightened, rubbery-legged. My thoughts were racing; I'd seen how fast violence springs to life when hunger, misery, and desperation infect the public mind. I'd begun wondering too about the aftereffects of empty stomachs. Obviously, peace and prosperity couldn't survive without food; even the most serene society could turn violent. What have hungry people to lose?[4]

What have they to lose? The frightening answer to Norm's rhetorical question is: their kindness—their humanity.

Norm had accidentally been witness to one of the opening salvos in a labor disputed that was to grow much, much worse over the next year. When he returned to the apartment he told George Champlin and Erv Upton of his disquietude. They were listening to a Chicago Cubs baseball game being broadcast on WHO radio, out of Des Moines, by a young sportscaster named Ronald Reagan. Norm had to squeeze in the recounting of his harrowing ordeal during breaks in the action. Immediately following the game the station cut over to an address originating at the Des Moines Coliseum. There Iowa's favorite son, Secretary of Agriculture Henry A. Wallace, was addressing a crowd of several thousand. Norm listened intently, his roommates less so. Secretary Wallace's closing remarks struck a special chord with Norm given the events of that day.

> "Only the merest quarter-turn of the heart separates us from a material abundance beyond the fondest dream of anyone present. Selfishness has ceased to be the mainspring of progress. There is something more. There is a new social machinery in the making. Let us maintain sweet and kindly hearts toward each other, however great the difficulties ahead."[5]

¤ ¤ ¤

Academically, Norm was doing very well. As his cousin Sina had observed when she was his teacher in seventh and eighth grades, "As a scholar he is no great shakes, but he's got grit."[6] A bachelor's degree is likely more a measure of fortitude than scholastic aptitude under any circumstance, but Norm was attending school during the darkest days of the Great Depression. Jobs were scarce. Jobs that paid cash were nonexistent. It took ample amounts of fortitude (spelled g-r-i-t) to find food; to get to class in the mornings after going to bed hungry; to study and make the grades.

Finding food was never far from Norm's mind. Indeed with his stomach frequently rumbling, the search could best be described as a full time preoccupation. He served paying customers at the University Coffee Shop for an hour and a half each morning. His pay was one cup of coffee, two pieces of bread, and five stewed prunes. This is where he met his future wife, Margaret Gibson. She was in the same situation—living from meal to meal. Soon after meeting they were a couple.

With their friends Norm and Margaret cobbled together a whole variety of means to earn a few cents or a few morsels of food. Norm served dinner at the Alpha Omicron Pi sorority for free meals. Margaret sought waitress work door-to-door in the retail area, called "Dinkytown," that neighbored the U of M campus. They cut coupons out of the university newspaper; three coupons and a dime bought a bottle of milk and three hamburgers at the civic minded White Castle Restaurant. Times were tough and demanded innovation and persistence. Sometimes even that was not enough.

In the early spring of 1934, Norm had the second brush with mortality in his young life. It started as a sore throat, but when his temperature soared Margaret and their buddy, Scott Pauley, got Norm over to the student health center. What they heard there was a frightening diagnosis—streptococcus. Though there had been some success treating the infection with sulfa compounds in Europe, this antibacterial treatment was not widely known or accepted. At the University hospital, Norm was treated with warm salt water gargles. Pneumonia, including streptococcal pneumonia, was the third leading cause of death in the United States in 1933. This was deadly serious, and everyone knew it. After weeks of fighting the ravages of the bacteria, unaided by the miracle chemicals of modern medicine, Norm's body and will to live finally prevailed. He headed home to Iowa. The spring semester of 1934 was a total wash.

17

GRIT IN THE TEETH

Wallace's war on the Dust Bowl.

Henry Wallace wrote the Foreword for the 1232 page volume *Soils and Men*, published by the U.S. Department of Agriculture in 1938. He was writing as Secretary of Agriculture, but one can easily imagine that he felt some long dead Iroquois Shaman channeling through his pen.

> The earth is the mother of us all—plants, animals, and men. The phosphorus and calcium of the earth build our skeletons and nervous systems. Everything else our bodies need except air and sun comes directly from the earth.
>
> Nature treats the earth kindly. Man treats her harshly. He overplows the cropland, overgrazes the pastureland, and overcuts the timberland. He destroys millions of acres completely. He pours fertility year after year into the cities, which in turn pour what they do not use down the sewers into the rivers and the ocean. The flood problem insofar as it is man-made is chiefly the result of overplowing, overgrazing, and overcutting of timber.
>
> This terribly destructive process is excusable in a young civilization. It is not excusable in the United States in the year 1938.
>
> We know what can be done and we are beginning to do it. As individuals we are beginning to do the necessary things. As a nation, we are beginning to do them. The public is waking up, and just in time. In another 30 years it might have been too late.
>
> The social lesson of soil waste is that no man has the right to destroy soil even if he does own it in fee simple. The soil requires a duty of man which we have been slow to recognize. . . .
>
> —Henry A. Wallace, Secretary of Agriculture[1]

Early on, the Roosevelt administration viewed the wind born devastation on the Great Plains as being much like the Mississippi River flood of 1927. That flood had been a massive event that from start to finish lasted almost eleven months. The rains had come to the central Mississippi river basin in late summer 1926 and stayed for months. The levee breached in 147 different places, water inundated 27 thousand square miles, and 246 people died. Over 700 thousand people, almost half of them black, were displaced, more or less permanently, as many homes were uninhabitable when the flood waters receded.

Relief camps were set up in 154 locations. The conditions in those camps were horrendous, particularly for black persons, some of whom were detained and forced to labor at gun point. Mincing no words, the relief effort was abysmal, in large part because of the nation's leadership. Calvin Coolidge and his cohorts could not even envision the institutionalization of kindness by a federal government.

LOUSIANA 1927
What has happened down here is the wind have changed
Clouds roll in from the north and it started to rain
Rained real hard and rained for a real long time
Six feet of water in the streets of Evangeline

The river rose all day
The river rose all night
Some people got lost in the flood
Some people got away alright
The river have busted through clear down to Plaquemines
Six feet of water in the streets of Evangeline

Louisiana, Louisiana
They're tryin' to wash us away
They're tryin' to wash us away
Louisiana, Louisiana
They're tryin' to wash us away
They're tryin' to wash us away

President Coolidge came down in a railroad train
With a little fat man with a note-pad in his hand

The President say, "Little fat man, ain't it a shame, what the river has done
To this poor crackers land."

> Louisiana, Louisiana
> They're tryin' to wash us away
> They're tryin' to wash us away
> Louisiana, Louisiana
> They're tryin' to wash us away
> They're tryin' to wash us away
> —Lyrics by Randall Newman[2]

The Coolidge administration's response was as anemic as the lyrics of Randal Newman's song *Louisiana 1927* imply—people who had lost everything had the government's sympathy, but little else. During the dust bowl's early days, the New Dealers realized that what was happening in the heartland was "the winds had changed." They were determined not to repeat mistakes the Coolidge and Hoover administrations had made by failing to take dramatic action in response to the 1927 flood event. While New Dealer's intentions were noble, they erred early on by conceptualizing the dust bowl as "an event." The flood had been "an event." It was an event that could not have been predicted at the time and could not have been controlled regardless of prediction. The dust bowl was a catastrophe of heretofore unparalleled proportions. Unlike the flood, it was a catastrophe caused by human hands—seventy plus years in the making. Most people in 1933 could not fathom the human causal factor. Also, it was not **an** event. It was many, many events that went on day, after day, after day for most of eight years.

Wallace's understanding and fight against the ravages of environmental abuse did not begin with him. For three decades before the dust began to fly, there were those who understood and were giving voice to warnings that human behavior was changing the earth's environment, and not in positive ways.

The first environmental progressive to be president was also a Roosevelt. Theodore and Franklin Roosevelt were fifth cousins once removed. In addition to their surnames their lives had some other remarkable similarities. Both served a stint as Assistant Secretary of the Navy, both were elected Governor of New York, and both were Presidents who believed in an expanded role for the Federal Government.

Of like mind was a Connecticut Yankee by the name of Gifford Pinchot, whom Theodore Roosevelt appointed the first director of the United States Forest Service. He may well have been Roosevelt's most trusted confidant.

> Among the many, many public officials who under my administration rendered literally invaluable service to the people of the United States, Gifford Pinchot on the whole, stood first.
>
> —Theodore Roosevelt[3]

In 1900, Pinchot founded the Society of American Foresters and is credited with coining the phrase "conservation ethic," which he described as "An ethic of resource use, allocation, and protection. The primary focus of the ethic is on maintaining the health of the natural world, its forests, fisheries, habitats, and biological diversity."

Another of America's early foresters sounded warning alarms about the nation's disregard for the natural order of the environment. Aldo Leopold was perhaps a more radical environmentalist than his mentor Pinchot. He not only embraced the "conservation ethic" he expanded it, "The land ethic simply enlarges the boundaries of the community to include soils, waters, plants, and animals, or collectively; the land."[4] Leopold had no political aspirations, and therefore no qualms whatsoever about asking questions that would today seem tame. But during the twentieth century's first decade, those questions made many Americans squirm uncomfortably.

> This sounds simple: do we not already sing our love for and obligation to the land of the free and the home of the brave? Yes, but just what and whom do we love? Certainly not the soil, which we are sending helter-skelter downriver. Certainly not the waters, which we assume have no function except to turn turbines, float barges, and carry off sewage. Certainly not the plants, of which we exterminate whole communities without batting an eye. Certainly not the animals, of which we have already extirpated many of the largest and most beautiful species. A land ethic of course cannot prevent the alteration, management, and use of these 'resources,' but it does affirm their right to continued existence, and, at least in spots, their continued existence in a natural state.
>
> —Aldo Leopold[5]

Pinchot went on to be elected Governor of Pennsylvania twice, and Leopold became known as the father of the Environmental Movement in America.

In addition to foresters, agriculturalists were seeing the warning signs of the impending disaster. George Washington Carver in an interview with Atlanta Journal reporter James H. Cobb said, "Conservation is one of our big problems in this section. You can't tear up everything just to get the dollar out of it without suffering as a result. It is a travesty to burn our woods and thereby burn up the fertilizer nature has provided for us. We must enrich our soil every year instead of merely depleting it. It is fundamental that nature will drive away those who commit sin against it."[6] Dr. Carver's statement was not truly prophetic, it was instead a statement of fact as howling winds and black blizzards of dust drove three generations of farmers from the high plains.

In Dodge City, Kansas there were only thirteen dust storm free days in the first four months of 1935. Tens of thousands of people would die of dust related respiratory illnesses. The over 345 thousand people, who packed what little belongings they had and abandoned their homes and farms on the high plains and move west toward California, would bear witness to the veracity of Dr. Carver's admonition. Though these farmers had "sinned against the soil" for most of three decades, they were not evil—just ignorant. No one yet had even heard of the "butterfly effect," and there were only a handful who believed that humans could change the weather.

As mentioned in an earlier chapter, perhaps the most fervent and effective of the "true believers" was Hugh Hammond Bennett, fondly called "Big Hugh." What was happening to the soils of North America had hit him as an epiphany. In the Spring of 1903 Big Hugh graduated from the University of North Carolina where he'd studied chemistry and geology. For a thousand dollars a year, he went to work for the Bureau of Soils in the U.S. Department of Agriculture. His job was supposed to be lab work, but there was a delay in filling the laboratory chemist position. The USDA contacted Bennett and asked if he would object to a temporary fieldwork assignment doing soil surveys. Big Hugh did not object. Heck, he was thrilled to have a job, any job. That temporary assignment changed the course of his career and the course of human history.

Bill McClendon of Bishopville, South Carolina, and I were stirring through the woods down there in middle Virginia when we noticed two pieces of land, side by side but sharply different in their soil quality. The slope of both areas was the same. The underlying rock was the same. There was indisputable evidence that the two pieces had been identical in soil makeup. But the soil of one piece was mellow, loamy, and moist enough even in dry weather to dig into with our bare hands. We noticed this area was wooded, well covered with forest litter, and had never been cultivated. The other area, right beside it, was clay, hard and almost like rock in dry weather. It had been cropped a long time. We figured both areas had been the same originally and that the clay of the cultivated area could have reached the surface only through the process of rainwash—that is, the gradual removal, with every heavy rain, of a thin sheet of topsoil. It was just so much muddy water running off the land after rains. And, by contrast we noticed the almost perfect protection nature provided against erosion with her dense cover of forest.

—Hugh Hammond Bennett[7]

Even as President Theodore Roosevelt was busy embracing the conservation ethic, Big Hugh's commonitions about erosion were unappreciated, misunderstood, and/or simply not believed. In 1909 the Department of Agriculture articulated their view on soils and erosion in the Bureau of Soils Bulletin #55. In that bulletin Professor Milton Whitney, Chief of the Bureau of Soils, stated, "The soil is the one indestructible, immutable asset that the Nation possesses. It is the one resource that cannot be exhausted; that cannot be used up."[8] In this institutional environment, Big Hugh's arguments for a national soil conservation effort could not get much traction at the Department of Agriculture. Years later, Dr. Bennett described how he felt when reading Bulletin #55 for the first time, "I didn't know so much costly misinformation could be put in a single brief sentence!"[9]

Perhaps in an effort to silence, or at least dislodge, the voice of the young and zealous soil conservation crusader, the USDA sent Hugh Bennett far afield. Between 1910 and 1920 he was given field assignments in the Panama Canal Zone, Cuba, Alaska, Honduras, Guatemala and elsewhere. If the intent had been censorship, the strategy was a miserable failure. His field work at these various research stations gave him reams of source material for publication.

In 1921, Bennett returned stateside when he accepted an appointment as Inspector for the Southern Division of the United State Department of Agriculture, Bureau of Soils. In this position, he began crusading in earnest. He published articles in popular farm magazines, such as *American Game*, *Country Gentleman*, and *Nature*. He wrote a monthly column for *Farm Journal* from late 1925 through 1926. Espousing a new and expanded notion of land stewardship, he published over forty items between 1920 and 1930.

Still viewed as an alarmist within the Bureau of Soils, Big Hugh found solace and support in the Forest Service. The Division of Forestry had been established, in large part, to "conserve resources" and therefore the service employed many conservationists. One of them, W. R. Chapline, co-authored with Hugh Bennett the Department's 1928 Circular #33: *Soil Erosion, A National Menace*. This was to become Bennett's best known and most effective publication, in no small measure because it was issued as the 1927 flood waters of the Mississippi River were finally receding. In their wake, people could see the effects of devastating soil erosion. The Circular was not technical. It did not discuss control measures. It did secure a $160 thousand congressional appropriation for soil erosion research. Not a minute too soon! By 1933, the research project was done. The verdict was in, just as the winds began to strip the Midwest's high plains naked.

Big Hugh became the most articulate of crusaders on the dangers of soil erosion and virtues of conservation. As the first director of the dust bowl inspired Soil Conservation Service in the New Deal's Department of Agriculture, he found a similar soul in his boss. All of these voices of reason (Pinchot, Leopold, Carver, Bennett, and others) were powerful in and of themselves. But in order to leverage change of awareness and change of public policy, they needed a focal point, and they found a tuned ear and open mind in Secretary Henry A. Wallace.

Henry had come by his conservationist proclivity quite naturally. In addition to his old friend, Dr. Carver, another two of his most cherished childhood mentors had been early conservationists. His grandfather, "Uncle Henry" Wallace was appointed President of the Third National Conservation Congress in 1910, by President Theodore Roosevelt. During that same period, Uncle Henry's good friend and Dr. Carver's college mentor, James (Tama Jim) Wilson, was appointed to serve as the Secretary of Agriculture. It was through their early efforts that the conservation ethic and environmental movement began to claw its way into the public consciousness.

In a 1935 meeting with Department of Agriculture staff, their Secretary articulated the growing awareness about the Dust Bowl's true nature.

> It has been the popular view of most people, including people in this administration and congress that the dust storms are akin to the floods of the Mississippi or the hurricanes that smash our coasts, but they are not the same. You see as a child I traipsed around with George Carver. He taught me that if you wanted your friends and family to grow strong and prosper you treated them with kindness and respect. Likewise, if you wanted your ground to nourish you and your family and your friends, you must nourish it with understanding and kindness. And if you wanted beautiful flowers and crops to spring forth from that ground, you must love them.
>
> I learned more about life during those two years of clinging to the hand and words of George Carver than I have learned in all the years since. What we are now seeing across the Midwestern prairies is that Carver's lessons about our power over our environments do not just apply at the individual or family or family farm level, but rather that power is applicable across the breadth of our continent, north to south; west to east. Human behavior is changing the weather, indeed, every aspect of our environment, and it is going to continue to do so no matter what we do. The trick for us is to figure out how to behave in a way that would make my old friend Carver proud.

Mother Nature's indignant response to the mistreatment of the Great Plains grasslands dictated Secretary Wallace's "Job #2"—implementation of the Soil Conservation Act. Just as Rex Tugwell had quarterbacked the Agricultural Emergency Act effort, Henry now turned to the zealous, affable, and articulate Dr. "Big Hugh" Bennett for leadership in the fight against "the national menace," that was soil erosion.

What Henry Wallace, Hugh Bennett, and Rex Tugwell all understood was that Public Law 46, stating that "soil erosion was a menace to the national welfare," had given sweeping powers and broad authority to the newly created Soil Conservation Service (SCS). What the law did not do was authorize sufficient funds to carry out the mandate. The SCS, with Big Hugh as Chief, had but twelve people on the payroll. Twelve people to carry out a mandate to save the nation's topsoil in forty-eight states and three territories—not likely. They began casting around for resources.

Two years earlier, Congress had also passed The Emergency Conservation Work Act, which the President had signed into law on March 31, 1933. The Act created the Civilian Conservation Corps (CCC). The Corps was a public works relief program for unemployed men between the ages of eighteen and twenty-five. Not coincidentally, the age group most likely to become violent and revolutionary when given to hunger pangs. In addition to keeping the peace and providing relief employment in the throes of the Great Depression, their focus was on natural resource conservation.

By the end of the CCC's second year over 500 thousand young men were working in 2650 camps located in every state as well as the territories of Hawaii, Alaska and Puerto Rico. Upon arrival at the camps, at least seventy percent of the enrollees had been malnourished and poorly clothed, but by 1935 the news was better. Crime on the streets of cities like Chicago was down almost fifty-five percent, the young men were working, eating well, gaining weight and muscle. They were paid $30 per month, but $25 of that was sent directly to the worker's families. This diffused the allotment of $72 million into communities all across the nation. The CCC also, incidentally, began preparing half a million young men of the "greatest generation" for a call to arms against the Empire of Japan and European Fascists only six short years later.

But in 1935 the war Wallace, Tugwell and Bennett were interested in fighting was not overseas. It was against the ravages of years and years of mismanagement of the nation's most precious natural resources. The CCC was just the army needed for the fight. As the nation's newspapers carried the haunting pictorials of the Dust Bowl and its refugees by the likes of photographer Dorthea Lange, making the case to use the CCC to fight the battle at hand was not too difficult.

"Migrant Mother"—The Dust Bowl and drought devastated some farm families in the early 1930's, such as this thirty-two year old mother of seven. Dorthea Lange, photographer, Nipomo, California, February, 1936. (Library of Congress, Prints & Photographs Division)

We used to think that unless rills and gullies appeared on the face of the land, the soil was still there, with no serious damage from accelerated erosion. Early in the present century Hugh Bennett showed that smooth land may become barren. Whole fields and the greater part of a countryside may lose all or nearly all of the topsoil to the streams and the sea, grain by grain, layer by layer, without a single rill or gully breaking forth to cry warning. Bennett detected "sheet erosion" all the way from Virginia to Oklahoma. Bennett and his helpers were in the vanguard of a new defense against an actual enemy. NOW we have seen the refugees from the thinned fields; we have learned the grim fact that when a soil "runs down," not only the soil but the people there are drained of the very essence of life and vitality.

—Henry Agard Wallace[10]

The photographic evidence engendered public and political support, but there still may have been a bureaucratic stumbling block. Funds for the CCC were allocated to the Department of Interior, not the Department of Agriculture. Rather than fight a turf war, Department of Interior Secretary Harold Ickes was prevailed upon to create within his department the Soil Erosion Service (SES). Of course, Hugh Bennett was appointed to direct the SES, which he did in addition to his service as director of the Department of Agriculture's Soil Conservation Service. Five million dollars and 150 CCC camps were transferred to Big Hugh's Soil Erosion Service almost immediately. Bennett, Wallace and Tugwell had the tools to get to work.

Within two years the CCC had treated a million acres, which was good, but not good enough. Characteristically, Henry Wallace used data to articulate the challenge in a *Survey Graphic Magazine* article titled "The War at Our Feet."

The Land We Are Losing—From Our 1,900,000,000 Acres

3 percent (57,200,000 acres) gone forever as farmland
12 percent (225,000,000 acres) topsoil, three fourths lost
41 percent (775,600,000 acres) more than one fourth gone

The Cropland We Hold—415,334,931 Arable Acres

Over half is too poor to farm for profit, much of it badly eroded; conservation practices urgently needed.
Nearly half can be safely cultivated under prevailing practices; or, in other words, our agricultural plant would have to be reduced by half if we wanted to save our soil.

BUT, under the best practices, 82 percent of our cropland can be safely cultivated (18 percent should be retired).

MOREOVER if the need arose, we have a national production reserve, improvable by drainage or irrigation, plus over 100 million acres of plowable pasture; which brings the potential resources of cultivable land, under the best practices, up to 447,466,000 acres, a little more than the cropland area of today.

—Henry A. Wallace[11]

With this publication Secretary Wallace threw the gauntlet at the feet of a nation's people who were beginning to awaken to the horrors of environmental abuse, as they were busy washing the dust of the high plains from their faces and out of their eyes.

18

Only Butterflies are Free

The completion of Dr. Lorenz' work on chaos theory and the butterfly effect.

On Wednesdays Dr. Lorenz taught an early morning graduate level class, "Physics of Atmospheres." Though an avid hiker, and capable of a very rapid pace, if early enough he always seemed to enjoyed a leisurely stroll across the MIT campus to his office. On November 8, 1972, he was scanning the front page of the newspaper he had picked up on the way in to work from his home in Cambridge. The headline read "Nixon in a Landslide." Another front page story chronicled how the Republican, Paul Cronin, had defeated a young Democrat anti-war candidate named John Kerry for the 5th Congressional District seat in the U.S. House of Representatives. After the September primary, Mr. Kerry's election seemed almost ordained. However, *The Sun*, a local newspaper in the heart of the district, had made it their mission to see that the brash young "carpetbagger" did not represent the people of northeastern Massachusetts.

As he rounded the corner off Ames Street, Dr. Lorenz was joined by Professor Stommel, whose eyes carried a hint of amusement. "Hey, I see that you are going to demonstrate how butterflies create weather."

Always a man a few words, Dr. Lorenz questioned, "Uhm, I'm not quite sure?"

Stommel grinned slightly as he handed Lorenz the just published agenda for the upcoming 139th meeting of the American Association for the Advancement of Science. Right there it was on the printed page:

AAAS Section on Environmental Sciences
Sheraton Park Hotel – Wilmington Room

Washington, DC

10:00 am – December 29, 1972

"Predictability: Does the Flap of a Butterfly's Wings in Brazil Set Off a Tornado in Texas?"

Edward N. Lorenz, ScD.

Professor of Meteorology

Massachusetts Institute of Technology[1]

Years later, his long time friend and colleague from Princeton, Dr. Jerry Mahlman, would remember Dr. Lorenz, "Of all the geniuses of that era, he was the quietest and most humble and the most kind."[2] This being the case, it was consistent with his self-effacing personality that Dr. Lorenz had submitted the manuscript of his proposed presentation without a title. It was his friend and the session convener, meteorologist Philip Merilees, who had this tongue-in-cheek title printed in the official conference program. Little did Dr. Merilees, nor anyone else at the time, know that the term "butterfly effect" would change the lexicon, and in the minds of most people be so totally misunderstood with regard to Chaos Theory.

"Well, I guess this means I'm going to have to change my introductory comments, huh?" was Dr. Lorenz' only comment as he handed the conference program back to Dr. Stommel.

As they turned to enter building #54, they were met at the door by one of students in the morning class. "Good morning gentlemen, I pulled an all-nighter and I just gotta to have another cup of coffee."

Affably, and making much ado of looking at his watch, Dr. Lorenz exhorted, "Now Kevin, don't be late."

Over his shoulder, as he trotted off across McDermott Court, "No worries, Dr. Lorenz, I'll be there."

¤ ¤ ¤

At 10:08am on December 29, 1972 in the Wilmington Room of the Sheraton Park Hotel, Edward Lorenz thanked Dr. Merilees for the kind introduction and, looking him squarely in the eye, began his address.

"Lest I appear **frivolous** in even posing the title question" Lorenz winked at Merilees and turned his attention to the audience, "let alone suggesting that it might have an affirmative answer, let me try to place it in proper perspective by offering two propositions.

First, if a single flap of a butterfly's wing can be instrumental in generating a tornado, so also can all the previous and subsequent flaps of its wings, as can the flaps of the wings of millions of other butterflies, not to mention the activities of other more powerful creatures, including our own species.

Second, if the flap of a butterfly's wing can be instrumental in generating a tornado, it can equally be instrumental in preventing a tornado.

More generally, I am proposing over the years minuscule disturbances neither increase nor decrease the frequency of occurrence of various weather events such as tornadoes; the most that they may do is to modify the sequence in which these events occur. The question which really interests us is whether they can even do this—whether for example two particular weather situations differing by as little as the immediate influence of a single butterfly will generally after sufficient time evolve into two situations differing by as much as the presence of a tornado. In more technical language, is the behavior of the atmosphere unstable with respect to perturbations of small amplitude?

The connection between this question and our ability to predict the weather is evident. Since we do not know exactly how many butterflies there are, nor where they are located, let alone which ones are flapping their wings at any instant, we cannot, if the answer to our question is affirmative, accurately predict the occurrence of tornadoes at a sufficiently distant future time."[3]

Dr. Lorenz went on to describe the conundrum of atmospheric instability confounded even further, with regard to predictability, by sensitive dependence on initial conditions— "the butterfly effect." Initially he had developed twelve formulas, but by the application of the model to increasingly simple systems he refined the math to these three simple equations:

$$dx/dt = \sigma(y - x)$$
$$dy/dt = x(p - z) - y$$
$$dz/dt = xy - \beta z \ [4]$$

These equations seem to express a system of entirely random behavior. However, when graphed the outcome always stayed on a double spiral curve, which came to be known as the Lorenz Attractor. The fact that the graphed results look strikingly like a butterfly is an intriguing happenstance.

Prior to the development of these equations there were only two known systems of order: the "steady state" system, in which the variables never change; and, the "periodic system," which results in an endlessly repeating pattern. Dr. Lorenz's equations are definitely ordered, as they always produce a double spiral, which never resolves to a single point, but it also never repeats itself. So, the formulas represented an entirely new system that was neither steady state nor periodic.

Because Dr. Lorenz was a meteorologist, his articles slanted toward the effect on atmospheric dynamics and, of course, were generally published in journals of meteorology. Therefore, his discovery of an entirely new "system" of order was not being shared with an audience of mathematicians or physicists. It was decades after the 1963 publication of his article, "Deterministic Nonperiodic Flow," in the *Journal of Atmospheric Science*, that his discoveries were acknowledged and studied by others in the scientific community. It was as if the world could not share Dr. Lorenz' revolutionary discoveries, until the world discovered Dr. Lorenz.

With that said, it is not surprising that the development of this revolutionary scientific system would hail from the field of meteorology. Weather demonstrates the "butterfly effect" because it is dependent on a number of variables such as temperature, humidity, wind currents, etc. All of these variables are, obviously, interrelated and interdependent. Temperature changes depend on humidity, wind speed, and wind direction. At the same time, humidity, wind speed and direction are dependent upon temperature. Therefore, each variable in some way becomes a function of itself, and the equations that relate these variables are nonlinear. What Dr. Lorenz discovered was that "sensitive dependence on initial conditions" is a function of the nonlinear relationship of the variables. The weather, like the graph of the Lorenz Attractor, repeats itself (periods of wet weather and periods of drought), but it does so in unpredictable ways.

Though it is logical that the theory has its roots in meteorology, the model is more generally applicable. At once both exquisitely simple and intricately complex, the implication is that given enough time every event, indeed every expression of energy everywhere, ripples through time and space to impact every subsequent event and expression of energy everywhere, forever—the "butterfly effect." However, the theory implies that because of the infinite number of preceding events (expressions of energy), and because even the most minuscule change in the way that energy is expressed (sensitive dependence on initial conditions), the effect over time produces enormously different results, which appear to be chaotic (chaos theory).

Chaos theory does not imply a random unfolding of the cosmos, rather the theory instructs that because of the infinite connectedness of all matter and energy, future events become virtually impossible to predict. Dr. Lorenz did realize that "Chaos" is applicable to more than just the weather as witnessed by this layman's explanation at one of his lectures:

> Before I define what systems are or are not chaotic let me present two examples that will help to clarify certain details. The first is a bit of old English verse often quoted as indicating an early recognition of possible chaotic behavior. It goes
>
> For want of a nail, the shoe was lost.
> For want of a shoe, the horse was lost.
> For want of a horse, the rider was lost.
> For want of a rider, the battle was lost.
> For want of a battle, the kingdom was lost.
> And all for the want of a nail.
>
> Let me say right now that I do not feel that this verse is describing true chaos, but better illustrates the simple phenomenon of instability. The verse assumes the loss of a nail to be detrimental, but if this were true chaos losing a nail might equally well lead to the loss or winning of the kingdom. Moreover, if this were chaos, subsequent small events like the loss of more nails could also lead to the loss or gain of a kingdom. Yet in the verse there is something rather final about the statement, "the kingdom was lost." The implication is that subsequent small events will not reverse the outcome.
>
> My second example which I feel better describes a chaotic process is a rather trivial anecdote. In it I am driving along a city street where there are frequent intersections with traffic lights. As I approach the next intersection, the light is green, and I expect to

proceed. However, a jaywalker, a pedestrian intent upon crossing the street between intersections, suddenly steps out. I stop to avoid hitting him, and he gets out of the way, but by then the light has turned red. I wait for the next green light and proceed, and as I approach the next intersection the light there is green. I continue, but as I cross the intersection a small truck on the side street runs through its red light and hits me.

Did the jaywalker cause the accident? Certainly it would not have occurred if he had not stepped out. Yet I find it hard to assign similar blame to him and the truck driver. There was an equal likelihood that the truck would have arrived at the intersection a minute sooner. In that case, if the jaywalker had not appeared, I also would have arrived a minute sooner, and would have been hit. Because the jaywalker did delay me, I would have reached the intersection after the truck and no accident would have occurred. Would the jaywalker then have prevented the accident?

Not only was the jaywalker equally likely to have led to an accident or the avoidance of one, but the actions of all other jaywalkers, at other times or on other streets, also bear similar likelihoods of being associated with accidents. Here I am intentionally disregarding the possibility of another type of accident, in which the jaywalker is the victim. To return to the butterfly, if a butterfly can cause or prevent a tornado, it can do so only in the sense that a jaywalker causes or prevents an accident. Moreover, just as important as the specified flap of a butterfly's wings are all subsequent flaps, and each flap of the wings of innumerable other butterflies, not to mention the actions of members of all other species, some far more powerful.[5]

In addition to recognizing the applicability of the "butterfly effect" to human behavior, Dr. Lorenz' final comment alludes to the power of even random acts of humanity. Clearly actions that are not so random may be even more remarkably powerful in terms of sensitive dependence on initial conditions and the environmental consequences of intentional, large scale human activity. If Dr. Lorenz had been asked about the predictability of Black Sunday on April 14, 1935, he likely would have responded that any undergraduate student of meteorology could have predicted that if you plowed up a half million square miles of grass, you would likely to have a dust storm during a drought when the wind blows. What they would not have been able to predict, with much certitude, was when there would be a drought and when the wind would blow. Given the initial condition of the top soil stripped naked, "if" a Black Sunday type event would occur becomes a virtual certainty; the "when" is not nearly so certain—perhaps Monday, or Tuesday, or Wednesday—one may suppose the best advice is, 'don't plow up all the grass.'

¤ ¤ ¤

Remaining remarkably active, physically and mentally, until his final two weeks, Edward Lorenz died peacefully in his home on April 16, 2008, at the age of ninety. In an obituary Dr. Kerry Emanuel fondly remembered his friend and colleague.

> By showing that certain deterministic systems have formal predictability limits, Ed put the last nail in the coffin of the Cartesian universe and fomented what some have called the third scientific revolution of the twentieth century, following on the heels of relativity and quantum physics. He was also a perfect gentleman, and through his intelligence, integrity and humility set a very high standard for his and succeeding generations.[6]

Whether intentional or not, Dr. Emanuel's statement about his old friend expressed something quite profound. Because of the butterfly effect, everything we do matters—forever. Just as Moses Carver's decision to rescue the baby George from his kidnappers would spare untold millions of people the horrors of hunger five generations hence, the expressions of energy that demonstrated Dr. Lorenz' "intelligence, integrity, and humility" had an impact upon his contemporaries, will impact succeeding generations, and someday, in some unpredictable way, will affect the flapping of a butterfly's wings in Brazil. Just as his theories have permanently altered human perceptions of the cosmos in which we live, his kindnesses too will ripple through time.

19

STORM Clouds

Profits: The reason to fight.

In the early morning hours of June 30, 1934, a plane landed at the Munich, Germany airport. An enraged Adolph Hitler and his entourage disembarked. The prior evening hungry, desperate, unemployed men had been rioting in the streets. That was bad enough, that these men were brown shirted Nazi Storm Troopers (Sturmbateilung) made matters worse. Hitler had ridden their penchant for violence to power during the Nazi revolution. Now however, they were still not employed, and their anti-capitalist sentiments, often expressed by Sturmbateilung leaders and echoed by the restless masses of storm troopers, caused great concern to the big business and industrial leadership that undergirded the Nazi regime. Hitler had promised his corporate patrons that he would put down the trade union movement and Marxists, which he had done. But now the Nazi storm troopers themselves were talking of a second revolution. They were sounding more and more like Marxists.

Just two weeks earlier, Vice Chancellor Franz von Papen in a speech at the University of Marburg asked, "Have we experienced an anti-Marxist revolution in order to put through a Marxist program?"[1] His question was answered with roars of applause from the ultraconservative audience. The industrialists, the military, and Adolph Hitler all agreed something had to be done.

On that fateful night of June 30th, Hitler unleashed his personal army, the Schutzstaffel (SS), and his personal secret police force, the Gestapo. The "Night of Long Knives" was on. Over the next three nights these "law enforcement officers" purged (read: killed) at least eighty-five "socialists" and imprisoned more than a thousand other "enemies of the state."

Initially, Nazi leaders Goring, Goebbels, Himmler and Heinrich feared how the public would react to the perceived excesses of the "law enforcement" effort. However, to their surprise and relief, the military and leading industrialists were almost giddy at the elimination of the perceived threat. Emboldened by that response, on July 13, 1934 Hitler address the German Reichstag (Parliament):

> "Let the nation know that its existence, which depends on its internal order and security, cannot be threatened with impunity by anyone! And let it be known for all time to come that if anyone raises his hand to strike the State, then certain death is his lot."[2]
>
> —Adolf Hitler

Law and order, Nazi style, prevailed.

¤ ¤ ¤

Half a world away, the Minneapolis Teamster Local 574 strike was two months old. The Teamsters had taken on the powerful Citizens' Alliance. The eight hundred member Alliance was made up of persons from the area's big industries, smaller businesses, bankers, merchants, and even some laborers. They had succeeded in making Minneapolis and St. Paul a stronghold of the open shop. The Citizens Alliance was well financed and boasted an efficient staff and a trained crew of undercover agents. It had been successful in breaking every strike in the city since the turn of the twentieth century. They had crushed the trucker stoppage of 1916 and claimed to have spent only $25,000 in doing so. But now, a generation later, they were faced with another aggressive challenge from the labor segment of the transportation industry.

There had been running brawls in the streets off and on since May 20th, when three trucks full of men and women strikers were duped into an ambush behind the Minneapolis Tribune Building. They were bludgeoned by the paramilitary arm or the Citizens Alliance, a group that had been deputized as "special police." The defeated where wheeled into the triage facility set up in the back of the striker's headquarters. Three women had suffered broken legs and all others were bloodied by clubs and fists.

In the following two days, the confrontations took a decidedly more dangerous turn. Thousands of strikers and union sympathizers confronted thousands of Citizens Alliance toughs and Minneapolis Police. Violence erupted and the ensuing riots turned into routes that came to be known as the "Battles of Deputies Run." The overwhelmed "law enforcement" forces had broken ranks and retreated at full run. Two deaths were recorded. One was Arthur Lyman, a man who had served as the attorney for the Citizens Alliance for the preceding sixteen years.

At that point, the rhetoric became super heated. "Communists capturing our streets . . . Minneapolis brought to its knees by a handful of agitators . . . Law and order must be enforced . . . Class domination over industry is not going to be tolerated," etcetera, etcetera, etcetera. The truck owners within the ranks of the Citizens Alliance wrapped themselves in a shroud of patriotism, and denounced the "Red Dictators" who are out to "starve our city into submission."

Humiliated by their retreat and loss of control, the city's police force decided to take definitive action. Exactly one week after Adolph Hitler justified the actions of the Schutzstaffel (SS) and the Gestapo in his speech to the German Reichstag, a truck was driven into the midst of a group of strikers. As the strikers approached to inspect the truck, a phalanx of police officers with sawed off 12-gauge shotguns stood from their hiding places below the sideboards and discharged their buckshot at point blank range. Sixty-nine of the strikers were felled immediately, many shot in the back as they tried to escape. Sixty-seven were wounded. Two were dead.

Perhaps sensing that the Minneapolis Police had gone too far, the Citizens Alliance sent a memorandum to the Governor charging the strikers were under the influence of communists and insisting that he step up to the plate on the side of the Alliance.

> "We demand to know whether you will support local authorities with military aid in the discharge of their duty, or support the efforts of the few to obstruct the flow of normal traffic in this city."[3]

Governor Olson was not amused either by the tone of the memorandum or the antics of those lined up against the Union. His letter clearly stated his point of view.

> I do not agree with you that a plea for living wage by a family man receiving only $12.00 a week is answered by calling that man a Communist.

Neither am I willing to join in the approval of shooting unarmed citizens of Minneapolis, strikers and bystanders alike, in their backs in order to carry out the wishes of the Citizen Alliance of Minneapolis.

I have never attended a meeting of Local 574 and am unable to agree or disagree as to your claim concerning who controls it. However, I have had numerous opportunities recently during strike negotiations to attend meetings of employers and in the past years have had considerable opportunity to observe the action of this organization known as the Citizens Alliance of Minneapolis, of which you are members.

This organization is controlled and dominated by a small clique of men who hate all organized labor and are determined to crush it. . . . [I]t gained its power because of its alliance with the big financial institutions, which control the two chain banking institutions of Minneapolis through the extension of stifling of credit. These chain institutions are able, aided by the manipulation of the Citizens Alliance clique, to dictate the very destiny of the majority of employers in the city of Minneapolis. . . .

The Agencies of government do not belong to you, as one would be led to believe from reading your communication. They belong to all the people, and I propose to use the governmental agencies under my jurisdiction, including the National Guard, for the protection of all the people of the city of Minneapolis, and all people outside the city, including farmers, who desire to do business within the city.

—Floyd B. Olson[4]

Chancellor Hitler and his fascists were in Berlin, but Governor Olson was at the State Capitol in St. Paul. The Governor did indeed dispatch 3700 armed National Guardsmen to the streets of Minneapolis. They were ordered to protect the strikers! These orders in practice served to replace the picketers with Guardsmen, who began issuing permits for the delivery of certain commodities. The Citizens Alliance was hopping mad. The deployment orders were clearly a statement of support for the strikers. (*Governor Olson had also personally contributed $500 to the strike fund, but this was not yet known by the Citizens Alliance membership.*)

The Teamsters were also furious. The National Guard issuance of permits for delivery trucks to move through the streets of Minneapolis was in essence breaking the strike. Almost surely Governor Olson sat across the river thinking, 'the road to hell is indeed paved with the best of intentions.'

The strike was finally resolved by the end of August 1934. The employers and Citizens Alliance nominally conceded defeat by granting recognition of the union and a very modest pay increase. Despite the use of state militia and much condemnation of the strike leaders as "radicals and Communists," the radicals prevailed.

¤ ¤ ¤

All these years after the rhetoric has had time to cool, it is worth now considering who were the people at the negotiating table in Minneapolis during that hot summer of 1934. The simple fact is that Teamsters Local 574 was under the control and direction of communists. Ray Dunne, Miles Dunne, Grant Dunne, Carl Skoglund and Farrell Dobbs were the core leadership of Teamsters Local 574. They were also all card carrying members of the Communist League of America and followers of the exiled Russian Communist, Leon Trotsky. Farrell Dobbs later visited Mr. Trotsky in exile, where the self-proclaimed "proletarian revolutionist," lived in his surprisingly "bourgeois" estate in Coyoacan, a neighborhood of Mexico City.

In 1940, the United States Congress conspired to codify its disdain for the Bill of Rights by enactment of the Smith Act. At the end of World War II, Carl Skoglund and Farrell Dobbs were both charged with violating the Smith Act, which made it unlawful to "Knowingly or willfully advocate, abet, advise or teach the duty, necessity, desirability or propriety of overthrowing the Government of the United States or of any State by force or violence, or for anyone to organize any association which teaches, advises or encourages such an overthrow, or for anyone to become a member of or to affiliate with any such association."

At the trial it was never brought to the jury's attention that during the campaign of 1928, the communist Farrell Dobbs, had been a strong supporter and campaigned for the Republican candidate, Herbert Hoover. Dobbs and Skoglund were both found guilty and served a year in a federal penitentiary. It seems that the Freedom of Speech guaranteed by the U.S. Constitution's First Amendment only applied if the political right wing agreed with what one had to say.

Imprisoned for voicing their beliefs, these men nevertheless remained staunch supporters of Leon Trotsky and active life-long communists. In retrospect, it is difficult to understand how these otherwise intelligent men could have been so duped by the dogma of the radical left. It is difficult to understand their allegiance to Leon Trotsky, for he was staunchly anti-union, at least he had been while in the Soviet Union. His uncompromising position was that in a "worker's state" the workers should have nothing to fear from the state, and therefore the State should fully control the unions. Trotsky led the left wing of the Soviet Communist Party and stood in opposition to Stalinist totalitarianism. Instead, he advocated "permanent political revolution" and espoused that "socialism cannot sustain itself without democracy."

The logic Trotsky employed to square all of these seemingly conflicting positions (unions must be fully controlled by the state vs. socialism cannot exist absent democracy) seems impossibly muddled. Muddled or not, he was perceived as a threat to Joseph Stalin's autocracy. Hence, Trotsky found himself purged from the party and exiled from the Soviet Union in February 1929.

Initially, Trotsky was one of the lucky few for whom "purge" meant "exile." Worldwide, communist idealism was being crushed under Stalin's megalomanic iron fist. Purges soon employed a more final disposition for the dispossessed. During the decade of the 1930s, it is estimated that two million Soviet citizens were executed or incarcerated in Siberian Gulags, where they were worked and starved to death. Of course, they were **all** guilty of "crimes against the state."

In the end, also "guilty" of action perceived by Stalin as treasonous, the same fate awaited Mr. Trotsky. Carrying out the death sentence imposed by the Soviet Government, NKVD agent Ramon Mercader assassinated Trotsky by sticking a pick ax through his skull. He was attacked in his Mexico City residence on August 20, 1940 and died at the hospital some twenty-eight hours later.

¤ ¤ ¤

While there is no doubt that the leaders of the Minneapolis strikers were Communists, on the other side of the strike's bargaining table, it would be all too easy to charge that the Citizens Alliance members were a bunch of Fascists. Well, even though they clearly took a page out of Adolph Hitler's *Mein Kampf* in terms of strategy, it would be inaccurate to paint the entire membership with the Nazi brush. Many of the members would not have been at all comfortable that far right on the political spectrum. Governor Olson's observation that the Citizens Alliance was controlled by a clique who sat on the boards of the big financial institutions, which in turn controlled the credit available to Minnesota businessmen, likely had more to do with the large membership and support of the Citizens Alliance than did far right-wing politics.

However, it is fair to ask where the business barons of the era stood with regard to the worldwide growth of fascism? That is not easy to pin down because individually and as a group they were so enigmatic. Yet as the Fascists armed the European continent for its second major war within two decades, it is necessary to point out that one of the unwritten rules of warfare has long been that a war should never be fought unless it is good for industrial profits.

Below is a listing of pre-war vs. intra-war profits for American companies during World War I.[5]

Company	Average Profits in the Last Pre-War Year	Average Profits During the Four Years of War
U. S. Steel	$105,331,000	$259,653,000
Du Pont	$6,092,000	$58,076,000
Bethlehem Steel	$6,840,000	$49,427,000
Anaconda Copper	$10,649,000	$34,549,000
Utah Copper	$5,776,000	$21,622,000
American Smelting	$11,566,000	$18,602,000
Republic Iron & Steel	$4,177,000	$17,548,000
International Mercantile	$6,690,000.00	$14,229,000
Atlas Powder	$485,000	$2,374,000
American and British Man.	$172,000	$325,000
Canadian Car & Foundry	$1,335,000	$2,201,000
Crocker Wheeler	$206,000	$666,000
Hercules Powder	$1,271,000	$7,430,000
Niles, Bement Pond	$656,000	$6,146,000
Scovill Mfg. Co.	$655,000	$7,678,000
General Motors	$6,954,000	$21,700,000

That was World War I, but World War II was truly a battle of good against evil, right? Well, perhaps it was not quite that simple. The U.S. Ambassador to Germany, Dr. William E. Dodd, wrote this observation in the diary he kept during his ambassadorship from 1933 to 1938.

> A clique of U.S. industrialists is hell-bent to bring a fascist state to supplant our democratic government and is working closely with the fascist regimes in Germany and Italy. I have had plenty of opportunity in my post in Berlin to witness how close some of our American ruling families are to the Nazi regime.
>
> Certain American industrialists had a great deal to do with bringing fascist regimes into being in both Germany and Italy. They extended aid to help Fascism occupy the seat of power, and they are helping to keep it there.[6]

Were U.S. Industrialists really "hell-bent" on bringing fascist states to Europe and America, or were they just doing business? Or is it plausible that they could not see any way to profit from the government controlled industrial structures proposed by Marxism, and thus viewed Fascism as a bastion against the perceived Communist threat? That question is not as preposterous as it may seem. There is much evidence to suggest that many of this nation's leading industrialists did, in fact, believe that Franklin Roosevelt was a Socialist at best and perhaps even a Communist. However, the evidence would incline one to believe that their motives were less political and more commercial. The following is excerpted from a report of the United States Senate Committee on the Judiciary in 1974:

> The activities of General Motors, Ford and Chrysler prior to and during World War II . . . are instructive. At that time, these three firms dominated motor vehicle production in both the United States and Germany. Due to its mass production capabilities, automobile manufacturing is one of the most crucial industries with respect to national defense. As a result, these firms retained the economic and political power to affect the shape of governmental relations both within and between these nations in a manner which maximized corporate global profits. In short, they were private governments unaccountable to the citizens of any country

yet possessing tremendous influence over the course of war and peace in the world. The substantial contribution of these firms to the American war effort in terms of tanks, aircraft components, and other military equipment is widely acknowledged. Less well known are the simultaneous contributions of their foreign subsidiaries to the Axis Powers. In sum, they maximized profits by supplying both sides with the materiel needed to conduct the war.

During the 1920s and 1930s, the Big Three automakers undertook an extensive program of multinational expansion. . . . By the mid-1930s, these three American companies owned automotive subsidiaries throughout Europe and the Far East; many of their largest facilities were located in the politically sensitive nations of Germany, Poland, Rumania, Austria, Hungary, Latvia, and Japan. . . . Due to their concentrated economic power over motor vehicle production in both Allied and Axis territories, the Big Three inevitably became major factors in the preparations and progress of the war. In Germany, for example, General Motors and Ford became an integral part of the Nazi war efforts. GM's plants in Germany built thousands of bomber and jet fighter propulsion systems for the Luftwaffe at the same time that its American plants produced aircraft engines for the U.S. Army Air Corps. . . .

Ford was also active in Nazi Germany's prewar preparations. In 1938, for instance, it opened a truck assembly plant in Berlin whose "real purpose," according to U.S. Army Intelligence, was producing "troop transport-type" vehicles for the Wehrmacht. That year Ford's chief executive received the Nazi German Eagle (first class). . . .

The outbreak of war in September 1939 resulted inevitably in the full conversion by GM and Ford of their Axis plants to the production of military aircraft and trucks. . . .On the ground, GM and Ford subsidiaries built nearly 90 percent of the armored "mule" 3-ton half-tracks and more than seventy percent of the Reich's medium and heavy-duty trucks. These vehicles, according to American intelligence reports, served as "the backbone of the German Army transportation system." . . .

After the cessation of hostilities, GM and Ford demanded reparations from the U.S. Government for wartime damages sustained by their Axis facilities as a result of Allied bombing. . . . Ford received a little less than $1 million, primarily as a result of damages sustained by its military truck complex at Cologne. . . .

Due to their multinational dominance of motor vehicle production, GM and Ford became principal suppliers for the forces of fascism as well as for the forces of democracy. It may, of course, be argued that participating in both sides of an international conflict, like the common corporate practice of investing in both political parties before an election, is an appropriate corporate activity. Had the Nazis won, General Motors and Ford would have appeared impeccably Nazi; as Hitler lost, these companies were able to re-emerge impeccably American. In either case, the viability of these corporations and the interests of their respective stockholders would have been preserved.[7]

By no means were the big three auto makers the only American based international corporations doing business with Europe's Fascists. The German based corporation, I. G. Farben, was the largest chemical manufacturing company in the world during the first four decades of the twentieth century. They owned holdings in America which included Bayer Co., General Aniline Works, BASF, Agfa Ansco, and Winthrop Chemical Company. In the 1930s they also entered into enormous contracts with Standard Oil, DuPont, Alcoa, and Dow Chemical that supplied them with the raw materials to help build the Nazi war machine and death camps.

¤ ¤ ¤

While raw materials were vital to the development of their economies, the Fascists realized that possession and manipulation of information was also a source of power. Toward that end they groomed the American media and technology giants.

For twenty-five years Karl von Wiegand was a leading reporter for the International News Service in Central Europe. In 1935 he provided a report to Ambassador Dodd which was forwarded, as classified information, directly to President Roosevelt. The following is an excerpt that details William Randolph Hearst's business dealings with the Italian Fascists and German Nazis.

"Gianini, President of the Italian Bank System of California, an ardent supporter of Mussolini, agreed to lend Hearst some millions of dollars, Hearst being thought at that time to be in embarrassing financial circumstances. . . .

Hearst then sent me (von Wiegand) to Rome for an interview with Mussolini, and asked me to engage him to write articles whenever he chose for the Hearst press at $1 a word. Mussolini was greatly pleased and he wrote articles over a number of years, and I delivered to him large checks from time to time. From that time on Hearst was considered by his correspondents as an ally of Mussolini. . . .

In 1934 he (Hearst) came with a big party, including his mistress, and spent the summer at Nauheim. Once more representatives of the German Government visited him, and finally Rosenberg (editor of the VOELKISCHER BEOBACHTER and representative of German foreign propaganda work) made an engagement for him to see the Chancellor, and he flew to Berlin one night in September. The next day he had an interview of nearly an hour with the Chancellor, and he reported to me that he was greatly impressed with the genius and friendliness of Hitler. . . .

A little later he asked me to negotiate a deal with Goebbels for supplying the German Propaganda Ministry with all the Hearst news service. I declined. Hearst then appointed Hillman, of London, to work out the deal, and I went to London to continue my work for the International News Service. Hillman arranged for the Propaganda Ministry to have all continental Hearst information in Europe delivered to its office at the same time it went to the Hearst press over the world. For this service Hearst was to receive $200,000 a year, and he at once began to bring pressure to bear on his correspondents to give only friendly accounts of what happened in Germany. . . ."[8]

Seventy-four years after this report was submitted to the President, and exactly sixty-four years to the day after the U.S. 3rd Army, 6th Armored

Division liberated the Buchenwald Concentration Camp, the following story appeared in several newspapers around the United States.

California returns 2 paintings Nazis stole, Hearst bought

Peter Hecht – Sacramento Bee

Saturday, April 11, 2009

California park officials say publishing tycoon William Randolph Hearst had no inkling of the hellish circumstances of the Oppenheimer family in Germany when he bought three paintings for his San Simeon castle in 1935.

He didn't know the Nazis had looted the works from Jakob and Rosa Oppenheimer's fine-art shop, Galerie van Diemen, in Berlin. Or that Jakob and Rosa had fled to France. Or that their grown children escaped to the United States and Argentina when the Gestapo came looking for them as the paintings were being auctioned, resold and shipped to California.

On Friday, Gov. Arnold Schwarzenegger and state park officials returned two of the paintings to Oppenheimer family heirs.

They also accepted the family's gift of the third painting. It will be displayed at the mansion at the Hearst San Simeon State Monument as a remembrance of the Oppenheimer family and a Holocaust-era injustice.

The long journey of the paintings back into the family's hands came far too late for Rosa and Jakob Oppenheimer. Jakob died in poverty in France in 1941. Rosa was arrested by German occupiers and put to death two years later at Auschwitz.

Friday, in a ceremony at the Leland Stanford Mansion in Sacramento, Schwarzenegger declared he was closing the book on a "sorrowful story" by returning the artworks.

Oppenheimer grandson Peter Bloch of Boyton Beach, Fla., and granddaughter Inge Blackshear of Buenos Aires accepted two paintings: a 1518 – 1594 Venetian work from the Jacopo Tintoretto school and a sixteenth century painting by an unknown Venetian artist.[9]

An emaciated and emancipated survivor drinking from a metal bowl in front of barracks at Buchenwald concentration camp just minutes after liberation. Courtesy of National Archives and Records Administration, College Park, Maryland.

¤ ¤ ¤

A more chilling pursuit of war profiteering can be found in the arrangements Europe's Fascists had with the International Business Machines Corporation (IBM).

Wireless to *The New York Times.*

> BERLIN, July 1. – Thomas J. Watson, president of the International Business Machines Corporation of New York and the new president of the International Chamber of Commerce, has achieved the distinction of being the first American whom Chancellor Adolf Hitler has decorated with the new order of merit of the German Eagle, created for "honoring foreign nationals who have made themselves deserving of the German Reich.[10]

By the time this New York Times article appeared in 1937, recognizing the honor bestowed by Chancellor Hitler on IBM founder and CEO, Thomas Watson, Nazi Germany had acquired the technological underpinnings necessary to pursue and execute the Holocaust. IBM owned the patents for the Hollerith punch card technology. There being no computers, IBM Hollerith D-11 card sorting machines had been utilized to organize the data from the 1933 German census. The punch cards contained information about the age, ethnicity, residence, etc. of each person living in Germany—the Nazis possessed in thousands of boxes of punch cards the name and location of every person of Jewish decent in the nation.

Ultimately over two thousand machines were placed throughout Germany by IBM's wholly owned German subsidiary, Deutsche Hollerith Maschinen Gesellschaft. Using mock-ups of cards and reports, IBM personnel worked closely with their customers to custom-design the applications to the specifications provided by the Nazis (e.g. name, address, occupation, number of children of all Jewish residents). IBM was the sole source for the machines and the 1.5 billion punch cards purchased by the Nazi government each year. IBM refused to sell the machines to the Germans, rather they entered into more profitable lease agreements, which included the provision of regular on-site maintenance and upgrading. Those sites included places like Hinzert and Dachau and Buchenwald. In order to maintain and improve the data management systems being employed in the process of purifying the Aryan race, IBM employees made regular visits to places where people were being systematically exterminated and provided the data management systems to record the deaths as well as property confiscated from the condemned. In order to maintain data backups, the IBM main offices in Berlin kept duplicate code books for the leased machines. In 1934 IBM aggressively targeted their advertisements to their Nazi clientele.

The IBM advertising slogan used in Germany was "Uberficht mit Hollerith Lochkarten" (See everything with Hollerith Punchcards). Posters carrying this slogan had the image of a single eye staring at a punchcard with the silhouette of a building and smokestack in the background.

How did Himmler's SS henchmen know where to find almost every Jew living in Germany? They simply ran queries for the census data on machines owned by IBM and stored on Hollerith punch cards.

All of that, of course, was being handled by German citizens working for IBM's German subsidiary. Surely no U.S. citizen working for IBM was aware of this insidious use of IBM technology. Well, that would be comforting, but it is simply untrue. Records indicate almost daily communication between IBM home offices in New York and the subsidiary offices in Berlin and Geneva. The communications generally regarded monitoring payments for services and additional business opportunities as they arose in Nazi occupied Europe. Business was very, very good as new death camps sprung up in conquered territories.

When the German Chargé d'Affaires, Dr. Hans Thomsen, and the First Secretary of the German Embassy, Mr. von Strempel hand-delivered Germany's declaration of war against the United States to Mr. Ray Atherton at his State Department office in Washington, DC on December 11, 1941, the "Trading With the Enemy Act" immediately forbid any conduct of business between the United States and Germany. However, being a multinational corporation, IBM determined that this law was not strictly applicable to them even though their home offices were located in New York City. Still, fearing legal and public relations repercussions, IBM shifted management of all its European business operations to their offices in "neutral" Geneva, Switzerland. Of course, as a simple matter of corporate communications protocol, the IBM Board of Directors and the CEO, Thomas Watson, continued to receive regular reports from Geneva.

All of this may seem totally preposterous in what has been perceived as the "war of good against evil," but the business reality is that Ford, General Motors, Standard Oil, IBM, even Coke-a-Cola and dozens of other "American" corporations were able to have their subsidiary operations in Axis controlled territories classified as "American property," thereby creating a legal protection against bombing or military destruction. A British embassy internal memorandum stated, "It is only too clear that where U.S. trade interests are involved, these are being allowed to take precedence over 'hemispheric defense,' and over cooperation with us."[11]

When the war ended, several companies sued the United States Government for damages done to their properties. Some of the law suits were successful. Hence, the corporations profited from selling munitions, equipment and materiel to all sides in the conflict. Then they arranged for the United States tax payer to reimbursement them for damages sustained to their properties by the very munitions they had sold to the various combatant countries.

¤ ¤ ¤

All this brings us back to the question, who was sitting around that Minneapolis conference table trying to negotiate a settlement of the strike during the summer of 1934?

Were the Teamster representatives communists? Yes they were.

But who were the Citizens Alliance representatives? Or perhaps more germane, who were the real power brokers Governor Olson observed pulling the strings of the Citizens Alliance? Even in light of all the preceding documentation, the evidence just does not support that American corporate bosses were "card-carrying" Fascists. They were clearly anti-communist, but fascist? Not likely. Their motives were simply not political enough to result in zealous extremism. Rather, they represented a corporate mentality of shameless, even soulless, profiteering. If they were willing to profit by selling Axis powers the war materiels used to kill 416,800 United States military personnel; profit by maintaining the data related to the extermination of Europe's Jews; then surely a few cracked heads and the destitute families of truck drivers being paid only $12 a week in Minneapolis was not much of a jolt to the corporate conscience.

¤ ¤ ¤

Is there a lesson here? Perhaps that avarice is evil. Perhaps that extremism, on either side of the political spectrum, leads to the most horrific acts of unkindness. Perhaps that political extremism is a natural and spontaneous outgrowth of people being forced to go without enough to eat.

Whatever the lessons, as he folded the Des Moines Register and laid it on the table, the twenty year old Norman Borlaug was deeply troubled by reports of the tumult in Minneapolis and Munich that August of 1934. As he sat at the kitchen table, while his mother boiled Mason jars in preparation for canning sweet peas, he worried. He worried about the people of Germany. He worried about the people of Minneapolis. He worried about hungry people in general. But most of all, he worried about his fiancée, Margaret Gibson.

20

The New Deal's Mystic

Wallace becomes the New Deal's unofficial "spiritual leader-philosopher."

I know that I'm often called a mystic, and in the years following my leaving the United Presbyterian Church, I would say I was probably a practical mystic. I've always believed that if you envision something that hasn't been, that can be, and bring it into being, that is a tremendously worthwhile thing to do. I'd go this far— I'd say I was a mystic in the same sense that George Carver was, who believed that God was in everything, and therefore, that if you went to God, you could find the answers. Maybe that belief is mysticism. I don't know.
—Henry Agard Wallace[1]

If for Dr. Carver the pursuit of education had been arduous and his spiritual enlightenment came easily, then the reverse must be said of his protégé. The youngest Henry adored his grandfather, the Reverend "Uncle Henry" Wallace. Intellectually, he accepted and understood his grandfather's liberal interpretation of Presbyterian doctrine, but he lacked the emotional connection with the church necessary for it to be the source of spiritual enlightenment—and if one could characterize Henry Agard Wallace's life in a single phrase, it would be "pursuit of enlightenment."

As eccentric as were Henry's diets, his spiritual quest was even more so. It would be wrong to say he dabbled with Christian Protestantism, Eastern Occultism, Native American Religions, Liberal Catholicism, astrology, Mysticism, Theosophy, Pantheism, Hinduism, Buddhism, Jewish Cabalism, Confucianism, and other forms of spirituality. The word 'dabble' would trivialize his seriousness, as well as the time and energy he devoted to his spiritual life. In addition to his grandfather and Dr. Carver, Henry exposed himself to the spiritual influences of William James, author of *Varieties of Religious Experiences*; Ralph Waldo Emerson; Helena Petrovna Blavatsky, founder of the Theosophical Society; Irving S. Cooper, Liberal Catholic Bishop for the United States; Nicholas Roerich, a Russian Theosophist and flimflam artist; the very, very eccentric Charles Roos, a "Native American Medicine Man" (actually of Finnish ancestry); L. Edward Johndro, an astrologer; and, William H. Dower, a Utopian physician.

Though he communicated most with the latter three, it would be a mistaken notion to assume they had the greatest influence on his spirituality. The influence of his family in these matters was made obvious by his 1930 joining of the Episcopal Church, where his sons sang in the choir. Overall, the eclectic nature of Henry's numerous spiritual influences is reflected in this 1948 back and forth with a reporter who asked if he was a Pantheist.

"What do you mean by Pantheism?" questioned Wallace.

"The belief that nature, science, and religion are as one," responded the reporter.

Grinning, Henry replied, "If that is Pantheism, I'm for it—you can put in some economics, too!"[2] (Dr. Carver would have been proud.)

¤ ¤ ¤

Whether or not one agrees with the characterization by some of his political opponents that Henry Wallace indulged in "spiritual window-shopping," it is fair to rhetorically ask, what did all his soul-searching come to? That would be a difficult question to answer by any means other than his own words.

As racist fascism was gestating across the European continent, Wallace authored *Statesmanship and Religion* which was published in 1934. In it he commented:

> No great religion, whether it be Christianity, Judaism, Hinduism, or Mohammedanism, can recognize ideals which set up a particular race or class as an object of religious worship. While admittedly there has been but little true Christianity in the world during the past five hundred years, yet it would seem that a follower of Christ least of all should recognize nationalism as the commander of his spiritual self. From the standpoint of true religion, it is

singularly unfortunate that so many faiths, churches and doctrines are confined by national boundaries and, therefore, take on national colorings. Any religion which recognizes above all the fatherhood of God and the brotherhood of man must of necessity have grave questionings concerning those national enterprises where the deepest spiritual fervor is evoked for purely nationalistic, race or class ends.[3]

There can be little doubt that these attitudes likely had their origins in one of his earliest friendships. While serving as Secretary of Agriculture, Wallace shared these thoughts, "Such botanists as Carver are exceedingly rare, but today they are increasingly important because the day fast approaches when the spirit of man must go out into understanding living things with as much fervor as it has gone forth into the understanding of steel, cement, machine tools, oil, gas, roads and airplanes. The ability to understand life in all its varied manifestations is the supreme criterion of man."[4]

This theme resonated in the halls of the Department of Agriculture during his early, exciting, frustrating, and heady days as Secretary. As the economic and meteorological crisis worsened and was quite literally starving America, Henry A. Wallace articulated a vision that embodied a new direction for agricultural economics, which was liberally sprinkled with spirituality. One day while denying the request of an attorney lobbying for some specific regulatory language, Secretary Wallace leaned forward across the table and in a kind but firm voice said, "No. Unless we learn to treat each other fairly this country is going to smash." When this story got around the Department one of the Public Information Officers, Paul Porter, who went on to serve as Chairman of the Federal Communications Commission during the closing days of World War II, commented, "I never saw anything like it. Don't it beat hell? He's a Christian!"[5] The irony of Mr. Porter's observation is that in 1933, Henry Wallace was at a point in his spiritual journey when he likely would not have called himself Christian.

In a speech to the World Fellowship of Faiths Conference in Chicago the Secretary observed, "Religion comes first and from it springs the arts, the sciences, the inventions, the divisions of wealth, and the attitudes between classes and toward other nations. The millennium is not yet here although the makings of it are clearly in our hands."[6]

One has to wonder if he may have been remembering the cooperative irrigation systems he found in western communities during his 1909 tour of the American West, when he made these comments to the Federal Council of Churches, "The world is one world. When cooperation becomes a living reality in the spiritual sense of the term, when we have defined certain broad objectives which we all want to attain, when we can feel the significance of the forces at work not merely in our own lives, not merely in our own class, not merely in our own nation, but in the world as a whole—then the vision of Isaiah and the insight of Christ will be on their way toward realization."[7]

As word of his "social gospel" spread through President Roosevelt's administration, Henry became known as the unofficial philosopher of the New Deal. He wore the metaphorical vestments of a man thus ordained when he returned to Des Moines in the Autumn of 1933. The Secretary spoke of a "new age of cooperation and generosity" to several thousand farmers congregated in the municipal Coliseum. The address was being broadcast on a local radio station and when he finished his prepared text a few moments early, he had to fill the dead air. He paused poignantly, stared intently into the audience and ad libbed, "Only the merest quarter-turn of the heart separates us from a material abundance beyond the fondest dream of anyone present. Selfishness has ceased to be the mainspring of progress. There is something more. There is a new social machinery in the making. Let us maintain sweet and kindly hearts toward each other, however great the difficulties ahead."[8]

¤ ¤ ¤

Sadly, even as Secretary Wallace spread the gospel of kindness into the yaw of the Great Depression, the Kwantung Army of the Empire of Japan had completed its occupation of Manchuria, and was settling in for a rape of that Chinese province which would last for another thirteen years. Meanwhile, on the European continent storm clouds were gathering as nations were pouring massive quantities of resource and wealth into their military industries.

Still, Secretary Wallace persisted in his 1934 book *New Frontiers*. In the three hundred page treatise, he tried to condense into broad strokes the objectives and philosophy of the New Deal. "What we approach is not a new continent but a new state of heart and mind resulting in new standards of accomplishment. We must invent, build and put to work new social machinery. This machinery will carry out the Sermon on the Mount as well as the present social machinery carries out and intensifies the law of the jungle."[9]

The oblique reference to social Darwinism may have been missed or misunderstood by the book's readers, but the reference to the Sermon on the Mount could not have been clearer in terms of his own life. His words were prolific. He authored twenty-one books, wrote hundreds of articles, and made thousands of speeches. The Henry Agard Wallace collection at the Library of Congress Manuscript Division contains 24,600 items. A lot of words—and his words mattered, but among the final words in the Sermon on the Mount, Jesus taught, "By their fruit ye shall know them."[10] And so it was with the spirituality of Henry Agard Wallace—to the very end of his life, his actions spoke even louder than his words.

PART III

THE HARVEST

21

Destiny's Appointment

*Borlaug's Great Depression adventures that shaped a man
who would feed the world.*

As a little collective, Norman Borlaug, Margaret Gibson, her brother
Bill, their friend Scott Pauly, and a few others, leveraged every possible
resource to cobble together the means to stay in school and get enough to
eat. 1935 was tough! Norm had returned to school that January with $35 in
his pockets. His tuition alone would gobble $25. The remaining $10 would
not buy the food and pay the rent for an entire semester. Norm wondered
how on earth he was going to be able to stay in school.

As if the situation were not already bad enough, the University Coffee
Shop, where they had been able to wait tables for a meager breakfast, had
gone broke and closed. In doing so, it was a local trope for the entire nation,
which had also gone broke and in many respects was also closed for business.
Masses of people were unemployed. They did not have money to buy goods
and services. Hence, businesses were not making enough money to offer
employment. Hence, more people became unemployed. It was an ugly cycle.

The anti-New Deal crowd clamored for tax breaks, rather than stimulus
spending through what they called "artificial make-work" programs. Main
street merchants were puzzled by the tax-break proposals. As the owner of
the coffee shop placed the "Out of Business" sign in the window, he scoffed
at the tax-break notions. Heck, he'd have loved to pay more taxes. Taxes
were derived from income. He did not have any of that.

As if ignoring the nay-sayers, the Federal Government stepped in to
prime the business pumps with cash. The Feds were only able, or willing,

to do so in ways consistent with the touted American work ethic. While Secretary of Agriculture Wallace was championing the radical ideas of agricultural production control and crop subsidies, Secretary of Interior Ickes was pushing employment in the Civilian Conservation Corps (CCC) upwards toward a half million men in 2600 different camps. Meanwhile, Eleanor Roosevelt's tenacious prodding of the New Deal power-brokers to do something about unemployed youth finally paid off. That 'something' was the National Youth Administration (NYA). Administratively attached to the Works Progress Administration (WPA), the NYA was headed by a prominent Alabama politico, Aubrey W. Williams. In this capacity, Williams mentored and became life-long friends with another politician who was tapped to head the Texas NYA program, Lyndon B. Johnson.

The NYA program provided on-the-job training in construction trades, metal and woodworking, office work, recreation, health care, and other occupations to 2.6 million adolescent girls and boys. It also created an on-campus work-study program that provided part-time employment opportunities for 2.1 million young men and women attending college. In most cases, the college work-study "wages" were paid as tuition credits. So, in essence, the program infused over $20 million per year directly into American Universities. Some of those Universities would likely have closed without this source of student support and cash.

Without the NYA support, Norman Borlaug would have had to pack his bags and go home in 1935. Instead, he stayed in school. He worked in the entomology department pinning up insect specimen on cork boards, cleaning up classes and labs, and running errands for professors. He earned about $2.25 a week, working fifteen hours. He was paid in 'chits' which were applied toward his tuition.

Many Congressional New Deal antagonists questioned why professors could not "run their own damned errands," or why students and faculty could not clean up after themselves? Why did the Federal Government need to pay another student to do those tasks? Wasn't this program just a big waste of taxpayer money?

Fifteen years later, hundreds of thousands of heretofore hungry citizens of Mexico would, as a result of Dr. Borlaug's efforts, have abundant food for the first time in their lives. They would likely not agree that the $2.25/week paid by the NYA for college student tuition had been a waste of taxpayer money.

¤ ¤ ¤

In 1936 Margaret suspended her studies, as her brother Bill had arranged for her to work as an assistant proofreader for the University of Minnesota Alumni Magazine. She explained her decision, "I was just sick of going to bed hungry."[1] Norm took a different NYA work-study job at the Department of Veterinary Medicine. He cleaned cages and fed animals. It paid his tuition.

That summer Norm secured a job with the Civilian Conservation Corps. There being no word processing or copy-and-paste technology, Margaret typed fifty-five separate letters of application on his behalf. They received just one response. Norm was offered $100 per month by the Northeastern Forest Experiment Station near New Haven, Connecticut. With not a second thought, he was off like a hungry greyhound the day after his last class.

¤ ¤ ¤

In the 1870's Amos Lawrence Hopkins, as owner of the Wabash Line, made a fortune in the railroad business. In 1887 he purchased Buxton Farms outside of Williamstown, Massachusetts. His brother soon purchased several adjoining pieces of property.

Twenty-one years after Mr. Hopkin's death, his widow sent this letter to Harry A. Garfield, the president of Williams College.

> 22 November 1933
> My dear Dr. Garfield,
>
> As you know, I am no longer able to come to W'mstown, but it is my old home and greatly loved by both my husband and myself. As a memorial to him, a graduate of the college, I want to give to Williams College our place, 'Buxton Farms.' It is free from debt and other incumbrances ‹sic›,and I feel it would be a valuable piece of property.[2]

This donation gave birth to the Hopkins Memorial Forest, straddling the confluence of Massachusetts, Vermont, and New York. It has been used primarily for research by the National Forest Service and Williams College Environmental Studies ever since.

In the summer of 1936 the twenty-two year-old Norman Borlaug was put in charge of a small crew of CCC recruits, who were charged with surveying, mapping, and inventorying the flora on the four-square-mile historic Hopkins Estate. It was a great job and a great summer for a crew of twenty-somethings in the heart of the Berkshire Hills.

Norm was offered a six month job extension, which he could ill afford to turn down. So, he sat out the fall semester of 1936, but in December he returned to the University of Minnesota with some big money in his wallet—$600!

¤ ¤ ¤

In 1937 Scott Pauly, Margaret Gibson and Norm were much like the rest of the country. They were taking the first tentative steps out of the Great Depression's grip of poverty. Norm and Scott still served meals at the sorority. They were not wealthy enough to turn down the free food, but things were definitely looking up. Norm wrestled for the U of M team, which was now coming into national prominence. He continued to do well in his forestry coursework.

Norm and Scott were actually offered summer jobs working with the U.S. Forest Service. After their final exams, they loaded Scott's car with the essentials and headed west. Scott was assigned to Montana Flathead National Forest, and Norm was to report some 230 miles south, at Big Creek Ranger Station in Idaho.

When Norm was growing up on the farm there were many days that he spent working in the fields alone, or rather with only a draft horse for company. But during those long sun-up to sundown days, he knew each evening he would retire into the kindly embrace of his close-knit family. When he arrived at the Big Creek Ranger Station he was given two weeks of boot-camp style training. He was taught fire fighting techniques, phone line maintenance, and radio operations. Then he was deployed.

He and a professional packer set out on two horses, leading three pack-mules loaded with Norm's provisions, into the Idaho wilderness. Two days and forty-five miles later they arrived at the Cold Mountain Lookout station. The next day the packer returned to Big Creek. Unlike those days following the plow horse, Norm was **alone**.

Norm's job was to mend the phone lines and watch for fires from a seven foot by seven foot box, made of wood and tin, sitting astride a seventy-two foot high aluminum structure. Access to the lookout was via a zig zag ladder intertwined through the structures long aluminum legs. He was responsible for spotting, and being the first responder, to any fires that broke out across the immense Chamberlain Basin. He learned in his training that first responder meant he would likely have to fight any fire alone for up to two days. Being several years before the first person was crazy enough to parachute into a forest fire situation, all reinforcements would arrive on horseback.

The first few weeks were spent repairing the winter damaged phone lines. The mountains were still wet from the annual twelve plus feet of snow that melted slowly and fed the giant Salmon River. Consequently, there was no significant fire danger and little need to spend time in the tower. When the phone was operational, at least he had daily contact with the ranger station. He also bent the rules a bit, the phone was for emergency use only, and had frequent conversations with a prospector who lived in a cabin on the far side of the basin. The Forest Service had put a phone line in to Charles "Matty" Mahan's cabin, as he was a reliable fire scout and ideally located for that purpose.

When fire season arrived, Norm spent many hours looking through the sites of the Osborne Firefinder, which was installed in the lookout tower. One afternoon dry thunderstorms raked Chamberlain Basin striking eighteen smokes. Norm would spot the fire and call in the location of each plume of smoke. Much to everyone's relief, they did not flare and the frenzied deployment of fire crews was not necessary.

However, on September 20th, Norm's last day at the lookout, a fire blazed. Using the Firefinder, Norm sited its exact coordinates, called that information in to the Big Creek Ranger Station, and took off on foot to do battle. Late in the day, as exhaustion was taking hold, he was joined by a full-time Forest Ranger from another lookout station, who arrived on horse. After several more hours of work, they managed a marginal containment. Then at about 7:00pm the Ranger, realizing it was Norm's last day on the job, sent him on his way. The night offered a full moon, which one might think was lucky, but perhaps it was not. After fighting the fire all day, Norm hiked all night long by the light of the moon. At 9:00 am, fourteen hours after leaving his comrade at the fire site, he dragged into the Ranger Station, exhausted to the very edge of physical collapse.

That summer, Norm learned a level of personal responsibility, self-sufficiency, and loneliness that few people encounter in a lifetime. He was twenty-three years old.

¤ ¤ ¤

Before Norm and Scott headed back across the northern tier toward Minnesota, Norm was stunned by a conversation with the Forest Superintendent, Hank Shank, "You will be finishing your degree work in December, right?"

"Yes sir, I kind of took the scenic route, but I had to lay out a few times to earn some money," replied Norm. He did not bother to mention his streptococcal induced brush with death.

"Well son, your timing is actually impeccable. A Junior Forester position will be opening up here next January, and it's yours if you want it."

Norm did not ride home in Scott Pauly's old Dodge—he flew on cloud nine.

This time Norm was certain. He knew what he was going to do with his life. The next January he was moving to Idaho to work for the U.S. Forest Service. His future was secure. When Scott and Norm arrived in Minneapolis, without taking time to unpack, Norm walked to Margaret's office at the Independent Press. He asked her to marry him. The next Friday, they did just that.

¤ ¤ ¤

By the time Norm was in his final semester he had become increasingly interested in forest pathology. He had read a good deal about Pine Blister Rust and Fusiform Rust. He had a good deal of hands-on opportunities to study Pine-Oak Gall Rust, which is indigenous to Minnesota's White Pine, Norway Pine, Austrian Pine, Scots Pine, and Jack Pine trees. The Cronartium quercuum, the fungus that causes Gall Rust, also attacks the oak trees of Minnesota as an alternate host. Spread by wind carried spores, it can sicken whole stands of trees and actually kill swaths of Jack Pine.

With just weeks to go before his graduation and departure to Idaho, Norm noticed that the Dean of the Plant Pathology Department, and one of the university's most authoritative figures, Dr. Elvin Charles Stakman, was offering a public lecture on "The Little Enemies that Destroy Our Crops."[3] The Borlaug family was still raising wheat down in Little Norway. Thinking that perhaps just as he had learned about chemical fertilizers during his high school years he might learn something about wheat rust that would help the folks back on the farm. He decided to attend the lecture. Besides, maybe he could pick up some information that would be applicable to his concerns about tree rusts.

The lecture at Northrop Auditorium was so compelling that it became one of those seminal events in Norm's life and career, though he did not know it at the time. He came home and enthusiastically told his bride about the fascinating Dr. Stakman and his lecture. He even waxed wistful about a desire to study with the man, but alas, he knew for sure that in less than a month they would be driving west toward their future lives in the forests of the northern Rocky Mountains.

Well, not quite—the economy's goblins were not yet entirely ready to release their choke hold on the nation. Contrary to present day stories told by revisionist history writers, the New Deal had actually worked extraordinarily well in the four years from 1933 through 1936. All of the main economic indicators had regained the levels of the late 1920s, except for unemployment which remained unacceptably high at fourteen percent. Even at that, one must remember that unemployment topped twenty-five percent on the day of Franklin Roosevelt's inauguration in 1933. The Gross National Product (GNP) was estimated at slightly over $100 billion in 1929. During Hoover's administration it shrank by almost fifty percent to just over $56 billion. Starting in 1933, it began to claw its way out of the gulf, adding almost $9 billion in new production each year. In 1937 the GNP had returned all the way back to $92 billion. Likewise, the stock market had gone a long way toward full recovery. In 1929 the Dow Jones Industrial average daily closing was pegged at 248.48. During the next four years stocks lost over seventy-five percent of their value. In 1932 the average closing value was 59.93. During the New Deal's first four years, the Dow added about thirty points to its average daily closing per year, and in 1936 it had reached 179.90. Even though unemployment figures remained high, total employment had rebounded dramatically. In 1928 approximately 31,300,000 Americans were employed. That shrank to 23,700,000 in 1932, but had recovered to 30,100,000 in 1937.

Then, the economy decided to act just like a bad dream. The nation had almost woken up in 1937, but not quite enough to shake the nightmare. In 1938 the Gross Domestic Product fell by 6.3%. Unemployment jumped from 14.3% to 19.1%. Manufacturing output fell by forty percent.

With all of this negative economic news, the Federal Government budget shrank from $9.2 billion to $8.4 billion. One of the federal departments that took a big budget hit in 1938 was the National Forest Service. Late one afternoon in the first week of January 1938, Margaret walked into their little one room apartment and found Norm sitting staring at a letter with a glum face and a lump in his throat. Due to budget constraints the Junior Forester position had been cut, and by necessity, the job offer was rescinded. The letter hit Norm like a kick in the gut. He felt, through no fault of their own, fate had conspired to throw the young couple all the way back to 1933, when he and Margaret met waiting tables at the University Coffee Shop for one cup of coffee, two pieces of toast, and five prunes.

Margaret sat on the arm of the chair, put her arms around Norm's neck, rested her head on top of his, and reassured him that things were not nearly that bad, not now—not ever again. She had a good job. They had an apartment they could afford and enough money to buy the food they needed. "What about going to see that fascinating professor who gave the lecture on wheat rust—I've forgotten his name?"

"Dr. Stakman, but I don't think he has any strings to pull with the Forest Service," Norm replied glumly.

"No silly, I mean to see about studying with him. You said that would be of great interest."

Now with a bit more vigor, "Well, maybe I could do that."

Within the week, Norm had made an appointment to meet with the fifty-three year old Dr. Stakman, who encouraged Norm to continue his study of pathology, but to broaden beyond forestry. Too much specialization would not be a good career move in the still tremulous economy. Obviously, the letter from the Forest Service validated Dr. Stakman's point. The professor arranged a graduate assistantship for Norm, working in the University of Minnesota plant pathology laboratory.

In that lab they studied slides of rust spores that had been gathered from locations strewn all the way from Mexico to Canada. Under those microscope lenses, they identified species and calculated the exact date each specimen had arrived at each location across the continent. Painstakingly, they mapped the annual migrations of the microbial crop destroying enemies.

Importantly, the modest wage Dr. Stakman arranged for Norm's labors salvaged his battered self-esteem. This was 1938—the man of the house was expected to be the family bread-winner, after all. More important still,

Norm pursued studies that would eventually lead to his Doctorate degree in 1942. Most important of all, a bond between this mentor and his young protégé was forged that would last forty-one years, change the science of food production, and the history of humanity—forever.

¤ ¤ ¤

The weather had raged insolently across North America for most of a decade. In September 1938, meteorology threw one more temper tantrum, as if to give Americans one last lesson in humility before the decade's end. On September 4, 1938 a tropical depression formed over the Cape Verde Islands in the eastern Atlantic. It rode the Tropic of Cancer wind currents westward across the warm ocean waters, gathering strength all along the way. On September 20th, sparing the Bahamas its brunt, the storm turned almost due north having strengthened to a Category 5 hurricane over the preceding sixteen days and 2500 miles.

The eye of the storm screamed northward at an extraordinary sixty-plus miles per hour. In the late afternoon of September 21, 1938, the hurricane slammed into New England with 120 mile per hour sustained winds. The storm surge pushed a twenty foot high wall of water up Narragansett Bay, completely inundating Providence, Rhode Island, which lays some thirty miles inland from Rhode Island Sound. Within a matter of hours, the storm killed over seven hundred people and injured thousands more. Nine thousand homes and twenty-six thousand automobiles were totally destroyed. Sixty-three thousand people were left homeless, with no means to escape the devastation. Rainfall ranged from ten to seventeen inches across the Connecticut River Valley. The liquefied soil, coupled with wind speeds approaching one hundred miles per hour many miles inland, resulted in the leveling of approximately 2 billion trees. A swath of flattened timber stretched three hundred miles long and one hundred miles wide from Long Island Sound to Maine.

Power lines lay on the ground and roads were impassable for months. In typical New Deal fashion, the federal government funded a huge relief effort to help New England dig out. The Feds created the Northeast Timber Salvage Administration (NTSA) and attached the program to the U.S. Department of Agriculture. They began immediately clearing the roads and trying to get the power grid back on-line. The NTSA set up 275 sawmills across the region, and by the summer of 1939 had salvaged 600 million board feet of lumber. That sounds like a whole heck of a lot of wood, but an estimated 1.65 billion board feet remained laying on the ground.

As Secretary of Agriculture, Henry Wallace knew that dumping that much timber on the market would bankrupt the entire lumber industry. He well remembered the lessons of the agricultural markets in the 1920s. The questioned remained, however, what could they do with all that wood? It had been an exceptionally dry winter and spring since the hurricane had hit. The debris field, which included thousands of square miles of forest, was one lightening strike or careless match away from an unimaginable conflagration.

The decision was made to deploy the Civilian Conservation Corps (CCC) and the Works Progress Administration (WPA) on an enormous clean-up operation. They would cut the slash from the down trees, and then sink the massive timbers in area lakes and ponds for salvage and use at a later date. (*During World War II the United States military required enormous quantities of lumber for barracks and packing crates. 631 million board feet of lumber was retrieved from the lakes and ponds of New England for the war effort.*)

The clean-up effort required leadership from foresters with fire fighting experience. So it was in June of 1939, Norm received a letter from Washington, DC. It was not a draft notice, but it may as well have been. There was no mistaking the letter's urgency, and his nation was calling Norm to action. The U.S. Forest Service needed him to report to their office in Gardener, Massachusetts, for a six month duty stint. They needed experienced foresters to train the young men with the CCC and WPA in the art and science of fire fighting.

Recognizing it as a call to national service, Norm took the letter to Dr. Stakman, who quite reluctantly agreed that even though the Forest Service could not mandate his participation, the only honorable choice was to report to duty. So, just as he had three years earlier, Norm set out to hitchhike from Minnesota to New England. This time, however, it would not be the idyllic interlude he had relished, surveying the Hopkins Estate in the Berkshires during that summer of 1936.

Within four days, Norm found himself thumbing a ride just outside of East Hartford, Connecticut. A kind of beat up 1927 Buick Standard Six pulled up to offer a lift.

"Where you headed?

"I'm on my way to Gardner—gonna work for the Forest Service for a while."

"Well, I can get you as far as Worcester, that's a bit more than half way."

Norm chuckled, "I've been thumbing all the way from Minneapolis— Worcester is a good deal more than half way for me."

"Yep, I suppose it sure is," replied the affable looking young man, a few years younger than Norm.

As he climbed into the car, "My name is Norman, but everyone except my professors call me Norm."

"I'm Edward, and everyone, *including* my professors call me Ed."

They did not talk much for a while, but as the car rolled on and the hours rolled by, the conversation just evolved. Norm asked a lot of questions about the storm and the destruction he was going to encounter in northern Massachusetts. Edward offered only cryptic responses. He was courteous, but a quiet sort of guy.

Ed was studying for his master's degree in math at Harvard. Norm shared that he was likewise doing graduate work, albeit in a quite different field of study. Actually, plant pathology interested Ed a good deal, and he asked several questions about plant diseases and rust. He seemed particularly interested in knowing about the impact of different kinds of weather on plant resistance to the various pathogens.

When they arrived in Worcester, Ed's route led east into Boston, and Norm's was due north to Gardener. They shook hands, Norm thanked Ed for the lift, and they wished each other well. When these two young men parted ways on that afternoon in 1939, not even knowing each other's last names, neither Ed Lorenz nor Norman Borlaug realized that though they were on very divergent courses in life, they would both change some of humanity's most fundamental perceptions of the world.

¤ ¤ ¤

For Norm it was a tough, hot summer at Camp DA-13, near Ashburnham, Massachusetts. There he trained young CCC enlistees in fire fighting techniques. Their efforts also included clearing the tangled masses of trees, branches and roots, which served to exacerbate the likelihood that they would need to bring their newly acquired fire fighting skills to bear. Sure enough, just as in the previous summer in the Idaho wilderness, a wild fire broke out on Norm's last day of work. Unlike the previous summer, the fire situation on the Massachusetts-New Hampshire state line was much more explosive. However, this time Norm had a crew that was ready to do battle.

Training for any kind of combat is one thing, actual engagement is quite another. Like any rookies, Norm's firefighters were shaky at first, but they realized that thousands of acres and perhaps thousands of lives were at stake. After the initial shock, they "sucked it up" and beat back the blazes. After almost twenty-four straight hours of doing battle, Norm reported to his boss, Dean Rowland, in Gardner, "Dean, I've had enough. You have a fire fighting crew and they proved yesterday they are good to go—and speaking of going, it is time for me to get on home to Margaret and back to school." Rowland was almost effusive with his appreciation as he bid Norman a reluctant farewell.

22

MR. SECRETARY

The political metamorphosis of Secretary Wallace.

Henry Wallace and Rexford Tugwell came to realize that compartmentalization of the challenges facing the nation's agricultural needs would likely not lead to success. As was his nature, Henry Wallace rose to the challenge with a flurry of hyperactivity that brought forward wide ranging proposals, creating a tapestry of programs addressing the complexities of feeding the nation's hungry, sustainable farm income, grazing rights on public lands, agricultural research and biodiversity. It was the most astonishing array of progressive action ever implemented in the history of human governance. The results were then and still today widely supported by farmers and agricultural communities throughout the country.

The Secretary was a whirlwind of activity that metaphorically challenged the storms raking the top soil off the high plains of the Midwest. No matter where one lived in 1934, Henry Wallace would soon be at the doorstep. He visited all forty-eight states traveling over 40 thousand miles by planes, trains, and automobiles. He delivered eighty-eight speeches on topics ranging from the benefits of "societal cooperation," to the need for "fire and vigor" in our spiritual lives, to the evils of what he termed the "tyranny of greed." He wrote twenty articles for magazines and professional journals and published two books.

His book *Statesmanship and Religion* was essentially a compilation of lectures he had delivered at the Chicago Theological Seminary. It embodied the notion of thoughtful and realistic idealism. In the first paragraph of the Preface, Wallace set the book's tone:

For the past few years we have been going through an economic and social crisis probably as severe as any that our civilization has ever had to face. It has come as a result, in large part, of our failure to learn how to live with abundance. We have conquered great physical obstacles and have taken possession of vast natural resources; we have the manpower, the machine-power, and the technique to convert these resources into a much higher standard of living; yet here we are bogged down for lack of a social machine that will help us distribute, fairly, the fruits of our labor.

—Henry Agard Wallace[1]

He also published a book that in many respects served as the New Deal manifesto and the blue print for another Democrat's administration some thirty years later—John F. Kennedy. The book was titled *New Frontiers*. He dictated the 83 thousand word first draft in just three months. More utile than spiritual, it was no less idealistic than *Statesmanship and Religion*.

In *New Frontiers* Wallace made the case that the United States government's ten year objective should be, "To manage the tariff, and the money system, to control railroad interest rates; and to encourage price and production policies that will maintain a continually balanced relationship between the income of agriculture, labor, and industry." To those who want to keep government out of business he commented, "The hard facts are that for years government has been in business, and business in government, to a point where it is impossible to untangle the mess." In recognizing "the paradox of want amid plenty," Wallace envisioned that business and government will both have to catch up to a new economics, in which unbridled competition would be relegated to pages of history texts. On this point Wallace did not equivocate in stating his belief that society will "recognize competitive individualists and competitive nations and deal with them, as the anachronisms they are, treating them kindly, firmly, and carefully."[2]

The Secretary's old nemesis, Herbert Hoover, also published a book in 1934. One would think *The Challenge to Liberty* was written in direct response to Wallace's *New Frontiers*. However, Hoover had not even seen Wallace's book while writing his own. The books were published within days of each other in the summer of 1934. It almost goes without saying that they espoused two visions that could not have been further apart. In his defense of "rugged individualism" and his attack on the direction and programs of the New Deal, Hoover states, "Those amateur sociologists who are misleading this nation by ignoring the biological foundations of human action are as far from common sense as an engineer who ignores physics in bridge building. . . . For at least the next several generations we dare not wholly abandon self-interest as a component of motive forces to initiative, to enterprise, to leadership."[3] From his point of view, Darwinian "survival of the fittest" not only had a place in the nation's economic schema, it was a revered place.

Even with two books in one year, Wallace's most influential work may well have been a pamphlet. "America Must Choose" articulated, in just twenty-six pages, the historical background and dynamics of the new international trade paradigms imposed by the worldwide economic depression. For Henry Wallace it was an uncharacteristically neutral exposition—a scholarly treatise, detailing the pros and cons of possible courses of action and the absolute peril of having no plan at all. In the Forward the President of the Foreign Policy Association, Raymond Leslie Buell, and the director of the World Peace Foundation, Raymond Thomas Rich, characterized the pamphlet thus:

> When the Foreign Policy Association and the World Peace Foundation asked the Secretary of Agriculture to put into writing his views on world relations, they expected something unusual, but not anything as stirring as this pamphlet.
> Secretary Wallace presents a vivid picture of the dilemma in which America now finds itself. We are confronted, he shows, by two possible extremes: We can restore international economic cooperation in order to find an outlet for our productive facilities, or we can turn our backs on the rest of the world and bend every effort to establish and maintain a tightly protected, self-sufficient nation.

The pamphlet rather timorously articulates Wallace's idealism, tempered by international economic and political reality:

> My own bias is international. It is an inborn attitude with me. I have very deeply the feeling that nations should be naturally friendly to each other and express that friendship in international

trade. At the same time we must recognize as realities that the world at the moment is ablaze with nationalist feeling, and that with our own tariff impediments it is highly unlikely that we shall move in an international direction very fast in the next few years. Therefore, we must push with the greatest vigor possible our retreat from surplus acres, and seek to arouse the intellectual stamina necessary to meet and triumph over unpopular facts.

The middle path between economic internationalism and nationalism is the path we shall probably take in the end. We need not go the whole way on a program involving an increase of a billion dollars a year in imports. There are intermediate points between internationalism and nationalism, and I do not think we can say just where we are headed yet. We shall be under increasing difficulties, no matter which way we tend, as our people become more and more familiar with the discomforts of the procedure.[4]

As Wallace's activity level reached fever pitch, and his scholarly credentials grew, his eccentricities became more widely known and were either loved or loathed; a source of fascination and exasperation among allies and enemies alike. In general, the press loved them. The normally dull Department of Agriculture beat became a source of journalistic inspiration. Reporters wrote about his youth, energy and a certain depth of presence that proved difficult to articulate:

- "He does not look his age."
- "He is a wiry young man with wiry reddish-brown hair that bristles in all directions from the part on the left side of his long head."
- "Despite a pleasant, natural and infectious smile, seriousness is the order of his tanned face."
- "In his gray-blue eyes a serious purpose seemed to have won only a slight victory over a quick understanding that is the mother of his humor."
- "There is a deep pathos in his face, but he is strong, fond of simple living, fond of walking."[5]

Even more confounding and delightful to reporters were behaviors that fell outside the expected norms. They wrote:

- ¤ "He cares so little for things of this world that he refuses to ride in the luxurious limousine provided for him by the government."
- ¤ "In Chicago recently he horrified his companion by insisting on walking from the hotel to the station, about half a mile distant. He carried his heavy suitcase and when his companion could no longer stagger under his, Wallace carried that, too."
- ¤ "Probably no other cabinet officer in this or any other administration would stop along a highway in the shade of a farmer's grove and revel in a choice of lunch of cheese, watermelon, tomato juice, popcorn and crackers. Imagine the consternation of the grocery boy in Sac City. 'Give me two pounds of cheese,' said the mild mannered cabinet member, who personally supervised purchase of a picnic lunch. The lad reeled off eight or nine varieties of cheese. 'Nothing fancy; just give me some ordinary rat cheese,' the customer replied."[5]

In combination, his outward appearance and behaviors painted a puzzling picture of his personality that seemed to many just a bit too baffling to grasp, though reporters tried, their observations ranged wildly:

- ¤ "a gloomy economist."
- ¤ "a clean toothed, smiling optimist."
- ¤ "a man of scientific curiosity and exactitude of mind."
- ¤ "essentially a mystic and a moralist."
- ¤ "a fluent easy speaker."
- ¤ "a man with no taste for speaking."
- ¤ "He is shy and modest by nature and he has been observed to resemble a schoolboy waiting for his turn to speak a piece."
- ¤ "He customarily either sits with his eyes half closed and stares into space or else fidgets and ruffles his tawny mane."
- ¤ "a self confident man, in his quiet way."[5]

Those who knew Wallace best understood him only slightly better than reporters. His long time friend and aide, Russell Lord, observed the conundrum that the journalistic portraits seldom seemed to jibe. "They wrote that he was simple, but exceedingly complex; that he wavered between ardor for the utmost advance of an independent civilization, with an abundance of material goods and gimcracks for everyone, and the simple desire to lie on green grass under trees and be let alone."[6]

As elusive as his personality seemed to be, there can be little doubt that it was what it was, whether reporters were present or not. On one of his trips "home" to Iowa his train had a layover in Chicago. Always the restless mind, the Vice President walked alone to a Chicago Public Library and began browsing. The head of the library's reference room recognized the famous visitor. He introduced Wallace to a book called *The American Faith*. Ernest Sutherland Bates had finished this last and perhaps his most important work less than an hour before he died in December 1939. Mr. Bates described the premise of his book: "Democracy did not arise out of 18th Century political and industrial conflicts, as a momentarily popular view misconceives. Its roots are to be found in the attempted revival of primitive Christianity by the radical lower-class sects of the Protestant Reformation..."[7]

The librarian, Mr. Hewitt, later said of his visit with the Vice President of the United States, "I liked the way he came in—as a citizen, without any show. He was very easy to talk to and very kind."[8]

On another occasion Wallace was walking across the lobby of the Mayflower Hotel. This time he had a small entourage in tow. A photographer who had just checked out of the hotel was staggering under the weight and awkward bulk of his gear. The Vice President approached and unassumingly asked, "May I help?" But without waiting for a response, he grabbed the largest black box, carried it to the street, shook the photographer's hand, then without a word turned and walked away down the street.

Whatever he was, at some level Wallace's president seemed to understand and appreciate him. Roosevelt said, "There is something satisfying about a man who can, without a hint of self-consciousness, go on national radio and praise 'the strength and quietness of grass'." The President found something simple, yet profound and touching, about the Easter gift he received from Wallace—a small box of seed corn with hand written instructions about how it should be planted in the soil of Hyde Park, New York.[9]

While there are a lot of smart people, indeed, there are a lot of very smart people in the world, what separates merely smart from the truly prodigious is energy. Before being stricken by amyotrophic lateral sclerosis late in life, Wallace only once found himself bedridden. On that occasion, he caught a bad cold after spending several hours pushing cars out of a mud hole during a 30° snow storm, which he and his young family encountered while returning from a Thanksgiving day visit with his wife Ilo's folks in Indianola, Iowa. His cold developed into a fever and tonsillitis and laid Wallace up for the better part of a week.

His creativity and energy set him apart from ordinary smart people, as well as his fellow cabinet members—"by their fruit ye shall know them." The fruit of his intellect and vitality while Secretary of Agriculture changed the role of the federal government, and the prosperity of the nation's farmers for generations to come. Even Secretary Wallace found it difficult to be succinct when writing about the complex array of the Agriculture Department's efforts.

> Not all of our advances have moved evenly together, without friction or duplication. Here in the Department of Agriculture we are doing all that we can now to make them move together for the good of the country as a whole.
> At the national level we have:
>
> 1. The Agricultural Adjustment Administration, which helps the farmer meet the costs of shifting from an exploitative system of agriculture to a conservation system.
> 2. The Soil Conservation Service, which provides technical assistance to farmers who need help in making physical adjustments in soil and crop management; and helps farmers with farm forestry and water facilities development; engages in submarginal land purchase and development.
> 3. The Farm Security Administration, which, through supervised loans, helps disadvantaged farmers solve problems of subsistence, insecurity of tenure, poor homes and inadequate farm management.
> 4. The Forest Service, which manages the national forests for conservation purposes, watershed protection, and public enjoyment; and offers guidance to private owners of forests.
> 5. The Taylor Grazing Administration, which governs grazing on the public grasslands.

6. The Bureau of Biological Survey, which establishes refuges for wildlife.

7. Research bureaus and a body of knowledge to provide the basis for intelligent action.

During the same period our efforts at the state level have included:

1. An awakened interest in conservation and the need for readjustment in land use that has resulted in:
    a. Passage of soil conservation district laws in 36 states. (173 districts have been set up in 25 states; Department is now cooperating with 146 districts according to terms outlined in memoranda of understanding, 108 million acres in districts.)
    b. Rural zoning laws in an ever-growing number of states.
    c. Revision of tax laws to provide incentives to wiser use of land.
    d. Revision of water laws to bring use of water into conformity with wise use of land.
    e. A law in one or two states defining tenant and landlord rights.
    f. Laws authorizing formation of grazing associations under state charters.
2. State colleges of agriculture with a developing conservation philosophy.
3. Agricultural extension services reaching into practically every agricultural county in the United States.
4. State Agricultural and Forestry Departments.

—Secretary Henry Agard Wallace[10]

¤ ¤ ¤

Wallace first shared thoughts about the "ever-normal granary" in a 1918 editorial published in *Wallaces' Farmer*. He had espoused the ethical and economic value of the 2 thousand year-old Confucian principal ever since. It appealed to both the spiritual mystic and the pragmatic farmer that coexisted in the person of Henry Wallace.

He borrowed the idea from the 1911 Columbia University doctoral thesis of Chen Huan Chang. The two volume work titled *The Economic Principles of Confucius and His School* described how China's first ever-normal granary had been established by a provincial statesman in 54 B.C. Chen wrote, "All provinces . . . should establish granaries. When the price of grain was low, they should buy it at the normal price, higher than the market price, in order to profit the farmers. When the price was high, they should sell it at the normal price, lower than the market price, in order to profit the consumers."[11] The story goes that the results were so favorable the emperor bestowed the title of "Marquis" upon the man who originated and implemented the win-win idea.

Over the years Henry revisited the ever-normal granary idea on the pages of *Wallaces' Farmer*:

- ¤ "If any government shall ever do anything really worthwhile with our food problem it will be by perfecting the plan tried by the Chinese three thousand years ago; that is, by building warehouses and storing food in years of abundance, and holding it until years of scarcity."(December 16, 1918);

- ¤ "Its principle had in it more of statesmanship than can be found in the vast majority of plans suggested for the relief of American agriculture." (October 6, 1926);

- ¤ "Some day the 'ever-normal granary' idea will be made to fit modern conditions." (January 21, 1927)[12]

While the Agricultural Adjustment Act of 1933 had taken steps toward embracing the Confucian granary management notion, it had primarily been directed at managing and disposing of agricultural surplus. In this regard it was quite successful. However, the disastrous drought and dust bowl across the middle of the nation demonstrated that managing shortages was a more compelling and complex matter. Therefore, once again, Henry pitched the ever-normal granary idea. In a radio address on June 6, 1934, he pointed out its effective application in China and urged the adoption of something similar here. Always prolific, over the next four years he wrote and spoke on this subject often.

Finally in 1938, through a process of assimilation and compromise, Congress cobbled together and passed the Agricultural Adjustment Act that included the fundamental framework for establishing this nation's "ever-normal granary" system. While it was far from a perfect piece of legislation, Secretary Wallace spun the achievement, "It tries in practical ways to bring balanced abundance to the people."[13]

Following the President's bill signing ceremony, Henry commented on a 1938 radio address, "We need a practical method to maintain balance, because that is the only way to have and to keep real abundance. That way is to use our surpluses to balance our shortages. This is the purpose of the Ever-Normal Granary plan of the new act."[14]

He looked upon the implementation of the "ever normal granary," under the auspices of the Agricultural Adjustment Act of 1938, as "the action of which I was most proud as Secretary of Agriculture."[15] And why not, for Henry it had been a long time coming. As since applied by American agriculture, the ever-normal granary consists of numerous activities intended to maintain an even balance in the production and prices of agricultural commodities. Several aspects of America's system, such as measures for soil conservation and the voluntary reduction of surplus crops, did not exist in Chang's description of the economic principals of Confucius. However, the basic Chinese idea of storing up surpluses from good years for use in bad has been applied under the auspices of the American system of commodity storage loans. Through this program the government loans money to farmers who, in years of overproduction, agree to keep a part of their crops in storage until a stronger demand develops. Another aspect of the Chinese program is evidenced in the American program for government crop insurance. Wheat, cotton, and flax farmers pay insurance premiums to the government. The premiums may be paid in kind or in cash. In turn, the government indemnifies the participating farmers in cases of catastrophic crop failure.

As World War II approached it was observed that the ever-normal granary provided the nation "with more security than a whole flotilla of battleships." It did then, and it still does today.

¤ ¤ ¤

By the late 1930s the communist scare was waning. Not because communism was any less threatening, but primarily because humans can only handle a limited number of monsters in the psyche closet at any one time. Racist imperialism had a choke hold across the ocean on the left. Fascism was rolling like a tumbleweed over the continent across the ocean on the right, seeding insanity and hatred in its path. In the middle, the atmospheric envelope shrouding North America was expressing Mother Nature's wrath. Humans, with shortsighted avarice, had disregarded her ancient balance— and she was angry! Winds choked people to death in the heartland and drowned people from the Florida coast all the way north to Rhode Island.

One such drowning came on Labor Day 1935. With sustained winds approaching 185 miles per hour, gusts in excess of 200, and barometric pressure all the way down to 892 millibars, which was the lowest barometric pressure ever recorded at that time. The category 5 hurricane smashed into the Florida Keys, releasing thousands of times more energy than the first splitting of the atom at the Trinity site near Alamogordo, New Mexico almost exactly ten years later. Living at the Works Progress Administration (WPA) camp on Islamorada, 718 World War I veterans were working on a extraordinary engineering project that would string together bridge spans the length of the entire Florida Keys. When finally completed, this stretch of elevated roadworks would be the furthest south reaches of U.S. Highway 1.

By 10:00pm on September 2, 1935 winds blasted the camp with granules of sand that quite literally stripped the flesh off the men's faces. Then the storm surge raked an eighteen foot high wall of water across the island. Along with 164 local residents, 259 veterans perished. Most of them had been among the Bonus Army that had been so ignominiously routed from their nation's capitol two years and eleven months prior. Only ninety of the veterans bodies were ever identified. For the others, their final indignity was mass cremation. Their ashen remains are now buried in the crypt in front of The Florida Keys Memorial honoring their service on Upper Matecumbe Key with these words engraved on a bronze plaque:

Dedicated to the memory of the civilians and war veterans whose lives were lost in the hurricane of September second 1935.

¤ ¤ ¤

In those chaotic times, marked by war, hunger, and mother nature seemingly gone mad, many found great comfort in a man who quietly but passionately spoke of fairness and kindness and peace and "the strength and quietness of grass." Henry Wallace's star was ascending. In his syndicated column "We the People" John Franklin Carter wrote, "He is as earthy as the black loam of the corn belt, as gaunt and grim as a pioneer. With all of that, he has an insatiable curiosity and one of the keenest minds in Washington, well disciplined and subtle, with interests and accomplishments which range from agrarian genetics to astronomy. . . . If the young men and women of this country look to the west for a liberal candidate for the Presidency, as they may in 1940, they will not be able to overlook Henry Wallace."[17]

Carter's prognostication was close, but no cigars.

23

Eniqmas of Opulence

Henry Ford, Mohandas Gandhi, Eleanor Roosevelt—not as remembered.

Enigma #1:

Henry Ford is best known for being perhaps the most remarkably successful entrepreneur of the Industrial Revolution—the inventor of the assembly line. Less well known is the fact that he also established and published a weekly "news" periodical, *The Dearborn Independent.* On May 22, 1920 the front page of Ford's newspaper carried the headline: "The International Jew: The World's Problem." This was the first front page article to appear in a series, which would be followed by ninety consecutive exposés on this topic. Some of the headlines give a good sense of how Mr. Ford used his periodical to express his deeply held anti-Semitism:

> "The Scope of the Jewish Dictatorship in the U.S."
> "When Editors were Independent of Jews"
> "The Jewish Element in Bootlegging Evil"
> "Jewish Hot-Beds of Bolshevism in the U.S."
> "Jewish Power and America's Money Famine"
> "Jewish Degradation of American Baseball"
> "Jew Wires Direct Tammany's Gentile Puppets"
> "Dr. Levy, a Jew, Admits his People's Error"
> "Will Jewish Zionism Bring Armageddon?"[1]

An anthology was soon published as a four volume series of books titled *The International Jew.* It was translated into over a dozen languages including German. The anti-Semitic ideas were warmly embraced by

Germany's embryonic Nazi movement. Hitler himself treasured a personal set of the books and had a framed photograph of Henry Ford hung in his office. Henry Ford was the only American to be mentioned in Hitler's *Mein Kampf*:

> Every year makes them [the Jews] more and more the controlling masters of the producers in a nation of one hundred and twenty millions (United States of America); only a single great man, Ford, to their fury, still maintains full independence.[2]

In 1938, on Ford's seventy-fifth birthday he received two representatives from the German government at his office in Dearborn, Michigan. There they bestowed upon Mr. Ford the Grosskreuz des Deutschen Adlerordens (Grand Cross of the Order of the German Eagle), which was the highest honor a foreigner could receive from the Reich. It was accompanied by a personal written greeting from Hitler himself.

It is difficult to fathom that this is the same Henry Ford who founded a school for African-American children on property he owned near Ways, Georgia. He named it for his close personal friend, George Washington Carver, who was the guest of honor at the school's dedication in 1939. It is exceedingly difficult to square the inherent unkindness found in the anti-Semitic ravings of *The International Jew*, with the kindness found in Henry Ford's cash gift to Tuskegee Institute for the installation of an elevator in Dorothy Hall, so that the elderly Dr. Carver could access his second floor laboratory. Henry Ford even traveled to Tuskegee Institute in 1941 to preside over the dedication ceremonies of the Carver Museum.

A twenty-four hour day has light and darkness, perhaps it is so with each of us.

¤ ¤ ¤

Enigma #2:

Mohandas Gandhi was born to tremendous wealth and privilege on October 2, 1869. His father was the prime minister to the Raja of three city-states on the Kathiawar Peninsula of India. In 1888, Gandhi studied law at University College London. Soon after obtaining a barrister (law) degree he found himself working for an Indian firm in Natal, South Africa, which was then part of the British Empire.

While in London and Natal, he experienced racial discrimination which left him greatly troubled. Yet in a February 15, 1905 letter to Dr. Porter, Medical Officer of Health for Johannesburg, he articulated his own enigmatic attitude about human races.

Why, of all places in Johannesburg, the Indian location should be chosen for dumping down all Kaffirs of the town, passes my comprehension. Of course, under my suggestion, the Town Council must withdraw the Kaffirs from the location. About this mixing of the Kaffirs with the Indians, I must confess I feel most strongly. I think it is very unfair to the Indian population, and it is an undue tax on even the proverbial patience of my countrymen.[3]
(‘Kaffir’ was a term used to identify several ethnic groups in colonial South Africa, such as the Zulu, Xhosa, Sotho, Tswana, and others. It was also used as an ethnic slur.)

Gandhi published a similarly disparaging statement in *The Indian Opinion* about a court's decision in June 1906.

You say that the magistrate's decision is unsatisfactory because it would enable a person, however unclean, to travel by a tram, and that even the Kaffirs would be able to do so. But the magistrate's decision is quite different. The Court declared that the Kaffirs have no legal right to travel by tram. And according to tram regulations, those in an unclean dress or in a drunken state are prohibited from boarding a tram. Thanks to the Court's decision, only clean Indians or coloured people other than Kaffirs, can now travel in the trams.[4]

Also in *The Indian Opinion* Gandhi mixed ethnicity issues with militancy.

In this instance of the fire-arms, the Asiatic has been most improperly bracketed with the natives. The British Indian does not need any such restrictions as are imposed by the Bill on the natives regarding the carrying of fire-arms. The prominent race can remain so by preventing the native from arming himself. Is there a slightest vestige of justification for so preventing the British Indian?[5]

Perhaps even more surprising is Gandhi's position on the appropriate role of Indians in the South African Zulu war of 1906. After the British introduced a new poll-tax, Zulus in South Africa killed two British officers. In response, the British declared a war against the Zulus. It was not a war at all, but rather the legalized sport hunting of unarmed humans of Zulu decent. Gandhi actively encouraged the British to recruit Indians to aid the British army in this slaughter. He argued that Indians should support the war efforts in order to legitimize their claims to full citizenship. The British, however, refused to commission Indians as army officers. Nonetheless, they accepted Gandhi's offer to let a detachment of Indians volunteer as a stretcher bearer corps, to treat wounded British soldiers. This corps was commanded by Gandhi himself.

> The corps had been formed at the instance of the Natal Government by way of experiment, in connection with the operations against the Natives consists of twenty three Indians. If the Government only realized what reserve force is being wasted, they would make use of it and give Indians the opportunity of a thorough training for actual warfare.
>
> —Mohandas Gandhi

In 1908, while incarcerated in a British prison, Gandhi disparaged his fellow inmates.

> Kaffirs are as a rule uncivilized—the convicts even more so. They are troublesome, very dirty and live almost like animals.[7]

This is the same Mohandas Gandhi who went on to become one of the most influential pacifist of the twentieth century. The same man who used passive resistance to break an empire's strangle hold on his homeland and create a new nation. The same man who was assigned the name Mahatma, meaning "great soul," by his loving followers of many ethnicities. The same man who eschewed the lawyer's three piece suits of his youth and settled in to the traditional dhoti kurta of India. The same man who expressed his egalitarian values so eloquently.

> ¤ I came to the conclusion long ago...that all religions were true and

also that all had some error in them, and whilst I hold by my own, I should hold others as dear as Hinduism. So we can only pray, if we are Hindus, not that a Christian should become a Hindu... But our innermost prayer should be a Hindu should be a better Hindu, a Muslim a better Muslim, a Christian a better Christian.[8]

¤ To call woman the weaker sex is a libel; it is man's injustice to woman. If by strength is meant brute strength, then, indeed, is woman less brute than man. If by strength is meant moral power, then woman is immeasurably man's superior. Has she not greater intuition, is she not more self-sacrificing, has she not greater powers of endurance, has she not greater courage? Without her, man could not be. If nonviolence is the law of our being, the future is with woman. Who can make a more effective appeal to the heart than woman?[9]

¤ The seven blunders that human society commits and cause all the violence: wealth without work, pleasure without conscience, knowledge without character, commerce without morality, science without humanity, worship without sacrifice, and politics without principles.[10]

Perhaps as the fires of youth burned low, a great spirit emerged from a troubled youth. Kindness did not come easily to Mohandas Gandhi, but it came. And when at last it did, he became the Mahatma.

¤ ¤ ¤

Enigma #3:

In New York City, on October 11, 1884, Eleanor Roosevelt was born into the preordained life of opulence of the "Oyster Bay" (Republican) branch of the Roosevelt family. Even the enormous wealth of the family could not stay certain tragedies in her early life. Her mother died of diphtheria when she was just eight years old and her brother succumbed to the same deadly bacteria less than a year later. Her father then took his own life in an alcohol induced stupor a year after that.

After their parents deaths, Eleanor and her surviving brother were raised by their maternal grandmother, Mary Ludlow Hall. Eleanor also developed a very close relationship with her Uncle Teddy.

The family's wealth secured the very best education possible. Eleanor's education up to the age of fifteen was provided primarily by a private tutor. She was then sent to a finishing school, Allenswood Academy, near London, England. While there she studied history, literature, geography, and French. The headmistress, Marie Souvestre, may very well have been the most powerful influence on Eleanor's developing mind and emerging political points of view. Ms. Souvestre was a fiercely independent woman, who over the course of their long relationship was Eleanor's teacher, mentor, parent, role model and friend.

When Eleanor returned to the United States in 1902, her Uncle Teddy, who was at that time President of the United States, hosted a débutante ball in her honor. It was there that she met her fifth cousin, Franklin Delano Roosevelt, of the Hyde Park (Democrat) Roosevelts. They would be married three years later.

She could have easily retired to the luxurious life of privilege her family's wealth would have allowed. Instead, she took a job as a social worker in the slums of New York City's east side. There she worked with the Junior League on the "Promotion of Settlement Movement." The movement focused on addressing the economic and social problems experienced by recent mass immigration to urban areas, which was one result of the industrial revolution. In New York City many of these people were, in fact, immigrants from other nations, only recently arriving through the gateway at Ellis Island.

While teaching immigrant children at the College Settlement on Rivington Street, she took her fiancée, Franklin D. Roosevelt on several visits to New York's Lower East Side. Having grown up entirely within wealth's cloister, neither had ever been exposed to human destitution before. They were horrified by the living conditions that were common place among the earth's poorest humans.

Coming from almost incalculable wealth, Eleanor became the most outspoken and most effect advocate for the nation's poor, for opportunity, for civil rights. When the Great Depression hit and over one quarter of the population slid into a state of grinding poverty, she was unwilling, indeed unable, to hide in the vestments of Darwinian Sociology, as many of the nation's wealthiest citizens chose to do. She viewed the contentiousness of philosophical arguments about "socialism" as being utterly irrelevant when measured against the gnawing hunger of a single child.

Secretary of the Treasury, Henry Morgenthau, Jr., coined the phrase "Lost Generation" to describe the youth of the Great Depression. However, it was the First Lady, Eleanor Roosevelt, who articulated the phrase's inherent warning, "I live in real terror when I think we may be losing this generation. We have got to bring these young people into the active life of the community and make them feel that they are necessary."[11]

With those words she planted the seed that would birth the National Youth Administration (NYA) in June 1935. It was created to address the problem of unemployment among the nation's Great Depression era youth. The NYA provided college tuition credit grants to students in exchange for work, at a rate of 15¢ per hour. Seemingly a pittance, those jobs and credits allowed tens of thousands of young people to continue studying while simultaneously preventing the pool of unemployed youth from getting even larger.

In the late summer of 1935, the young Norman Borlaug was one of the first in line to apply for the program in Minneapolis, Minnesota. Years later he recalled, "NYA is what saved me. And it was a valuable education within itself. We worked for different professors. I worked for a while with a veterinarian, another time with an entomologist. Those experiences helped round out my education."[12]

Putting aside all of the political dogma about spending government money, in Norm's case, the program worked; he worked; he did not go hungry; he got an education. That education became the vehicle whereby he forwarded the inherent kindness of the Borlaug home. As a result, hundreds of millions of people around the world would be spared the horrors of starvation. By any measure, American taxpayers realized a pretty darn good return, due to Eleanor Roosevelt's insistence on that investment of 15¢ an hour.

There are a few, a precious few, who just seem to be born understanding the dynamic and power of kindness and those few may spring from any social economic echelon. Eleanor Roosevelt was one. Born to enormous wealth she had the greatest empathy for humanity's most impoverished. Once in a great while there are angels born to walk among us.

24

Mr. Vice President

Wallace becomes Vice President of the United States and tours Mexico.

By early 1940, no one had emerged as an undisputed leader in the campaign for president around whom the Democratic troops would rally. Actually, the same can be said for the loyal opposition. The Republicans did not have a leading contender for their presidential nominee. There was no fervor for Roosevelt to break with presidential tradition and run for a third term. But there was also little enthusiasm about a change of course during those turbulent times. Earnest students of history can have legitimate differences of opinion about how Roosevelt approached this conundrum. Some might say that he took a passive "wait-and-see—only-if-I'm-drafted-to-serve" role. Others may say that was all theatrics, and in realty he manipulated the process to assure his renomination. If the former position is true, then indeed his party did draft him for nomination number three. If the latter approach is what actually happened, then Henry Wallace was one of the major pawns in the political game of chess.

If, indeed, it was a game of political chess, then Henry Wallace was a willing pawn. There almost seemed a malaise over the entire prospect of a presidential campaign in 1940. Roosevelt refused to announce his intentions. Other Democrats who may have been interested in a run at the nation's highest office were somewhat frozen in place by what appeared to be the incumbent's reticence. Wallace was invited to speak at a Jackson Day dinner in Des Moines on January 8, 1940. When taking questions at the end of his short presentation a questioner pressed him about his own possible candidacy. He responded in his characteristically laconic style, "I hope the nominee in 1940 will be President Roosevelt."[1] Upon hearing of this remark, the White House issued a mild rebuke. Wallace did not even bother to offer up a tongue in cheek apology. Unofficially a White House staffer reported back to Wallace that the "gentleman in the oval office was much pleased."

In these decades neither of the major political parties could be defined on purely ideological grounds. That is to say that both parties had strong liberal and conservative constituencies. This dynamic was a holdover from the "party of Lincoln" and the political dichotomies imposed by the Civil War and the "reconstruction" era. Though there were many very liberal and powerful Republicans, there were likewise many conservative democrats who controlled most committee chairmanships in Congress due to appointments predicated upon the seniority system.

During the 1920s the conservative wing of the Republican party held sway in the Executive Branch. Whether or not their policies exacerbated a dynamic that led to the financial collapse, there can be little doubt their ideology paralyzed them in terms of responding to the new economic realities. This forced the populace, out of sheer desperation, to embrace the liberal inclinations of the left wing of the Democratic Party. That said, in the hearts of the majority, the nation clung to its historical right-of-center political inclinations. This created a split-personality dynamic among much of the electorate.

Farmers in the Midwest and South were at their very core uneasy with much of the Agricultural Adjustment Act (AAA). Eighty percent of those farmers were signed up and benefiting directly from AAA programs. But the rugged individualist residing in the hearts of many was extremely ambivalent about the notion of being saved financially, and thus able to feed their families, as a result of the expanded role of government emanating from Washington, DC.

The AAA programs issued cash payments to more than 6 million farmers. In the depths of the Great Depression the relief offered by government largess was indeed welcomed as a last-resort lifeline, but misgivings began to reemerge as the economy slowly improved.

In the late 1930s Henry Wallace did not share those misgivings, though he clearly sensed the nation's shift back to the right.

Any political figure which sees clearly the nature of the reactionary forces, which are more interested in holding onto the past of violence than molding the future constructively, can operate successfully politically in a democracy like the United States of America only during the brief period following the time when the reactionaries have demonstrated their ineptitude in terms of great unemployment and misery in the midst of plenty. This was the secret of the temporary power of the New Deal.

—Henry A. Wallace[2]

Expressing this realization that the "Deal" was no longer "New," Henry Wallace continued his view of the "good fight." Even though he countered the electorate's shift back toward the right with his own shift to the left, there were many who espoused the belief that he would be the next president, and perhaps even a good one.

Early in 1937 Richard Wilson wrote in the Des Moines Register, "A new Henry A. Wallace has been born out of the four years of the New Deal. A bit less frank, a bit more genial, he has begun to realize the importance of politics and has become a definite possibility for the presidential nomination in 1940."[3]

In July of 1937 the nation's most read magazine, the *Saturday Evening Post*, featured an article by Stanley High. Under the title "Will It Be Wallace?" High wrote, "It is an axiom of American politics that booms which bloom early are subject to frost, but if the boom withers; if, in 1940, Mr. Roosevelt's hands are laid on some other head, it will not be because Mr. Wallace has faltered in his understanding of the New Deal gospel or has failed, in his special field, to do a job of almost presidential proportions."[4]

Later that same year *Look Magazine* featured an article titled "Henry Agard Wallace: A Scientific Farmer and a White House Possibility."[5] It was an almost fawning biographical piece about Henry and his family.

On slow news days, newspapers across the country would often roll-out a file article featuring the relative strengths and weaknesses of various political figures. Quite often, these articles featured Henry Wallace and analyzed his potential as a candidate for the presidency. Their own analyses often perplexed the reporters because, simply put, the Secretary of Agriculture was just too enigmatic for most journalists on the political beat. The *Baltimore Sun*'s political reporter, Gerald W. Johnson, best captured their confoundedness with this description of Wallace:

A politician who really does not care about making political friends is, in the opinion of Washington, a flat contradiction of terms. Hence, in the case of Henry A. Wallace appearances must be deceptive. Behind the figure presented to the public gaze there must be another and very different man; yet no one, not even the most highly trained observers of the nation's press, has perceived that other man. Hence the frank bewilderment. Hence correspondents' confession that although they see him every day, and talk to him, and watch him, they don't know him.[6]

Secretary Wallace may have seemed politically obtuse. More likely, however, he eschewed the drama of political maneuvering simply because he found it distasteful. To him the value of politics was a matter of policy rather than personality. The following excerpt from a letter he sent to President Roosevelt in the late summer of 1939 should dispel any notion that Wallace did not understand the political game afoot. The game which he chose not to play, at least not overtly.

It is still true that the Democrats in order to win must have a progressive candidate but it is also true that the 10 million progressives are not the only ones on the fence. There are many million other people who are very close to the farm, the small town and the small business men in the cities who were with us enthusiastically in 1932, to a somewhat lesser extent in 1936 and who are now raising many questions about government spending, labor policies, etc. These people temperamentally are not progressives but they are fine people whose votes we must have. We must make some kind of suitable accommodation with these people.

On a straight division of the electorate on a basis of the broadly liberal and the generally conservative, the definite majority is conservative. The Gallup poll shows that. So also does the way Garner runs in the Democratic polls. We have to have some means of getting basic, general support, and then covering that foundation with a liberal superstructure."[7]

¤ ¤ ¤

Within days of receiving Wallace's political consultation letter, the

President was awoken a few minutes before 3:00am on September 1st and informed that 1.5 million German troops supported by 2315 aircraft, 2750 tanks, and an additional 51 thousand troops from Slovakia had just poured across their border with Poland.

In a land grab that showed the true colors of Stalin and the Bolshevik gangsters who ran the Soviet Union, the Red Army invaded Poland from the east on September 19th. Within a month Poland was crushed between the two forces. However, as one would expect of such political opposites, the Nazi and Communist alliance was short lived. Both the creation and the dissolution of that alliance would prove to be a human tragedy of almost unimaginable proportions over the next six years.

World War II had arrived in Europe and in the awareness of the American people. This theater, more so than the six year old war in the western Pacific and China, would cast a long, dark shadow across the 1940 presidential campaign.

On April 9, 1940 Nazi forces invaded and crushed the nations of Norway and Denmark in a single day. The next day they turned their attention to the Low Countries: Netherlands, Belgium, and Luxembourg. By June 5th they managed to outflank the defenders at the "invincible" Maginot line and swarmed into France.

Fascist Italy joined the fracas on June 10th. Knowing that his armed forces were not prepared for war, Italian dictator Benito Mussolini instructed Marshal Badoglio, Army Chief of Staff, "I only need a few thousand dead so that I can sit at the peace conference as a man who has fought."[8] Of the 500,100 killed and wounded during these two bloody months, 1247 of the dead and 2631 of the wounded were Italians—a very acceptable level of loss to feed Mussolini's lust for power and money.

Paris fell to the Fascist onslaught on June 14th and France officially capitulated on June 25th. On July 10th, sorties of the German Luftwaffe crossed the channel from airfields near Calais and began the ruthless bombardment of the British Isle. The Democrat's convened their national convention in Chicago five days later. One might wonder who would even want to be president under those circumstances.

¤ ¤ ¤

By early spring of 1940 the White House inner circle had already decided that Roosevelt would be the nominee. The events in Europe crystallized the decision but altered the strategy. The appearance of national unity was not likely in an election year, so they had to settle on unity of the party. In order to demonstrate that, Roosevelt had to be "drafted" at the Chicago convention. For the sake of the press, both domestic and international, it was essential that the draft appear to be spontaneous and unanimous.

In retrospect, it seems fantastic and astounding that the White House deployed only two operatives to the party's national convention. Secretary of Commerce, Harry Hopkins, set up shop in a suite at the Blackstone Hotel and Secretary of Agriculture Wallace rented a couple of rooms in the nearby Stevens Hotel. From there they endeavored to orchestrate the drafting of the party platform and the third nomination of Franklin Roosevelt. Unbeknownst to Wallace, Hopkins carried in his pocket the President's coup de grace—a handwritten, signed note to his party stating that he did not wish to serve a third term. Perhaps these two gentlemen did not understand, perhaps nobody on earth understood, the momentous nature of their task. The future of democracy, the future of humanity stood in the balance.

¤ ¤ ¤

Compared to the scripted and choreographed exercises in tedium that evolved with the advent of television news, national political conventions of that era were rough and tumble affairs. That was certainly the case with both major party conventions in 1940.

The Republican Convention was held in Philadelphia from June 24 through June 28. Two days prior to the opening ceremonies the Gallup poll reported on Republican preferences—Thomas Dewey: 47%; Wendell Willkie: 29%; Robert Taft, Arthur Vandenberg, and Herbert Hoover all hovered just below 10%. On the opening day, only three hundred of the one thousand convention delegates were pledged to a particular candidate. The names of ten men were put in nomination. On the first ballot Dewey received 360 delegate votes; Taft had 189; and, Willkie mustered only 105. Frantic and feverish "politicken" went on between ballots, with patronage promises being handed out as freely as campaign buttons. Rather than a clear leader emerging, the fourth ballot was even more balanced, but Willkie had for the first time won a round: Willkie: 306; Taft: 254; Dewey: 250. Still no one was even close to the 500 needed to secure the nomination. On the fifth ballot Dewey's support evaporated. He received only 57 votes. With 429 votes Willkie emerged 52 votes ahead of Taft. A spontaneous chant arose from the peanut gallery, "We want Willkie! We want Willkie! We want Willkie!" Another vote was taken quickly and Willkie obtained the support of 629 delegates. So, on the sixth ballot the Republican National Convention nominated an attorney from New York who had never campaigned for a political office in his life.

¤ ¤ ¤

It might have been expected that the Democrat's would not have such a ruckus at their convention, given that they had an incumbent president. Come on—it was a convention full of Democrats! Though there were no constitutionally imposed term limits, many in the party had serious reservations about breaking the two term tradition that had begun with George Washington. The strong conservative wing of the party were by now in open revolt against the New Deal. A powerful group with isolationist leanings had no illusions about Roosevelt's belief that United States' involvement in the wars around the world was inevitable. These issues, coupled with Roosevelt's position that he would not campaign for the nomination, rather he must be "drafted" by the conventioneers, created the backdrop for the historical gathering in Chicago.

Three men's names were put in nomination: President Roosevelt, Vice President John Garner, a staunch conservative from Texas; and, James Farley, the Democratic National Committee Chairman. The nomination of Farley was more of an honorary tribute to him, than a serious challenge to Roosevelt. Farley had been, and still was, a supporter of the New Deal. He was also a Roman Catholic, and no one in 1940 believed that America was yet ready to elect a Catholic president.

The convention started badly for the "Draft Roosevelt" crowd. Chicago Mayor Ed Kelly gave a speech trying to rally the troops for Roosevelt's third nomination. There was no typical floor demonstration of support, no horns blowing, no people chanting. There was only a few moments of polite applause. On the other hand, the party's conservative wing staged a rowdy demonstration for their man John Garner. But when Farley's name was mentioned at the close of the nominating speech, the convention floor erupted spontaneously. This was likely a way of thanking him for his years of successful service as the Postmaster General and party chairman. It was also an opportunity to give voice to the pent up frustration at having no real choice except to renominate Franklin Roosevelt. By the next morning Farley and Harry Hopkins had tamped down the notion that there was any other alternative. Wallace meanwhile played the role of policy-wonk in crafting the party platform. He was not consulted about an appropriate Vice Presidential nominee.

On Tuesday night the Roosevelt supporters staged a comeback of sorts. Senator Alben Barkley was designated to give the evening's keynote. It was a traditional rouse-the-troops political speech. A very good orator, Barkley had the crowd flying high. Then he pulled from his pocket the note Harry Hopkins had given him earlier in the day. He read the President's letter. "I haven't any desire or purpose to continue as president..."[9] The convention delegates were too stunned to even gasp. Then over the public address system a voice roared, "No! No! No!—We want Roosevelt! We want Roosevelt! We want Roosevelt!" The voice belonged to a man by the name of Thomas Garry who had been stationed, with microphone in hand in a basement closet, awaiting his cue—the anticipated moment of stunned silence on the convention floor. It was a bit of tawdry political theatrics, but it worked. The incumbent president received 946 votes on the first ballot.

By Wednesday morning, the conservatives, feeling somewhat bamboozled, determined that **they** would select the next Vice President. Given the state of world affairs, this was not a decision of small import, made even more serious by the general awareness that the President's health was increasingly challenged by the pressures of the office, and what is now known as post-polio syndrome. There was growing and legitimate concern that Roosevelt's health would fail, that he might not be able to survive a third term.

Roosevelt called Secretary of State Cordell Hull and offered him the position of Vice President. He knew, of course, given Hull's own health concerns that this was a courtesy call only. Hull responded simply, "No, by God—by God, no!"[10] Now Roosevelt was politically freed to designate his true first choice. The call went to the private line in Harry Hopkins suite at the Blackstone Hotel. New York Supreme Court Justice, Sam Rosenman, was dispatched to the Stevens Hotel to inform Secretary Wallace of the decision. It was 2:00am on Thursday, July 18, 1940. Wallace began immediately drafting his acceptance speech—perhaps a bit prematurely.

Roosevelt remained at the White House. He was "drafted" as the party's nominee. He did not plan to go to Chicago, not even to give an acceptance speech. Nevertheless, he began to lobby his selection for Vice President. He called James Farley, the party chairman, whose own name had been submitted to the convention as a presidential nominee just two days prior.

Roosevelt, "Henry Wallace is the best man to nominate in this emergency."

Farley responded, "Mr. President, the party needs Jesse Jones. He is a conservative from Texas. He will be a much bigger vote getter than Wallace come November."

"Well, I think Henry is perfect. I like him. He's the kind of fellow I want around. He's honest. He thinks right. He's a digger," insisted the President.

"But Mr. President, people here think of him as a wild-eyed mystic."

Roosevelt did not attempt to veil the growing impatience that could be heard in his voice, "He's not a mystic. He's a philosopher. He's got ideas. He thinks right. He'll help people think."[11]

As he hung up the phone, Farley realized that Wallace would indeed make people think. In fact, that was exactly what the Wallace detractors feared. The party's far right wing feared being required to think and feared those who think too much—they are much harder to control. Regardless, the President's mind was made up.

The reaction on the convention floor, and in telegrams to the White House, was so negative and so profound that the President's men waffled badly. The party conservatives were in open revolt and the isolationists were only a centimeter behind. Feeling the whole convention slipping away, Harry Hopkins called the President to warn him that Wallace would likely not be nominated that evening. Roosevelt responded, "Well, damn it to hell, they will go for Wallace or I won't run, and you can jolly well tell them so."[12] When Hopkins hung up the phone he realized that unlike the disingenuous letter he had carried in his coat pocket to Chicago, this time the President was most certainly sincere.

Eleanor Roosevelt arrived on the scene, waded into this quagmire, and even she seemed to waiver. She was overheard on a phone conversation saying, "Wallace won't do."

The president called Farley again, "I've given my word. What do you do when you give your word?"

"I keep it. If you gave your word to Wallace you should keep it; but it was a mistake to give it."[13] responded Farley laconically.

That evening Speaker of the U.S. House of Representatives, William Bankhead of Alabama, was nominated first. This was an interesting twist, because even though a successful democrat from the deep south, he was far too progressive to be supported by most of the Southern Democrats at the convention. Nevertheless, there was a rousing floor demonstration staged in his support. Next, the distinguished, very rich, and staunchly conservative Secretary of Commerce, Jesse Jones, was nominated. The party's right wing went wild. By the time Indiana Governor Paul McNutt went to the podium to nominate Henry Wallace, a mob mentality ruled. Every mention of Bankhead and Jones drew crazed cheers. Every mention of Wallace was greeted with boos and catcalls.

Ilo Wallace was seated on the stage. This was her first ever political convention. In tears, she leaned over and asked Eleanor Roosevelt, "Why are they booing my Henry?"[14] The almost surrealistically ironic answer to that question was that they were not booing Henry. In fact, those delegates who knew him personally, almost to a man, liked the man. Even those who disagreed with his politics, admired and respected him as a kind soul, of genuine integrity and character. No indeed, the crowd was not booing Henry Wallace, they were booing Franklin Roosevelt.

Though they fully realized they had no choice, Roosevelt's third nomination crammed down their throats rankled. Wallace just happened to be the convenient target upon whom the delegates could unleash their pent-up frustration with the situation in the convention hall, on the farms, and in the banks and businesses back home. As if that were not enough, the anxiety among the party activists at the specter of an international conflagration cannot even be estimated. Understanding all of that, in the Oval Office the President listened with growing disdain to the proceedings being broadcast on the radio.

At about 9:00pm Eastern Standard Time, Roosevelt's patience took leave. He pulled out a piece of stationary and hastily drafted a handwritten letter. In part it said, "When it thought in terms of dollars instead of in terms of human values the Democrat Party has consistently failed. It cannot face both directions at the same time. By declining the honor of the nomination for the Presidency, I can restore that opportunity to the convention. I so do."[15] He handed the letter to his chief of staff, Sam Rosenman. For the second time in twenty-four hours, Roosevelt was calling the conventioneer's bluff, but this time the President absolutely was not bluffing.

As Roosevelt somewhat agitatedly resumed playing solitaire, Rosenman, with much more agitation, began making frantic phone calls to Chicago. As word of the President's letter to the Convention spread around the floor, Eleanor Roosevelt took the stage to speak, as she so often did on her husband's behalf, "We people in the United States have got to realize that we face now a grave and serious situation.... We cannot tell from day to day what may come.... This is no ordinary time, no time for thinking about anything except what we can best do for the country as a whole, and that responsibility is on each and every one of us as individuals."[16]

Suddenly, the collective memory of newsreel images of Nazi tanks rolling over Poland and Norway and Denmark and Luxembourg and Belgium and France settled in on the Convention Center in Chicago. Within the hour, delegates to the 1940 Democratic National Convention nominated Henry Agard Wallace as their candidate for Vice President of the United States. The following day, when asked at a press conference how he felt about his humiliating reception by the conventioneers, Henry commented through a toothy grin, "It was a convention of Democrats, after all."

¤ ¤ ¤

Roosevelt had insisted that the Democrats draft him to be their candidate. It seems that he approached the election with the same mindset. The electorate needed to draft him to continue as their president. He essentially refused to campaign for the post. On the other hand, the campaign schedule assigned the Vice Presidential candidate was torrid, yet by modern standards amazingly understated. Wallace had a campaign staff of exactly two people in addition to himself.

Like the Republican nominee, Wendell Willkie, Wallace had never run for an elected office in his life. Both men, much to the surprise of the opposing party, proved to be very good on the campaign trail. The campaign of 1940 almost seemed like a childish challenge between the two major political parties, "My novice can beat your novice." However, there was much more at stake for the nation and the world than political Rookie-of-the-Year honors.

Wallace realized that it was not his job to appease Midwest farmers, who almost instinctively resented the government agriculture programs from which they were willingly and thankfully receiving cash benefits. A large percentage of those farmers were first generation Americans of German descent. Among them there was a growing and powerful pro-German sentiment for appeasing, rather than opposing, Adolf Hitler. At his very core Henry Wallace was repulsed by the tenets of Fascism. At some level his own personal slide further to the political left was more driven by that revulsion than by American conservatives reactionary response to the New Deal.

If his campaign job was not to carry the Midwestern farm states, what then was it? Understanding the larger historical context of the campaign Wallace realized, with the concurrence of the President, that he had to counter the pro-isolationist sentiment in the country. He had to make a case against the Fascists and a case for military intervention, should it become necessary. With this goal in mind, he began the assault before a friendly audience back home in Des Moines.

> Adolph Hitler is the implacable enemy of all democracy. Franklin Roosevelt is its eager servant and faithful defender before the whole world. . . . This is a fight between freedom and democracy and the materialistic religion of darkness. Against this dark and blood faith we of the New World set the faith of Americanism, of Protestantism, of Catholicism, of Judaism. Our faith is based on the belief that the possibilities of an individual are not determined by race, social background or wealth.[17]

Frequently citing the influence of his childhood mentor and friend, George Carver, Wallace time and again used campaign speeches to blast the "false eugenics" and "pseudo-sciences" employed by the Fascists to justify their genocidal racism. He hammered the message home in a famous speech, "Racial Theories and the Genetic Basis of Democracy," which he delivered to the "Committee for Democracy and Intellectual Freedom" at the Waldorf-Astoria in New York City.

> The cause of liberty and the cause of true science must always be one and the same. For science cannot flourish except in an atmosphere of freedom, and freedom cannot survive unless there is an honest facing of facts. The immediate reason for this meeting is the profound shock you have had, and the deep feeling of protest

that stirs in you, as you think of the treatment some of your fellow scientists are receiving in other countries. Men who have made great contributions to human knowledge and culture have been deprived of their positions and their homes, put into concentration camps, driven out of their native lands. Their lifework has been reviled.

In those same countries, other men, who call themselves scientists, have been willing to play the game of the dictators by twisting science into a mumbo-jumbo of dangerous nonsense. These men are furnishing pseudo-scientific support for the exaltation of one race and one nation as conquerors. . . .

Thus the dictatorial regime in Germany, masquerading its propaganda in pseudo-scientific terms, is teaching the German boys and girls to believe that their race and their nation are superior to all others, and by implication that that nation and that race have a right to dominate all others. That is the claim. What ground does it have in scientific fact? . . .

When I was a small boy, George Carver, a Negro who is now a chemist at Tuskegee Institute, was a good friend of my father's at the Iowa State College. Carver at that time was specializing in botany, and he would take me along on some of his botanizing trips. It was he who first introduced me to the mysteries of botany and plant fertilization. Later on I was to have an intimate acquaintance with plants myself, because I spent a good many years breeding corn. Perhaps that was partly because this scientist, who belonged to another race, had deepened my appreciation of plants in a way I could never forget.

Carver was born in slavery, and to this day he does not definitely know his own age. In his work as a chemist in the South, he correctly sensed the coming interest in the industrial use of the products of the farm—a field of research which our government is now pushing. I mention Carver simply because he is one example of a truth of which we who meet here today are deeply convinced. Superior ability is not the exclusive possession of any one race or any one class. It may arise anywhere, provided men are given the right opportunities. . . .

Democracy—and that term includes free science—must apply itself to meeting the *material* need of men for work, for income, for goods, for health, for security, and to meeting their *spiritual* need for dignity, for knowledge, for self-expression, for adventure and for reverence. *And it must succeed.* The danger that it will be overthrown in favor of another system is in direct proportion to its failure to meet these needs. We may talk all we like about the beauties of democracy, the ideals of democracy, the rightness of democracy. In the long run, democracy or any other political system will be measured by its deeds, not its words. . . .

Let us dedicate ourselves anew to the belief that there are extraordinary possibilities in both man and nature which have not yet been realized, and which can be made manifest only if the individualistic yet co-operative genius of democratic institutions is preserved. Let us dedicate ourselves anew to making it possible for those who are gifted in art, science and religion to approach the unknown with true reverence, and not under the compulsion of producing immediate results for the glorification of one man, one group, one race or one nation.[18] (Partial excerpt of speech.)

In his simple eloquence, Wallace had captured the dichotomy of his own feelings and the feelings of the nation. In his heart he had always been a pacifist as witnessed by his waggish comment in a letter congratulating a young Iowan on his graduation from the Naval Academy, "Personally, I am quite a pacifist and I shall be interested in talking with you sometime about the fallacies of my position."[19] Whether or not he ever had that conversation is not known, but by 1940 the specter of a world dominated by Fascists and Imperialists forced him to reconsider. And reconsideration of the nation's isolationist leanings is what he urged upon the American people throughout the course of the campaign.

Assuming the unlikely role as the champion for intervention, Wallace adroitly articulated, in whistle stops all across the nation, a need to win the war and a reason to win the peace.

As an expression of his egalitarian inclinations while campaigning in Mesilla, New Mexico, Wallace folded his prepared comments and stuffed them in his pocket. He looked out at the faces smiling up at him. He delivered an extemporaneous speech in Spanish. It was the first time a major candidate of either party had spoken Spanish in public—it would most certainly not be the last. His Spanish was not so good, but it was good enough. The crowd cheered wildly and a few days later fifty-seven percent of the New Mexico electorate went to the polls and voted for Roosevelt.

Meanwhile, Wendell Willkie had mounted a much more effective campaign than anyone expected of a political greenhorn. By the middle of October, it was clear that the race was a good deal tighter than the Democrats had anticipated. For political reasons, more international than domestic, the President had up to that point eschewed the campaign. On October 18th he came out of the Rose Garden, and he came out swinging. In a speech at Madison Square Garden he named the three whom he considered the most dangerous people in America—the three congressional isolationists who were blocking his "preparedness program." Preparedness was euphemistic code talk for funding a national war arsenal. Roosevelt led the crowd in chanting the rhyming names of his isolationist nemeses, "Marton, Barton, and Fish."

"Who stands in the way of protecting our American ideals?" the President asked rhetorically.

"Marton, Barton, and Fish!"

"Who wants to appease the Fascists of Europe?"

"Marton, Barton, and Fish!" the crowd picked up the chant.

"Who observes the aggression of petty dictators around the world but say 'it's not our concern'?"

"Marton, Barton, and Fish!"

"Who watches the Nazi planes night after night bomb our brothers and sisters of Great Britain and in the morning say there is nothing we can do?"

"Marton, Barton, and Fish!"

He was the master politician and everyone watching could see that he loved the stump.

To drive the message of the isolationist danger home, the next day Roosevelt returned to Washington to attend the lottery for the first peace time draft in the nation's history. He watched over Secretary of War Henry Stimson's shoulder as the first capsule from a large glass bowl was drawn. The President then, in a voice resonating the statesman's solemnity, offered a few words, "You who will enter this peacetime army will be the inheritors of a proud history and an honorable tradition. You will be members of an army that first came together to achieve independence and to establish certain fundamental rights for all men."[20]

Meanwhile, all around the nation little children at play began chanting "Marton, Barton, and Fish" rather than "ring-around-the-rosy." Willkie acknowledged, "Those three little words tied me more effectively to the isolationists than anything else said during the whole campaign."[21]

Though there was doubt in the minds of all the major players on election eve, of the 50 million people who went to the polls on November 5th, fifty-five percent of them voted to reelect the President for an unprecedented third term.

¤ ¤ ¤

Henry Wallace grew up working. As the first born son he was assigned and assumed many chores around the home. He shoveled coal into the furnace in the winter, pumped water into two tanks upstairs for drinking and bathing, cared for the sow and her piglets, milked the cow, and fed the horses. Like his mentor, George Carver, by the age of ten Henry was also the master of the family garden.

It could be said that his first full time job was in the summer of his fifteenth year, when he accepted the challenge of the "Corn Professor," Perry G. Holden. He spent the entire summer tending five acres of corn planted from sample ears of the famous Reid Yellow Dent. He irrigated, weeded and detasseled the entire five acres by hand. He harvested, calculated and graphed yield, and in the end debunked the myth that pretty had anything whatsoever to do with corn quality and vigor.

The summer of 1909, between his Junior and Senior years at Iowa State, he was assigned a tour of the American west as a roving reporter for *Wallaces' Farmer*. After graduating the next summer he walked the entire state of Iowa, again as a reporter for the family paper. He became a full time writer and editor for the paper upon his return and the chief editor in 1916. He was twenty-eight years of age.

From the time he was ten years old in 1898 until November 6, 1940, Henry Wallace had either been in school full time, working full time, or both at the same time. President Roosevelt had insisted that he resign his position as Secretary of Agriculture during the campaign of 1940. It was considered unseemly for a political appointee to retain the appointed position and salary while campaigning for an elected position. Of course, the campaign was more than a full time job, but when it was over, Henry Wallace found himself unemployed for the first time in over thirty years. He was far to hyperactive to tolerate seventy-five days of idleness awaiting the inauguration on January 20, 1941.

From his days as editor of *Wallaces' Farmer*, Henry had kept a copy of Webster's Unabridged Dictionary in his office. On page 1543 the volume offers forty distinct definitions for the word 'rest.' As a journalist, author and Secretary of Agriculture, Henry understood and had used virtually all of those definitions at one time or another. It is one thing to have a word in one's vocabulary and quite another to possess the concept in one's behavioral repertoire. After the election Henry and Ilo wanted to spend some time together and get away for a rest. Henry's idea of rest was to travel to Costa Rica and Guatemala where he would be immersed in the language he had been studying for several years. Ilo wondered exactly how restful practicing Spanish would be.

He informed Roosevelt of their plans to spend some time in Latin America and the President thought it a grand idea, with the exception of the planned destinations. Roosevelt wanted the Wallaces to go to Mexico, and while there represent him at the presidential inauguration of Manuel Avila Camacho. It was hastily arranged to have Wallace put on the State Department payroll as "ambassador extraordinary." He was to be paid $50 per day plus 5ᶜ per mile. The Wallaces would be driving their own car. They would be followed by their friends Jim and Helen LaCron in another car. In addition to being long time friends, Jim had been Henry's personal assistant at the Department of Agriculture. He too was a student of the Spanish language.

As they crossed the border at Laredo, Texas on November 25, 1940, no one would have ever dreamed that this trip would change human history at least as much as the events at Pearl Harbor one year and sixteen days later.

Politically, the visit was a smashing success. The visit of the Spanish speaking Vice President-elect went a long way toward mending a difficult and suspicious relationship between Mexico and the United States. President Camacho had just won a fiercely contested, and likely corrupt, election against General Juan Andreu Almazan. General Almazan had been supported by the recently created Revolutionary Party of National Unification. This party was little more than a proxy for European Fascists, particularly those in Spain, who viewed the 1939 election in Mexico as an opportunity to get a foothold in the western hemisphere; a foothold on the southern border of the United States no less.

As was typical of elections involving Fascist factions, the campaign was marred by bloodshed. During a joint appearance of Camacho and Almazan in Los Mochis on the west coast of Sinaloa, a gun battle broke out. Though neither candidate was hit, dozens of people lay dead and wounded when the fire fight ended. The Mexican military had a tradition of political intervention, and there was good reason to fear another Mexican Revolution that could have taken the nation toward either the extreme left or extreme right. Either scenario was not palatable to the Roosevelt administration, given the state of international affairs around the globe.

Everywhere Wallace and LaCron put in an appearance the people were thrilled with their command of the Spanish language, their genuine interest in the nation and its people, and their kindly demeanor. Even before assuming office, Wallace was becoming an international star.

The Wallaces, driving their green Plymouth, had no official entourage except the LaCrons following in their own car. The Mexicans were somewhat taken back, and yet at the same time delighted, by their unpretentious "ambassador extraordinary." They did, however, insist upon some police escort which seemed a provident course of action, given the bloodshed of the recent campaign. In Monterrey the Wallaces and LaCrons were greeted by 150 thousand flag waving residents and a storm of confetti.

Along the way Wallace would confound his police escorts by pulling up short to walk out into fields to inspect crops and talk to farmers. He would wade into groups of schoolchildren on the playgrounds and chat amicably. He laughed out loud when one wide eyed little girl turned to her teacher and said with incredulity, "¡Este gringo habla Español!" ("This Yankee ‹white guy› speaks Spanish!")

In Mexico City when the Wallaces and LaCrons entered the hall for the inauguration ceremonies, every member of the Mexican Congress rose to a standing ovation. Much to his surprise, Wallace was asked to speak to the assembly. His impromptu remarks in Spanish carried the day, "The most practical ideal for the people of this hemisphere is Pan-Americanism. Without hemispheric solidarity we can have no assurance of peace. Without peace, we cannot build in orderly fashion for that prosperity of agriculture, labor, and business which we all so keenly desire."[22]

For most of their journey they were accompanied by Mexican Minister of Agriculture, Marte Gómez. Gómez offered a two week crash course in land reform. For Mexico, it had been a disaster.

¤ ¤ ¤

The War of Mexican Independence from Spain had been a strange affair. On September 16, 1810, "liberal" revolutionaries began fighting ineptly against the Spanish Colonial Government. In the wake of the Napoleonic Wars, Spain revolted against itself. During the Spanish Civil War of 1820 – 23 much of the Spanish empire just dissolved. Many Mexicans of Spanish descent saw this as a threat to their source of wealth and power. General Agustin de Iturbide, who had fought for the Spanish Colonial government against the revolutionaries, seized the opportunity to switch sides, declare independence for Mexico, and at the same time leave the Spanish power elite in place as the landowners and governors of the new nation. Under the Plan of Iguala the independence of the Mexican Empire was recognized by Spain.

The constitutional monarchy that was established under the auspices of the plan recognized Roman Catholicism as the official religion and left virtually all state power and land ownership in the hands of the "criollo" class. Criollos were persons born in Mexico deemed to have limpieza de sangre (cleanliness of blood), meaning they were of "pure" unmixed Iberian Christian ancestry. In some respects, the newly established Mexican Empire codified a caste system with those of pure Spanish ancestry at the top.

Most of the indigenous peoples and people of mixed heritage were, to some extent, "Latinized" by the time of Mexico's independence. Nevertheless, they were second and third class citizens in every respect. Economically they were little more than debt-slaves to wealthy land owners, including the church. The masses chaffed under the yoke of debt, and political unrest was the norm. In 1856 the state broke with the Catholic Church. The Leredo Law allowed church owned land, not used specifically for religious purposes, to be confiscated and sold to private individuals. Virtually all of the buyers were Criollos, so there was no substantive relief for peasants under this first effort at land reform. Peonage, Mexican style, lived on.

In the early twentieth century President Obregon led a radical process he called "Mexicanization." Agrarian reform and land redistribution was one of its main goals. Redistribution was slow. By 1928 approximately 12.5 million acres had been distributed to approximately half a million people in 1500 communities. That calculates to only about twenty-five acres per farmer. The pace of land redistribution quickened dramatically during the administration of President Larzo Cardenas (1934 – 1940). Forty-five million acres of land changed hands, four million of which were expropriated from American owned agricultural firms. This phase of redistribution effectively brought to an end Mexico's version of industrial tenant farming. However, the recipients of the land did not receive the mechanized equipment nor capital necessary to effectively operate their newly acquired properties. As Mexico's population was poised on the verge of explosive growth, their agricultural production plummeted.

The best corn fields Wallace and LaCron saw produced only twenty bushels per acre. That was the very best—most farms were producing ten bushels per acre or less. What was even more distressing to the analytical Mr. Wallace was his calculation that with modern equipment and techniques an Iowan farmer in 1940 required ten hours of labor to produce one bushel of corn. That same bushel, given the state of Mexican agricultural technology, required over two hundred hours of labor. What Wallace and LaCron saw left them profoundly disturbed. They knew that hungry masses provided fertile ground for revolution. They knew that something had to be done— and done soon.

25

THE FARM BOY AT DUPONT

Dr. Norman Borlaug's work at DuPont during World War II.

After Norm returned from Massachusetts, he and Margaret moved into married student housing. They had a two room apartment in the brand new Thatcher Hall. He finished his Master of Science degree in May 1940. With his parents, sisters, and bride in the audience, the graduation ceremony was one of the proudest moments of Norm's life. Though much of the world was diving head long in to the abyss of war, things were looking up nicely for the young Borlaugs.

His mentor, Dr. Stakman, insisted that Norm continue his studies in pursuit of a Doctorate degree. The "General College," where Norm had matriculated his first semester after failing the University of Minnesota entrance exam, was not yet called a Junior College. It was, however, moving in that direction. It had just established a "University Farm School." This program allowed farm kids who had graduated from high school to pursue higher education after harvest and before planting seasons on the farm. Figuring that Norm had succeeded academically, beyond their expectations, and that he could relate to the mind-blowing experiences most of the students would have upon leaving the farm and arriving on campus, the General College administration recruited Norm to teach.

Having been a wrestler on a now nationally ranked team, Norm was recognized on campus as something of a star athlete. The Athletic Director, Marshall Ryman, recruited him to start a wrestling program at the St. Paul campus. There, the "farm boys" wrestled against local high school teams and even managed to win a few meets.

All in all it was a great experience for the farm kids, as well as for Norm, who later recounted, "University Farm School was a great thing. It benefited a critical portion of Minnesota's youth and did a huge amount of good. I'm still mad as hell the university abandoned it after World War II." One could never fault Norman Borlaug for lacking passion.

The economic pressures on the young couple were essentially resolved with Margret's salary from her work as an editor, and Norm's earnings from teaching. It is a wondrous thing what having enough food and less anxiety about hunger can do for cerebration. Norm's complicated and intricate studies of Fusarium lini, a soil fungus that destroys flax, was easier, more fun, and more interesting than all of his heretofore studies combined.

Margaret and Norm did not know at the time that these two years (1940 – 41) would likely be the most idyllic in their lives together. Though they would be married for almost seventy years, world events, fate, and callings to great actions, would conspire to occasion frequent intervals of separation. They would come to understand that life is an odd combination of comings and goings. But all that lay in the newlyweds' future—a future their crystal ball had not yet revealed.

¤ ¤ ¤

Just as Norm was approaching completion of his doctoral research, opportunity knocked in the person of Dr. Frank Kaufert. Dr. Stakman arranged a meeting with Dr. Kaufert, who had actually taught an undergraduate forestry class that Norm had taken years earlier. He had since been working as the director of the biochemical laboratory for E.I. du Pont de Nemours and Company, in Wilmington, Delaware.

Dr. Kaufert had just accepted a position as a full professor at the University of Minnesota. He had been extended the professional courtesy by the DuPont Company of recommending his successor. Though Norm had yet to complete his dissertation, Dr. Stakman was encouraging Kaufert to nominate Borlaug as the next director of DuPont's biochemical lab. Now only twenty-seven years old, and lacking the full credentials (Ph.D.), Norm was absolutely floored by the suggestion. Even more so when he learned the fortune DuPont was offering to pay the incumbent in this position—$2800 per year.

Though he had some doubts, Margaret's voice of reason prevailed. "You are only a couple of months from graduation, you have no other prospects, and at the very least, it's a good place to see if you like working in industry." It is amazing how great a single opportunity appears when "you have no other prospects."

In early December, 1941 the couple had packed their belongings in their "new" 1935 Pontiac and headed east. As they drove through Philadelphia, just thirty miles shy of their new digs in Wilmington, they heard the newspaper boy hawking a special edition, "Pearl Harbor Bombed!" It was December 7, 1941, and like almost everyone of their generation, they never ever forgot exactly where they were, and exactly what they were doing, when they heard those fateful words.

¤ ¤ ¤

At 8:30 the next morning, Norm reported to his first day as director of the DuPont biochemical laboratory. At 12:30pm all work ground to a halt as everyone present crowded around radios to hear their President address a joint session of Congress.

Mr. Vice President, Mr. Speaker, members of the Senate and the House of Representatives: Yesterday, December 7th, 1941— **a date which will live in infamy**—the United States of America was suddenly and deliberately attacked by naval and air forces of the Empire of Japan.

The United States was at peace with that nation, and, at the solicitation of Japan, was still in conversation with its Government and its Emperor looking toward maintenance of peace in the Pacific. Indeed, one hour after Japanese air squadrons had commenced bombing in the American island of Oahu, the Japanese Ambassador to the United States and his colleague delivered to our Secretary of State a formal reply to a recent American message. And while this replay stated that it seemed useless to continue the existing diplomatic negotiations, it contained no threat or hint of war or of armed attack.

It will be recorded that the distance of Hawaii from Japan makes it obvious that the attack was deliberately planned many days or even weeks ago. During the intervening time the Japanese Government has deliberately sought to deceive the United States by false statements and expressions of hope for continued peace.

The attack yesterday on the Hawaiian Islands has caused severe damage to American naval and military forces. I regret to tell you that very many American lives have been lost. In addition American ships have been reported torpedoed on the high seas between San Francisco and Honolulu.

Yesterday the Japanese Government also launched an attack against Malaya.

Last night Japanese forces attacked Hong Kong.

Last night Japanese forces attacked Guam.

Last night Japanese forces attacked the Philippine Islands.

Last night Japanese attacked Wake Island.

And this morning the Japanese attacked Midway Island.

Japan has, therefore, undertaken a surprise offensive extending throughout the Pacific area. The facts of yesterday and today speak for themselves. The people of the United States have already formed their opinions and well understand the implications to the very life and safety of our nation.

As Commander-in-Chief of the Army and Navy, I have directed that all measures be taken for our defense.

But always will our whole nation remember the character of the onslaught against us. No matter how long it may take us to overcome this premeditated invasion, the American people in their righteous might will win through to absolute victory.

I believe that I interpret the will of the Congress and of the people when I assert that we will not only defend ourselves to the uttermost but will make it very certain that this form of treachery shall never again endanger us.

Hostilities exist. There is no blinking at the fact that our people, our territory and our interests are in grave danger.

With confidence in our armed forces—with the unbounding determination of our people—we will gain the inevitable triumph— so help us God.

I ask that the Congress declare that since the unprovoked and dastardly attack by Japan on Sunday, December 7th, 1941, a state of war has existed between the United States and the Japanese Empire.[1]

Three days later, on the morning of November 11, 1941 Germany formally declared war against the United States when Reich Foreign Minister, Joachim von Ribbentrop, delivered this "diplomatic note" to the American Charge d'Affaires in Berlin, Leland B. Morris.

The government of the United States of America, having violated in the most flagrant manner and in ever increasing measure all rules of neutrality in favor of the adversaries of Germany, and having continually been guilty of the most severe provocations toward Germany ever since the outbreak of the European war, brought on by the British declaration of war against Germany on September 3, 1939, has finally resorted to open military acts of aggression.

On September 11, 1941, the President of the United States of America publicly declared that he had ordered the American Navy and Air Force to shoot on sight any German war vessel. In his speech of October 27, 1941, he once more expressly affirmed that this order was in force.

Acting under this order, American naval vessels have systematically attacked German naval forces since early September 1941. Thus, American destroyers, as for instance, the *Greer*, the *Kearny* and the *Reuben James*, have opened fire on German submarines according to plan. The American Secretary of the Navy, Mr. Knox, himself confirmed that the American destroyers attacked German submarines.

Furthermore, the naval forces of the United States of America, under order of their government and contrary to international law, have treated and seized German merchant ships on the high seas as enemy ships.

The German government therefore establishes the following facts:

Although Germany on her part has strictly adhered to the rules of international law in her relations with the United States of America during every period of the present war, the government of the United States of America from initial violations of neutrality has finally proceeded to open acts of war against Germany. It has thereby virtually created a state of war.

The government of the Reich consequently breaks off diplomatic relations with the United States of America and declares that under these circumstances brought about by President Roosevelt, Germany too, as from today, considers herself as being in a state of war with the United States of America.[2]

About two hours later Chancellor Hitler in an address to the Reichstag, explained that the attack on Pearl Harbor was, in fact, the fault of the failed "New Deal" and Franklin Roosevelt's manipulation by Jews—of course.

In the same way, it was not America that discovered Europe, but the other way around. And all that which America did not get from Europe may seem worthy of admiration to a Jewified mixed race, but Europe regards that merely as symptomatic of decay in artistic and cultural life, the product of Jewish or Negroid blood mixture. . . .

In scarcely five years, economic problems had been solved in Germany and unemployment had been overcome. During the same period, President Roosevelt had increased the State Debt of his country to an enormous extent, the decreased value of the dollar, had brought about a further disintegration of economic life, without diminishing the unemployment figures. But this is hardly remarkable when one realizes that the intellects appointed by this man, or more accurately, who appointed him, are members of that same group who, as Jews, are interested only in disruption and never in order. . . .

Roosevelt's New Deal legislation was all-wrong. It was actually the biggest failure ever experienced by one man. There can be no doubt that a continuation of this economic policy would have undone this President in peace time, in spite of all his dialectical skill.

In a European State he would surely have come eventually before a State Court on a charge of deliberate waste of the national wealth; and he would have scarcely escaped at the hands of a civil court, on a charge of criminal business methods. . . .

Roosevelt was fully aware of the danger threatening the card castle of his economic system with collapse, and that he was therefore urgently in need of a diversion in foreign policy. The circle of Jews around Roosevelt encouraged him in this. With Old Testament vindictiveness they regarded the United States as the instrument that they and he could use to prepare a second Purim [slaughter of enemies] against the nations of Europe, which were increasingly anti-Jewish. So it was that the Jews, in all of their satanic baseness, gathered around this man, and he relied on them. Thus began the increasing efforts of the American President to create conflicts, to do everything to prevent conflicts from being peacefully solved. For years this man harbored one desire—that a conflict should break out somewhere in the world. . . .

The fact that the Japanese Government, which has been negotiating for years with this man [Franklin D. Roosevelt], has at last become tired of being mocked by him in such an unworthy way, fills us all, the German people, and all other decent people in the world, with deep satisfaction. . . . Germany and Italy have been finally compelled, in view of this, and in loyalty to the Tripartite Pact, to carry on the struggle against the U.S.A. and England jointly and side by side with Japan for the defense and thus for the maintenance of the liberty and independence of their nations and empires. . . . As a consequence of the further extension of President Roosevelt's policy, which is aimed at unrestricted world domination and dictatorship, the U.S.A. together with England have not hesitated from using any means to dispute the rights of the German, Italian and Japanese nations to the basis of their natural existence. . . . Not only because we are the ally of Japan, but also because Germany and Italy have enough insight and strength to comprehend that, in these historic times, the existence or non-existence of the nations, is being decided perhaps forever.[3] (Partial excerpt of speech.)

At the end of Hitler's 11,955 word ranting diatribe, the Reichstag exploded to their feet with thunderous cheers and applause. Meanwhile, at almost exactly the same hour in Rome, Il Duce, Benito Mussolini, issued a more subdued declaration of war.

This is another day of solemn decision in Italy's history and of memorable events destined to give a new course to the history of continents.

The powers of the steel pact, Fascist Italy and Nationalist Socialist Germany, ever closely linked, participate from today on the side of heroic Japan against the United States of America.

The Tripartite Pact becomes a military alliance which draws around its colors 250,000,000 men determined to do all in order to win.

Neither the Axis nor Japan wanted an extension of the conflict.

One man, one man only, a real tyrannical democrat, through a series of infinite provocations, betraying with a supreme fraud the population of his country, wanted the war and had prepared for it day by day with diabolical obstinacy.

The formidable blows that on the immense Pacific expanse have been already inflicted on American forces show how prepared are the soldiers of the Empire of the Rising Sun.

I say to you, and you will understand, that it is a privilege to fight with them.

Today, the Tripartite Pact, with the plenitude of its forces and its moral and material resources, is a formidable instrument for the war and a certainty for victory.

Tomorrow, the Tripartite Pact will become an instrument of just peace between the peoples.

Italians! Once more arise and be worthy of this historical hour!

We shall win.[4]

¤ ¤ ¤

The world had been set aflame by hatred. Hate which a farm kid from Little Norway could hardly fathom. Whether comprehending the world's insanity or not, within a matter of weeks Norm's position, as DuPont's main microbiologist, was classified "Essential to the War Effort" under the auspices of the War Manpower Commission. For the second time in his life, he was pressed into service for his nation. Unlike his Massachusetts "tour of duty" with the Forest Service in 1939, this was not a time-limited assignment, and there was no opting-out.

By no means did Norm begrudge his participation in the war effort. He also realized that the people on the home-front had to continue to care for and about each other. He recalled, "With millions being called up for military duty, those of us still in civilian life had to fill in. I, for example, spent three nights a week substituting for Boy Scout leaders who were away in uniform. Someone needed to keep the activities going."

Norm knew that the war would be won someday, but even in a world gone utterly mad, kindness, especially with young people, would ultimately win the peace.

¤ ¤ ¤

The work at DuPont was interesting and rewarding. Norm contributed to the war effort in ways that can now only be reckoned.

He was involved in analyzing a powder captured from Nazi forces in the Soviet Union. Typhus was killing more Russian people than the Nazi armed forces. Yet, the German troops were not infected. The Soviets noticed that the bodies of killed and captured Germans were not infested with lice. It had long been known that lice were the carriers of typhus, but how to rid millions of people of lice without daily bathing was a total mystery. Historically, typhus outbreaks were frequently concurrent with prolonged military campaigns, when soldiers and civilians alike did not have access to sanitary bathing. On humans, lice live primarily in pubic, underarm and head hair.

Norm and the chemists at DuPont broke the code and identified the chemical composition of the powder. They called it AL63. Huge quantities of it were quickly manufactured and distributed to Allied troops and civilians in territories controlled by the allies all over the world. Millions of people used the powder on the hairy parts of their bodies.

When British and Canadian Forces liberated the concentration camp at Bergen-Belsen in lower Saxony, typhus had already broken out. The horrors they found were described by BBC reporter, Richard Dimbleby.

> Here over an acre of ground lay dead and dying people. You could not see which was which. . . . The living lay with their heads against the corpses and around them moved the awful, ghostly procession of emaciated, aimless people, with nothing to do and with no hope of life, unable to move out of your way, unable to look at the terrible sights around them. . . . Babies had been born here, tiny wizened things that could not live. . . . A mother, driven mad,

screamed at a British sentry to give her milk for her child, and thrust the tiny mite into his arms, then ran off, crying terribly. He opened the bundle and found the baby had been dead for days. This day at Belsen was the most horrible of my life.[5]

Historically, typhus pandemics had been notoriously difficult to control once the outbreak occurred. By the time the Allied forces arrived on April 15, 1945, typhus had already claimed the lives of at least 20 thousand of the Belsen prisoners, including the fifteen year old Anne Frank and her sister Margot. Another 13,994 former prisoners would die after liberation. The military's secret AL63 powder was used to kill the lice on everyone who came in contact with the prison camp. Though the bacteria 'Salmonella Enterica Serovar Typhi' was obviously present and virulent, there was no continental epidemic subsequent to World War II, as there had been after World War I, when 25 million Europeans were infected and 3 million died. Typhus was virtually stopped in the tracks of the dead body lice. Hundreds of thousands, perhaps millions, of human lives were saved.

This was Norm's first participation in an initiative that saved a multitude of lives. By no means was it to be his last. Nor was this his last encounter with the controversy that often follows bold, life-saving action. With good reason, humanity saw the use of AL63 as a positive thing. However, the name of this chemical became synonymous with the human tendency toward massive, indulgent excess—the same tendency that precipitated the Great Depression. In fact, too much of a good thing is often a bad thing—sometimes a very bad thing. The enormous overuse of this chemical had dire consequences for the environment, particularly riparian environments, where it accumulated and decimated amphibious wildlife. The chemicals that the DuPont chemists disaggregated from the white powder seized from German soldiers in 1942, were Dichloro-Diphenyl-Trichloroethane—more commonly known as DDT.

Controversy aside, it cannot be doubted that Norm's motivation was a reflection of the times in which he lived and the immediate need to save desperate people from the horrors of an agonizing death. This motivation became a theme that would resonate throughout the remainder of his life.

Another of Norm's assignments came from the need to use ocean currents as the transport vehicle for food delivery. Due to enemy air and sea patrols, the U.S. Navy was unable to land supplies for the allied forces on Guadalcanal. Cartons of foodstuffs were being dumped in the ocean as the tide was rolling in. Theoretically, the marines would be able to pull the crates of supplies out of the surf as they washed onto the beaches. However, as often as not, the seals on the cartons had dissolved in the ocean water and the contents were spoiled. Norm's instructions were quite simple, "Fix that!" And he did. His team found a polyvinyl acetate glue that is virtually impervious to water. Thousands of tons of food were spared the ruin of salt water. Polyvinyl acetate is still today the industry standard adhesive for food packaging and labeling.

The military was also confronted with mold and fungus, which was rotting everything from food stuffs, to canvas tents, to soldiers' feet, particularly in the Pacific theater. Norm and his team tested every matter they could lay their hands on. What they found that resisted the jungle rot is actually somewhat surprising, given that it has a wood pulp base. Nevertheless, cellulose acetate worked, and it worked well. The problem was that it was rare and the United States had no significant industrial production capabilities.

Vice President Henry Wallace was the chairman of the Board of Economic Warfare and his friend and political ally, Donald M. Nelson, chaired the War Production Board. When the need to produce massive amounts of cellulose acetate was presented to these boards, there was some hand ringing about the cost of bringing a whole new industry on-line. Secretary of Commerce, Jesse Jones, continued his pattern of resisting anything that he viewed as adding "superfluous costs" to the war effort.

Jones contended that all loans had to be secured and that deficit spending by the federal government was ruining capitalism. Born to wealth, Jones was by far the richest man on Roosevelt's cabinet. He had never served in the military and could not imagine the pain of marching in wet combat boots, without toenails, which had long since succumbed to fungal infection.

After a brief equivocation, the government charged forward with funding the development of an industry that supplied the troops with a defense against a tiny, but insidious enemy. An enemy that could disable as many soldiers as all of the rifles of the Axis Powers. In addition to saving the lives of thousands of soldiers, today the cellulose acetate industry produces apparel linings, blouses, dresses, wedding and party attire, home furnishings, draperies, upholstery, slip covers, ink reservoirs for fiber-tip pens, diapers, surgical products, and even Lego bricks. Over the next six decades, the taxes paid on the profits earned from these products have repaid Uncle Sam a thousand fold. Perhaps if Secretary Jesse Jones could return for a single day, he would acknowledge a more than satisfactory return on the federal government's investment.

¤ ¤ ¤

Twice during the course of the war Norm received orders to report for military duty. As soon as this happened, the DuPont folks would run down to the draft board waving the letter from the War Manpower Commission designating Borlaug's position as "Essential to the War Effort." The battles Norm was to fight overseas, were yet in his future—he stayed stateside for the duration of World War II.

Norm genuinely enjoyed his work at DuPont. He made his post-war plans to continue with the company. This time he was sure. His career choice was made. His future was secure. He wasn't going to be a high school science teacher and coach. He wasn't going to be a forester in the wildernesses of the American west. He wasn't going to be a university professor in Minnesota. He was going to be a microbiologist and work for DuPont. But fate and for the third time Dr. Elvin Stakman had other ideas.

26

BENEVOLENCE

Establishment of the Rockefeller Foundation.

In his 1886 book, *The Gospel of Wealth*, Andrew Carnegie wrote, "The best means of benefiting the community is to place within its reach the ladders upon which the aspiring can rise—free libraries, parks, and means of recreation by which men are helped in body and mind; works of art certain to give pleasure and improve the public taste; and public institutions of various kinds, which will improve the general condition of the people; in this manner returning their surplus wealth to the masses of their fellows in the forms best calculated to do them lasting good . . . yet the day is not far distant when the man who dies leaving behind him millions of available wealth, which was free for him to administer during life, will pass away 'unwept, unhonored, and unsung,' no matter what uses he leaves the dross which he cannot take with him. Of such as these the public verdict will be: 'The man who dies thus rich dies disgraced.' Such, in my opinion, is the true gospel concerning wealth, obedience to which is destined some day to solve the problem of the rich and the poor, and to bring 'Peace on earth, among men good will.'"

John Davison Rockefeller was born on July 8, 1839 in Richford, New York. He was by no means born rich. All of his children and grandchildren would be. He combined intellect, ambition, and energy with a great sense of timing. Riding the ascending cusp of the industrial revolution, in 1863 Rockefeller and several partners borrowed money and built an oil refinery on the east bank of the Cuyahoga River in Cleveland. Already there was a robust demand for petroleum products, but no one at the time could have begun to imagine the demand that would result from the coming of the internal combustion engine. Well before that engine rolled off of Ford's assembly lines, Rockefeller had already amassed a fortune worth tens of millions of dollars as primary share holder in Standard Oil, Inc.

J.D. Rockefeller, Sr. was an enigmatic character to be sure. Some considered him a cut-throat industrialist; others saw in him the most forward thinking philanthropist of the era. In fairness, both points of view could be supported by the facts of his life. At sixteen years of age he took a job as an assistant bookkeeper with Hewitt & Tuttle, a produce firm. He earned $50 for three months work. Acceding to his socialist inclinations, he tithed ten percent of those earnings to his church; a practice he would maintain with various benevolent causes for the remainder of his life.

In 1889 Rockefeller read Andrew Carnegie's essay, "The Gospel of Wealth" that had been published three years earlier. Greatly impressed, he found in Carnegie a mentor for the organization of his philanthropic endeavors. That same year he gave the University of Chicago the first gift of many, which would eventually come to total over $80 million. In 1901 he founded the Rockefeller Institute for Medical Research in New York. In 1906 a trusted business advisor, Fredrick T. Gates, warned Rockefeller that his wealth was growing so fast he needed to set up "permanent corporate philanthropies for the good of mankind" lest his heirs "dissipate their inheritances or become intoxicated with power."

It is doubtful that Mr. Gates was actually worried about Rockefeller's only son, John D. Rockefeller, Jr., who was something of a financial wizard in his own right, and had become one of his father's closest financial advisors. In 1909 the father and son founded the Rockefeller Sanitary Commission, which was credited with eventually eradicating hookworm disease that had long plagued the American South.

The Rockefeller Foundation was officially established on May 14, 1913, under the auspices of a charter granted by the State of New York and signed by Governor William Sulzer. The Senior Rockefeller endowed the foundation with nearly $250 million, and Junior became its first president. During the course of his life, Rockefeller, Jr. would give over $537 million to various causes supported by the foundation.

During the Foundation's first thirty years it focused primarily on public health, medical training, higher education, social sciences, and the arts. Then in January 1941 the Vice President-elect, just back from recent trip to Mexico, strode into their offices with another idea.

27

Comestibles Por Mexico

Vice President Wallace pitches an idea to feed Mexico—the Rockefeller Foundation establishes the Mexican Agricultural Project.

For a variety of reasons Henry Wallace believed in writing reports. First, long before becoming Secretary of Agriculture, he was a journalist. He understood the power of the written word. Second, he found that the process of writing helped him clarify his own thoughts, experiences, and possible courses of action. He was also aware of the historical context in which he was working, and in his own mind many of his reports were primarily documents of historical record. Finally, and perhaps most importantly during Henry's years in Washington, he became convinced that the recommendations in written reports received more serious attention at the White House than his frequent conversations with the President and his staff.

Upon returning from Mexico Henry submitted the report of the "ambassador extraordinary" to the Secretary of State, Cordell Hull, and President Roosevelt. He also sent a copy over to his colleague, Secretary Morgenthau, at Treasury, owing to the fact that what the Vice President-elect was proposing would cost some money.

His traveling companion, Jim LaCron, had helped draft the report before Henry and Ilo flew back to Washington. Jim's wife, Helen, had the misfortune of contracting malaria while on their tour and was hospitalized in Mexico City. While his wife convalesced, Jim remained in Mexico City, staying at the residence of Ambassador Joseph Daniels. As was often the case after a bout with malaria, Mrs. LaCron's health never fully recovered. Instead of returning to Washington, the LaCrons returned to their home in

Des Moines. Wallace's most trusted aide and confidant would never return to work full-time on the Washington scene.

For the first time in almost a decade, Henry submitted an article for publication in *Wallaces' Farmer.* With minor modifications, it was the report that he had provided to the President and Secretary of State. The report dealt almost exclusively with the plight of Mexican agriculture and was virtually silent about the diplomatic successes the American officials had enjoyed.

When Henry went to the White House to meet with Roosevelt, he found that both Secretaries Hull and Morgenthau were to be included in the conversation. Initially, the President was most interested in the diplomatic side of things. He was delighted to hear that Wallace had been invited to speak at the Mexican Presidential inauguration, albeit extemporaneously. He was thrilled to learn that Minister of Agriculture Gómez had been assigned as their "tour guide." But as Henry spoke of the desperate state of affairs regarding Mexican food production, the light bulb went off in the President's head. He realized the grave threat posed by a hungry population living and starving just south of an invisible line, stretching thousands of miles across the Southwestern frontier.

The gentlemen gathered in the Oval office that morning could easily envision an invasion, of sorts, by thousands, perhaps millions of hungry illegal immigrants searching for work and money to send back to families in Mexico. Wallace also carefully pointed out the dangers of right and left wing extremism in the throes of a possible famine—as if they did not already have enough international worries in January 1941.

After Wallace finished his report, Secretary Hull shared his most recent intelligence information on Mexico. He offered a level of detail that astounded Wallace, who wondered just what kind of operation was really taking place at the recently visited United States Embassy in Mexico City. Hull reported that the latest round of agrarian reform and land redistribution under President Cárdenas was viewed as communist inspired. The radical right of Mexico, and elsewhere, were active in undermining the effort and were delighted with its apparent failure. It was the State Department's contention that should there be a coup d'état, or even another revolution, it would likely be spawned on the far right. They had reliable evidence that European Fascists had made considerable inroads in Latin America, particularly in Argentina, Paraguay, Uruguay, Mexico, as well as some places in the Caribbean.

Therefore, the unstated goal of the State Department was to encourage Mexico to step back from the agrarian reforms of the preceding six years. However, they did not believe that they would have a receptive ear within the current administration of President Camacho. Instead, their long term goal was to "assist" the Partido Revolutionario Instutional (Institutional Revolutionary Party) with identification of a leader who would be more amenable to reversing course when "elected" president six years hence. (*The Mexican Constitution limits the service of the President to one six year term.*) Though flabbergasted, Wallace was only mildly surprised by the State Department's calculation. He argued, that if a Fascist inspired revolution was pending famine, they likely would not have to wait six years. He believed the state of agriculture in Mexico was so desperate that collapse of the food production and distribution system was imminent.

Roosevelt had been listening carefully, then with his typical "can do" bravado interjected, "Well, Mr. Vice President, I believe you still have quite a few friends over at Agriculture, I guess your boys are going to have to figure out a way to send some of our surplus to Mexico at a cost even a bankrupt nation can afford." Waggling the cigarette holder clinched in his teeth, and clearly still troubled by the specter of thousands of hungry illegal immigrants crossing the southern border, the President added, "Gentlemen, we are also going to need a mechanism to legally import labor from Mexico for a while. Besides, once we get drawn into the fighting and making soldiers out of farm boys, we are going to need the help."

(*In August 1942 the United States and Mexico signed a contract establishing the "Mexican Farm Labor Program," more commonly known as the "Bracero Program." Over the twenty-two year life of the program 4.5 million guest workers would legally cross the border to obtain jobs on farms and railroads in the United States.*)

Secretary Hull cautioned this whole food and labor plan might be a little tricky, inasmuch as the administration of former Mexican President Cárdenas had confiscated over 4 million acres from American owned agricultural firms for redistribution to peasant farmers, and the Mexican government had expropriated all oil resources and expelled all U.S. owned oil interests from Mexico. The big boys in oil and agriculture were more than a bit miffed.

Roosevelt surprised his Cabinet members with his level of detailed understanding about the oil situation south of the border. He knew that not only had the oil company representatives challenged President Cardenas authority to end an oil workers strike, they had actually mocked him during a December 1937 meeting at the Presidential Palace in Mexico City. Roosevelt had seen reports that when this occurred Cardenas stated, "Sirs, we are finished!"[1] He had palace guards immediately and unceremoniously escort his oil company visitors out of the building.

On March 18, 1938, exactly four months after the oil company executives' boorish behavior, President Cardenas announced that all mineral and oil reserves found within the soil of Mexico belonged to the nation. In retaliation U.S. oil companies mounted a ferocious public relations campaign against Mexico, urging the boycott of Mexican goods particularly oil products. Secretary Hull pointed out that turkey had come home to roost, because it had forced Mexico to establish business ties for the exportation of oil to Fascist nations in Europe. Thus the door had been opened for enhanced Fascist influence in Latin America.

Wallace continued to press his main point that the United States needed to seize the initiative, "Gentlemen—weapons, men and material will win a war, but food will win the peace. The food production capacity of Mexico will not, cannot meet their future population needs. We must act. I propose establishing agricultural research facilities in Mexico to develop hybridized corn and grain crops specifically for the Mexican soils and climate."

At this point Secretary Morgenthau chimed in that Treasury was almost ready to unveil the new Series E United States Savings Bonds. They would be marketed as "Defense Bonds" with the idea that people would be more likely to purchase the bonds if they believed the funds would be used to enhance national defense. He then explained that in reality the receipts from the sale of the bonds would be used to remove currency from circulation in the economy as a hedge against inflation. That being the case, he pointed out that if it became widely known that the government was funding research projects that **might** feed Mexicans at some indeterminate point in the future, uncomfortable questions would likely be raised about the real purpose for the sale of those bonds. That concern, coupled with the fact that hunger within the United States was far from eradicated, hammered the last nail in the coffin of Henry's idea for an overt U.S. government role in feeding Mexico.

In summing up, the President turned to Wallace, "Henry, you know the federal government probably doesn't have as much money available as John D's boys have on ice up in the City."

The next Vice President asked, "Do I have your approval to approach them about funding this project then?"

"Absolutely, that is exactly what needs to be done now." As the group rose to leave the Oval Office, the President added, "Oh, and Henry."

"Yes Mr. President?"

"Make this happen—the world is counting on you."

Perhaps no truer words were ever spoken.

In point of fact, Wallace had already been casting about to determine possible foundation interest in his proposed project for Mexico. He had in hand a preliminary commitment from Mexican Agriculture Minister Gómez on behalf of his government to match resources. Mexico had land and could build research facilities and living quarters for staff. What they lacked was the scientific expertise and the cash to pay the researchers.

Wallace did not believe this would be an extraordinarily expensive undertaking. Having anticipated the potential political roadblocks discussed in the Oval Office, he had already placed a call to John A. Ferrell, associate director of the Rockefeller Foundation International Health Division. Always the agriculturalist, Wallace knew that before you plant the seeds you have to till the soil.

¤ ¤ ¤

In 1940 the United States Constitution mentioned the Vice President in only four clauses:

> Article 1, Section 3, Clause 4—The Vice President of the United States shall be President of the Senate, but shall have no Vote, unless they be equally divided.
>
> Article 1, Section 3, Clause 5—The Senate shall choose their other Officers, and also a President pro tempore, in the Absence of the Vice President, or when he shall exercise the Office of the President of the United States.
>
> Article 2, Section 1, Clause 6—In Case of the Removal of the President from Office, or of his Death, Resignation, or Inability to discharge the Powers and Duties of the said Office, the Same shall devolve on the Vice President, and the Congress may by Law provide for the Case of Removal, Death, Resignation or Inability, both of the President and Vice President, declaring what Officer

shall then act as President, and such Officer shall act accordingly, until the Disability be removed, or a President shall be elected.

Article 2, Section 4—The President, Vice President and all civil Officers of the United States, shall be removed from Office on Impeachment for, and Conviction of, Treason, Bribery, or other High crimes and misdemeanors.[2]

The constitution primarily charges the Vice President with the responsibility to preside over the Senate. In reality, because of Senate rules, the Vice President is not allowed to debate or address the Senate. The Senate elects a President pro tempore from among their ranks and they frankly prefer that the Vice President not even bother to come over to the Capitol unless there is likely to be a tie vote. In which case, the Vice President would exercise his second duty, casting the deciding vote. This arrangement was just fine with Vice President Wallace. When he told his mother that it was his duty as Vice President to preside over the Senate, her response was, "Oh, you poor boy."[3]

Wallace's disdain for the Senate rules, unlimited debate on any issue, and the committee structure governed by the seniority system was captured in his comment, "One of the most futile occupations I know is presiding over the Senate." This attitude about the institution did not extend to the individual members. His liberal politics aside, he maintained respectful and positive relationships with most Senators, who were themselves mostly from the conservative side of the political spectrum.

Wallace's predecessor had been John "Cactus Jack" Garner. He once described the Vice Presidency as ". . . not worth a warm bucket of piss." Garner described the reporter who cleaned-up his statement, by replacing the word "piss" with "spit," as a "pantywaist."[4] While Garner viewed his service as Vice President with considerable disdain, he got along marvelously with the Senators. In no small measure because he kept an open bar in his office at the capitol and Senators could drop by any time of the day or night for a stiff shot of their favorite alcoholic libation.

On the other extreme, Henry Wallace was a teetotaler. The day after being sworn in as the nation's 33rd Vice President he closed the bar. This did not win him a bunch of friends among the Senators. He endeavored, therefore, to engage the members of Congress' upper house in healthier and more sober activities. He tried to get them to play volleyball, but was never able to get enough players together at the same time to make a game. This was perhaps due in part to lack of interest, but also reflected the reality of the complicated Senate calendars.

Henry reasoned that a more individualized sport might be easier to arrange and a better fit for the Senator's various schedules. So, he tried to establish a boxing club among members of the United States Senate. Wall Doxey, the Senate Sergeant at Arms, privately expressed his misgivings about this activity. He felt that the chance of a "lucky punch" posed a potentially unacceptable risk for the nation in general, and the Senate in particular. Not long after expressing these concerns, Henry Wallace landed a left uppercut to the chin of Louisiana Senator Allen Ellender. It knocked him down—it knocked him out. With that incident the Sergeant at Arms' objections prevailed, and the short-lived Senate boxing club was suspended forthwith.

Soon thereafter, Henry and his friends, Milo Perkins and Jim LaCron, when he was in Washington, took up the sport of boomerang throwing—of all things. From time to time, they were joined by colleagues, reporters, and visitors at Potomac Park. The press loved it. This activity from Down Under was just one of those fun and frivolous activities that everyone seemed to enjoy—no pressure.

As Vice President, Wallace only had two other constitutional duties: 1) wait around for the President to either die or become incapacitated; 2) avoid being convicted of treason, bribery, or other high crimes and misdemeanors. With good reason, he was far more concerned about the former than the latter.

To put it bluntly, after eight years of a frenetic activity level as Secretary of Agriculture, the Vice President was bored. Soon he decided to take the President at his word and take a little train trip up to "the city." In New York he met with Raymond Fosdick, the president of the Rockefeller Foundation. After the congratulatory small talk about his recent inauguration, the Vice President steered the conversation toward his recent trip to Mexico. He talked about the warmth of his reception and the kindness of the people. He talked about the population growth and agrarian reforms Mexico had undertaken during the century's first four decades. He talked about nutrition as a most critical aspect of health care. Saving until last the topic about which he had the most expertise—enhanced food production through hybridization and improved agricultural technology.

By 1941 Wallace's childhood experiments with growing and hybridizing corn had begun to pay off in earnest. The little fledgling Hi-Bred Seed Company he had left in the care of his Iowa friends, J.J. Newlin, Nelson Urban, Raymond Baker, Roswell (Bob) Garst, and Fred Lehmann back in 1933 had grown into a behemoth. In 1933 less than one percent of all corn harvested was the product of hybrid seed. Even at that, their little seed company had grossed a whopping $20,000 that year. By 1941, seventy-eight percent of all corn planted in the corn belt was hybridized. Pioneer Hi-Bred revenues had grown to $2.5 million. Corn production had increased from 24.1 bushels per acre to over thirty-one bushels during that same period.

Yes, indeed, Henry Wallace knew a thing or two about enhancing crop yields through hybridization. He explained to Mr. Fosdick that the United States could not just take a bunch of seeds from Iowa and give them to Mexico. That simply would not work. Successful hybridization had to be done locally to accommodate local soil and climatic conditions. He made the case that Mexican farmers were only producing ten bushels per acre. For a modest investment in agricultural research, enormous benefits could be realized in terms of food production.

Mr. Fosdick listened courteously, without interrupting or interjecting any thoughts of his own. When Henry was done with his spiel, Fosdick told him that he had been preaching to the choir. The Rockefeller Foundation had come to recognize that their historic focus on health programs was realizing many great successes. What they had come to believe, however, was that their success against the likes of yellow fever, hookworm, and malaria may have been saving people from diseases only to be condemned to a life of hunger or a slow excruciatingly painful death by starvation.

At the mention of malaria, Fosdick paused to inquire about Helen LaCron's health. Henry related the events surrounding her infection with malaria and how they had to rush her out of the back country to the hospital in Mexico City when they realized the severity of her illness.

Mr. Fosdick resumed with the issue at hand, "You know, Mr. Vice President, the Foundation has for some time been supporting family planning and birth control research."

To which Wallace replied, "That will surely be a most important endeavor, but for a whole host of cultural and economic reasons I believe humanity is a century, perhaps two, away from embracing population control in a serious way—in the mean time, we better figure out how to feed 'em."

On the spot, Mr. Fosdick made a commitment of $20,000 to put the wheels in motion for a project to help feed Mexico. The Vice President left feeling gratified that in fact he could do something of value in his current job.

¤ ¤ ¤

Within days the Rockefeller Foundation appointed a commission of three men. Richard Bradfield (professor of soil sciences at Cornell University), Paul Mangelsdorf (professor of plant genetics and economic botany at Harvard University) and Norman Borlaug's mentor, Elvin Stakman from the University of Minnesota, were sent to Mexico to conduct the initial survey of the task at hand.

Vice President Wallace called his friend, Minister Gómez, in Mexico to let him know that some American scientists were coming down with more benevolent intentions than the oil barons of the decade prior. Of course, Gómez knew that it was the wealth of the grand-daddy of all oil barons, John D. Rockefeller, that was making this endeavor possible.

Upon returning from Mexico, the commission submitted its report to Mr. Fosdick and the Rockefeller Foundation trustees. One of the survey commission members, Richard Bradfield, summarized the Foundation's new direction:

> I am convinced that the post war services of American agronomists will not be confined within the United States.... When the war is over, there will be millions to feed, large communities of people to be resettled, and farms to be supplied with seed, fertilizer, machinery, and livestock. A roster of qualified personnel for assisting with such work is already being prepared. ... [T]he leaders of some of our large philanthropic foundations have become convinced that the best way to improve the health and well being of people is first to improve their agriculture.[5]

The story was picked up by *Wallaces' Farmer* and Dr. Bradfield's comment was quoted therein. Sitting at the corner of his desk in the Vice President's office, Henry Wallace grinned when he read the article. A year later the Rockefeller Foundation appropriated $192,800 for staffing and equipping the first experimental station. In partnership with the Mexican Ministry of Agriculture, the Mexican Agricultural Project (MAP) was underway.

The cocoons had opened and millions of butterflies were ready to emerge.

28

Winning The Peace

Vice President Wallace's role during World War II.

As early in his term as April 1941, Vice President Wallace was busy mounting a full court press for creating a sustainable peace in the post-war world. The United States military had not yet joined the fight, when the Vice President commented in a speech to the Foreign Policy Administration, "After the victory, what of the peace? The battle of the peace will be more difficult to win than the battle of the war. All Europe will be a mad swirl of chaotic forces. Unless we are prepared to help in the reorganization of a shattered world, these forces will leap from continent to continent and destroy even the United States."[1] Sitting in the audience and hearing these words was the U.S. Army Chief of Staff, General George C. Marshall.

Over and over, the Vice President hammered on the theme that the Allies had to do whatever was necessary to defeat racist fascism and imperialism around the world. But he always stressed that the actions taken by the United States during the course of the war, and immediately afterward, would set the geopolitical stage for decades to come. Consistent with his own spirituality, his messages keeled toward pacifism, opportunity, abundance, and kindness. In an April 1942 memo to President Roosevelt, Wallace was blunt in stating that we are writing the post-war world as we go along. The end of the war will be our second chance. We can choose to circumnavigate the pitfalls that followed World War I. We can now work toward establishing a world where security, stability, efficiency and abundance will prevail.

It is important to note that Henry Wallace was the first Vice

President in America's history with a real job. President Roosevelt viewed the Vice President with such high regard that he made sure Henry's talents were not wasted sitting around "waiting for the President to die." Roosevelt created the Supply Priorities and Allocations Board (SPAB) and designated Wallace its Chair. Wallace was also appointed chairman of the Board of Economic Warfare (BEW) and the Economic Defense Board (EDB). He also represented all of these boards on the War Production Board (WPB).

¤ ¤ ¤

In 1923, Kahlil Gibran's *The Prophet*, gave voice to Uncle Henry Wallace's dream of a prosperous nation, founded upon the principals of an agrarian society.

> Would that I could gather your houses into my hand, and like a sower scatter them in forests and meadow.
> Would the valleys were your streets, and the green paths you alleys, that you might seek one another through vineyards, and come with the fragrance of the earth in your garments.
> But these things are not yet to be. . . .[2]

Another of history's quirky ironies seems to lie the fact that as Vice President, Henry A. Wallace oversaw the death knell of his grandfather's dream. If twenty years of rural economic depression and seven years of drought and dust storms had not been enough to break the back of that gentle agrarian dream, the attack on Pearl Harbor sealed its fate. On December 8, 1941, with Vice President Wallace chairing the meeting, the Supply Allocations and Priorities Board (SAPB) issued the following statement.

> A united people will harness the unparalleled might of the United States to one slogan—VICTORY. From this moment we are engaged in a victory program. We can talk and act no longer in terms of a defense program. Victory is our one and only objective, and everything else is subordinate to it.[3]

And thus the nation was committed to total war mobilization. Every industry, including agriculture, would convert to the war effort. Hundreds of thousands of young men and women left farms for jobs making bombers and battleships, cannons and rifles, bullets and boots. Several million more would use those weapons and supplies as they fought bloody battle after bloody battle across North Africa, Europe, Southeast Asia and the Pacific. Many died, most would never return to the farm, and Uncle Henry's dream died too.

¤ ¤ ¤

Given the Vice President's critical roles in the nation's war efforts, when Wallace went public with his concerns about the post-war world on May 8, 1942, he was not just some talking-head Vice President of an earlier era. He was the man, designated by the Roosevelt Administration, to "inform the war with moral purpose." His speech "The Price of Free World Victory" delivered in New York City at the Free World Association meeting did just that.

> This is a fight between a slave world and a free world. Just as the United States in 1862 could not remain half slave and half free, so in 1942 the world must make its decision for a complete victory one way or the other. . . .
>
> The people are on the march toward even fuller freedom than the most fortunate peoples of the earth have hitherto enjoyed. No Nazi counterrevolution will stop it. The common man will smoke the Hitler stooges out into the open in the United States, in Latin America, and in India. He will destroy their influence. No Lavals, no Mussolinis will be tolerated in a Free World. . . .
>
> The people, in their millennial and revolutionary march toward manifesting here on earth the dignity that is in every human soul, hold as their credo the Four Freedoms enunciated by President Roosevelt in his message to Congress on January 6, 1941. These Four Freedoms are the very core of the revolution for which the United Nations have taken their stand. We who live in the United States may think there is nothing very revolutionary about freedom of religion, freedom of expression, and freedom from the fear of secret police. But when we begin to think about the significance of freedom from want for the average man, then we know that the revolution of the past 150 years has not been completed, either here in the United States or in any other nation in the world. We know that

this revolution cannot stop until freedom from want has actually been attained.

And now, as we move forward toward realizing the Four Freedoms of this people's revolution, I would like to speak about four duties. It is my belief that every freedom, every right, every privilege has its price, its corresponding duty without which it cannot be enjoyed. The four duties of the people's revolution, as I see them today, are these:

The duty to produce to the limit.

The duty to transport as rapidly as possible to the field of battle.

The duty to fight with all that is in us.

The duty to build a peace—just, charitable and enduring.

The fourth duty is that which inspires the other three. . . .

Some have spoken of the "American Century." I say that the century on which we are entering—the century which will come out of this war—can be and must be the century of the common man. Everywhere the common man must learn to build his own industries with his own hands in a practical fashion. Everywhere the common man must learn to increase his productivity so that he and his children can eventually pay to the world community all that they have received. . . .

If we really believe that we are fighting for a people's peace, all the rest becomes easy. Production, yes—it will be easy to get production without either strikes or sabotage, production with the wholehearted co-operation between willing arms and keen brains; enthusiasm, zip, energy geared to the tempo of keeping at it everlastingly, day after day. Hitler knows as well as those of us who sit in on the War Production Board meetings that we here in the United States are winning the battle of production.

I need say little about the duty to fight. Some people declare, and Hitler believes, that the American people have grown soft in the last generation. Hitler agents continually preach in South America that we are cowards, unable to use, like the "brave" German soldiers, the weapons of modern war. It is true that American youth hates war with a holy hatred. But because of that fact and because Hitler and the German people stand as the very symbol of war, we shall fight with a tireless enthusiasm until war and the possibility of war have been removed from this planet. . . .

The American fighting men, and all the fighting men of the United Nations, will need to summon all their courage during the next few months. I am convinced that the summer and fall of 1942 will be a time of supreme crisis for us all. . . .

There can be no half measures. North, South, East, West and Middle West—the will of the American people is for complete victory.

No compromise with Satan is possible. We shall not rest until all the victims under the Nazi yoke are freed. We shall fight for a complete peace as well as a complete victory.

The people's revolution is on the march, and the devil and all his angels cannot prevail against it. They cannot prevail, for on the side of the people is the Lord.

He giveth power to the faint; to them that have no might He increaseth strength. . . . They that wait upon the Lord shall mount up with wings as eagles; they shall run, and not be weary; they shall walk and not be faint.

Strong in the strength of the Lord, we who fight in the people's cause will never stop until that cause is won.[4] (Partial excerpt of speech.)

In that brief half hour, behind that podium in the dining hall of the Hotel Commodore, Vice President Wallace articulated the moral authority to win the war **and** win the peace. He articulated his belief in "the century of the common man."

¤ ¤ ¤

It is exceedingly bizarre that two of the most famous and articulate pacifists of the twentieth century laid the groundwork for development of nuclear weapons. That the pacifist, Henry Wallace, believed fervently in complete and total victory cannot be questioned, as witnessed by his involvement in the development of the nuclear weapon from its earliest conception. The origins of an insane global arms race, that drove humanity to the brink of its own annihilation, is found in a letter sent to President Roosevelt by another pacifist, Albert Einstein. In his August 2, 1939 letter,

Einstein warned of the possibility that nuclear fusion could be used to create "extremely powerful bombs."

Albert Einstein
Old Grove Road
Peconic, Long Island
August 2nd, 1939

F.D. Roosevelt
President of the United States
White House
Washington, D.C.

Sir:

Some recent work by E. Fermi and L. Szilard, which has been communicated to me in manuscript, leads me to expect that the element uranium may be turned into a new and important source of energy in the immediate future. Certain aspects of the situation which has arisen seem to call for watchfulness and if necessary, quick action on the part of the Administration. I believe therefore that it is my duty to bring to your attention the following facts and recommendations.

In the course of the last four months it has been made probable through the work of Joliot in France as well as Fermi and Szilard in America—that it may be possible to set up a nuclear chain reaction in a large mass of uranium, by which vast amounts of power and large quantities of new radium-like elements would be generated. Now it appears almost certain that this could be achieved in the immediate future.

This new phenomenon would also lead to the construction of bombs, and it is conceivable—though much less certain—that extremely powerful bombs of this type may thus be constructed. A single bomb of this type, carried by boat and exploded in a port, might very well destroy the whole port together with some of the surrounding territory. However, such bombs might very well prove too heavy for transportion by air.

The United States has only very poor ores of uranium in moderate quantities. There is some good ore in Canada and former Czechoslovakia, while the most important source of uranium is in the Belgian Congo.

In view of this situation you may think it desirable to have some permanent contact maintained between the Administration and the group of physicists working on chain reactions in America. One possible way of achieving this might be for you to entrust the task with a person who has your confidence and who could perhaps serve in an unofficial capacity. His task might comprise the following:

a) to approach Government Departments, keep them informed of the further development, and put forward recommendations for Government action, giving particular attention to the problem of securing a supply of uranium ore for the United States.

b) to speed up the experimental work, which is at present being carried on within the limits of the budgets of University laboratories, by providing funds, if such funds be required, through his contacts with private persons who are willing to make contributions for this cause, and perhaps also by obtaining co-operation of industrial laboratories which have necessary equipment.

I understand that Germany has actually stopped the sale of uranium from the Czechoslovakian mines which she has taken over. That she should have taken such early action might perhaps be understood on the ground that the son of the German Under-Secretary of State, von Weizsacker, is attached to the Kaiser-Wilhelm Institute in Berlin, where some of the American work on uranium is now being repeated.

Yours very truly,

(Signature)

Albert Einstein

A few weeks later the President responded to Dr. Einstein.

THE WHITE HOUSE
WASHINGTON

October 19, 1939

My dear Professor:

I want to thank you for your recent letter and the most

interesting and important enclosure.

I found this data of such import that I have convened a Board consisting of the head of the Bureau of Standards and a chosen representative of the Army and Navy to thoroughly investigate the possibilities of your suggestion regarding the element of uranium.

I am glad to say that Dr. Sachs will cooperate and work with this Committee and I feel this is the most practical and effective method of dealing with the subject.

Please accept my sincere thanks.

(Signature)
Franklin D. Roosevelt

Dr. Albert Einstein,
Old Grove Road,
Nassau Point,
Poconic, Long Island,
New York.

Over the ensuing two years, the science progressed to the point of making Dr. Einstein's prognostication a virtual certainty. An atomic bomb was a scientific possibility, and someone was going to build it. German scientists, under the watchful eye of the Himmler's Gestapo, were already hard at work.

On October 9, 1941 Vice President Wallace arranged a meeting between Vannevar Bush, head of the Office of Scientific Research and Development, and President Roosevelt. Together Wallace and Bush laid out the case for the president. A uranium bomb, with an explosive core of only twenty-five pounds, would yield an explosive force equivalent to 1,800 tons of TNT. For one of the very few times in his life, the President was struck dumb.

In that meeting, the three men discussed the implications of creating and using such a device, as well as the issues of post-World War II control of the technology. True to form, the president appointed a board to manage the entire affair, code named "Manhattan Project." Members of the top secret board were: Secretary of War, Henry L. Stimson; Army Chief of Staff, George C. Marshall; President of Harvard University, James Bryant Conant; head of the Office of Scientific Research and Development, Vannevar Bush; and Vice President Wallace.

The pacifist Vice President and the career military man, General George C. Marshall, viewed each other with great respect. There can be little doubt that Wallace's non-stop agricultural economics lessons and pontifications about the common man's right to self-determination, had a profound impact upon thoughts of the man who would author and oversee implementation of the famous Marshall Plan; the plan that pulled Europe back from a decade long return-visit with its own Dark Ages; the plan that was a renaissance—in every sense of the word.

¤ ¤ ¤

Two years after the cessation of hostilities, Secretary of State Marshall toured war-torn Europe. He found very, very few signs of hope across the breadth of the continent. He was much dismayed and used the occasion of Harvard's Commencement ceremonies on June 5, 1947 to articulate a plan for bold, expansive, and expensive action. Standing on the steps of Memorial Church in Harvard Yard he opened the dialog that would change Europe:

> The people of this country are distant from the troubled areas of the earth, and it is hard for them to comprehend the plight and consequent reactions of the long-suffering peoples of Europe and the effect of those reactions on their governments in connection with our efforts to promote peace in the world.
>
> In considering the requirements for the rehabilitation of Europe, the physical loss of life, the visible destruction of cities, factories, mines, and railroads was correctly estimated, but it has become obvious during recent months that this visible destruction was probably less serious than the dislocation of the entire fabric of European economy. For the past ten years conditions have been highly abnormal. The feverish preparation for war and the more feverish maintenance of the war effort engulfed all aspects of national economies. Machinery has fallen into disrepair or is entirely obsolete. Under the arbitrary and destructive Nazi rule, virtually every possible enterprise was geared into the German war machine. Long-standing commercial ties, private institutions, banks, insurance companies, and shipping companies disappeared through loss of capital, absorption through nationalization, or

by simple destruction. In many countries, confidence in the local currency has been severely shaken. The breakdown of the business structure of Europe during the war was complete. . . .

The town and city industries are not producing adequate goods to exchange with the food-producing farmer. Raw materials and fuel are in short supply. Machinery, as I have said, is lacking or worn out. The farmer or the peasant cannot find the goods for sale which he desires to purchase. So the sale of his farm produce for money which he cannot use seems to him an unprofitable transaction. He, therefore, has withdrawn many fields from crop cultivation and he's using them for grazing. He feeds more grain to stock and finds for himself and his family an ample supply of food, however short he may be on clothing and the other ordinary gadgets of civilization.

Meanwhile, people in the cities are short of food and fuel, and in some places approaching the starvation levels. . . . The modern system of the division of labor upon which the exchange of products is based is in danger of breaking down. The truth of the matter is that Europe's requirements for the next three or four years of foreign food and other essential products—principally from America—are so much greater than her present ability to pay that she must have substantial additional help or face economic, social, and political deterioration of a very grave character. . . .

It is logical that the United States should do whatever it is able to do to assist in the return of normal economic health in the world, without which there can be no political stability and no assured peace. Our policy is directed not against any country or doctrine but against hunger, poverty, desperation, and chaos. Its purpose should be the revival of a working economy in the world so as to permit the emergence of political and social conditions in which free institutions can exist. . . .

Any government that is willing to assist in the task of recovery will find full cooperation, I am sure, on the part of the United States Government. Any government which maneuvers to block the recovery of other countries cannot expect help from us. . . .

Furthermore, governments, political parties, or groups which seek to perpetuate human misery in order to profit there from politically or otherwise will encounter the opposition of the United States. . . .

Political passion and prejudice should have no part. With foresight, and a willingness on the part of our people to face up to the vast responsibility which history has clearly placed upon our country, the difficulties I have outlined can and will be overcome. . . .

It is virtually impossible at this distance merely by reading, or listening, or even seeing photographs and motion pictures, to grasp at all the real significance of the situation. And yet the whole future of the world hangs on a proper judgment. It hangs, I think, to a large extent on the realization of the American people, of just what are the various dominant factors. What are the reactions of the people? What are the justifications of those reactions? What are the sufferings? What is needed? What can best be done? What must be done?[5] (Partial excerpt of speech.)

The soldier and General, who had for half the decade overseen the deployment of millions of tons of armaments all across Europe, was returning to that continent with "plowshares and pruning hooks."

¤ ¤ ¤

Even as the Marshall Plan was unfolding across the European continent, planning for the next world war was well underway. This time two World War II allies were faced off eyeball to eyeball, and the first blink could easily have been the prelude to an apocalypse.

The most bombed place on earth is likely the state of Nevada. Between January 27, 1951 and September 23, 1992, 1021 nuclear devices were detonated at a test site some sixty-five miles northwest of Las Vegas. As many as five devices in a single day were set off, and during the height of the testing program in the mid-1960s at least one nuclear bomb was being exploded approximately every three days. The reported explosive yield from all those bombs was approximately 21,980 kilotons. By way of comparison, the nuclear bombs that destroyed Hiroshima and Nagasaki yielded fifteen and twenty-one kiloton explosions respectively. (*A kiloton is the explosive force equivalent of 1000 tons of TNT.*)

The mindless failure of diplomacy and statesmanship in the years immediately following World War II led to a nuclear arms race primarily between the United States and the Soviet Union. In addition to the more than one thousand nuclear weapons actually detonated by the United States, over 32 thousand nuclear weapons were stockpiled and pointed at the nation's enemies. The Soviet Union's insanity reached its apex in the late 1980s when they had over 40 thousand nuclear weapons in their inventory.

Though neither nation released the human version of hell on earth against one another, it would be ridiculous to say that reason prevailed. This was nuclear war by proxy—"our bombs can kill more gophers than your bombs." It was utterly unreasonable and the costs were staggering:

- ⊐ Worldwide, the average number of earthquakes of 5.8 or greater (Richter scale) between 1900 and 1950 was sixty-eight per year. After nuclear testing began the average rose to 127 per year between 1950 and 1988. The cost of life and property damage of these additional earthquakes is incalculable.
- ⊐ In the United States there were approximately 15 thousand cancer related deaths due to radioactive fallout and an additional 20 thousand non-fatal cancers. The lion's share of these cancers cropped up in the down-wind states of Montana, Idaho, and Utah.
- ⊐ At least 6500 United States troops were intentionally exposed to radioactive fall-out during the 1951 Buster-Jangle nuclear bomb series of tests.
- ⊐ During the forty years of nuclear testing, the United States Government spent $5.821 trillion on the nuclear arms program. That is more money than has been spent on Medicare and veterans' benefits combined, and only $2.3 trillion less than the total outlays on Social Security since 1940. $5.8 trillion stacked tightly in bricks made of one dollar bills would be enough to build a wall 8.7 feet high around the earth's equator.

Of course, at the end of the Cold War the United States realized an enormous "peace dividend" when all of the spending on nuclear weapons was no longer viewed as necessary. Well, not really. During the Cold War the United States spent $4.2 billion building nuclear bombs each year. The federal government could not or would not turn off the corporate welfare spigot and in 2007 the United States directed $6.4 billion to the production of more nuclear bombs! Reason did not prevail during the Cold War—it has not prevailed yet.

29

A Moment of Grief

Vice President Wallace learns of George Washington Carver's death.

The War Production Board met on the morning of Wednesday, January 6, 1943. Secretary of Agriculture Claude Wickard arrived about ten minutes late, he excused himself, and handed the Vice President a folded note marked "Personal."

Nine board members and one administrative assistant were present that morning. The chairman, Donald M. Nelson, sat at the head of the table. Vice President Wallace sat immediately to his left. Over, the door directly behind the chairman, stretched a banner with the War Production Board motto blazoned in bold letters: TIME IS SHORT.

The meeting continued as Wallace unfolded and read his message. Slowly his shoulders slumped and his face turned a tad ashen, as he stared at the paper.

Sensing his friends distress, "Are you alright Mr. Vice President?" inquired the Chairman.

"Oh—I'm sorry—I was—" struggling for composure, "I just learned that old George Carver died yesterday, down at the Tuskegee Institute," replied the Vice President.

"You knew him as a kid, didn't you?" questioned Secretary Wickard, who had been aware of the note's sad contents before he handed it to Wallace.

Haltingly, with pauses between thoughts, "Yes—yes I did—Carver became friends with my mother and father when he was studying at Iowa

State, a long time ago." The board room was silent as everyone turned their attention to the saddened Vice President. "He'd come over to eat dinner with us from time to time. I was just a little tyke, you know, about five years old— I'd dare say I learned more about plants, and about life, and about kindness, traipsing around the woods with Carver during those years than I've learned in all the years since." He paused, gazing out the window, "He was a good man. He was a credit to his race—he was a credit to humanity. He was my friend. The world is a better place for his having shared it with us, and he will be missed—I will miss him."

All of the nine men present sat quietly for a moment. Perhaps contemplating a personal loss of their own; perhaps contemplating the loss of one of America's best men; perhaps just letting the Vice President have a moment to gather himself. At the end of the meeting, each of the Board members filed passed Henry's chair and offered a word and a firm handshake. Even the Vice President's political adversary and often personal antagonist, Secretary of Commerce Jesse Jones was a gentleman, "Henry, you have my condolences. Please offer my best wishes to Dr. Carver's Tuskegee family when you contact them."

"Thank you, Jesse, I'll do that."

¤ ¤ ¤

Because it claims us all, rich and poor; liberal and conservative; intelligent and not so much; death is the great equalizer. Mortality puts all of the petty squabbles and differences of opinion in a kind of perspective that allows antagonists to momentarily put aside the discord, albeit only for a moment. For that moment the arch-rivals Henry Wallace and Jesse Jones were friends.

30

M.A.P. To The Future

"You can't build a peaceful world on empty stomachs and human misery.
—Norman Borlaug[1]

The wisdom of our actions in the first three years of peace will determine the course of world history for half a century.
—Henry A. Wallace[2]

In 1943, the need to win the war **and** win the peace, served as the backdrop, as well as the context, in which the Rockefeller Foundation pressed forward with their plans to help Mexico feed itself. Dr. George Harrar, a graduate of the University of Minnesota, and a former student and protégé of Dr. Stackman's, was tapped to lead the Mexican Agricultural Project (M.A.P.). World War II raged on.

On April 10, 1944 the Red Army of the Soviet Union over-ran the German forces holding Odessa; May 12, 1944 German troops surrendered in the Crimea: June 4, 1944 Allied troops captured Rome; June 6, 1944 Allied forces mounted the largest amphibious invasion in history and successfully established a beachhead in Normandy, France; June 13, 1944 U.S. troops began an amphibious assault on the Japanese held island of Saipan; June 19, 1944 Japanese forces were badly defeated in the air and naval Battle of the Philippine Sea; July 25, 1944 Allied forces broke out of Normandy and raced eastward toward Paris and two days later liberated Cherbourg on the north coast of Normandy; July 3, 1944 the Soviets retook Minsk; July 7, 1944 Japanese troops surrendered on Saipan; July 9, 1944 British troops forced the Nazi retreat to liberate Caen. The war's tide had turned.

It was becoming increasingly clear, though the U.S. government and military were not about to say so just yet, that the war was being won. This could not, by any stretch of the imagination, have been said for the peace. In July 1944, the War Manpower Board released Dr. Norman Borlaug from his obligation to work at DuPont, in order to allow him to contribute his expertise to the Rockefeller Foundation efforts in Mexico. With much consternation, and after much consideration, Norm and Margaret decided that Mexico and the Rockefeller Foundation lay in their future. Norm was not going to be a microbiologist for with DuPont Corporation after all. Indeed, he would spend the next sixty plus years as an agricultural research scientist, yet in 1944 he had no inkling of how far that journey would lead.

¤ ¤ ¤

By the time Norm agreed to go to work for the Foundation, they had been trying to lure him away from DuPont for almost two years, though he had not been at liberty to vacate his "essential to the war effort" position. The timing of Norm's departure for Mexico, in September 1944, could not have been more inauspicious in terms of his personal life.

Margaret was pregnant with their second child. (Their daughter, Norma Jean, had been born two years earlier.) Deciding that health care facilities in Mexico might not be adequate, Margaret and Norma Jean stayed behind. On November 9th their son, Scott, was born with severe spina bifida. Immediately upon receiving the news Norm caught an airplane home. Longevity was not Scott's lot in this life.

Now, it is possible to take a person's temperature, blood pressure, and pulse. But there is no meter to measure grief. Be that as it may, there can be little doubt that a parent's grief, at losing a child, is likely the source of the "broken heart" idiom. It is impossible to articulate how this loss impacted the Borlaug's lives, only that it did. For the Borlaugs—Norm, Margaret and "little Jeanie"—life did go on, and somewhere out of the darkness of an infant's death, they once again found meaning. They made a life for themselves in Mexico. Though not as serene as the previous years in Minneapolis and Wilmington, they became comfortable in a culture and an environment a long, long way from Little Norway. Then on March 29, 1947, William Gibson Borlaug arrived in this world and made their little family four.

¤ ¤ ¤

Being exponents of a "management by objective" approach, the Rockefeller Foundation articulated a clear and simple goal—simple in terms of understanding the goal, not so simple with regard to achievement. The purpose of the Mexican Agriculture Project was "to improve the yield of basic food crops in Mexico." Toward that end, Dr. Harrar articulated three strategies:

1. Engage in on-going research in an effort to produce ever better varieties of corn, wheat, potatoes, and other crops, as well as to improve methods of growing those crops;

2. Persistent outreach to teach Mexican farmers about the latest developments in agricultural sciences and persuade those farmers to put into use those new developments and methodologies; and,

3. Train a corps of indigenous agronomists, plant protectionists, and other agricultural professionals, who would ultimately be able to assume responsibility for the well being of agriculture in Mexico.

The third strategy was accomplished by offering hundreds of Rockefeller Foundation sponsored fellowships and scholarships, enabling Mexican students to study at U.S. universities, and thereby exposing them to cutting edge agricultural technologies. The Foundation also incorporated a comprehensive internship program into the M.A.P. at the experimental farms near Champingo, about thirty kilometers east of Mexico City. These activities not only enabled accomplishment of the third strategy, but also served to perpetuate the long term success of the first two strategies.

Upon his arrival, Norm found challenges even greater than he had expected. He had been told that crop yields in Mexico were low and static, soils were impoverished, and fertilizer technology virtually nonexistent. He had some inkling of Mexico's history with agrarian reform and the massive land distribution program of the 1930s (45 million acres of land changed hands between 1934 and 1940). However, Norm had not envisioned the extent to which the new landowners were under-capitalized. Perhaps had he been fluent in Spanish, he may have guessed their lot by the moniker applied to the new farmer class. They were called "campesinos," which roughly translates as "peasant farmer" in Spanish. On the other end of the spectrum, the researchers assigned to work with Norm were known as "limpo sacos" or "clean shirts." This elitist cultural ethic was also a handicap to the Foundation's efforts during their early days in Mexico.

Norm modeled a get-your-hands-dirty approach to agricultural science. This, in addition to his cajoling, broke down the "limpo saco" mentality over a fairly short period of time. The capitalization of the new model of small scale farming was not nearly so easy to master. Poor people, subsistence farming on twenty-five acres of land, could not and likely never would be able to afford to buy a tractor of their own. Heck, Mexican agriculture was at such low ebb, the vast majority of farmers could not even consider buying fertilizer, much less any kind of farm machinery. In point of fact, what Norm found in Mexico was a vastly more primitive agriculture than he had known during the horse-drawn plow days of his youth, on the Borlaug farms in Iowa.

Exacerbating all of these issues was a reality that stunned Norm. Coming from a family that valued education above almost all else, it seemed unfathomable to Norm that only about twenty percent of the Mexican farmers were literate. In a letter to Margaret, Norm expressed his bewilderment at the challenge that lay ahead.

> "These places I've seen have clubbed my mind—they are so poor and depressing. No wonder the people are the way they are. Can you imagine a poor Mexican guy struggling to feed his family? I don't know what we can do to help these people, but we've got to do something!"[3]

Adopting "we've got to do something" as a mantra, Norm rolled up his sleeves, put together a team and went to work on developing a better wheat.

¤ ¤ ¤

Historically the conventional wisdom of science has been inclined to the myths borne of its practitioners biases:

The earth is the center of the universe;
all animal (other than human) behavior is only instinctive;
Space is a vacuum;
Lightening never strikes the same place twice;

Humans use only ten percent of their brains;

The soil is the one indestructible, immutable asset that the Nation possesses—it is the one resource that cannot be exhausted—that cannot be used up.

Across time it seems "conventional wisdom" becomes less so.

In Mexico, Norm had to challenge certain myths of cultural and scientific consensus related to agriculture. First and perhaps most strange among the myths, was the belief that seeds required a period of "rest" after harvesting, in order to store energy for germination. The logic of this escaped Norm. If seeds were storing energy, what was the energy's source? Seeds stored in burlap bags in dark sheds were not getting energy from the sun, or from the soil, or even from the air. On the other hand, seeds of corn found in caves hundreds of years old, were able to grow and produce crops of dark colored "Indian" corn. Did those kernels store the energy for centuries?

Second, the M.A.P. wheat team had to confront the resistance to move the project forward quickly. The bureaucrats held that haste would be too costly, and scientists argued that it would not result in development of the ideal strain of wheat.

Third, it was widely believed that grain crops were by necessity, and in all cases, photoperiodistic. Photoperiodicity is the physiological reaction of organisms to the length of day or night. Unlike the nonsense about seeds storing energy, this belief at least had a solid scientific basis. There are "long-day" plants, including oats and wheat, and "short-day" plants, such as corn, cotton and rice. There are even a few plants (e.g. cucumbers and tomatoes) that are "day-neutral." A plant's regulating mechanism is actually powered by hours of darkness rather than hours of daylight. So, the idea that wheat is photoperiodistic was observable. Still, the mythology that Norm's team had to confront held that wheat, indeed, all plant's photoperiodicity is preordained and unalterably coded in the plant's genes.

Using innovate processes, Norm's M.A.P. team had within twelve years hybridized wheat varieties that were equally productive at 22° North, in the Yaqui valley, and 12° North, near Champingo. Not only was the length of daily sunlight substantially different, given the 10° difference (800 miles north to south), but the Yaqui valley is only 120 feet above sea level, whereas Champingo is at an altitude of almost 8 thousand feet. The climates also differ greatly between these growing environments, from relatively hot temperatures in the north, where virtually all moisture was supplied through irrigation, to cool mountain climates in central Mexico, where it rained heavily two to three times a week and there was always a morning dew.

How was it possible to produce wheat that could perform equally well in such different environments? Well, Norm refused to accept the conventional wisdom. He was also willing to get dirt under his fingernails and take innovate risks, which were more than a bit frustrating at times— but my how they paid off.

Norm took the M.A.P. stated goal at face value: "improve the yield of basic food crops in Mexico." All around him he saw people without enough to eat, more mouths to feed each day, and agricultural output descending into an abyss. Improving yield was not some far-off hypothetical. It was a real and urgent need.

Given that urgency, and the recent history of almost total crop destruction by wheat rust, Norm initiated an untried "high-volume crossbreeding" approach. Most plant scientists would endeavor to cross, at most, a few dozen varieties each growing season. The M.A.P. team obtained seeds from all over the world and tediously crossed literally thousands of different lines each year. By doing so, they dramatically increased the odds that a few, perhaps only one, strain would have high yield potential, demonstrate resistance to wheat rust, and exhibit "vigor" in subsequent generations.

Reasoning that it is better to be pleasantly surprised than disappointed by overly optimistic expectations, Norm cautioned his team members, "Cross breeding is a hit-or-miss process. It is time consuming and mind-warpingly tedious. There's only one chance in thousands of ever finding what you want, and actually no guarantee of success at all."[4]

Each member of the team had to be taught to remove, with surgical precision, the pollen laden male stamen from each bisexual wheat flower. Otherwise, the plant would pollinate itself. In order to prevent wind or insect instigated cross-pollination with other plants, a small paper bag was then secured tightly around each head of wheat. After two days the bags were removed and the pistil (female organ) of the emasculated flower was pollinated, by hand, with the chosen wheat variety for crossbreeding. The exact parent plant stock was fastidiously recorded for every single crossbred plant. Likewise, the rust resistance, productivity, and viability of the second generation seeds were recorded in excruciating detail—"mind-warpingly tedious"—indeed!

¤ ¤ ¤

The bombs had yet to fall on Hiroshima and Nagasaki that horrible summer of 1945. Therefore, Edward Lorenz was still at his station in the Pacific. He was still trying to predict the weather for the Army Air Corp. He had yet to articulate the theory of "sensitive dependence on initial conditions." It is thus surprising that one day, while explaining to a group of Champingo College staff the reasoning behind the "high-volume crossbreeding" approach, Norm almost seemed to intuit the highly random and chaotic essence of the "butterfly effect."

> There are millions of wheat plants here. Each head will grow a couple of dozen grains of seed, and there will not be one seed in billions that will be totally acceptable for what we need in Mexico. Perfection is a butterfly the academics chase and never catch. If we go on looking for the ideal wheat for Mexico, your countrymen will go on being hungry for a long time. We will have to do the best we can with what we have.[5]

Perhaps remembering the anguish borne of his own hunger pangs during his early years at the University of Minnesota; or perhaps remembering the hollow-eyed capitulation of hungry men sitting on the ground at Gateway Park in downtown Minneapolis, just waiting for the morsels of food that they could scavenge from the discarded trash; whatever the reason, waiting while hundreds of thousands of Mexicans went hungry day after day, was not much to Norm's liking.

His impatience led to another major innovation by the M.A.P. team—shuttle breeding. Over 1100 miles separate the southernmost tip of Mexico from the northern frontier with the United States. Ecosystems range from tropical forests to high desert xeric shrub lands. Norm reasoned that this north to south diversity offered an opportunity to produce two generations of wheat each year, rather than only one. This in turn would halve the time necessary to develop an acceptable wheat hybrid for Mexico.

He proposed shuttling the seed from the M.A.P. experiment stations near Mexico City to Obregon, in the northern state of Sonora. His teams would grow the hybrid crops in the southern highlands during the summer, and plant their offspring in the northern lowlands in late fall. Accountants bemoaned the doubled cost of operating two stations so far apart. Theoreticians forewarned that the seeds needed to rest. Agronomists cautioned that the crops would not do well at such different altitudes and latitudes. All the while, the people of Mexico continued to go hungry, and Norm's teams just pushed ahead, with surprising results.

Because they chose the best of the best in each generation to seed the next crop, the team was fortuitously developing high yield wheat that was resistant to rust diseases and highly tolerant to different altitudes, different soils, different climates, and different lengths of daylight hours. They learned that photoperiodicity is indeed coded on the DNA, but they also learned, figuratively speaking, that double helix could be stretched a bit.

¤ ¤ ¤

In August 1946, the United States Secretary of Commerce, Henry A. Wallace, was personally invited to attend the ceremonies marking the end of Mexican President Manuel Avila Camacho's term. They had become friends six years earlier when the U.S. Vice President-elect had addressed the Mexican Congreso de la Unión during Camacho's inauguration. They had communicated frequently during the ensuing six years, so needless to say, Henry was honored by the invite.

During that earlier visit, Wallace and his traveling companion, Jim LaCron, had also befriended Marte Gomez who was the Minister of Agriculture. Again during Wallace's 1946 visit, Minister Gomez took him under wing and served as his unofficial tour guide. Secretary Wallace was adamant about wanting to visit the Centro Internacional de Mejoramiento de Maíz y Trigo (CIMMYT) (English: International Center for Improvement of Corn and Wheat). The CIMMYT hosted the Rockefeller Foundation's Mexican Agriculture Project. During this visit, Henry Wallace met his fellow Iowan, Dr. Norman Borlaug, for the first time.

It had been Wallace's distress with the state of Mexican agriculture in 1940, and his vision of creating a better corn, that brought the Mexican Agriculture Project to fruition. Norm knew well the history of the Vice President's advocacy with the Rockefeller Foundation and was almost star-struck at this first meeting. Wallace broke the ice by asking, "What's a good Iowa boy like you doing working on **wheat**?"[6]

They both laughed, but it was an "inside joke," understood only by Iowan farm boys.

At one point during the visit, Secretary Wallace stood looking out across the almost mature heads of wheat, waving gently in the breeze. A stronger gust blew across the field into the faces of Wallace and his entourage. Norm noticed the Secretary standing a few feet from the group and though looking out across the field, he was clearly not really looking at it. Norm sidled over toward the guest of honor, and Wallace began to speak. He told Norm of the day he, Roswell Bob Garst, and Charlie Rippey were at Charlie's farm, inspecting a corn crop, which was planted alternately with two rows of Reid Yellow Dent, two rows of hybridized corn, and so on across the field. As they watched, a sudden blast of wind laid waste the Reid Yellow Dent, while the hybrid corn came through relatively unscathed. Wallace turned and looked Norm directly in the eye and said, "You know Dr. Borlaug, it's ironic that improved yield cannot be the only goal for hybridization, though at the end of the day, what you have in the harvest basket is all that really matters."

Secretary of Commerce, Henry Wallace speaks with Dr. Borlaug about his work with Centro Internacional de Mejoramiento de Maíz y Trigo. Courtesy World Food Prize, Des Moines, Iowa.

Clearly remembering Henry Wallace's eloquently simple observation, in 1953 when Norm was offered access to some Japanese dwarf winter wheat seed, he jumped at the chance to work the dwarf traits into the genome of the Mexican wheat. The M.A.P. team crossbred and re-crossbred the Japanese wheat with the Mexican wheat. The resulting "dwarf-Mexican" wheat was less susceptible to wind damage and more drought tolerant. Astoundingly, the dwarf wheat doubled the yield of its predecessor generations from 4500 kilos to 9000 kilos per hectare.

When Dr. Norman Borlaug arrived in Mexico in 1944, the nation had been importing half its wheat consumption, and that was still not enough to adequately feed its people. In 1956, Mexico became self-sufficient in wheat production and would export one half million tons eight years later.

From somewhere in the "beyond," George Washington Carver was remembering his first publication, "Plants Modified by Man." He also remembered towing little Henry Wallace along on "botinizing" expeditions. The angel smiled to himself, thinking of seeds sown.

31

Abundance

*"We began by observing that 'hope is always buried in tragedy'.
Maybe strife in return arrives with success."*
—*Good News India*, November 2002[1]

Some 71 million years ago, the India tectonic plate began to drift northward toward Asia. Ten million years ago it made landfall on the southern edge of the Eurasian Plate. It continues its northern journey still. In the process, it is pushing skyward the tallest mountain range in the world. A land mass of over 2.1 million square miles lays south of the Himalayan Mountains (including Sri Lanka). It is now the most densely populated area on earth.

For centuries the Asian subcontinent was not a nation or even a cluster of nations. During the last three thousand years there have been hundreds of combinations of janpadas, empires, kingdoms, dynasties, sultanates, confederacies, colonies, theocracies, military dictatorships, and democracies. The European empires began to chisel their way into the mix in 1502. First to arrive were the Portuguese, followed in quick succession by the British, Dutch, French, and Danes.

At no time has the entire subcontinent come under the rule of a single government, either indigenous or imposed. The area has historically been the nexus of some of humanities greatest cultures and religions. In their pursuit of Dharma, the almost 1.6 billion people who live on the subcontinent have embraced an eclectic array of spiritualism. Four major world religions, Hinduism, Buddhism, Jainism, and Sikhism originated in this area. Traders and conquerors brought Zoroastrianism, Judaism, Christianity, and Islam during the first millennium. Bahá'ís, Jains, Vedic Brahmanism, and numerous tribal religions spice the theological milieu. Therefore, in addition to the political, commercial, and ethnic contentions, the peoples of the Asian subcontinent have also used religious bigotry as a rationale for slaughtering each other from time to time.

¤ ¤ ¤

Modern India was born in the ruins of the Bengal Famine of 1943. Early in the twentieth century, the British empire had become the dominant colonial force in all of south Asia. While vestiges of the French, Spanish and Dutch empires remained, they were waning and a far cry from the "glory" years at the height of their empirical power.

By 1940, perhaps unbeknownst to the British, their empire too was entering its twilight years. Not only was the idea of the colonial power's "inherent superiority" being questioned by people all over the world, the Japanese Empire's war machine hastened the demise of European imperialism.

In February 1942, the occupying forces of the United Kingdom in Singapore suffered a disastrous defeat at the hands of the Japanese military. The Japanese then went on to capture virtually all of Malaysia and Burma from the British as the year progressed. Prior to 1942, about twenty percent of Bengal's rice consumption was being imported from Burma. With the occupation of Burma by the Japanese, this source was completely choked off.

Fearing a Japanese invasion of Bengal, British forces removed most rice stockpiles from the province and embargoed what remained for military use only. On October 16, 1942 the east coast of Bengal and Orissa was hit by a powerful cyclone. Rice fields were disastrously flooded some forty miles inland. The autumn rice crop failed. This resulted in the populace eating their surplus, including the seed that were to be planted in the winter of 1942 – 43. All the while, the Bengal civilian government, motivated by profits, failed to stop exporting food produced in Bengal. Hundreds of thousands of people began to starve.

British military officials stepped in to organize the provision of 110 million free meals. It was far too little, far too late, and things got worse rather quickly. By the end of 1943 almost 4 million Bengali people had starved to death. The incompetence of the local civil authorities, and the callousness of the British government in London, cannot be overstated. "If food is so

—— 345 ——

scarce, why hasn't Gandhi died yet?" was British Prime Minister Winston Churchill's response to an urgent request by the Secretary of State for India, Leo Amery, and British Field Marshall Archibald Wavell to release food stocks for India. As the Indian subjects of Great Britain starved, extra food produced in the British Empire was sent to aid civilians in famine stricken Greece.

The Bengal famine did not need to occur. Much like the early days of the Great Depression in the United States, adequate supplies of food grains were available. Huge stores existed in other locations throughout India. The combination of avarice and incompetence by the local and British authorities perhaps caused, and most certainly exacerbated, the massive death toll. When World War II was over, and the true nature of the famine was understood, the governmental structures in place to rule much of the Asian subcontinent simply could not withstand the anger and condemnation of over one billion people.

In 1916, Mohandas Gandhi had returned to India from South Africa, after his service to the British Army during the Zulu War. Upon returning to his homeland, his removal of the lawyer's three piece suit was a metaphorical act, symbolizing the disrobing of his spirit and intellect from his sycophantic relationship with India's British rulers. In 1918 he began organizing a populist independence movement in India. Characterized by non-violence and passive resistance, the movement acquired the support of hundreds of thousands of followers over the next two decades.

Then, in the aftermath of the Second World War and the Bengal Famine debacle, civilian insurgencies sprung up in virtually every 'Princely State' under control of the British Raj. Most of these mini-revolts eschewed Gandhi's pacifism. Following military mutinies by the Royal Air Force, the Royal Indian Navy and the Royal Indian Air Force, the newly elected Labour Government in Britain realized that the war-weary British people simply could not project the military force necessary to suppress the insurgencies and extend the Empire's rule of India.

On July 18, 1947 King George VI gave assent to the Indian Independence Act, which had been passed by the British Parliament earlier in the year. The act stipulated the partition of India and the independence of the dominions of Pakistan and India. When word of the impending independence spread, spontaneous celebrations broke out all across the region. Within days the rejoicing ended, and Muslims, Hindus and Sikhs began killing each other. Of course, they did so as a means of expressing and demonstrating their religious superiority.

The conventional wisdom held that the only way to avoid the sectarian violence was to huddle with one's own kind. Hence, millions of refugees packed up their meager belongings and scrambled to cross the newly drawn borders. In Punjab, the new border lines divided the Sikh regions in half. Disenfranchised populations, particularly when coupled with hunger and recent memories of massive starvation, are extremely dangerous. As Norman Borlaug observed several years prior, "What does a hungry man have to lose?" Massive sectarian bloodshed followed. In all, half a million people were killed in the ensuing carnage. To put the deaths of 500 thousand people in perspective, the citizenry of the United States was horrified and traumatized by the murder of 2974 people by religious zealots on September 11, 2001.

¤ ¤ ¤

Smiling Buddha was the secret code name for the first nuclear test explosion in India on May 18, 1974. The explosion was detonated near the town of Pokhran, which is provocatively close to Pakistan, in the heart of the shared Thar desert. By 2008, India had as many as a hundred nuclear warheads, about seventy-five of them were fully assembled and capable of almost immediate deployment.

India also boasts at least nine ballistic missile systems capable of delivering nuclear warheads. One of those missiles, the Surya, is an intercontinental ballistic system, theoretically capable of delivering a nuclear payload anywhere within a 12 thousand kilometer distance. Thus making virtually any location in Asia, Africa, and Europe a possible target. India also maintains a fleet of submarines and battleships with nuclear weapons capabilities, and is one of only four nations that maintains a nuclear strategic bomber fleet. The Indian Air Force has four types of fighter jets, including the absolutely masterful Sukhoi Su-30MK, which are capable of delivering nuclear tipped weapons.

Though they had fallen far behind technologically, Pakistan was not about to sit by idly and watch their adversary's growing military might. On April 6, 1998 they conducted their first test of the Ghauri. Pakistani media reported the missile had a 1100 kilometer test flight and an apogee of 350 kilometers. However, information on the impact point indicates that the flight distance was no more than 800 kilometers. Pakistan claimed that the missile was designed and produced indigenously. It was, in fact, a North Korean produced No-dong missile. With an 800 kilometer effective range, Mumbai, Ahmadabad, and New Delhi became easy targets for Pakistan.

A few weeks later, on the afternoon of Monday, May 11, 1998 Indian Prime Minister Atal Behari Vajpayee stunned the world by announcing that earlier that day India had conducted three nuclear tests. International observers were even more astonished by the announcement two days later that two additional tests had been conducted.

Obviously, the saber rattling did not go unnoticed by India's northern neighbors. On Wednesday, May 28, 1998 Pakistani Prime Minister Mohammad Nawaz Sharif announced, "Today, we have settled a score and have carried out five successful nuclear tests. . . . Our security, and the peace and stability of the entire region, was gravely threatened. As any self-respecting nation, we had no choice left for us. Our hand was forced by the present Indian leadership's reckless actions. We could not ignore the magnitude of the threat. . . . Under no circumstances would the Pakistani nation compromise on matters pertaining to its life and existence. Our decision to exercise the nuclear option has been taken in the interest of national self-defense. These weapons are to deter aggression, whether nuclear or conventional."[2] This was a meticulously crafted statement. In military/diplomat speak, the phrase "whether nuclear or conventional" implies a willingness to use nuclear weapons if attacked by conventional weapons, or perhaps even as a first strike.

With regard to the "Smiling Buddha" project, Siddhártha Gautama Buddha once counseled his followers, "Holding on to anger is like grasping a hot coal with the intent of throwing it at someone else; you are the one who gets burned."[3] It is a fair bet that on May 19, 1974 the spirit of the Holy Buddha was **not** smiling, but he may have been thinking, "I told you so!" on May 29, 1998.

By 2010 every living thing in both India and Pakistan lived in target range of a nuclear weapon. In this volatile mix, humanity can ill afford to allow any wiggle room for starvation's chicanery.

¤ ¤ ¤

Realizing the success of the dwarf-Mexican wheat offered even greater potential, in the early 1960s, Dr. Borlaug began asking a couple of critical questions. How can the new cereal strains be put into extensive production in order to feed hungry people around the world? By doing so, can we achieve a temporary respite from hunger and deprivation, thus creating the breathing space necessary to deal with the "Population Monster" and the subsequent environmental and social ills that spark conflict between people and nations?[4]

Pakistan had sent trainees to Mexico to participate in the Rockefeller Foundation international training program. In 1960 the Pakistani trainees had returned home with varieties of Mexican wheat and began testing them on the Asian subcontinent for a couple of years. The Pakistanis shared information about their experimental plantings with Dr. M.S. Swaminathan, director of India's national wheat research program. In March 1963, he arranged to have Dr. Borlaug invited to meet with Indian government officials.

When Borlaug visited the subcontinent, he made stops in both Pakistan and India. He inspected fields, reviewed agricultural practices, and met with government officials. His official report guardedly projected that something **might** be done to help farmers feed the burgeoning populations. However, he predicted that planting of hybrid dwarf wheat would be the least problematic issue. He saw three main barriers to success: fertilizer; credit for farmers to make the necessary purchases before planting; and, fair prices for harvested crops brought to market. In all three areas, government institutional mindsets were greater barriers than farmer willingness.

The main point of optimism in the report was the fact that the science worked. The two Pakistanis who had been trained at the Mexican facilities, Manzoor Bajwa and M. Nur Chaudry, had somewhat surreptitiously managed to cultivate a couple acres of the dwarf wheat, applying the entire prescribed protocol of fertilizer, irrigation and weed control. They had not been allowed to do so at the primary experimental station, but at their "secret" plots Borlaug saw a prodigious crop. A crop, that on just four small plots of land, was a flicker of hope for over 1.3 billion people.

As it turned out, "hope" was enough for the Ford Foundation to join with the Rockefeller Foundation to fund an effort to help India and Pakistan improve their cereal grain production. Dr. Borlaug put together a team led by Dr. Glenn Anderson from Canada and Dr. Ignacio Narvaez from Mexico. The team included several Mexican scientists who had participated in the early days of the Mexican Agricultural Project Scholarship and Internship programs. They began their efforts not a week too soon.

In 1964 the teams began planting experimental plots in locations all across India and Pakistan. The results informed them which varieties of the Mexican wheat would be most productive. Little did they know that meteorology and bigotry were conspiring against the people of south Asia. In 1965 a dry period began across the subcontinent that would continue for twenty-two years. From 1965 through 1987 India endured nine droughts. Rainfall in 1965 was over eighteen percent below normal over almost forty percent of the subcontinent. Again in 1966 over thirty-five percent of the land mass received thirteen percent less rainfall than average. During both of these years, India received over 5 million tons of emergency wheat grain from the United States, under the auspices of the Food for Peace program. Even at that, 1.5 million people starved to death as a result of the drought driven famine.

As if the famine was not dire enough, an astounding failure of statesmanship by the leaders of both countries led to a second Indo-Pakistani War in 1965. It began with skirmishes between policemen on either side of the border separating India's state of Gujarat from Pakistan. Of course, the will of Allah and the pride of Hindu would not allow either nation to stand down. The conflict escalated and, tellingly, ended up focusing on the fertile Jammu and Kashmir, which were not being impacted by the drought that was withering much of the rest of India.

Both sides were armed almost exclusively with American and British made tanks, planes, and artillery. The corporate merchants of death made a killing, literally and figuratively. In all, 328 tanks and over 120 fighter jets were destroyed, hundreds of thousands of rounds of ammunition were fired, and almost 7 thousand soldiers were killed.

The war was ended by a United Nations mandated cease fire. Officially, the war resulted in no permanent territorial changes. Unofficially, international corporations that sell war made billions and billions of dollars in profits.

Meanwhile, Dr. Borlaug was back in Mexico arranging for a convoy of thirty-five trucks to carry the selected varieties of wheat seeds from Cuidad Obregón to a Los Angeles dock for shipment. The convoy was held up by the Mexican police, next blocked by U.S. border agents attempting to enforce a ban on seed importation, and then stopped by the California National Guard when race riots in Watts prevented access to the Los Angeles harbor. Finally, the seeds arrived at the dock, were loaded on the ship, and set sail toward the Indian Ocean. Though valuable time had been lost on the land leg of the journey, there was hope that shipment would arrive in time for planting. Otherwise, the consequences in terms of lost lives would be horrendous. Borlaug recalls that after the ship sailed, "I went to bed thinking the problem was at last solved, and woke up to the news that war had broken out between India and Pakistan."[5]

During the waxing months of 1965 Borlaug's teams had been scrambling around two continents and two oceans trying to arrange the delivery of 250 tons of dwarf-Mexican wheat seed to Pakistan and 200 tons to India. They knew full well that the drought tolerant dwarf wheat would save millions of lives if planted in time to make a crop. Then as the teams began planting in fertile valleys of northern India and eastern Pakistan, the roar of cannons just a few miles away, almost made them cry.

With these events as the backdrop, Dr. Borlaug's teams, as well as the Ford and Rockefeller Foundations, could easily have surrendered to the notion that this was a cursed enterprise. No one would have condemned them had they just pulled up stakes and walked away. This was, however, one of those propitious moments in history, when butterflies flew into the darkness of a tragedy and emerged on the other side carrying the pollen of hope.

¤ ¤ ¤

One afternoon in late November of 1965, Dr. Borlaug and Dr. Ignacio Narvaez stood on a ditch bank several miles east of New Delhi watching the irrigation of a field of newly sprouted Lerma Rojo 64, a variety of dwarf-Mexican wheat. Dr. Swaminathan, India's Director of Wheat Research, drove up in a beat up old Ford pick-up. As if seeing him arrive in the truck by himself was not odd enough, his normally affable smile was replaced with an unreadable expression. He stepped out of the truck, said a quiet hello, and handed Norm an obituary dated November 21, 1965. It had been sent to Dr. Swaminathan by one of his friends at the Indian Embassy in Washington, DC.

> Services were held yesterday at St. Stephens Episcopal Church in Ridgefield, Connecticut for Henry Agard Wallace. The former Secretary of Agriculture, Secretary of Commerce, Vice President and Progressive Party Candidate for the presidency, passed away on November 18th. He was diagnosed with amyotrophic lateral

sclerosis (ALS—Lou Gehrig's disease) a little over a year ago. As was his penchant, he viewed even this challenge as an opportunity to better humanity. He spent many weeks over the last year working with doctors and researchers at the National Institutes of Health, allowing himself and the disease to be studied. He kept meticulous records of the progression that an NIH spokesman indicates will be invaluable in furthering our understanding of ALS.

Henry Wallace grew up among the farmers of Iowa and spent the lion's share of his life's energy encouraging humanity to reconsider our relationship with food production and our relationships with each other. Consistent with this life-long endeavor, just hours before his passing, he scribbled on a yellow pad of paper a final few thoughts about human kindness. "Here as I write I look to the east through my New York farm window and see the ridge which is Ridgefield, Connecticut. Everyone has been so utterly good and kind to me, both here and at NIH. After listening to the radio and reading the newspapers and looking at TV, the mind becomes oppressed by the viciousness of man. But there is another aspect of man—kindliness to those in great need. This ALSer has had a rich experience with the goodness of man as exhibited toward those who are unfortunate."[6] Soon after scripting these words, his family returned him to the Danbury Hospital where he died peacefully at 11:15 am.

Many dignitaries were among the three hundred plus people attending the simple twenty minute service to pay their last respects and support Wallace's loving family. He was always a controversial character on the American political scene. Even those with whom Wallace did not frequently see eye to eye remember him kindly—remember him as a man of character and good will.

In a statement issued by the White House, President Johnson characterized Wallace as "an original American voice whose points of view were not always popular, but they were always sincere."[7]

Dr. Paul Mangelsdorf, of Harvard University noted, "It was Wallace's fate to be often regarded as a 'dreamer' when actually he was only seeing in his own pragmatic realistic way some of the shapes of things to come, and more often than not, he was right!"[8]

Secretary of Agriculture Orville Freeman commented, "History cannot ignore him and we shall not forget him. No single individual has contributed more to the abundance we enjoy today than Henry Wallace."[9]

All of these accolades notwithstanding, Vice President Hubert Humphrey, seemed to best sum up Wallace's life and his passing, "Henry Wallace was a scientist and statesman, a politician and a philosopher who was devoted and dedicated to peace—but above all, he was a good man."[10]

Henry Agard Wallace (October 7, 1888 – November 18, 1965), rest in peace.

After reading the article, Norm handed it to Dr. Narvaez, walked over to the edge of the ditch, and sat down. After a moment his two colleagues joined him, Navaez sitting to his left and Swaminathan on the right. Not a word was spoken for several minutes. The three men just sat watching the water flow through the check from the ditch into the wheat field. Norm broke the silence, "We would not be here today if it were not for Henry Wallace. Hell, Ignacio, you and I would never have even met—there would never have been a Mexican Agricultural Project, were it not for his foresight." They sat quietly for another moment before Norm continued, "He was a complicated old coot, and in his time his complexity and eccentricities caused many to misunderstand him. But his quest for a better corn was the metaphor of his life. Wallace spent his life hybridizing corn and trying to hybridize the way humans treat each other." The sounds of the breeze, the birds, and the gurgling water passing into the field were a subconscious reminder of the earth's life. "Gentlemen, the world may never know what we are trying to do here, and they will almost certainly never know that we are here today because Henry Wallace lived—but we know—and I guess if old Henry were here right now, he'd probably say 'It's time to get back to work.'"

The three men stood and dusted off the seats of their pants. Dr. Swaminathan offered each a handshake, climbed back into the pickup and drove away.

☐ ☐ ☐

Only about 17 thousand acres in India and Pakistan were planted with the dwarf Mexican wheat in 1965, but those acres demonstrated a seventy percent increase in yield. More importantly, they produced the seeds for the

1966 planting by farmers who were growing more enthusiastic about the prospects of those stunted varieties of wheat from across the ocean. In the fall of 1966 over 600 thousand acres were planted. Even though both nation's "statesmen" tried to diddled the farmers with regard to access to fertilizer and reduced crop prices, Dr. Borlaug managed to cajole resolutions that resulted in a ninety-eight percent increase in wheat yields.

¤ ¤ ¤

During this time, while Norman Borlaug was endeavoring to harvest the seeds sown by his predecessors, George Washington Carver and Henry Agard Wallace, others were sounding alarms about the rate of growth of the human population. Paul Ehrlich in his book *The Population Bomb* stated bluntly that food production could not possibly keep up with increases in human population, and that it was "a fantasy" that India would be able to feed itself ever again. In even more draconian terms, William and Paul Paddock predicted, in their 1967 book, *Famine 1975! America's Decision; Who Will Survive*, that mass starvation was inevitable, that India was beyond hope, and efforts to avert the disasters should be focused on more promising geographical locales.

As if bearing witness to these dire forecasts, in 1964 Pakistan harvested only 3.4 million tons of wheat. However, using varieties of dwarf wheat and the Mexican Agricultural Project prescribed agricultural protocols, Pakistan became self sufficient in wheat production by 1968. Forty years later Pakistan produced 18 million tons of wheat. Likewise, India became self-sufficient in food grain production by 1990, producing 176.4 million tons compared to 82 million tons in 1960. In the year 2000 India produced a whopping 201.8 million tons, which allowed for storing 40 million tons in their version of Confucius' ever-normal granary.

So, were Mssrs. Ehrlich, Paddock and Paddock wrong? Not entirely—instead, the seeds of kindness, being carried by Dr. Carver's butterflies, had just bought humanity some more time to defuse the population bomb. Failure to do so, can only be considered the ultimate unkindness.

32

Always A Good Boy

The Nobel Peace Prize.

Alfred Nobel was born on October 21, 1833 in Stockholm, Sweden. His father, Immanuel Nobel had declared bankruptcy earlier that year. Immanuel was, however, endowed with a unique genius which resulted in his amassing and losing several fortunes during the course of his life. He was a Swedish engineer and inventor; a builder of bridges and the inventor of plywood and the rotary lathe.

Immanuel became interested in the use of explosives for rock removal in construction projects, but he soon learned that military use was a more lucrative market for explosives. The Russian Czar secured Mr. Nobel's expertise with explosives for the purpose of mining the Gulf of Finland during the Crimean War, in order to keep the British Royal Navy out of firing range.

Immanuel's son, Alfred was present when his father demonstrated the effectiveness of the sea mine. Little boys love big bangs, hence, his lifelong interest in the use of explosives. As a young man in his early twenties, Alfred studied in Paris. There he met a young Italian chemist, Ascanio Sobrero, who had invented nitroglycerine about three years earlier. The liquid was whole orders of magnitude more explosive, and volatile, than the black powder that had powered most of Immanuel Nobel's explosions. Alfred Nobel saw immediately the commercial application of nitroglycerin, particularly for mining. However, he also realized the chemical's inherent volatility made it much too dangerous for practical application.

Undeterred, Alfred Nobel returned to Stockholm and began work on creating a commercially viable explosive using nitroglycerin as the base.

The trick was finding a way to limit the chemical's volatility. He conducted experiments that often did not end so well. One such experiment in 1863 killed several people, including his younger brother, Emil. Unlike perhaps ninety-nine percent of humanity, who would have been mortified by the catastrophe and walked away from the whole idea, Alfred Nobel pressed on. He learned that by mixing a fine sand called Kieselguhr with nitroglycerin the explosive liquid became a paste that could be shaped into rods. The rods were quite stable and would only ignite by intentional detonation. He then invented the "blasting cap" which was ignited by a black powder fuse.

Alfred Nobel's research coincided with the development of the pneumatic drill and diamond tipped drill bits. In combination, these inventions dramatically reduced the labor and cost necessary for drilling tunnels and building bridges. His explosive could be packed into small deep holes cut by the new drills which greatly facilitated blasting away rock for construction and mining projects. He patented and began the mass production and marketing of his new invention—dynamite.

Business was good, but governments have long been most enthusiastic about military spending, and it did not take long for them to see the tremendous military potential of this new high explosive. Soon the primary customers for his products were nationalistic war industries. In that arena, and during that era of militarism, business was very, very good. Capitalizing on this market, Alfred Nobel established factories in ninety different locations strewn across twenty different nations. The armaments business was so lucrative that by the 1880s he branched into different weapons systems including rockets, cannons and ballistite (smokeless gun powder).

All the while, he enigmatically flirted with, and modestly supported, the European pacifist movement. In 1876 he met and became friends with the first lady of European pacifism, Bertha von Suttner. In 1889 she authored the peace movement's manifesto, *Lay Down Your Arms*. Nobel told von Suttner of his wish to produce material or a machine which "would have such a devastating effect that war from then on, would be impossible."

In an 1891 letter to Baroness von Suttner, Nobel stated, "Perhaps my factories will put an end to war sooner than your congresses: on the day that two army corps can mutually annihilate each other in a second, all civilized nations will surely recoil with horror and disband their troops."[1] The wars of the next half century would provide indubitable evidence that Nobel grossly overestimated the civil behavior of "civilized nations." Even so, he was one of the first people to articulate the idea of military deterrence, which seventy years later, became the cornerstone of the nuclear arms race—Mutually Assured Destruction (MAD). MAD is a military strategy in which a full-scale use of nuclear weapons by opposing sides would effectively result in the annihilation of all combatants, likely even all human civilization. MAD—Indeed!

It is fair to ask how Nobel could resolve his pacifist inclinations with his business enterprises, which merchandised war materiel. In this life he did not, but he did use the occasion of his death to find that reconciliation. He also likely ascribed to the nineteenth century assertion that the scientist was not responsible for how his findings were used; that each scholarly discovery is neutral in itself, but can be used both for good and bad objectives. Of course, Albert Einstein had a famous and dramatic struggle with this same dilemma, as do many in the scientific communities of the Twenty-first century. Work on the human genome being an obvious case in point.

The eclectic Alfred Nobel also expressed his pacifist notions in plays and poetry he authored. He was, therefore, mortified when he read his own obituary. In 1888 Alfred's older brother, Ludvig, died. A French journalist mistakenly thought Alfred had died and wrote an obituary titled *Le marchand de la mort est mort* ("The merchant of death is dead"). The obituary went on to say, "Dr. Alfred Nobel, who became rich by finding ways to kill more people faster than ever before, died yesterday."[2] This shattered the fragile compartmentalization of Nobel's life. In the eyes of others, his espoused pacifism did not stand discretely separate from his business ventures with explosives and armaments. Realizing that his wealth had been obtained in large part by the selling of misery, he determined that same wealth should be employed to, in some way, assuage human wretchedness.

(*In fact, Ludvig Nobel deserved an obituary that would have given him much credit for his kind and humanitarian spirit. Ludvig and another brother, Robert, had made a fortune in the oil business in Baku, Azerbaijan. He introduced profit sharing and worked actively to improve working conditions in his factories. His humanitarian social approach was unique for the time. In 1885 he started a cooperative bank, Sparkasse, for the company's workers. In Baku, social areas were built for the workers like dining rooms, billiard rooms, libraries and conference rooms where speeches and discussions were held. Near his home, Villa Petrolea, several houses for the workers were built and a shuttle boat was offered between the city and the harbour. The company donated funds for schools and ran a hospital. Ludvig and Robert created a large park, which still exists in the "Black City" section of Baku, near Villa Petrolea.*)

Having read his personal legacy, as articulated in the premature obituary, Alfred Nobel spent two years working on a plan to dispose of his estate upon his actual death. The well known peace prize criteria is laid out in his last will, which he signed on November 27, 1895, "...to the person who shall have done the most or the best work for fraternity between nations, for the abolition or reduction of standing armies and for the holding and promotion of peace congresses." When he informed friend and confidant, the Baroness von Suttner, of his decision, she expressed her delight, "Whether I am around then or not does not matter; what we have given, you and I, is going to live on."[3]

Alfred Nobel's will left an inheritance of approximately 2 million Swedish krona to twenty-three surviving heirs. The disposition of the remaining 31 million krona was thusly specified:

> The whole of my remaining realizable estate shall be dealt with in the following way: the capital, invested in safe securities by my executors, shall constitute a fund, the interest on which shall be annually distributed in the form of prizes to those who, during the preceding year, shall have conferred the greatest benefit on mankind. The said interest shall be divided into five equal parts, which shall be apportioned as follows: one part to the person who shall have made the most important discovery or invention within the field of physics; one part to the person who shall have made the most important chemical discovery or improvement; one part to the person who shall have made the most important discovery within the domain of physiology or medicine; one part to the person who shall have produced in the field of literature the most outstanding work in an ideal direction; and one part to the person who shall have done the most or the best work for fraternity between nations, for the abolition or reduction of standing armies and for the holding and promotion of peace congresses. The prizes for physics and chemistry shall be awarded by the Swedish Academy of Sciences; that for physiological or medical work by the Caroline Institute in Stockholm; that for literature by the Academy in Stockholm, and that for champions of peace by a committee of five persons to be elected by the Norwegian Storting. It is my express wish that in

awarding the prizes no consideration whatever shall be given to the nationality of the candidates, but that the most worthy shall receive the prize, whether he be a Scandinavian or not.

As Executors of my testamentary dispositions, I hereby appoint Mr. Ragnar Sohlman, resident at Bofors, Varmland, and Mr. Rudolf Lilljequist, 31 Malmskillnadsgatan, Stockholm, and at Bengtsfors near Uddevalla. To compensate for their pains and attention, I grant to Mr. Ragnar Sohlman, who will presumably have to devote most time to this matter, One Hundred Thousand Crowns, and to Mr. Rudolf Lilljequist, Fifty Thousand Crowns.[4]

To say the will was "controversial", when it was read subsequent to Nobel's death on December 10, 1896, would be a monumental understatement. For obvious reasons, some of Alfred Nobel's relatives contested the will and opposed the creation of a foundation to award prizes. King Oscar II of Sweden opposed the will because it was not considered "patriotic." Perhaps the King was most distressed with the sentence, "It is my express wish that in awarding the prizes no consideration whatever shall be given to the nationality of the candidates, but that the most worthy shall receive the prize, whether he be a Scandinavian or not." The Swedish King may also have felt slighted by the assignment of some responsibility and authority to the Norwegian Storting (parliament). It has always been a mystery why, being a Swede, Nobel endowed the Norwegian Storting responsibility for administering one of the five prizes, the Nobel Peace Prize. Adding to the controversy, Nobel did not consult before his death with the entities he identified as responsible for awarding the prizes. The reading of the will came as a complete surprise to the Swedish Academy of Sciences, the Caroline Institute in Stockholm, the Academy in Stockholm, and the Norwegian Storting. Therefore, the will was also even resisted in some in these venues.

Credit for perseverance must be given to Nobel's young assistant and testament executor, Ragnar Sohlman. The estate was scattered about in eight European nations. Armed with a signed copy of the will and a handgun, Sohlman raced certain members of the Nobel family, as well as foreign government officials who wished to seize the wealth, to Paris and then to St. Petersburg. Fortuitously, he managed to withdraw Nobel's assets and deposit the cash, bank notes, titles and deeds in a bank vault in Stockholm.

It then took almost five years for Mr. Sohlman and Mr. Rudolf Lilljequist to resolve the conflicts and persuade the awarding entities to honor the stipulations in Nobel's Last Will and Testament.

¤ ¤ ¤

The first prizes were awarded on December 10, 1901. Sixty-nine years later Norman Borlaug joined an elite group of recipients of the Nobel Peace Prize for, in the words of the committee, "[H]is contributions to the 'green revolution' that was having such an impact on food production particularly in Asia and in Latin America."[5]

On October 20, 1970 Margaret Borlaug showed up unexpectedly at the Toluca experimental farm, thirty miles from their home in Champingo, Mexico to tell her husband that it had just been announced that he was the 1970 winner of the Nobel Peace Prize. Borlaug was utterly amazed and frankly flabbergasted. It had never crossed Norm's mind that a dirt farmer from Iowa would be considered for such an honor, even though he had foreshadowed the event by his comment, "You can't build a peaceful world on empty stomachs and human misery." The Borlaug's lives of relative obscurity in their little home in Mexico would never be the same.

In addition to his wife, Norm shared credit with his old mentors, Henry Wallace, George Harrar, Dave Bartelma, and E.C. Stackman. It was the latter who commented, "Norm, one of the things I admire about you is that your collar size and your hat size haven't changed. You are the same humble, dedicated person whom I knew as a student at the university."[6]

In his acceptance speech, Dr. Borlaug gave voice to Henry Wallace's concern that at some point, producing more food will just not be enough.

> "There can be no permanent progress in the battle against hunger until agencies that fight for increased food production and those that fight for population control unite in a common effort. Fighting alone, they may win temporary skirmishes, but united they can win a decisive and lasting victory to provide food and other amenities of a progressive civilization for the benefit of mankind.
>
> Then, indeed, Alfred Nobel's efforts to promote brotherhood between nations and their peoples will become a reality."[7]

In addition to the beautiful medal and a cash prize, fame and its unavoidable consequences are also bestowed upon the recipient of a Nobel Prize. So it was with Norm and Margaret. There can be no argument that they managed to leverage that notoriety for the greatest good. Even so, sometimes Norm wistfully shares Henry Wallace's affinity for 'the strength and quietness of grass.'

> "The Nobel Prize hit me like a typhoon. I sometimes think fondly of that summer of complete isolation on Cold Mountain."
>
> —Dr. Norman Borlaug[8]

As one might expect, thousands of congratulatory messages and accolades were received. Of those, Norm likely most cherished his Mother's comment. Upon hearing that Norm would return to Norway, the nation from whence his great-grandparents had fled famine 116 years earlier, to receive the Nobel Peace Prize, the eighty-two year old Clara Vaala Borlaug said simply, "Norm was always a good boy."[9]

33

Tʜᴇ Evil Mᴇɴ Do

Kindness and evil juxtaposed.

"Friends, Romans, countrymen, lend me your ears;
I come to bury Caesar, not to praise him.
The evil that men do lives after them;
the good is oft interred with their bones..."
—William Shakespeare[1]

Shakespeare's Mark Anthony articulated a certain pathos about the human spirit, and the resulting sense of dread focuses attention on the darkness rather than the dawn. Some truly evil men lived and even rose to positions of enormous power all over the world during the course of the twentieth century. Literally millions of words have been written recounting their deeds. Deeds so unimaginably horrible that the wake of their trauma ripples still through families, communities, nations and time. When one reads a history text of the century past, it seems nothing else was as important or had as much impact as the evil men do. Perhaps by the brutal imposition of their will upon individuals and whole nations, sociopaths and tyrants so traumatized the populace as to cause a kind of mass, cross-generational post-traumatic stress disorder.

Against an historical backdrop of almost unfathomable cruelty, Clara Borlaug's son just kept right on being a "good boy." Norm was working hard, helping hundreds of millions of hungry people all around the globe learn to feed themselves. Though history hones its collective focus on the bad guys, George Carver, Henry Wallace and Norman Borlaug too threw some stones in the pond of humanity during the twentieth century. However, because of the human inclination to perseverate on the sensational, those ripples went almost unnoticed.

A short article buried on page three of the November 23, 1894 edition of the New York Times reported:

> CHICAGO, Nov. 22 – There is no longer a doubt that a part, at least, of the story told in Philadelphia by H.H. Holmes, the insurance swindler, is true. It is certain that Anna Williams did come to Chicago to join her sister Minnie, and that she was seen several times in Holmes's company, but whether she was murdered is a point that can only be cleared when her sister Minnie is brought to light.[2]

Over the next two years a sordid story of evil unraveled revealing that Dr. H.H. Holmes was actually one Herman Mudgett, and that his crimes were far more haunting than mere insurance fraud and use of false identity. In fact, Minnie Williams fate was the same as her sister Anna, neither surviving Mr. Mudgett's psychopathic bloodlust.

Mr. Mudgett's life of crime began in medical school. He purchased life insurance on cadavers being used at the school then stole and mutilated the corpses to make it appear they had died of some horrible accident. Mr. Mudgett would then claim the insurance money for the policy that listed him as the beneficiary. It was a far more innocent time, and it seems folks just could not fathom anything so perverse and thus, on numerous occasions, various insurance companies awarded settlement funds to Mr. Mudgett, who always used a nom de guerre.

If this scheme could work with cadavers, why not with the wealthy living after they were cajoled into willing considerable portions of their estates to Mr. Mudgett? As he cultivated these relationships, he always assumed a fictitious name, most often Dr. H.H. Holmes. He admitted responsibility for the seduction, kidnapping, torture, murder and mutilation of at least twenty-seven women and children, and likely many dozens more.

The grisly details of his torture and mutilation chambers are almost unfathomable by the normal human psyche. Superficially it would seem that Mr. Mudgett, who passed himself off as a doctor, chemist, and pharmacist set out to use the 1893 Chicago World's Fair as the venue to make his fortune. In reality, his more fiendish schemes entailed using the throngs of people who descended upon Chicago's World's Fair as the cloak to hide his larceny, sadism, and murder.

One of his victims was the tall and stunningly beautiful Julia Conner, who was the wife of one of Dr. Holmes employees. Using the alias Dr. H. H. Holmes, Mr. Mudgett had acquired a large piece of property in close proximity to the planned site of the Chicago World's Fair. There he had a strange and complex building shoddily erected that became derisively known as "the castle." At street level it housed a drug store, restaurant, barber shop, and plate glass company. The second floor was a combination boarding house-hotel. All of these enterprises hid a more sinister purpose. Ned Conner who worked as a jeweler in the drug store had a troubled marriage and when he separated from his lovely wife, she and her eight year old daughter, Pearl, soon took up with the utterly charming and erudite Dr. Holmes.

In November 1891 Julie found herself pregnant and the only possible father was Dr. Holmes. When she confronted him with their predicament he quickly agreed to marry her with the condition that she agree to an abortion, which, being a doctor, he would perform himself. On Christmas eve he escorted her to his "operating room" where he made her comfortable with a light dose of chloroform. However, he continued to dribble the liquid toxin onto the cloth until the duped Ms. Conner lapsed into a coma, thereby allowing Dr. Holmes to proceed with his macabre dissection of her body unimpeded.

That same evening Dr. Homes furtively sleuthed down the hallway of his boarding house to Julia's rooms. Letting himself in with his pass key he used the remaining chloroform and quickly dispensed with Julia's daughter, Pearl, who almost certainly lay dreaming of a visit from Santa Claus.

A couple of days after Christmas Dr. Holmes summoned an associate, Charles Chappell, who specialized in the art of carving all muscle and fiber from human bones and assembling the skeletons for display in doctor's offices and medical laboratories. He had acquired this skill while quite legitimately articulating cadavers for medical research at Cook County Hospital. No doubt, Mr. Chappell also employed these techniques on bodies stolen from cemeteries, as the demand for cadavers by medical schools was sizable, the market robust, and grave robbing a very profitable enterprise.

Upon arrival at "the castle" Dr. Holmes escorted Mr. Chappell to a secret room where he found the body of an unusually tall woman laid out on an operating table. Years later Chappell described what he found, "The body looked like that of a jack rabbit which had been skinned by splitting the skin down the face and rolling back off the entire body. In some places considerable of the flesh had been taken off with it."[3]

That Holmes claimed to be a physician allowed Chappell to rationalize that he had simply been doing a dissection for research purposes. Thus in good conscience Chappell accepted payment of thirty-six dollars for cleansing the bones and returning a fully articulated skeleton to the "good doctor" several days later. Holmes then sold the skeleton to Hahneman Medical College in Chicago for several multiples of what he had paid Chappell. Murder, like grave robbing, was also good business.

Almost to a person, each of his victims sensed something sinister, perhaps even dangerous about Mr. Mudgett, whom all knew by some other name. Though subconsciously almost able to acknowledge that they were in the presence of some kind of unfathomable evil, his victims were nevertheless seduced by a most compelling form of charisma-gilded deceit. So much so, that it seems they often served as unwitting accomplices in their own murders, at least until the very last moments when their erred judgment became clear but their fate sealed.

When Chicago police detectives searched "the castle" in July 1895 they found second floor rooms with no windows fitted with air tight doors. They found a walk-in vault made of iron fitted with a gas jet. The shut off valve located outside the iron walls in Mr. Mudgett's personal apartment. They found Lucy Burbank's bank book with a balance of $23,000. The unfortunate Ms. Burbank, however, was never found. In the basement they identified an acid vat containing the remains of eight ribs and a human skull, a sound proof vault, a blood stained surgical table, surgical tools, bone saws, and a pair of charred high heeled shoes. The inspectors also unearthed eighteen ribs of a child, a number of vertebrae, a shoulder blade, a foot bone, and a hip socket. In pits of ash and calcium oxide (*perhaps used to burn clothing, perhaps to torture his victims*) they found more human remains, pieces of a girl's dress, bloodstained overalls, wads of human hair, and a piece of gold jewelry that had been purchased by Mudgett himself and given to one of his many victims.

Just prior to his execution, Mr. Mudgett, still insisting on using the alias Dr. H. H. Holmes, described himself, "I was born with the devil in me. I could not help the fact that I was a murderer, no more than the poet can help the inspiration to sing—I was born with the "Evil One" standing as my sponsor beside the bed where I was ushered into the world, and he has been with me since."

¤ ¤ ¤

Meanwhile, 342 miles west, in Ames, Iowa, a young George Washington Carver was conducting the research that would be published as his Master's degree dissertation. In a mere seven page single spaced typed document, he set in motion a series of events that could not have stood in sharper contrast to the evil being perpetrated by Mr. Mudgett in Chicago. As a result of his work, a series of events would unfold that altered the course of human history in ways no one at Iowa State College of Agriculture and Mechanic Arts could have begun to contemplate. Even today the aftereffect seems so profound and enormous as to almost defy comprehension. In part, George's thesis stated:

> With the light that our past and present experience has given, the wide range of possibilities is beginning to dawn upon us. Horticulture has, indeed, a broad foundation upon which to build a mighty structure. The agents . . . in brief, these:
> 1. A change in environment.
> 2. Cross fertilization.
> 3. Cultivation.
> 4. In and in breeding and selection.
> No. 4 is by no means of minor importance since scientists have established beyond question that not only such a thing exists in the plant kingdom as heredity, but that it is very characteristic. . . . Its first appearance is, to be sure, a sport, but by selection, budding, and grafting, the type can be fixed so that it will reproduce itself with unerring certainty, and some of them have been so well fixed as to come fairly true from seed and this is likewise true of all characteristics.
> With these few milestones to guide us in our course, dare we not predict that the day is not far distant when man's workshop need no longer be chaos, but will be able to use the tools nature has placed before him from a purely scientific basis free from all conjecture.

Why should not the horticulturalist know just how to build up the size, flavor, vigor, and hardiness of his fruits and shrubs?[4] . . .

From a retrospective perch over a century later, Carver's observations and rhetorical questions are amusing in their elementary simplicity. However, at the time they were thunderbolts that would shake the very ground upon which farmers grew their crops. His life's work would guide and contribute to an agricultural transformation that would directly impact the lives of every single human on earth within a few decades. Yet unlike Mr. Mudgett's evil, Mr. Carver's early works, and the most profound kindnesses buried therein, went largely unnoticed.

Because of the butterfly effect, with their actions both men cast ripples upon the cosmos, but it seems mostly the evil has been remembered.

¤ ¤ ¤

During the course of the twentieth century a number of incredibly evil sociopaths rose to power over great nations. Men like Joseph Stalin, Mao Zedong, Pol Pot, Ismail Enver Pasha, Ante Pavelic, Idi Amin Dada Oumee, Anastasio Somoza Debayle, François Duvalier (father) and Jean-Claude Duvalier (son), and dozens more instigated the democidal slaughter and starvation of over 200 million humans. (*Democide is defined as the murder of any person or people by a government, including genocide, politicide, and mass murder.*)

The atrocities of Adolf Hitler's Nazi thugs are the most studied and reported in human history. Herr Hitler was the quintessential practitioner of government sponsored slaughter, not because he was the greatest mass murderer in history (that "honor" likely belongs to Mao Zedong), but rather because of the Nazi penchant for the industrialization of democide. With assembly line efficiency, and the help of IBM Hollerith punch cards, they kept meticulous records of their victims and their profits. The records of the Treblinka death camp are most instructive in this regard.

Each gas chamber built at Treblinka in the summer of 1942 had a capacity of approximately two hundred individuals—more if the individuals were sufficiently emaciated. With all six chambers operating, 1200 people could be gassed simultaneously. The gassing process required about thirty minutes, and another thirty minutes to remove the bodies. Therefore, a train load of 5 thousand people could be executed in just over four hours. In the first 163 days of operation, 713,555 prisoners were killed at Treblinka.

Another 1,235,000 persons would be gassed before the inflow of victims slowed in August of 1943.

As millions of Jews were being killed, the Nazi Economics and Administration Office took an interest in the economic aspect of 'confiscation of property' from murdered persons. An undated report by Odilo Globocnik gives an idea of the extent of profits obtained as well as the level of detailed record keeping.

Personal Staff Reich Leader SS
Files Administration
File No. Secret 115
[initialed by Himmler]
Valuables Turned In from the "Operation Reinhardt"
　　　Valuables from the "Operation Reinhardt" have been handed in at the SS WVHA Berlin for transmission to the Reich Bank or to the Reich Ministry of Economy as follows:
　　　a. RM, (Reichsmarks) total value – RM 53,013,133.51
　　　b. Foreign currency, in notes, from all main countries of the earth (particularly the half million dollars are noteworthy), total value – RM 1,452,904.65
　　　c. Foreign currency in coined gold, total RM 843,802.75
　　　d. Precious metals (about 1,800 kg. gold and about 10,000 kg. silver in ingots), total value – RM 5,353,943.00
　　　e. Other valuables such as jewels, watches, glasses, etc., in particular, the number of watches, about 16,000 watches in working condition and about 51,000 watches in need of repair, is noteworthy; they have been placed at the disposal of the troops – RM 26,089,800.00
　　　f. About 1,000 boxcars of textiles, total value – RM 13,294,400.00
　　　Total – RM 100,047,983.91
[Signed] GLOBOCNIK
SS Gruppenführer and Major General of the Police[5]

In a February 6, 1943 memo to Heinrich Himmler, Chief of the Economics and Administration Office, SS Obergruppenführer Oswald Pohl, issued a detailed list of items looted from the victims of the Nazi murder factories.

Men's clothing:

- overcoats – 99,000
- jackets – 57,000
- vests – 27,000
- pants – 62,000
- drawers – 38,000
- shirts – 132,000
- pullover – 9,000
- scarves – 2,000
- pajamas – 6,000
- collars – 10,000
- gloves – 2,000 pairs
- socks – 10,000 pairs
- shoes – 31,000 pairs

Women's clothing:

- Coats – 155,000 pieces
- dresses – 119,000 pieces
- blouses – 30,000 pieces
- pullovers – 60,000 pieces
- drawers – 49,000 pieces
- panties – 60,000 pieces
- jackets – 26,000 pieces
- shirts – 30,000 pieces
- chemises – 125,000 pieces
- pajamas – 27,000 pieces
- aprons – 36,000 pieces
- brassieres – 25,000 pieces
- underwear – 22,000 pieces
- kerchiefs – 85,000 pieces
- shoes – 111,000 pieces

Children's clothing:

- overcoats – 15,000
- boys' jackets – 11,000
- boys' pants – 3,000
- shirts – 3,000
- scarves – 4,000
- pullovers – 1,000
- drawers – 1,000
- girls' dresses – 9,000
- girls' chemises – 5,000
- aprons – 2,000
- drawers – 5,000
- stockings – 10,000 pairs
- shoes – 22,000 pairs[6]

Pohl closed the memo by actually apologizing for the unexpectedly low numbers!

In an April 2, 1947 affidavit for the Nuremberg trials, Pohl explained that he had been working under the direction of Himmler and was responsible for managing the economic aspects of the "Final Solution." He indicated that he was completely aware of the source of the valuables and the precedent activities that produced the plunder.

> It was never doubted that this loot was taken from Jews exterminated in the concentration camps. . . . As I learned in 1943, gold teeth and crowns of inmates of concentration camps were broken out of their mouths after liquidation. This gold was melted down and delivered to the Reich Bank. . . . When I received all the vouchers, setting out the economic assets received, I realized the extent of the operation. I realized that the greatest part of the textile goods listed in these reports had been taken from people who had been violently put to death and that the purpose of the operation had been the extermination of the Jews.[7]

The genocide was so remunerative that one might argue with Herr

Pohl's contention that ". . .the purpose of the operation had been the extermination of the Jews." Certainly, a case could be made that many of the Nazi hierarchy never accepted the pseudo-science, false-eugenic basis for the genocide. Rather, they supported mass murder because it was a profitable industry—the Nazi's cash cow—and thus, Adolf Hitler's Third Reich perpetrated the democidal extermination of 21 million people.

¤ ¤ ¤

Half a world away from this terror, Henry Wallace was preaching the gospel of kindness. In speeches across the breadth of the continent he reminded people that "We are writing the post-war world as we go along. The end of the war will be our second chance. We can choose to circumnavigate the pitfalls that followed World War I. We can now work toward establishing a world where security, stability, efficiency and abundance will prevail."[8]

While acknowledging that having good thoughts and kindly hearts toward each other was a necessary precursor to creating a sustainable peace, he stressed that good and kind intentions were not enough. "The battle of the peace will be more difficult to win than the battle of the war. . . ." He emphasized the absolute necessity of taking bold and progressive action.

When Vice President-elect Wallace and Jim LaCron saw the dismal state of affairs on Mexican farms in 1940, they did not just shake their heads and bemoan the situation. Wallace pushed for action. Recognizing that enduring peace without abundant food was not a possibility, the Rockefeller Foundation rose to the Vice President's challenge.

On the same day Vice President Wallace first met with Rockefeller Foundation President, Raymond Fosdick to propose a plan of action to save Mexican agriculture and the Mexican people, Adolf Hitler met with his military leaders to discuss final plans for the Axis Power's invasion of the Soviet Union. Operation Barbarossa would result in tens of millions of deaths. The Mexican Agricultural Project would spare tens of millions of people from starvation. February 3, 1941 is remembered for the horror that was planned and unleashed on eastern Europe. The meeting between Mr. Wallace and Mr. Fosdick does not even rate a mention in most historical texts.

Likewise, on the day Drs. Stackman, Manglesdorf, and Bradfield returned from Mexico after conducting the Rockefeller Foundation's initial survey for the Mexican Agricultural Project, Hermann Goering issued the following order to Reinhard Heydrich:

> I hereby charge you with making all necessary preparations with regard to organizational, technical and material matters for bringing about a complete solution of the Jewish question within the German sphere of influence in Europe. . . . I request you further to send me, in the near future, an overall plan covering the organizational, technical and material measures necessary for the accomplishment of the final solution of the Jewish question which we desire.[9]

Thousands of books have been written about the planning and implementation of the holocaust, but the mere existence of the Rockefeller Foundation's Mexican Agricultural Project is all but unknown.

Just as the first of 3,172 Nazi built V-2 rockets began raining death upon European cities controlled by Allied forces in September 1944, the thirty-year-old Norman Borlaug departed from Wilmington, Delaware to join the four man Rockefeller Foundation team charged with the assignment to "make Mexico capable of feeding itself." It seems almost implausible that the latter of those two events would have a far more profound impact upon humanity, but it did.

Unlike the V-2 rockets, Borlaug's adventure is a virtually unknown event in the history of the twentieth century. However, that his journey, which began on Monday, September 11, 1944, had a huge butterfly effect can hardly be argued.

Twenty-six years later, while the American press and public fixated upon the evil antics brought to light during the mass murder trial of Charles Manson, Susan Atkins, Leslie Van Houten, and Patricia Krenwinkel in Los Angles, the Nobel Selection Committee announced that Dr. Norman Borlaug would be the 1970 Peace Prize recipient. Today most baby-boomers recall a considerable amount of detail about Charlie Manson's vision of "Helter Skelter." But ask who won the 1970 Nobel Peace Prize—who spared over 2 billion people the agony of starvation, and few Americans even know the name.

"The evil men do lives after them..."

34

THE HARVEST

*Norman Borlaug is the living embodiment of the human
quest for a hunger free world.
His life is his message.*

—*Dr. M.S. Swaminatha*[1]

In one of the bestselling books of 1968, *The Population Bomb*, Paul Ehrlich predicted "The battle to feed all of humanity is over. . . . In the 1970s and 1980s hundreds of millions of people will starve to death in spite of any crash programs embarked upon now. . . . I have yet to meet anyone familiar with the situation who thinks India will be self-sufficient in food by 1971." He was absolutely certain that "India couldn't possibly feed two hundred million **more** hungry mouths by 1980."[2]

Ehrlich's predictions were born from his observations of India's drought in the mid-1960s. Two consecutive years of drought in 1965 and 1966 threatened the lives of millions of people on the Asian subcontinent. In point of fact, the Borlaug team was a year too late arriving with their drought and rust resistant strains of dwarf wheat. Even given the team's best efforts, it is estimated that 1.5 million people starved.

But from that drought sprung seeds of hope. In 1966, 13.2% less rain than normal fell on the farmlands of India. Yet in the fall of that year, 600 thousand acres were planted with Borlaug's dwarf winter wheat. The yield was the largest in Indian history. Had it not been so, had their agriculture continued to use the traditional wheat seeds and traditional agricultural technologies, at least another two million people would have starved by the end of 1967.

The real test, however, came some twenty years later. Starting in

1985 a much worse drought cycle began and lasted for three years. In 1985 7.1% less rain than normal fell, and by 1987 the rainfall deficit had grown to 19.4%. In 1960 India's total food grain production had been about 82 million metric tons. Twenty-five years later, using varieties of the drought tolerant dwarf wheat, India managed to produce 137.6 million metric tons. During the second year of the drought cycle, 1986, production grew to 142.6 million metric tons, and during the worst year of the drought, India still managed to produce 136.2 million metric tons. This time, the Borlaug team's wheat seeds saved hundreds of millions of lives across the Asian subcontinent.

Dr. Borlaug and the Rockefeller Foundation could have devised a scheme to sell the dwarf wheat product of the Mexican Agricultural Project. Dr. Borlaug could have used those wheat seeds, and his knowledge, to become one of the wealthiest men on earth. Instead, they took the seeds to Pakistan and India, the Middle East and Latin America, China and central Asia. They taught farmers how to feed their people. Soon thereafter, Mexican Agricultural Project (MAP) techniques were adapted by agronomists to growing rice, and then sorghum and oats and rye, as well as other crops.

Borlaug and his team were directly responsible for the fact that global food production expanded faster than the human population in the last half of the twentieth century. Had it not been so, Mr. Ehrlich's mass starvations would have been a certainty.

Dr. Borlaug's success in helping the world feed itself cannot be construed as an indication that he refuted *The Population Bomb* dynamics. To the contrary, he had long been an advocate of population control. In his 1970 Nobel Peace Prize acceptance speech he stated:

> There can be no permanent progress in the battle against hunger until the agencies that fight for increased food production and those that fight for population control unite in a common effort. Fighting alone, they may win temporary skirmishes, but united they can win a decisive and lasting victory to provide food and other amenities of a progressive civilization for the benefit of all mankind.[3]

That being said, Dr. Borlaug knew from personal experience that hunger hurts. While he understood that the human population must be controlled, he also knew that starvation is the cruelest imaginable means to that end. As he said, "Food is the moral right of all who are born into this world. . . . [It is]the first essential component of social justice. . . ."[4] Mass starvation is not now, has never been, an acceptable method for population control.

By the time Dr. Borlaug received the Nobel Peace Prize in 1970 it was estimated that his seeds and his kindness had saved hundreds of millions from the savageries of starvation—and still counting. By the time he was awarded the Presidential Medal of Freedom in 1977 the estimated lives saved had risen to 1 billion people—and still counting. On December 14, 2006 the United States Congress passed Public Law 109-395. It stated in part:

> Dr. Borlaug has saved more lives than any other person who has ever lived, and likely has saved more lives in the Islamic world than any other human being in history. Due to a lifetime of work that has led to the saving and preservation of an untold amount of lives, Dr. Norman E. Borlaug is deserving of America's highest civilian award: **the congressional gold medal.**[5]

By 2006, when Dr. Borlaug received the Congressional Gold Medal, the estimated lives saved was approaching 2 billion—and still counting.

Even with all the accolades, Norman Borlaug would be first to admit that he could not have saved billions of lives had it not been for the seeds of kindness passed down by Henry Wallace. And Henry Wallace would not have delivered those seeds had it not been for his childhood friend and mentor, George Washington Carver. And George Washington Carver would never have gotten an education, or even been alive, had it not been for the often courageous and colorblind offerings of kindness by the likes of Henry C. (Harry) and May Wallace, Louis Pammel, Etta Mae Budd, James "Tama Jim" Wilson, Mr. and Mrs. W.A. Liston, Dr. and Mrs. Milholland, Andrew and "Aunt Mariah" Watkins, Moses and Susan Carver.

Of course, the butterflies of kindness did not begin with any of these people either. It cannot be known when these seeds were germinated—it cannot be known where they will lead. That is the chaotic reality of the butterfly effect as kindness flies through generations. What can be known is that by the early twenty-first century, 2 billion people were spared the horrors of daily hunger. Spared, because this group of people made a conscious decision. They chose action. They chose kindness.

Moses Carver chose to act, and rescued an infant from certain death at the hands of his kidnappers. Susan Carver chose to raise a little boy, nurturing his intellect and spirit. Aunt Mariah Watkins treated that boy with stern kindness and made sure he understood from whence he came. Etta Mae Budd, Louis Pammel, James Wilson, the Listons, and the Millhollands all acted to secure an education for a young black man and to assure that he was treated fairly in that pursuit. In turn, George Carver passed on his enthusiasm and knowledge about plants to a little boy. He also passed along a kindness of spirit that would be one of the hallmarks of Henry Wallace's life. And Henry Wallace acted accordingly as Secretary of Agriculture and Vice President of the United States. His compassion for the common man, all common men everywhere in the world, led to actions by Norman Borlaug. Borlaug's actions and resolve translated into the greatest of all kindnesses. He shared food with a hungry world.

Directly and indirectly, the evil men of the twentieth century caused the deaths of some 200 million people. Two hundred million people, most guilty of nothing other than being of a different race, or religion, or ethnicity, or political persuasion. Evil extremists prescribed death as the penalty for being different, and 200 million people died. Yet, 200 million lives, given to evil excess, sums to just ten percent of the 2 billion lives saved by the seeds and the kindnesses passed on to humanity through George Washington Carver, Henry Agard Wallace and Norman Ernest Borlaug.

William Shakespeare's Mark Antony was partially right. The evil that men do does, indeed, live after them. But he was also partially wrong. The good is never, **never** interred with the bones. Because you see, the seeds of kindness continue to ride through generations on the wings of butterflies. And like the seeds we sow, those butterflies are multiplying, always multiplying.

Two billion—and still counting!

Epilogue

From the chaos of kindness to warm and caring environments.

Perhaps Aldous Huxley best captured my feelings upon completion of this book. Late in his life he commented, "It's a bit embarrassing to have been concerned with the human problem all one's life and find at the end that one has no more to offer by way of advice than 'Try to be a little kinder.'"[1]

As the "kindness movement" began gathering steam in the early 1990s I had the honor of working with a remarkable school administrator in the Las Cruces (New Mexico) Public Schools. Jean de la Pena became a mentor and friend, and first exposed me to the idea that kindness could be institutionalized within an organization. This could happen when (forgive my use of this overused metaphor) a "critical mass" of the people in an organization embrace the idea of treating each other with kindness. In a middle school, that had historically been "difficult," I observed over a four year period that a tipping point was indeed reached and the institutional culture keeled toward kindness. Jean characterized the resulting behavioral milieu as a "warm and caring environment."

At first, the school's faculty and staff were confused by the term. Later, many of us would roll our eyes at Jean's use of the term during morning staff meetings in the school's library. Finally, without anyone really saying, "Hey, something is happening here," our principal's unflagging proselytizing about the power of the decision to create warm and caring environments was causing a gradual metamorphosis of the school. I took from that experience an awareness that creating warm and caring environments is a decision anyone can make. It is likely the most powerful decision anyone will ever make. At its core, both its cause and its effect, is the decision to be kind.

As the story goes, the phrase "practice random acts of kindness" originated circa 1983, in the San Francisco Bay area, when writer-editor Anne Herbert scribbled her thought on a place mat in a local restaurant. Another version of the story claims that in the spring of 1993, Bakersfield College professor, Chuck Wall, was driving to campus to teach his human relations class. On this day, the professor was inspired by the emotionally numbing news he heard on the radio about yet another "random act of senseless violence." Professor Wall was struck by the idea that replacing the word 'violence' with the word 'kindness' might completely change a human dynamic. On that day he gave the class of eighteen students an unusual assignment. They were told to "commit one random act of senseless kindness." Though the students were utterly confused and requested more direction, Professor Wall just told them to figure it out for themselves and report back to the class the following week. The rest of the story is almost legendary—the class became so animated in their discussions during the ensuing weeks that a movement was born.

Perhaps both stories of origin are correct. Given the tens of billions of humans who have inhabited this earth, it is possible that there is almost no such thing as a truly original thought. While the exact genesis of this iteration of the movement is subject to question, there can be no doubt that the idea of kindness predates both Anne Herbert and Chuck Wall.

"Blessed are the merciful . . . " —Jesus[2]

"Kindness is the mark of faith; and whoever has not kindness has not faith" —Mohammad[3]

"My religion is very simple. My religion is kindness." —Dalai Lama[4]

"No act of kindness, no matter how small, is ever wasted." —Aesop (circa 600 BC)[5]

"That best portion of a good man's life—his little, nameless, unremembered acts of kindness and of love." —William Wordsworth[6]

"Every time you opt in to kindness
Make one connection, used to divide us
It echoes all over the world." —Dar Williams[7]

"Let no one ever come to you without leaving better and happier. Be the living expression of God's kindness: kindness in your face, kindness in your eyes, kindness in your smile." —Mother Teresa[8]

"Constant kindness can accomplish much. As the sun makes ice melt, kindness causes misunderstanding, mistrust, and hostility to evaporate." —Albert Schweitzer[9]

"There is a new social machinery in the making. Let us maintain sweet and kindly hearts toward each other, however great the difficulties ahead." —Henry Agard Wallace[10]

Whatever the source, there can be little doubt that the idea of acting kindly has entered the lexicon, and perhaps even the behavioral expectation of popular culture during the decades on each side of the new millennium. A book, *Random Acts of Kindness*, was released by Conari Press in 1993. The Random Acts of Kindness Foundation was established as a private not-for-profit corporation in 1993. The World Kindness Movement (WKM) started in 1997 when representatives from several countries gathered at a kindness centered conference in Tokyo. Twenty countries are currently members of the WKM. In 2000, the popular movie *Pay It Forward* espoused the ripple effect notion of kind deeds. Ben's Bells project was born when three-year-old Ben Packard suddenly died of croup. In his parent's search for some way to snatch meaning from their son's short life they hit upon the idea of Ben's Bells, to, in their own words, "Inspire, educate, and motivate each other to realize the impact of intentional kindness and to empower individuals to act accordingly to that awareness, thereby changing our world."[11] The Kindness Offensive (TKO) is a group in North London that has orchestrated large scale random acts of kindness for individuals and groups of people. In turn, the Kindness Offensive inspired the "One Million Random Acts of Kindness Campaign" (RAK) sponsored by BBC Radio in 2008.

It is clear that "random acts of senseless kindness" are preferable to "random acts of senseless violence," and that this idea is invading the collective consciousness. Additionally, it must be admitted that the phrase is catchy and sounds nifty. It fits nicely on a bumper sticker, coffee mug, or tee shirt. However, in terms of the decision to create warm and caring environments the phrase, but not the intent, is just **nonsense**. "Why?"

First, it seems to me there is no such thing as a senseless act of kindness. While one can never know or predict the impact of any particular act of kindness, because of the butterfly effect, that there will be an impact is an absolute certainty. If kindness is its own purpose, how can it be senseless?

Second, to succeed in the quest of creating warm and caring environments, I would propose that there should be nothing random about the decision to be kind. Dr. Edward Lorenz' formula ($dx/dt = -10(y - x) \ldots dy/dt = Rx - y - xz \ldots dz/dt = xy - (8/3)z$) provided the mathematical basis for chaos—the butterfly effect. In essence every expression of energy, everywhere, impacts every subsequent expression of energy, forever. However, the impact is so chaotic as to seem essentially "random." Random acts of kindness would contribute to the already chaotic array of behavioral expectations, hence likely creating neurotic, rather than caring environments.

Finally, and perhaps most importantly, if a person is capable of acting kindly on one occasion, it begs the question, why not act kindly on every occasion? Chaos can be limited by making the decision to always be kind. Kindness need not be random. One can rise each morning and commit to treat everyone encountered with kindness. In the quotes above, Mother Teresa and Albert Schweitzer both articulated a recognition of the non-random power of consistency—of "constant kindness."

Rather than acts of random kindness and senseless beauty, wouldn't we be better to courageously practice consistent acts of kindness and produce thoughtful works of beauty? Every thought we think, every word we speak, every action we take, matters, and it only matters forever.

A Word Personal

Dr. Borlaug's passing on September 12, 2009.

On the day I was putting the "finishing touches" on this manuscript's first draft, Dr. Norman Borlaug died at the age of ninety-five. I was not aware of his passing until the next morning when I saw a three paragraph article on page two of the *Santa Fe New Mexican*. I spent much of the day with a lump in my throat. Though I never had the honor of meeting him, I felt that I'd come to know him over the preceding year as a result of the research for this book.

On page three of the same newspaper was an article detailing the protests of thousands of angry people gathered at the steps of the nation's capitol in Washington, DC. They vented their emotions on signs that carried unkind and thinly veiled threats against the government, the nation, and the president. One such sign had a picture of a AR-15 assault rifle with the caption, "We came unarmed from Montana and Utah . . . this time!"

Politicians pandered to and manipulated the crowd's ugly mood with speeches referring to the president and the administration alternately as socialists and fascists. Well, with socialists on the left and fascists on the far right of the political spectrum, it seems that the politico's thinking and rhetoric was hopelessly muddled.

We were at a time when people all across America were engaging in angry screaming matches over silly political differences of opinion and superficial lines drawn in the sand. With his passing, perhaps we should reflect on a quote from Dr. Borlaug's December 11, 1970 Nobel Lecture:

> We must recognize the fact that adequate food is only the first requisite for life. For a decent and humane life we must also provide

an opportunity for good education, remunerative employment, comfortable housing, good clothing and effective and compassionate medical care.

As Dr. Swaminathan of India said, "Norman Borlaug is the living embodiment of the human quest for a hunger free world. His life is his message." Indeed it was, through his actions and his kindness he made the world a better place. We will miss him—I will miss him.

Appendix

Perpetrators of twentieth century democides.

Idi Amin Dada Oumee
AKA 'Big Daddy'; 'Butcher of Africa; 'Conqueror of the British Empire'; 'Lord of All the Beasts of the Earth and Fishes of the Sea'.
Country: Uganda.
Democide deaths: 300,000 (1971 – 1979)

Ion Antonescu
AKA 'Conducator' (Leader); 'Red Dog'.
Country: Romania.
Democide deaths: 300,000 Romanian Jews (1940 – 1945)

Théoneste Bagosora
AKA 'Colonel Death'; 'Rwanda's Milosevic'
Country: Rwanda.
Democide deaths: 800,000 (1994)

François Duvalier (father) and Jean-Claude Duvalier (son)
AKA 'Papa Doc' (François); AKA 'Baby Doc' (Jean-Claude).
Country: Haiti.
Democide deaths: 40,000 (1957 – 1986)

Francisco Franco Bahamonde
AKA 'El Caudillo' (The Leader).
Country: Spain.
Democide deaths: 150,000 (1937 – 1975)

Adolf Hitler
AKA 'Der Fuhrer'
Country: Germany
Democide deaths: 21,000,000 (1934 – 1945)

Saddam Hussein
Full name Saddam Hussein al-Majid al-Tikriti. AKA 'Great Uncle'; 'Lion of Babylon'; 'Lion of Iraq'; 'Beast of Baghdad'.
Country: Iraq.
Democide deaths: 400,000 (1979 – 2003)

Vladimir Lenin
Country: Russia
Democide deaths: 4,000,000 (1918 – 1924)

José Efraín Ríos Montt
AKA 'The General'.
Country: Guatemala.
Democide deaths: 70,000 (1982 – 1983)

Benito Mussolini
AKA 'Il Duce'
Country: Italy
Democide deaths: 400,000 Italians & 30,000 Ethopians (1922 – 1943)

Ismail Enver Pasha
Country: Turkey.
Armenian Democide: 1,100,000 deaths (1914 – 1918)

Ante Pavelic
AKA 'Butcher of the Balkans'
Country: Croatia (Yugoslavia)
Democide deaths: 30,000 Jews, 29,000 Gypsies, and 600,000 Serbs (1941 – 1945)

Anastasio Somoza Debayle
Country: Nicaragua.
Democide deaths: 50,000 (1967 – 1979)

Joseph Stalin
AKA 'Man of Steel', 'Shining sun', 'Staff of Life', 'Great Teacher and Friend', Hope of the Future for the Workers and Peasants of the World', 'Genius of Mankind', 'Greatest Genius of All Times and Peoples'
Country: Russia
Democidal deaths: 20,000,000 (1924 – 1953)

Suharto
AKA 'Pak Harto' (Father Harto); 'The Smiling General'; 'Bapak Pembangunan' (Father of Development). (Following a pilgrimage to Mecca in 1991, Suharto took the name Haji Mohammed Suharto.)
Country: Indonesia.
Democide deaths: 400,000 (1966 – 1998)

Rafael Trujillo
Full name Rafael Leónidas Trujillo Molina. AKA 'El Jefe' (the chief);'El Chivo' (the goat); 'Chapita' (bottle top).
Country: Dominican Republic.
Democide deaths: 20,000 (1937)

Jorge Rafaél Videla (with Argentine Junta)
AKA 'The Bone'; 'Pink Panther'.
Country: Argentina.
Democide deaths: 30,000 (1976 – 1981)

Agha Mohammad Yahya Khan
Country: Pakistan.
Democide deaths: 300,000 (1971)

Mao Zedong
AKA 'Chairman Mao'
Country: China
Democide deaths: 40,000,000 (1943 – 1976)

Empire of Japan
Country: Japan
Because of the way the Japanese military fought during World War II, as well as the way Japanese occupation forces behaved, an accurate estimate of democide is almost impossible. It is safe to assume, however, that the number of democidal

deaths exceeded 17 million people on the Korean Peninsula, China, Southeast Asia, and islands of the Pacific and Indian Oceans.
Democide deaths: 17,000,000 (1931 – 1945)

Pol Pot
Country: Cambodia
Democide deaths: 2,000,000

NOTES

Chapter 2

1. Sparks, Edwin E. The Wizard of the Goober and the Yam. American Life, November 1923, (p.16)
2. G.S. Scofield, Brothers Will You Meet Me (aka "Battle Hymn of the Republic"). Our Monthly Casket. 1858. ("John Brown's Body" lyrics author unknown.) Available at www.trans-video.net/-rwillisa/SayBrother.htm. Accessed 2010 May 17.
3. Reynolds, David. *John Brown, Abolitionist: The Man Who Killed Slavery, Sparked the Civil War, and Seeded Civil Rights.* New York: Alfred A Knoph; 2005. (p.1)
4. Du Bois, W.E.B. *John Brown.* New York: Modern Library; 2001. (Preface)
5. Ralph Waldo Emerson. "Boston Hymn". The Atlantic Monthly 1863.

Chapter 3

1. Thomas Dartmouth "Daddy" Rice. Jump Jim Crow (Live Performances) 1828. Available at en.wikipedia.org/wiki/Jump_Jim_Crow. Accessed 2010 May 17.
2. United States Constitution. Amendment 13. Amendment 14. Amendment 15.
3. Black Codes. Available at en.wikipedia.org/wiki/Black_codes. Accessed 2010 May 16.
4. Black Codes. Available at en.wikipedia.org/wiki/Black_codes. Accessed 2010 May 16.
5. Pennsylvania Campaign Poster, 1866. Available at en.wikipedia.org/wiki/File:Freedman%27s_bureau.jpg. Accessed 2010 May 16.
6. List of Jim Crow Law examples by State. Available at en.wikipedia.org/wiki/List_of_Jim_Crow_law_examples_by_State. Accessed 2010 May 6.
7. Harry S. Truman. Available at en.wikipedia.org/wiki/Harry_S_Truman. Accessed 2010 May 6.

Chapter 4

1. Fuller, Robert P and Mattes, Merrill J. The Early Life of George Washington Carver. manuscript in GWC Papers at Tuskegee Institute Archives. 26 November, 1957. (p. 29)

2. Wellman, Paul I. Friends of Old Days in Kansas Saw Budding Genius of Negro Scientist. Kansas City Star, September 9, 1942. (typed copy of article)

Chapter 5

1. Lorenz, Edward. Deterministic Nonperiodic Flow. Journal of Atmospheric Sciences 1963, March.

Chapter 6

1. *Holy Bible, Revised Standard Version.* Luke 3: 5-6
2. George Washington Carver. National Park Service, United States Department of the Interior, George Washington Carver National Monument. www.nps.gov/gwca/forteachers/upload/Carver%20the%20Artist%20Curriculum-2.pdf
3. Guzman, Jessie P. Investigative Trip Interview Notes, 1948. (pp. 92-93) Available from: George Washington Carver Papers, Tuskegee Institute Archives.
4. Uttinger, Kate. 2009. Leben a Journal of Reformation Life: George Washington Carver. Available at http://www.leben.us/index.php/component/content/article/58-volume-3-issue-3/230-george-washington-carver. Accessed 2010 September 15.
5. Gary R. Kremer, editor. *George Washington Carver In His Own Words.* Columbia (Mo.): University of Missouri Press; 1987. (p. 51)
6. Fuller, Robert P and Mattes, Merrill J. The Early Life of George Washington Carver. manuscript in GWC Papers at Tuskegee Institute Archives. 26 November, 1957. (p. 97)
7. Fuller, Robert P and Mattes, Merrill J. The Early Life of George Washington Carver. manuscript in GWC Papers at Tuskegee Institute Archives. 26 November, 1957. (p. 98)
8. Holt, Rackham. *George Washington Carver: An American Biography.* New York; Doubleday, Doran and Company; 1943. (pp. 95-97)
9. Gross, John O. George Washington Carver Papers.[letter from John L. Hillman to John L. Horsely, 27 January ca. 1939] Available from Simpson College Archives, Indianola, Iowa.
10. Crisp, Lucy Cherry. Lucy Cherry Crisp Papers [letter from Willis D. Weatherford to Lucy Cherry Crisp, 18 January 1939.] Available at: East Carolina Manuscript Collection, Greenville, North Carolina.
11. Sam Wellman's Biography Site. 1999. Heroes of History, Essential Facts about George Washington Carver. Available at www.heroesofhistory.com/page50.html. Accessed 2010 May 16.
12. Lord, Russell. *The Wallaces of Iowa.* Boston: Houghton Mifflin; 1947. (p. 125)

Chapter 7

1. Lee, James R. 1997. The Buffalo Harvest. Available at www1.american.edu/TED/ice/buffalo.htm#rl. Accessed 2010 May 16.

2. Cook, Maurice G. Hugh Hammond Bennett: the Father of Soil Conservation. Available at www.soil.ncsu.edu/about/century/hugh.html. Accessed 2010 May 16.
3. Burchard, Peter Duncan, Principal Investigator. George Washington Carver: For His Time and Ours Special History Study: Natural History Related to George Washington Carver National Monument Diamond, Missouri. National Park Service, United States Department of the Interior: Washington, DC.; 2005. (p. 20)

Chapter 8

1. Culver, John C., Hyde, John. *American Dreamer, A Life of Henry A. Wallace.* New York: W.W. Norton and Company; 2000. (p. 19)
2. Holdmeyer, Frank. 2003 February 19. The Center for Prairie Studies: The Legacy of Henry A. Wallace. Available at web.grinnell.edu/cps/resources/transcripts/frank_holdmeyer.htm. Accessed 2010 May 17.
3. Greenwood, Véronique. 2004. Yale Scientific: "Amino Acids, Alleles, & Antibodies – The Work of the Connecticut Agricultural Experiment Station. Available at ysm.research.yale.edu//article.jsp?articleID=319. Accessed 2010 May 17.
4. Graham, Rod. 2000 October 2. The Gazette Online, The Newspaper of the John Hopkins University: From Kansas Farm Boy to 'Dr. Vitamin'. Available at www.jhu.edu/-gazette/2000/oct0200/02mccoll.html. Accessed 2010 May 17.
5. Herbert Hoover. Available at en.wikipedia.org/wiki/President_Hoover. Accessed 2010 May 17.
6. Schapsmeier, Edward L. and Fredrick H. Henry A. Wallace of Iowa: The Agrarian Years, 1910 – 1940. Ames (IA): Iowa State University Press; 1968. (p. 18)

Chapter 9

1. Wallace, Henry A. "The Reminiscences of Henry Agard Wallace." Columbia University Oral History Collection: New York; 1951, 1953. (p. 56)
2. Wallace, Henry A. "The Reminiscences of Henry Agard Wallace." Columbia University Oral History Collection: New York; 1951, 1953. (p. 56)
3. Culver, John C., Hyde, John. *American Dreamer, A Life of Henry A. Wallace.* New York: W.W. Norton and Company; 2000. (p. 6)
4. Culver, John C., Hyde, John. *American Dreamer, A Life of Henry A. Wallace.* New York: W.W. Norton and Company; 2000. (p. 20)
5. Culver, John C., Hyde, John. *American Dreamer, A Life of Henry A. Wallace.* New York: W.W. Norton and Company; 2000. (p. 29)
6. Culver, John C., Hyde, John. *American Dreamer, A Life of Henry A. Wallace.* New York: W.W. Norton and Company; 2000. (p. 38)

Chapter 10

1. Lord, Russell. *The Wallaces of Iowa.* Boston: Houghton Mifflin; 1947. (pp. 216 – 17)

2. George Washington Carver Papers, [letter from John N. Garner to George Washington Carver, 31 August 1939.] Tuskegee, Alabama: Tuskegee University. Available from: Tuskegee Institute Archives, Tuskegee, Alabama; Box 45.

3. Wallace, Henry A. Editorial. Wallaces' Farmer. November 4, 1924.

4. Schapsmeier, Edward L. and Fredrick H. Henry A. Wallace of Iowa: The Agrarian Years, 1910 – 1940. Ames (IA): Iowa State University Press; 1968. (p. 104)

5. Baruch, Bernard. BrainyQuote: BrainyMedia.com; 2010. Available at www.brainyquote. com/quotes/quotes/b/bernardbar161320.html. Accessed 2010 May 17.

6. Culver, John C., Hyde, John. American Dreamer, A Life of Henry A. Wallace. New York: W.W. Norton and Company; 2000. (p. 93)

7. Mann, Horace. BrainyQuote: BrainyMedia.com; 2010. Available at www.brainyquote. com/quotes/quotes/h/horacemann133541.html. Accessed 2010 May 17.

8. Culver, John C., Hyde, John. American Dreamer, A Life of Henry A. Wallace. New York: W.W. Norton and Company; 2000. (p. 90)

9. Lee, Harold. Roswell Garst. Ames (Iowa): Iowa State University Press; 1984. (p. 40)

CHAPTER 11

1. Hesser, Leon. The Man Who Fed the World. Dallas: Durban House Publishing Company; 2006. (pp. 9 – 10)

2. Vietmeyer, Noel. BORLAUG – The Mild-Mannered Maverick Who Fed a Billion People. Lorton (VA): Bracing Books; 2008. (p. 64)

3. Webster's New Universal Unabridged Dictionary. New York: Simon and Schuster; 1983.

4. Vietmeyer, Noel. BORLAUG – The Mild-Mannered Maverick Who Fed a Billion People. Lorton (VA): Bracing Books; 2008. (p. 40)

5. Vietmeyer, Noel. BORLAUG – The Mild-Mannered Maverick Who Fed a Billion People. Lorton (VA): Bracing Books; 2008. (p. 79)

CHAPTER 12

1. Herbert Hoover. BrainyQuote: BrainyMedia.com; 2010. Available at www.brainyquote. com/quotes/quotes/h/herberthoo153649.html. Accessed 2010 May 17.

2. Egan, Timothy. The Worst Hard Time. New York: A Mariner Book, Houghton Mifflin Company; 2006. (pp. 58, 78, 129)

3. Herbert Hoover. Timeline of the Great Depression, The American Experience. PBS; November 29, 2001. Available at www.andrew.cmu.edu/course/88-301/classical_ model/timeline.html. Accessed 2010 May 17.

4. Burke, Adam. 2008 April 27. Bankrupt in the Richest Nation, Farmers Rampage in Plymouth County. The Iowa Independent. Available at iowaindependent.com/2260/ bankrupt-in-the-richest-nation-farmers-rampage-in-plymouth-county. Accessed 2010 May 17.

5. Smedley Butler. 2010. Available at en.wikipedia.org/wiki/Smedley_Butler. Accessed 2010 May 17.

6. Search Through Roland Marchand's File Cabinet. n.d. The Bonus Army in Washington. Available at marchand.ucdavis.edu/lessons/bonusarmy/bonus_army.html. Accessed 2010 May 17.

7. Search Through Roland Marchand's File Cabinet. n.d. The Bonus Army in Washington. Available at marchand.ucdavis.edu/lessons/bonusarmy/bonus_army.html. Accessed 2010 May 17.

8. United States Constitution. 1st Amendment.

9. Search Through Roland Marchand's File Cabinet. n.d. The Bonus Army in Washington. Available atmarchand.ucdavis.edu/lessons/bonusarmy/bonus_army.html. Accessed 2010 May 17.

10. Search Through Roland Marchand's File Cabinet. n.d. The Bonus Army in Washington. Available at marchand.ucdavis.edu/lessons/bonusarmy/bonus_army.html. Accessed 2010 May 17.

11. Search Through Roland Marchand's File Cabinet. n.d. The Bonus Army in Washington. Available at marchand.ucdavis.edu/lessons/bonusarmy/bonus_army.html. Accessed 2010 May 17.

12. Search Through Roland Marchand's File Cabinet. n.d. The Bonus Army in Washington. Available at marchand.ucdavis.edu/lessons/bonusarmy/bonus_army.html. Accessed 2010 May 17.

13. Allen, John, editor. Did the US Government ever support the troops? Veterans Today; October 7, 2005. Available at www.veteranstoday.com/modules.php?name=News&file=article&sid=832. Accessed 2010 May 17.

14. Wheeler, Linda. 1999 April 12. WashingtonPost.com: Routing a Ragtag Army. Available at www.washingtonpost.com/wp-srv/local/2000/bonus0412.htm. Accessed 2010 May 17.

15. Weaver, John D. Bonus March. American Heritage Magazine 1963 June; 14(4). Available at www.americanheritage.com/articles/magazine/ah/1963/4/1963_4_18.shtml. Accessed 2010 May 17.

16. Weaver, John D. Bonus March. American Heritage Magazine 1963 June; 14(4). Available at www.americanheritage.com/articles/magazine/ah/1963/4/1963_4_18.shtml. Accessed 2010 May 17.

17. Search Through Roland Marchand's File Cabinet. n.d. The Bonus Army in Washington. Available at marchand.ucdavis.edu/lessons/bonusarmy/bonus_army.html. Accessed 2010 May 17.

18. Kingseed, Wyatt. The 'Bonus Army' War in Washington. American History Magazine 2004 June. Available at www.historynet.com/the-bonus-army-war-in-washington.htm. Accessed 2010 May 17.

19. Army Officer Appointment Acceptance and Oath of Office. About.com: US Military. Available at usmilitary.about.com/od/army/l/blofficeroath.htm. Accessed 2010 May 17.

20. United States Constitution. Article 2. Section 2. Clause 1.

21. Kingseed, Wyatt. The 'Bonus Army' War in Washington. American History Magazine 2004 June. Available at www.historynet.com/the-bonus-army-war-in-washington.htm. Accessed 2010 May 17.

22. The Bonus Army. EyeWitness to History, 2000. Available at www. eyewitnesstohistory.com/snprelief4.htm. Accessed 2010 May 17.
23. Search Through Roland Marchand's File Cabinet. n.d. The Bonus Army in Washington. Available at marchand.ucdavis.edu/lessons/bonusarmy/bonus_army. html. Accessed 2010 May 17.
24. Associated Press. New York Times, July 29, 1932. Search Through Roland Marchand's File Cabinet. n.d. The Bonus Army in Washington. Available at marchand.ucdavis. edu/lessons/bonusarmy/bonus_army.html. Accessed 2010 May 17.
25. Kingseed, Wyatt. The 'Bonus Army' War in Washington. American History Magazine 2004 June. Available at www.historynet.com/the-bonus-army-war-in-washington.htm. Accessed 2010 May 17.
26. Famous Legal Orders In American History: The Bonus Army. 2009 February 24. Available at www.yeree.com/nw/010/article/join/2009-02-24/4457.html. Accessed 2010 May 17.

Chapter 13

1. Wordsworth, William. *Poems in Two Volumes*. London: Paternoster-Row; 1807.
2. Lord, Russell. *The Wallaces of Iowa*. Boston: Houghton Mifflin; 1947. (pp. 320 – 21)
3. Culver, John C., Hyde, John. *American Dreamer, A Life of Henry A. Wallace*. New York: W.W. Norton and Company; 2000. (pp. 104 – 105)
4. Culver, John C., Hyde, John. *American Dreamer, A Life of Henry A. Wallace*. New York: W.W. Norton and Company; 2000. (p. 105)
5. Harris, Joel Chandler, Church, Frederick S., Moser, James H. *Uncle Remus: His Songs and His Sayings – The Folk-Lore of the Old Plantation*. New York: D. Appleton and Company; 1886. (p. 30)
6. Culver, John C., Hyde, John. *American Dreamer, A Life of Henry A. Wallace*. New York: W.W. Norton and Company; 2000. (p. 106)
7. Wallace, Henry A. "The Reminiscences of Henry Agard Wallace." Columbia University Oral History Collection: New York; 1951, 1953.(pp.188 – 89)
8. Moley, Raymond. *27 Masters of Politics*. New York: Funk & Wagnalls; 1949. (p. 80)
9. Wallace, Henry A. "The Reminiscences of Henry Agard Wallace." Columbia University Oral History Collection: New York; 1951, 1953. (pp. 190 – 91)
10. Lord, Russell. *The Wallaces of Iowa*. Boston: Houghton Mifflin; 1947. (pp. 324 – 325)

Chapter 14

1. Roosevelt, Franklin D. First Inaugural Address (excerpts). Saturday, March 4, 1933. Available at www.bartleby.com/124/pres49.html. Accessed 2010 May 19.
2. Wallace, Henry A. "The Reminiscences of Henry Agard Wallace." Columbia University Oral History Collection: New York; 1951, 1953. (p. 207)
3. Tugwell, Rexford G.. *Roosevelt's Revolution*. New York: Macmillan Publishers; 1977. (p. 68)

4. Culver, John C., Hyde, John. *American Dreamer, A Life of Henry A. Wallace*. New York: W.W. Norton and Company; 2000. (p. 114)

5. Wallace, Henry A. *New Frontiers*. New York: Reynal and Hitchcock; 1934. (p. 167)

6. Culver, John C., Hyde, John. *American Dreamer, A Life of Henry A. Wallace*. New York: W.W. Norton and Company; 2000. (p. 115)

7. Culver, John C., Hyde, John. *American Dreamer, A Life of Henry A. Wallace*. New York: W.W. Norton and Company; 2000. (p. 115)

8. Wallace, Henry A. *New Frontiers*. New York: Reynal and Hitchcock; 1934. (p. 161)

9. Wallace, Henry A. *New Frontiers*. New York: Reynal and Hitchcock; 1934. (p. 200)

Chapter 15

1. Salsola Kali. Available at en.wikipedia.org/wiki/Salsola_kali. Accessed 2010 May 19.

2. Milk Thistle. Available at en.wikipedia.org/wiki/Milk_thistle. Accessed 2010 May 19.

3. Unruh, Barbara A. Black Sunday. Available at www.perryton.com/black.htm. Accessed 2010 May 19.

4. Egan, Timothy. *The Worst Hard Time*. New York: A Mariner Book, Houghton Mifflin Company; 2006. (p. 217)

5. Lewis(Allen), Kathleen. Black Sunday. Available at www.perryton.com/black.htm. Accessed 2010 May 19.

6. Associated Press: Church Crowd In Panic As Liberal Beclouded; April 14, 1935. Available at www.perryton.com/black.htm. Accessed 2010 May 19.

7. Ochiltree County Herald. Black Blizzard Breaks All Records; April 18, 1935. Available at www.perryton.com/black.htm. Accessed 2010 May 19.

8. Time Magazine. Wheat and Dust; Monday, April 22, 1935. Available at www.time.com/time/magazine/article/0,9171,762264,00.html. Accessed 2010 May 19.

9. Geiger, Robert. Associated Press: Writer Caught in Dust; April 14, 1935. Available at www.perryton.com/black.htm. Accessed 2010 May 19.

10. Geiger, Robert. Associated Press: April 15, 1935. Available at www.legendsofamerica.com/20th-dustbowl.html

11. Amarillo Daily News: 'Worst' Duster Whips Across Panhandle; April 15, 1935. Available at www.perryton.com/black.htm

12. Ganzel, Bill. Wessels Living History Farm: Tall Tales; 2003. Available at www.livinghistoryfarm.org/farminginthe30s/water_09.html. Accessed 2010 May 19.

13. Carver, George Washington. Negro Farmer Magazine: Being Kind to the Soil; January 31, 1914. Available at www.stthomas.edu/recycle/LAND.HTM. Accessed 2010 May 19.

14. Egan, Timothy. *The Worst Hard Time*. New York: A Mariner Book, Houghton Mifflin Company; 2006. (p. 226)

15 Egan, Timothy. *The Worst Hard Time*. New York: A Mariner Book, Houghton Mifflin Company; 2006. (p. 226)

16. Brink, Wellington. *Big Hugh: The Father of Soil Conservation*. New York: The MacMillan Company; 1951.

17. Peterson, John W. The United States Experience in Controlling Erosion: Involvement

of Government, Rural vs. Urban Controls, and the Blurring of Those Differences: Prepared for presentation at the 2002 ISCO Conference, May 26 – 31, 2002, Beijing, PRC. Available atwaswc.ait.ac.th/article/United%20States%20Experience%20in%20 Controlling%20Erosio .pdf. Accessed 2010 May 19.

18. Egan, Timothy. *The Worst Hard Time*. New York: A Mariner Book, Houghton Mifflin Company; 2006. (p. 228)

Chapter 16

1. Borlaug, Norman. May 12, 2008. Academy of Achievement, A Museum of Living History: Ending World Hunger, Interview with Norman Borlaug. Available at www. achievement.org/autodoc/printmember/bor0int-1. Accessed 2010 May 19.
2. Joyce, Henry. Historic Hudson Valley: Kykuit, the Rockefeller Estate. Available at www.hudsonvalley.org/content/view/68/132/. Accessed 2010 May 19.
3. United States Constitution. Article 1. Section 8.
4. Vietmeyer, Noel. *BORLAUG – The Mild-Mannered Maverick Who Fed a Billion People*. Lorton (VA): Bracing Books; 2008. (p. 134)
5. Lord, Russell. *The Wallaces of Iowa*. Boston: Houghton Mifflin; 1947. (p. 363)
6. Vietmeyer, Noel. *BORLAUG – The Mild-Mannered Maverick Who Fed a Billion People*. Lorton (VA): Bracing Books; 2008. (p. 81)

Chapter 17

1. Wallace, Henry A. In: *Soils and Men Yearbook of Agriculture 1938*. United States Department of Agriculture: United States Government Printing Office; 1938. (Foreword)
2. Newmann, Randall. Good Old Boys (album): Louisiana 1927 (lyrics); 1974. Available at www.lyricsdepot.com/randy-newman/louisiana-1927.html. Accessed 2010 May 20.
3. Grey Towers National Historic Site Gifford Pinchot. U.S. Department of Agriculture Forest Service. Last Modified: Thursday, 04 June 2009. Available at www.fs.fed.us/ na/gt/local-links/historical-info/gifford/gifford.shtml. Accessed 2010 May 20.
4. Leopold, Aldo. "The Land Ethic," in *A Sand County Almanac*. New York: Oxford University Press; 1966. (p. 239)
5. Leopold, Aldo. "The Land Ethic," in *A Sand County Almanac*. New York: Oxford University Press; 1966. (p. 240)
6. Cobb, James H., Jr. "Ford and Carver Point South's Way," Atlanta Journal, March 17, 1940.
7. Cook, Maurice G. Hugh Hammond Bennett: the Father of Soil Conservation. Available at www.soil.ncsu.edu/about/century/hugh.html. Accessed 2010 May 20.
8. Cook, Maurice G. Hugh Hammond Bennett: the Father of Soil Conservation. Available at www.soil.ncsu.edu/about/century/hugh.html. Accessed 2010 May 16
9. Cook, Maurice G. Hugh Hammond Bennett: the Father of Soil Conservation. Available at www.soil.ncsu.edu/about/century/hugh.html. Accessed 2010 May 20.
10. Wallace, Henry A. "The War at our Feet." Survey Graphic Magazine of Social Interpretation 1940 February 1.

11. Wallace, Henry A. "The War at our Feet." Survey Graphic Magazine of Social Interpretation 1940 February 1.

Chapter 18

1. Agenda of the AAAS Section on Environmental Sciences: American Association for the Advancement of Science the 139th meeting; 1972 December 29. Available at eapsweb. mit.edu/research/Lorenz/Butterfly_1972.pdf. Accessed 2010 May 20.
2. Globe Staff. Edward Lorenz, 90, MIT Professor Developed Chaos Theory. The Boston Globe 2008 April 17. Available at www.boston.com/bostonglobe/obituaries/ articles/2008/04/17/edward_lorenz_90_mit_professor_developed_chaos_theory/. Accessed 2010 May 20.
3. Lorenz, Edward N. Predictability: Does the Flap of A Butterfly's Wings in Brazil Set off a Tornado in Texas? Proceedings of AAAS Section on Environmental Sciences, New Approaches to Global Weather: GARP; 1972 December 29; Boston, MA. Available at eapsweb.mit.edu/research/Lorenz/Butterfly_1972.pdf. Accessed 2010 May 20.
4. Elert, Glenn. 1995 – 2007. Strange and Complex. In: The Chaos Hypertextbook. Available at hypertextbook.com/chaos/21.shtml. Accessed 2010 May 20.
5. Lorenz, Edward N. The Butterfly Effect. Proceedings of the Premio Felice Pietro Chisesi e Caterina Tomassoni award lecture; April, 2008; Rome, Italy. Université of Rome; 2008. Available at eapsweb.mit.edu/research/Lorenz/Miscellaneous/ Tomassoni_2008.pdf. Accessed 2010 May 20.
6. Obituary. Edward Lorenz, Father Of Chaos Theory And Butterfly Effect, 90. TechTalk Serving the MIT Community 2008April30; 52(24):2.

Chapter 19

1. The History Place. 1997. Holocaust Timeline: Night of Long Knives. Available at www. historyplace.com/worldwar2/holocaust/h-roehm.htm. Accessed 2010 May 21.
2. Night of Long Knives. Available at en.wikipedia.org/wiki/Night_of_the_Long_Knives. Accessed 2010 May 21.
3. O'Connell, Thomas Gerald. Toward the Cooperative Commonwealth: An Introductory History of the Farmer-Labor Movement in Minnesota (1917 – 1948) [dissertation thesis]. Brattleboro (VT): Union Institute and University; 1979. Available at justcomm.org/fla-hist.htm#2.3. Accessed 2010 May 21.
4. O'Connell, Thomas Gerald. Toward the Cooperative Commonwealth: An Introductory History of the Farmer-Labor Movement in Minnesota (1917 – 1948) [dissertation thesis]. Brattleboro (VT): Union Institute and University; 1979. Available at justcomm.org/fla-hist.htm#2.3. Accessed 2010 May 21.
5. Butler, Smedley D. (General). War is a Racket. New York: Round Table Press; 1935.
6. Price, R.G. 2004. Fascism Part II: The Rise of American Fascism. Available at www. rationalrevolution.net/articles/rise_of_american_fascism.htm. Accessed 2010 May 21.

7. Price, R.G. 2004. Fascism Part II: The Rise of American Fascism. Available at www. rationalrevolution.net/articles/rise_of_american_fascism.htm. Accessed 2010 May 21.
8. Price, R.G. 2004. Fascism Part II: The Rise of American Fascism. Available at www. rationalrevolution.net/articles/rise_of_american_fascism.htm. Accessed 2010 May 21.
9. Hecht, Peter. California returns 2 paintings Nazis stole, Hearst bought. Sacramento Bee 2009 April 11. Available at www.mcclatchydc.com/200/story/65929.html. Accessed 2010 May 21.
10. Thomas J. Watson Is Decorated by Hitler For Work in Bettering Economic Relations. The New York Times July 2, 1937: p. 8.
11. Price, R.G. 2004. Fascism Part II: The Rise of American Fascism. Available at www. rationalrevolution.net/articles/rise_of_american_fascism.htm. Accessed 2010 May 21.

CHAPTER 20

1. Wallace, Henry A. "The Reminiscences of Henry Agard Wallace." Columbia University Oral History Collection: New York; 1951, 1953. (p. 49)
2. Lord, Russell. *The Wallaces of Iowa.* Boston: Houghton Mifflin; 1947. (p. 432)
3. Wallace, Henry A. *Statesmanship and Religion.* New York: Round Table Press; 1934. (p. 80)
4. Culver, John C., Hyde, John. *American Dreamer, A Life of Henry A. Wallace.* New York: W.W. Norton and Company; 2000. (p. 14)
5. Lord, Russell. *The Wallaces of Iowa.* Boston: Houghton Mifflin; 1947. (p. 338)
6. Culver, John C., Hyde, John. *American Dreamer, A Life of Henry A. Wallace.* New York: W.W. Norton and Company; 2000. (p. 129)
7. Culver, John C., Hyde, John. *American Dreamer, A Life of Henry A. Wallace.* New York: W.W. Norton and Company; 2000. (p. 129)
8. Culver, John C., Hyde, John. *American Dreamer, A Life of Henry A. Wallace.* New York: W.W. Norton and Company; 2000. (p. 129)
9. Wallace, Henry A. *New Frontiers.* New York: Reynal and Hitchcock; 1934. (p. 11)
10. *Holy Bible, Revised Standard Version.* Matthew 7: 15-20.

CHAPTER 21

1. Vietmeyer, Noel. BORLAUG – *The Mild-Mannered Maverick Who Fed a Billion People.* Lorton (VA): Bracing Books; 2008. (p. 160)
2. Art, Henry W. The Amos Lawrence Hopkins Memorial Forest: An Eclectic History of its First Century (1887 – 1987). Williamstown (MA): Williams College; 1994. Available at www.williams.edu/CES/hopkins/history/eclectic.htm and www. williams.edu/CES/hopkins/history/eclectictext.htm. Accessed 2010 May 21.
3. Vietmeyer, Noel. BORLAUG – *The Mild-Mannered Maverick Who Fed a Billion People.* Lorton (VA): Bracing Books; 2008. (p. 204)

Chapter 22

1. Wallace, Henry A. *Statesmanship and Religion.* New York: Round Table Press; 1934. (Preface)
2. Wallace, Henry A. *New Frontiers.* New York: Reynal and Hitchcock; 1934. (Quotes from book review in Time Magazine, October 15, 1934. Available at www.time.com/time/magazine/article/0,9171,748058,00.html. Accessed 2010 May 21.)
3. Hoover, Herbert. *The Challenge to Liberty.* New York: Charles Scribner's Sons; 1934. (Quotes from book review in Time Magazine, October 15, 1934. Available at www.time.com/time/magazine/article/0,9171,748058,00.html. Accessed 2010 May 21.)
4. Wallace, Henry A. *America Must Choose.* New York: Foreign Policy Association; 1934.
5. Culver, John C., Hyde, John. *American Dreamer A Life of Henry A. Wallace.* New York: W.W. Norton and Company; 2000. Various journalist quotes. (pp. 150 – 152)
6. Lord, Russell. *The Wallaces of Iowa.* Boston: Houghton Mifflin; 1947. (p. 440)
7. Bates, Ernest Southerland. *American Faith.* New York. Norton Publishing, 1940. (Quote from book review in Time Magazine, May 6, 1940.)
8. Culver, John C., Hyde, John. *American Dreamer, A Life of Henry A. Wallace.* New York: W.W. Norton and Company; 2000. Various journalist quotes. (p. 253)
9. Culver, John C., Hyde, John. *American Dreamer, A Life of Henry A. Wallace.* New York: W.W. Norton and Company; 2000. Various journalist quotes. (p. 204)
10. Wallace, Henry A. The War at our Feet. Survey Graphic Magazine of Social Interpretation 1940 February 1.
11. Chang, Chen Huan. *The Economic Principles of Confucius and His School.* New York: Columbia Univ. Press; 1911.
12. Wallace, Henry A. Ever-Normal Granary. Wallaces' Farmer 1918December6; 1926October6; 1927 January21. Available at www.columbia.edu/itc/eacp/japanworks/chinawh/web/s10/ideas.pdf. Accessed 2010May21.
13 Culver, John C., Hyde, John. *American Dreamer, A Life of Henry A. Wallace.* New York: W.W. Norton and Company; 2000. (p. 178)
14 Culver, John C., Hyde, John. *American Dreamer, A Life of Henry A. Wallace.* New York: W.W. Norton and Company; 2000. (p. 178)
15. Wallace, Henry A. "The Reminiscences of Henry Agard Wallace." Columbia University Oral History Collection: New York; 1951, 1953.(pg 5166)
16. A Short History of SNAP. 2009April30. United States Department of Agriculture, Food and Nutrition Service. Available at www.fns.usda.gov/snap/rules/Legislation/about.htm. Accessed 2010 May 21.
17 Carter, John Franklin. *New Dealers.* New York: Simon and Schuster; 1934. (p. 84)

Chapter 23

1. *The International Jew: The World's Foremost Problem.* Dearborn (MI): Dearborn Publishing; November 1920. "Being a reprint of a series of articles appearing in the Dearborn independent from May 22 to October 2, 1920."

2. Hitler, Adolph. *Mein Kampf*. München (Germany): Eher-Verlag; 1925. (p. 639)

3. Gandhi, Mohandas, Dr. Porter, Medical Officer of Health for Johannesburg, Johannesburg (South Africa). Personal Communication. February 15, 1905. Available at en.wikiquote.org/wiki/Gandhi. Accessed 2010 May 23.

4. Gandhi, Mohandas. The Indian Opinion 2 June 1906. Available at en.wikiquote.org/wiki/Gandhi. Accessed 2010 May 23.

5. Gandhi, Mohandas. The Indian Opinion 25 March 1905. Available at en.wikiquote.org/wiki/Gandhi. Accessed 2010 May 23.

6. Singh, G. B. *Gandhi: Behind the Mask of Divinity*. Anherst (NY): Prometheus Books; 2004. (p.106)

7. Gandhi, Mohandas. *The Collected Works of Mahatma Gandhi*, Volume VIII. New Delhi (India): Publications Division, Ministry of Information & Broadcasting, Government of India; 1908 March 1 – 1908 July 29. (pp. 135 – 36)

8. Gandhi, Mohandas. Young India 19 January 1928. Available at en.wikiquote.org/wiki/Gandhi. Accessed 2010 May 23.

9 Gandhi, Mohandas. Young India 4 October 1930. Available at en.wikiquote.org/wiki/Gandhi. Accessed 2010 May 23.

10. Gandhi, Mohandas *The Collected Works of Mahatma Gandhi*, Volume 33. New Delhi (India): Publications Division, Ministry of Information & Broadcasting, Government of India; 1925September 25 – 1926 February 10.

11. Black, Allida M. *Casting Her Own Shadow*. New York: Columbia University Press; 1996. (p. 30)

12. Hesser, Leon. *The Man Who Fed the World*. Dallas: Durban House Publishing Company; 2006. (p. 22)

CHAPTER 24

1. Lord, Russell. *The Wallaces of Iowa*. Boston: Houghton Mifflin; 1947. (p. 474)

2. Wallace, Henry A. "The Reminiscences of Henry Agard Wallace." Columbia University Oral History Collection: New York; 1951, 1953. (pp. 5191 – 5192)

3. Culver, John C., Hyde, John. *American Dreamer, A Life of Henry A. Wallace*. New York: W.W. Norton and Company; 2000. (p. 195)

4. High, Stanley. Saturday Evening Post. Will It Be Wallace? Saturday Evening Post 1937 July 3.

5. Culver, John C., Hyde, John. *American Dreamer, A Life of Henry A. Wallace*. New York: W.W. Norton and Company; 2000. (p. 196)

6. Lord, Russell. *The Wallaces of Iowa*. Boston: Houghton Mifflin; 1947. (pp. 431 – 32)

7. Wallace, Henry A. "The Reminiscences of Henry Agard Wallace." Columbia University Oral History Collection: New York; 1951, 1953. (p. 558)

8. De Waal, Frans. *Peacemaking Among Primates*. Cambridge (MA): Harvard University Press; 1990. (Pg. 244)

9. Culver, John C., Hyde, John. *American Dreamer, A Life of Henry A. Wallace*. New York: W.W. Norton and Company; 2000. (p. 216)

10. Culver, John C., Hyde, John. *American Dreamer, A Life of Henry A. Wallace.* New York: W.W. Norton and Company; 2000. (p. 217)
11. Farley, James A. *Jim Farley's Story: The Roosevelt Years.* New York: McGraw-Hill, 1948. (p. 302).
12. Tully, Grace. *FDR, My Boss.* New York: Scribners; 1949. (p. 239)
13. Farley, James A. *Jim Farley's Story: The Roosevelt Years.* New York: McGraw-Hill, 1948. (p. 300)
14. Roosevelt, Eleanor. *This I Remember.* New York: Harper; 1949. (p. 218)
15. Rosenman, Samuel. *Working with Roosevelt.* New York: Da Capo Press, 1952. (p. 219)
16. Roosevelt, Eleanor. The New York Times, July 19, 1940. Available at www.gwu. edu/-erpapers/teachinger/q-and-a/q22-erspeech.cfm. Accessed 2010 May 24.
17. Culver, John C., Hyde, John. *American Dreamer, A Life of Henry A. Wallace.* New York: W.W. Norton and Company; 2000. (p. 235)
18. Wallace. Henry A. *Democracy Reborn.* Edited by Russell Lord. New York: Reynal & Hitchcock; 1943. (p. 152)
19. Culver, John C., Hyde, John. *American Dreamer, A Life of Henry A. Wallace.* New York: W.W. Norton and Company; 2000. (p. 94)
20. Rosenman, Samuel. *Working with Roosevelt.* New York: Da Capo Press, 1952. (p. 242)
21. Culver, John C., Hyde, John. *American Dreamer, A Life of Henry A. Wallace.* New York: W.W. Norton and Company; 2000. (p. 243)
22. Daniels, Josephus. *Shirt-Sleeve Diplomat.* Chapel Hill (NC): University of North Carolina Press; 1947. (p. 349)

CHAPTER 25

1. Roosevelt, Franklin D. The History Place. 1996 – 2010. The History Place Great Speeches Collection: Franklin D. Roosevelt For a Declaration of War. Available at www.historyplace.com/speeches/fdr-infamy.htm. Accessed 2010 May 25.
2. Ribbentrop, Joachim von. The History Place. 1996. World War II in Europe: German Declaration of War against the United States. Available at www.historyplace.com/ worldwar2/timeline/germany-declares.htm. Accessed 2010 May 25.
3. Hitler, Adolf. *The Journal of Historical Review*, Winter 1988 – 89 (Vol. 8, No. 4), pp. 389 – 416.
4. Mussolini, Benito. Mussolini's War Statement – Declaration of War against USA. The New York Times, December 12, 1941.
5. Dimbleby, Richard. "Liberation of Belsen." BBC News; April 15, 1945. Available at en.wikipedia.org/wiki/Bergen-Belsen_concentration_camp. Accessed 2010 May 25.

CHAPTER 27

1. Cárdenas, Lázaro (President of Mexico 1934 – 1940). Available at en.wikipedia.org/ wiki/Expropiaci%C3%B3n_Petrolera. Accessed 2010 May 25.

2. United States Constitution. Article 1. Section 3. Clause 4; Article 1. Section 3. Clause 5; Article 1. Section 3. Clause 6; Article 2. Section 4.
3. Culver, John C., Hyde, John. *American Dreamer, A Life of Henry A. Wallace*. New York: W.W. Norton and Company; 2000. (p. 246)
4. Garner, John Nance. Available at en.wikipedia.org/wiki/John_Nance_Garner. Accessed 2010 May 25.
5. Jack R. Kloppenburg, Jr. *First the Seed: The Political Economy of Plant Biotechnology, 1492 – 2000*. Cambridge (England): Cambridge University Press; 1988. (p. 158)

Chapter 28

1. Culver, John C., Hyde, John. *American Dreamer, A Life of Henry A. Wallace*. New York: W.W. Norton and Company; 2000. (p. 257)
2. Gibran, Kahlil. *The Prophet*. New York: Alfred A. Knopf, Inc.;1978. (p. 31)
3. Nelson, Donald. *Arsenal of Democracy: The Story of American War Production*. New York: Harcourt, Brace; 1946. (p. 184)
4. Wallace. Henry A. *Democracy Reborn*. Edited by Russell Lord. New York: Reynal & Hitchcock; 1943. (p. 190)
5. Marshall, George C. Commencement Address (The Marshall Plan Speech). Cambridge (MA): Harvard University; June 5, 1947. Available at www.famousquotes.me.uk/speeches/George_C_Marshall/. Accessed 2010 May 25.

Chapter 30

1. Borlaug, Norman E. 2003. "Penn and Teller: Bullshit! Eat This!" 4 April 2003: Season 1, Episode 11. Available at en.wikiquote.org/wiki/Norman_Borlaug. Accessed 2010 May 26.
2. Higgins, Andrew C. 1998. Henry A. Wallace Institute for Alternative Agriculture. Henry A. Wallace: Practitioner and Prophet, Wallace Quotes. Available at www1.american.edu/epiphany/quotes.html. Accessed 2010 May 26.
3. Hesser, Leon. *The Man Who Fed the World*. Dallas: Durban House Publishing Company; 2006. (pg 39)
4. Hesser, Leon. *The Man Who Fed the World*. Dallas: Durban House Publishing Company; 2006. (p. 44)
5. Hesser, Leon. *The Man Who Fed the World*. Dallas: Durban House Publishing Company; 2006. (p. 46)
6. Quinn, Kenneth M. 2007. World Food Prize Foundation: Dr. Norman E. Borlaug:20th Century Lessons for the 21st Century World. Available at www.worldfoodprize.org/borlaug/borlaug-history.htm. Accessed 2010 May 26.

Chapter 31

1. Good News India: From famine to plenty, from humiliation to dignity. November 2002.

Available at www.goodnewsindia.com/Pages/content/milestones/greenRev.html. Accessed 2010 May 26.

2. Sublette, Carey. Pakistan's Nuclear Weapons Program – 1998: The Year of Testing. 2001 September 10. Available at nuclearweaponarchive.org/Pakistan/PakTests.html. Accessed 2010 May 26.

3. Buddha, Siddhartha Gautama. BrainyMedia.com: Brainy Quote. 2010 Available at www.brainyquote.com/words/gr/grasping170332.html. Accessed 2010 May 26.

4. Hesser, Leon. *The Man Who Fed the World*. Dallas: Durban House Publishing Company; 2006. (p. 76)

5. Easterbrook, Gregg. Forgotten Benefactor of Humanity. The Atlantic Monthly January 1997; 279;1;75 – 82.

6. Culver, John C., Hyde, John. *American Dreamer, A Life of Henry A. Wallace*. New York: W.W. Norton and Company; 2000. (p. 530)

7. Culver, John C., Hyde, John. *American Dreamer, A Life of Henry A. Wallace*. New York: W.W. Norton and Company; 2000. (p. 531)

8. Culver, John C., Hyde, John. *American Dreamer, A Life of Henry A. Wallace*. New York: W.W. Norton and Company; 2000. (p. 531)

9. Culver, John C., Hyde, John. *American Dreamer, A Life of Henry A. Wallace*. New York: W.W. Norton and Company; 2000. (p. 531)

10. Culver, John C., Hyde, John. *American Dreamer, A Life of Henry A. Wallace*. New York: W.W. Norton and Company; 2000. (p. 531)

CHAPTER 32

1. Tägil, Sven. 2010. Nobelprize.org: War and Peace in the Thinking of Alfred Nobel. Available at nobelprize.org/alfred_nobel/biographical/articles/tagil/index.html. Accessed 2010 May 27.

2. Rooney, Sean. 2007 December 21. associatedcontent – The people's media company: Alfred Nobel & the Creation of the Nobel Prizes. Available at www.associatedcontent.com/article/494459/alfred_nobel_the_creation_of_the_nobel. html. Accessed 2010 May 27.

3. Tägil, Sven. 2010. Nobelprize.org: War and Peace in the Thinking of Alfred Nobel. Available at nobelprize.org/alfred_nobel/biographical/articles/tagil/index.html. Accessed 2010 May 27.

4. Nobel, Alfred. 2009. Nobelprize.org: Full text of Alfred Nobel's Will. Available at nobelprize.org/alfred_nobel/will/will-full.html. Accessed 2010 May 27.

5. Lundestad, Geir. Nobelprize.org: The Nobel Peace Prize, 1901 – 2000. Available at Nobel Peace nobelprize.org/nobel_prizes/peace/articles/lundestad-review/index.html. Accessed 2010 May 27.

6. Hesser, Leon. *The Man Who Fed the World*. Dallas: Durban House Publishing Company; 2006. (p. 135)

7. Hesser, Leon. *The Man Who Fed the World*. Dallas: Durban House Publishing Company; 2006. (p. 133)

8. Hesser, Leon. *The Man Who Fed the World*. Dallas: Durban House Publishing Company; 2006. (p. 135)
9. Hesser, Leon. *The Man Who Fed the World*. Dallas: Durban House Publishing Company; 2006. (p. 131)

Chapter 33

1. Shakespeare, William. *Mr. William Shakespeare's Comedies, Histories, and Tragedies*. London: Worshipful Company of Stationers and Newspaper Makers; 1623. (p.109)
2. Holmes's Record In The Past; The Pitezel Swindle Not the First in Which He Has Been Involved. The New York Times; November 23, 1894. Available at query.nytimes. com/gst/abstract.html?res=9905E5DE1E31E033A25750C2A9679D94659ED7CF&scp =1&sq=The+Pitezel+Swindle+Not+the+First+in+Which+He+Has+Been+Involved&st =p. Accessed 2010 May 28.
3. Larson, Eric. *The Devil in the White City*. New York: Vintage Books, a Division of Random House; 2003. (p.151)
4. Carver, George Washington. Plants Modified by Man [Master's Thesis]. Ames (IA): Iowa State University. 1894. (pp.5 – 6) Available at Iowa State University e-Library Digital Collections.
5. Potyondi, Stephen. 2006. University of Alberta: Ziel Treblinka / "Final Destination Treblinka". Available at www.holocaust-history.org/operation-reinhard/final-destination-treblinka. Accessed 2010 May 28.
6. Potyondi, Stephen. 2006. University of Alberta: Ziel Treblinka / "Final Destination Treblinka". Available at www.holocaust-history.org/operation-reinhard/final-destination-treblinka. Accessed 2010 May 28.
7. Opinion and Judgement of the United States Military Tribunal II, in *Trials of War Criminals Before the Nuremberg Military Tribunals Under Control Council Law* No. 10. Vol. 5: United States v. Oswald Pohl, et. al. (Case 4: 'Pohl Case'), p. 980-992. Available at www.mazal.org/archive.nmt/05/NMT05-T0980.htm.
8. Culver, John C., Hyde, John. *American Dreamer, A Life of Henry A. Wallace*. New York: W.W. Norton and Company; 2000. (p. 275)
9. Goering, Hermann. The Third Reich, Berlin. Personal communication. July 31, 1941. From: The Final Solution 1941 – 45; 2005. Available at www.leninimports.com/the_final_solution.html#thedecision. Accessed 2010 May 28.

Chapter 34

1. AgBioWorld. 2005. Quotes on Norman Borlaug; Professor M.S. Swaminathan. Available at www.agbioworld.org/biotech-info/topics/borlaug/quotes.html. Accessed 2010 May 28.
2. Ehrlich, Paul. *The Population Bomb*. New York: Buccaneer Books; 1968. (p.xi)
3. Hesser, Leon. *The Man Who Fed the World*. Dallas: Durban House Publishing Company; 2006. (p. 133)

4. Borlaug, Norman. BrainyQuote: BrainyMedia.com; 2010. Available at www. brainyquote.com/quotes/authors/n/norman_borlaug.html. Accessed 2010 May 28.

5. United States Congress: Public Law 109-395; December 14, 2006.

Epiloque

1. Huxley, Aldous. BrainyQuotes: BrainyMedia.com; 2010. Available at www.brainyquote. com/quotes/quotes/a/aldoushuxl392818.html. Accessed 2010 May 29.

2. *Holy Bible, Revised Standard Version.* Matthew 5: 3-12.

3. Mohammad. Islam for Today. Words of Wisdom from Prophet Mohammad: Fifty Hadiths selected by Dr. Shahid Athar. Available at www.islamfortoday.com/athar16. htm. Accessed 2010 May 29.

4. Dalai Lama. 2009. PhilosophersNotes: The Religion of Kindness by Dalai Lama. Available at philosophersnotes.com/ideas/show/the-religion-of-kindness. Accessed 2010 May 29.

5 Aesop. BrainyQuotes: BrainyMedia.com; 2010.Available at www.brainyquote.com/ quotes/quotes/a/aesop109734.html. Accessed 2010 May 29.

6. Wordsworth, William. Inspirational Words of Wisdom: Kindness Quotes. Available at www.wow4u.com/kindness/index.html. Accessed 2010 May 29.

7. Williams, Dar. My Better Self (album): Echoes (song lyrics); 2005.

8. Mother Teresa. 2004. High Thoughts by Mother Teresa. Available at www. thehighcalling.org/Library/ViewLibrary.asp?LibraryID=1843. Accessed 2010 May 29.

9. Schweitzer, Albert. Creative Commons: QuotationsBook. Available at www. quotationsbook.com/quote/bookmark_users/21999/. Accessed 2010 May 29.

10. Lord, Russell. *The Wallaces of Iowa.* Boston: Houghton Mifflin; 1947. (p. 363)

11. Ben's Bells Project. Welcome to Ben's Bells (Mission Statement). Available at www. bensbells.org/. Accessed 2010 May 29.

Acknowledgements

First I owe a debt of gratitude, and perhaps what is left of my vision to my spouse, Carla, who was the daily editor, consultant and critic. She placed one hand between my shoulder blades to push me along and the other hand in front of my chest to right me when I stumbled.

I want to thank my sister-in-law, Marline, for her editorial read and insights about the flow of the story. Likewise, I must thank my life-long friend Dr. Bill Baker for reading one of the early versions of the manuscript and having the courage to tell me that it still needed a whole lot of work.

My new friend, Sherry James, shared extraordinary insights about her old friend, Norman Borlaug. That, coupled with her insights about the publishing industry, has earned my appreciation.

The William Mitchell College of Law Intellectual Property Clinic and my daughter, Carissa, did the yeoman's job of getting the permissions for the use of copyrighted materials. To paraphrase Clara Vaala Borlaug, "she was always a good girl."

I must thank the staff and the New Mexico Division of Vocational Rehabilitation for putting up with me and my pontifications about kindness for the better part of four years.

Finally, I want to acknowledge Jim Smith and Carl Condit at Sunstone Press for taking a chance on an exceedingly strange book because "strange can be good." They encouraged and assisted, but most importantly they remind all who enter their offices to "breathe" and they proudly display a refrigerator magnet which admonishes everyone to "be nice or leave."

CPSIA information can be obtained at www.ICGtesting.com
Printed in the USA
LVOW08s1748050614

388781LV00003B/594/P